THE MAYANS MORNING OF TERROR AT CUMORAH

The Demise of Civilizations Who Refused to Call Upon God

STEVEN SEGO

THE MAYANS MORNING OF TERROR AT CUMORAH!
The Demise of Civilizations Who Refused to Call Upon God
Copyright © 2024   Steven Sego

Library of Congress Control Number: 2024932405
                        Paperback: 978-1-961119-62-8
                        eBook: 978-1-961119-63-5

Printed in the United States of America

Contents

·····················

DISCLAIMER

Before you dive into this book, I strongly encourage you to seek opinions from your friends, politicians, clergy, relatives, attorney, or anyone you trust for an honest and unbiased perspective. Keep in mind that everything expressed in this book is solely my opinion and may differ from the conclusions reached by others.

If you choose to act on any recommendations without the guidance of a licensed attorney, you do so entirely at your own risk. The publisher, author, distributors, and bookstores present this information exclusively for educational purposes.

I am not an attorney, nor do I claim to be. I am not attempting to practice law without a license. This book reflects only my opinions, thoughts, and conclusions based on sound knowledge and/or experience. The information provided here is intended for educational purposes, and the responsibility for any actions taken based on the book's content rests solely with you.

Steven Sego

ABOUT THE BOOK

The primary aim of this book is to convey to the reader a profound understanding of God's proximity to us, elucidated through the meticulous observation of two civilizations that self-destructed in the past. These societies, in their final moments, turned away from God, opting to attribute more power to the devil—an attempt to conceal and rationalize their sins by playing the card of ignorance.

My upbringing involved echoing the beliefs of my older brothers, accepting my father's words as gospel truth. Like most youngsters, I caught the bus every morning and attended church with my father, imbibing the teachings that emphasized dedicating at least one day a week to respecting and honoring God for His myriad blessings. This was deemed the least we could do, especially given what Christ has done and continues to do for our enlightenment and well-being.

I embarked on a mission to Hong Kong, China, from 1977-1979, teaching the gospel in Cantonese. It was during this period that I developed a profound love for the Chinese people, recognizing their easygoing nature. However, a significant challenge surfaced—their difficulty in comprehending the Book of Mormon. As a world traveler, I learned that people, regardless of nationality, share common traits, yet one aspect where they differ is the availability of knowledge about their Redeemer, Jesus Christ.

Drawing an analogy from little league baseball, where I advised my son Jordan to keep an eye on the ball, I underscore the importance of knowing where Jesus Christ is at all times. Just as keeping focus on the ball influences the game's outcome, understanding Christ's role and utilizing His teachings can determine the outcome of life's ultimate home run.

I am certain that if people worldwide knew where to find the Truth, they would embrace it. The Truth becomes transparent when the light of Christ or the Spirit of Truth illuminates minds and spirits. Simplifying the understanding of scriptures, government, and unraveling the mysteries of God is of utmost importance to me. The exhilarating moments when the Spirit of Truth enlightens someone are unparalleled. Through prayer, scripture study, meditation, and repentance, I have cultivated empathy and a godly love for every struggling soul seeking understanding.

It is these convictions that have led me to pen this third book, "The Mayan's Morning of Terror at Cumorah! The Demise of Civilizations When They Refuse to Call Upon God." Many are raised in a similar fashion, guided by parental teachings that they accept without questioning. While there is nothing inherently wrong with this, often, even the parents themselves lack a complete understanding.

In our quest to understand the Ancient Inhabitants of America, who predated us, we encounter a narrative of two thriving civilizations, both highly favored and blessed by God for 1,000 to 1,500 years. However, their downward spiraling course towards destruction unfolded as they turned their backs on God, succumbing to the influence of evil spirits. This demise resulted from selfishness, the pursuit of wealth and power, involvement in secret societies, treason, and internal strife.

As of 2023, a parallel narrative unfolds for us, echoing the same destructive patterns. The author contends that God's word against us, the Gentiles, has been foretold thousands of years in advance, and this divine judgment will materialize unless there is a collective change and repentance. The author emphasizes that God orchestrates events precisely, including the timing and individuals through whom His judgment will manifest.

Motivated by a deep yearning and a sense of obligation to share the gospel of Jesus Christ plainly, the author feels compelled to convey the truth to the world as a final call before God concludes His work. Positioned 247 years into the seventh day/millennium, the author anticipates Christ's intervention and the fulfillment of prophecies, including the so-called "Global Warming" sought by Satanists.

This book aims to counter liberal experts who dismiss God's role in all things, particularly those who discredit, ignore, and mock Joseph Smith and the divine revelations he received. The author asserts that in the "Fulness of Times," Joseph Smith's teachings are more pertinent than ever. The book seeks to dispel myths around evolution, ancient history, fallen angels, Nephilim, giants, and aliens, portraying these as deceptive narratives propagated by Satan to divert attention from spiritual truths.

The narrative explores the significance of Adam as the father of all living, emphasizing that those not in God's lineage cannot interfere with the Earth. Addressing the predecessors of our current civilizations, the author delves into their origin, worship practices, blessings, and eventual downfall due to forgetting God. This historical exploration aims to draw parallels with contemporary times, urging the Gentiles to reflect on the consequences of forsaking God.

Furthermore, the book serves as a warning to the Gentiles about the South American people, identified as remnants of the tribe of Joseph. The Americas, according to the author, constitute their lands of inheritance. A call for repentance is sounded, cautioning that failure to change their secret practices could result in Almighty God acting against the Gentiles, with the remnants of the Tribe of Joseph becoming a scourge until the Gentiles are either driven out or compelled to join forces.

In my unwavering conviction, Joseph Smith was a Holy Prophet of God, and the Book of Mormon stands as an absolute truth. While the Catholic Church engaged in the destruction of records and suppression of the Nephites/Mayans, Lamanites/Aztecs, and Jaredites/Giants/Olmecs, Joseph Smith, through divine guidance, unearthed the full history embedded in the abridged plates of Nephi.

As the world yearns for the truth about these ancient civilizations, my aim is to illuminate the historical timeline intricately detailed in the Book of Mormon. Despite experts relying on opinion, carbon dating, and fragmented discoveries, this book strives to present a cohesive narrative grounded in the translated records by Joseph Smith. The reader is urged to discern the truth, relying on facts, common sense, and the promptings of the Holy Ghost.

The book serves as a guide to understanding how the Spirit of Truth imparts knowledge and wisdom, making each reader an expert in their own right. It emphasizes the limitations of education without the guiding influence of the Spirit of Truth. The narrative underscores the importance of calling upon God for true knowledge and sound doctrine, challenging the deceptive narratives perpetuated by those who reject divine guidance.

A personal motivation underscores this work: to assist my family in seeing the Whole Truth. Through prayer, I hope for a divine revelation for my wife, and I extend this enlightening opportunity to all readers. The book emphasizes the omniscience of Almighty God, capable of declaring events thousands of years in advance. It highlights the divine placement of Joseph Smith in New York and the preservation of the Nephite/Mayan record through the intervention of the angel Moroni.

While the Catholic Church sought to erase the memory of Jesus Christ, God chose to hide sufficient records, ensuring their emergence through Joseph Smith. The small portion translated by Joseph Smith serves as a test of faith for the Gentiles. Those who believe, exercise faith, and listen to the Spirit of Truth will receive additional knowledge and unravel more mysteries of God.

This testimony to the world affirms the undeniable truth contained in this book, comparing it to the certainty of the sun rising each morning.

ACKNOWLEDGMENTS

I extend my sincere gratitude to the diligent historians whose tireless efforts have shed light on the mysteries of ancient American civilizations. Their varied approaches, from precise discoveries to revealing road systems and ancient cities through platforms like YouTube, contribute significantly to our understanding. Regardless of differing beliefs, be it evolution or humble followers of Christ, every contribution, intentional or accidental, forms a vital piece of the intricate puzzle.

Special thanks to the supportive publishers, graphic designers, and individuals who share my commitment to uncovering the truth, unafraid and unashamed to embrace it. Kaitlin Harding of TLF deserves appreciation for her unwavering support and friendship, consistently encouraging and presenting this information to publishers worldwide. This collaborative effort is a testament to the fact that no one accomplishes such work in isolation, requiring a diverse range of talents.

I express my gratitude to printers, designers, writers, directors, editors, attorneys, finance professionals, media specialists, historians, family, and friends who believe in and contribute to this mission of bringing truth to light. Your collective voices resonate as the voice of God.

Utmost honor and glory are reserved for my Father in Heaven and His Son, Jesus Christ. Acknowledging God's hand in all things, His words through scriptures, and revelations from His holy prophets shape my thinking and understanding. Witnessing the hand of God at work daily, exposing darkness and revealing truth, strengthens my faith. I am profoundly grateful for my Living God and His Son,

Jesus Christ, both actively present in our lives. I am certain that in a few years, He will reveal Himself, and we will hear His resounding declaration: "Enough!"

In prayer, I hope that all may become believers, embracing His gospel and recognizing Joseph Smith's pivotal role in restoring the Priesthood, bringing forth records of ancient civilizations, and translating the only known record available to the world. Christ's trial of His people challenges us to believe. To the many individuals I acknowledge, you know who you are, and once again, thank you.

Chapter 1

After The Flood

"And it came to pass that I saw a man, and he was dressed in a white robe; and he came and stood before me."" And it came to pass that he spake unto me, and bade me follow him."" And it came to pass that as I followed him I beheld myself that I was in a **dark and dreary waste**[the war torn world of force and slavery]."" And after I had traveled for the space of many hours in **darkness**[ignorance], I began to **pray unto the Lord** that he would have mercy on me, according to the multitude of his tender mercies."" And it came to pass after I had **prayed unto the Lord** I beheld a **large and spacious field**."" And it came to pass that I beheld a **tree, whose fruit**[freedom] **was desirable to make one happy**."" And it came to pass that I did go forth and **partake of the fruit**[freedom] thereof; and I beheld that it was most sweet[precious], above all that I ever before tasted. Yea, and I beheld that the fruit thereof was **white, to exceed all the whiteness that I had ever seen**."" And as I partook of the fruit[knowledge & freedom] thereof it filled my soul with exceedingly great joy; wherefore, I began to be desirous that my family should partake[have freedom and knowledge] of it also; for I knew that it was **desirable above all other fruit**." (1 Nephi 8:5-12, Book of Mormon)

"And I beheld a **rod of iron**[the word of God], and it extended along the bank of the river, and led to the tree[Kingdom of God] by which I stood."" And I also beheld a **strait and narrow path**[faith in Christ], which came along by the rod of iron, even to the tree by which I stood; and it also led by the head of the fountain[cross roads of free-agency to choose], unto a large and spacious field[the earth], as if it had been a **world**.""And I saw numberless concourses of people, many of whom were pressing forward, that they might obtain the path[access to knowledge & freedom] which led unto the tree[Kingdom of God]by which I stood.""And it came to pass that they did **come forth, and commence in the path which led to the tree**.""And it came to pass that there **arose a mist of darkness**[many lies and disinformation]; yea even **an exceedingly great mist of darkness**, insomuch that **they**[people who were not diligent, giving in to lusts and imaginative desires] **who had commenced in the path did lose their way, that they wandered off and were lost**.""And I beheld **others pressing forward, and they came forth and caught hold of the end of the rod of iron; and they did press forward through the mist of darkness, clinging to the rod of iron**, even until they did come forth and partake of the fruit[freedom] of the tree[Kingdom of God].""And after they had partaken of the fruit of the tree they did **cast their eyes about**[needing others' approval]**as if they were ashamed**.""And I also cast my eyes round about, and beheld, **on the other side of the river of water**[lies and filth], **a great and spacious building**[wealth and riches]; **and it stood as it were in the air**[pride], **high above the earth**[in defiance of the Creator, in scorn of God].""And it was **filled with people, both old and young, both male and female**; and their manner of dress was exceedingly fine; and they were in **the attitude of mocking and pointing their fingers towards those who had come at and were partaking of the fruit**[people who were desiring Freedom].""And **after they had tasted of the fruit they were ashamed**, **because of those**[liberals, democrats, liars, the proud and ignorant people who have been deceived already] **scoffing at them; they fell away into forbidden paths**[drugs, evolution, homosexuality, child abuse and sex trafficking, pedophilia, abortions, murder, fraud, witchcraft, Satanic worship and sacrifice, disinformation, the secret orders, etc.] **and were lost**.""

(1 Nephi 8:19-28, Book of Mormon)

*"And now I, Nephi, do not speak all the words of my Father[Lehi]." "But, to be short in writing, behold, he saw **other multitudes pressing forward**; and they came and caught hold of the end of the **rod of iron**; and **they did press their way forward**[holding to what is right, by virtue of God-given], **continually holding fast to the rod of iron**, [word of God], until they came forth and fell down[gave their lives by sacrificing their lives in protection of their Liberties] and **partook of the fruit of the tree**." "And he also saw **other multitudes feeling their way towards that great and spacious building**[world with it's lies, riches, power, treachery, flattery, temptations]." "And it came to pass that **many were** **drowned in the depths of the fountain: and many were lost from his view, wandering in strange roads**." "And great was the multitude that did enter into that **strange building**. And after they did enter into that building they did **point the finger of scorn**[ridicule and discrediting the source of truth] **at me and those that were partaking of the fruit** [Unalienable Rights that were God-given, and freedom] also**; but we heeded them** not[didn't pay any attention to the lies, because they had knowledge and faith in Christ]." " These are the words of my Father: **For as many as heeded them, had fallen away**."*

(1 Nephi 8:30-34, Book of Mormon)

As we go through this life and try to make sense of what God is doing, and sorting through all of the lies, and disinformation, the fraud, the deceitfulness etc., It is a continuous effort to not be distracted from what we know the truth to be. We all must realize that the truth originates from Christ, because He is the Truth, the Way and the Life. We need to understand and remember that there is created on purpose by Satan, and his helpers, demons, traitors, liars etc., a "Great Mist of Darkness" to get us to believe a lie. This is what Liberals, Anti-God people, those who want to deceive and make the masses as miserable as themselves. None of us are going to be 100% perfect in our facts, but by knowing 98% of the facts, will give us confidence in going forward in the faith of Jesus Christ, and the 2% of the Assumptions will fall into place in due time. We must seek the source of Truth, use our common sense, search the scriptures and call on our God, in the name of His

Son, Jesus Christ, and He will make the Truth known unto us through His Spirit, The Spirit of Truth, The Holy Ghost.

We all know the story about Noah and how he built an ark to preserve his family and samples of animals of every kind and of every size, except those who lived in the water, from drowning in the great flood. Noah was considered by God as a perfect man or at least as perfect as one could be for his day. *"These are the generations of Noah: Noah was a just man and perfect in his generations, and Noah walked with God."(Genesis 6:9, KJV)*

Noah was commanded by God to build an ark, and the measurements given by God to complete this task proved that this boat was going to be huge. This ark was going to be big enough to take two of each species of animals. Some people automatically picture in their minds the size of some of the species like the elephant, rhinoceros, hippopotamus, giraffe, and tigers. So they automatically imagine the size the boat would have to be. Suppose Noah only took babies of each species, male and female. The boat would still be huge because of the many, many species there were and are. Kent Hovind concurs that it probably was babies that were taken on the ark, which makes sense as Noah and his family were on the ark for about a year, long enough for the animals to be old enough by the time the boat settled on solid ground, ready and mature enough to breed and multiply.

Despite the goodness of God in providing as, He did for His family, it only takes one to abuse what is prepared or planned. This happened when Cain killed Abel. *"And Cain talked with Abel his brother: and it came to pass, when they were in the field, that Cain rose up against Abel his brother, and slew him. And the Lord said unto Cain, Where is Abel thy brother? And he said, I know not: Am I my brother's keeper?" (Genesis 4:8–9, KJV).*

Cain covenanted with Satan, and this was where the secret orders began. Cain had posterity of his own, one of which was Lamech, who killed a man and then entered into secret oaths with his wives. *"And Lamech said unto his wives, Adah and Zillah, Hear my voice; ye wives of Lamech, hearken unto my speech: for I have slain a man to my wounding, and a young man to my hurt" (Genesis 4:23, KJV).*

It was from the time of Cain that men began to be evil and seek to gain honor, glory, riches, and power over one another. Cain was the first liberal. Most of the people became evil very quickly. They became violent and mean, except for a certain few, such as Seth, who was a good man. From Seth were born sons and daughters up to Methuselah, who lived 969 years. He had a son also named Lamech, who was a good man. Lamech had Noah when he was 595 years old and then lived a total of 777 years before he died.

> *"There were **giants** in the earth in those days; and also after that, when the sons of God[those obedient to the commandments] came in unto the daughters of men[worldly women], and they bare children to them,the same became mighty men which were of old, men of renown[large and mighty men]."(Genesis 6:4, KJV)*

> *"But Noah found grace in the eyes of the Lord.""These are the generations of Noah: Noah was a just man[son of God] and perfect in his generations, and **Noah walked with God**.[kept his commandments](Genesis 6:28-29, KJV)*

Lamech was the last good man who lived before Noah. All the rest had become evil and violent and served Satan. *"And Noah begat three sons, **Shem**, **Ham**, and **Japheth**. The earth also was corrupt before God, and the whole earth was filled with violence. And God looked upon the earth, and, behold, it was corrupt; for all flesh had corrupted his way upon the earth. And God said unto Noah, The end of all flesh is come before me; for the earth is filled with violence through them; and behold, I will destroy them with the earth"* (Genesis 6:10–13, KJV).

So God commanded Noah to build an ark. It was really strange to the people around, seeing a man and his family building such a weird, huge contraption on dry land, as the whole world was one landmass, and it had never rained before. So you can imagine the name-calling, the derogatory statements made, the disrespect by others, and of course the unbelief of the masses. To them, Noah was probably called mental and foolish, but he endured because he talked directly with God and observed His commandments.

Noah spent about 120 years preaching and building the ark when the day finally came to enter into it with all the animals. It probably took a lot of work caring and quartering all of them. Lastly, Noah went in with his wife and his three sons, Shem, Ham, and Japheth, each one having a wife. The total number of people that entered the Ark was eight.

> *"In the selfsame day entered Noah, and Shem, and Ham, and Japheth, the sons of Noah, and Noah's wife, and the three wives of his sons with them, into the ark" (Genesis 7:13, KJV). "Which sometime were disobedient, when once the long suffering of God waited in the days of Noah, while the ark was a preparing, wherein few, that is, **eight souls** were saved by water" (1 Peter 3:20, KJV). "And spared not the old world, but saved **Noah the eighth person**, a preacher of righteousness, bringing in the flood **upon the world of the ungodly**" (2 Peter 2:5, KJV).*

From these verses, we know that only eight people got onto the ark, and all the rest were drowned in the flood, including people, animals of every kind, and fowls of the air.

> *And the flood was forty days upon the earth; and the waters increased, and bare up the ark, and it was lift up above the earth. And the waters prevailed, and were increased greatly upon the earth; and the ark went upon the face of the waters. And the waters prevailed exceedingly upon the earth; and all the high hills, that were under the whole heaven, were covered. Fifteen cubits upward did the waters prevail; and the mountains were covered. And **all flesh died** that moved upon the earth, both fowl, and of cattle, and of beast, and of every creeping thing that creepeth upon the earth, and every man: All in whose nostrils was the breath of life, of all that was in the dry land, died. And every living substance was destroyed which was upon the face of the ground, both man, and cattle, and the creeping things, and the fowl of the heaven; and they were destroyed from the earth: and **Noah only remained alive**, and **they that were with him** in the ark. And the waters prevailed upon the earth an hundred and fifty days. (Genesis 7:17–24, KJV)*

Noah, with his family, stayed in that ark from the 17th day of the 2nd month of the year, which we call February, until the 2nd month of the next year before he was able to come out of the ark. It rained for 150 days straight before it quit or abated, which is about July 17, before the ark rested in the mountains of Ararat. It was about October 1 before Noah could even begin to see the tops of the mountains. Forty days after that, Noah was able to open a window and send forth the dove and the raven. The dove came back, but the raven didn't.

It was 7-days later when he sent the dove out the second time, and the dove came back with the olive branch. Then on the 1st day of the 1st month, which we know as January, Noah removed the cover from the ark. Then on February 27, Noah was finally able leave the ark. It was only Noah and his family who left the ark. They were the only living family on the face of the whole earth. There were no other people but them, which included Noah and his wife; Shem, Ham, and Japheth; and each of their wives, making a total of eight people. Noah and his family were told to go forth and multiply on the face of the earth, the animals likewise. They were preserved to act as breeding stock.

Every man, woman, and child descended from Noah and his three sons. That means, today, no matter the nationality, color, or origin, we are one family and one race. *"And **the sons of Noah**, that **went forth of the ark**, were **Shem**, and **Ham**, and **Japheth**: and Ham is the father of Canaan. These are the three sons of Noah: and **of them was the whole earth overspread**"* (Genesis 9:18–19, KJV).

There are no different races; just colors, languages, and customs separate us. The whites came from the lineage of Shem, the orientals from the lineage of Japheth, and the blacks from the lineage of Ham. You wonder why Ham was black. The truth was that Ham did something foolish, even though he knew better, which caused him to be cursed with black skin.

*And Noah began to be a husbandman, and he planted a vineyard: And he drank of the wine, and was drunken; and he was uncovered within his tent. And **Ham, the father of Canaan**, saw the nakedness of his father, and told his two brethren without. And Shem and Japheth took a garment, and laid it upon both their shoulders, and went backward, and covered the nakedness of their father; and their faces were backward, and they saw not their father's nakedness. And Noah awoke from his wine, and knew what his younger son had done unto* *him. And he said, **Cursed be Canaan**; a servant of servants shall he be unto his brethren. (Genesis 9:20–25, KJV)*

*And Noah awoke from his wine and knew what his youngest son had done unto him, and he said, Cursed be Canaan; a servant of servants shall he be unto his brethren. And he said, Blessed be the Lord God of Shem; and Canaan shall be his servant, and **a veil of darkness shall cover him**, that he shall be known among men. (Genesis 9:29–30, JST of the KJV)*

Noah lived a total of 950 years, and he died. Noah lived 350 years after the flood, so he was 600 years old when he entered the Ark. *""And Noah lived **after the flood three hundred and fifty years.**"" And all the days of Noah were nine hundred and fifty years[**950**]: and he died."(Genesis 9:28-29, KJV)* Noah was 500 years old when he fathered Shem, Ham and Japheth. *"And Noah was five hundred years[**500**] old: and Noah begat Shem, Ham, and Japheth."(Genesis 5:32, KJV).* Shem, Ham, and Japheth were at least 100-years old when they entered the Ark, because Noah, their father, was 600-years old at this time. When Noah died 350-years after the flood, they would have been at least 450-years old, in that range, being as there was probably a year or two between the siblings, as they began to inherit the land and spread out upon the face of it.

There were after that, at least two generations from Ham to the birth of **Nimrod** who founded the City of Babel, on the ***"Plains of Shinar"***. He also had the wild idea to build the Tower with the intentions of outfoxing God , and invading God's Kingdom, that they could see directly above them. Nimrod was not a righteous man, but he sought to fight against God, as to this day, Pagan's worship his constellation in the form of stars or witchcraft.

Noah, nor his immediate sons would have been involved in building the Tower of Babel, and we know that at least each of them were 450 years old at the time their father, Noah, died. There were three generations from the time of Ham to Nimrod, Nimrod being Ham's great grandson. Today's generations average 100-years approximately, probably more like 80-90 years, so the generations in Noah's day were much longer. Noah lived after the flood to the ripe old age of 950-years, and his sons were already at least 450-years old.

So multiply 450 two times, you have 900 years, give or take a few to the time that God decided to confound their language and scatter the inhabitants to the countries of the world. Included in this number 900, is enough time for Nimrod to get big enough and mature enough to become devilish.

> *"And the sons of **Ham**; **Cush**, and Mizraim, and Phut, and **Canaan**.""And the sons of **Cush**; Seba, and Havilah, and Sabtah, and **Raamah**, and Sabtecha: and the sons of **Raamah**; Sheba, and Dedan.""And **Cush** begat **<u>Nimrod</u>**: he began to be a mighty one in the earth.""He was a mighty hunter before the Lord: wherefore it is said, Even as **Nimrod the mighty hunter**[wicked man] **before the Lord'""<u>And the beginning of his kingdom was</u> **Babel**</u>, and Erech, and Accad, and Calneh, **in the land of <u>Shinar</u>**."(Genesis 10:6-10. KJV)*

900-1000 years is plenty of time to people a whole continent, including all of the descendants of Japheth, and Shem. During this time frame, it would be impossible for this huge number of people to dwell in the land of Shinar, unless the land of Shinar, included all of the land of Iraq. Also the size of the people were hard to imagine after living upwards to over 450 years maybe more. After all, Noah lived to be 950-years, as also did Noah's predecessors back to Adam.

At this time, because they were all family, everyone spoke the same language; they were just different colors because of the curse of Ham. Because Ham was cursed, all of Ham's posterity carried the mark of the black skin. Ham's posterity is not responsible for Ham's sins, but it is because of Ham's sins that his posterity has to deal with what Ham did. The same happened when Adam and Eve transgressed in the Garden of Eden. It is not Adam's transgressions that we are responsible for, but it is because of Adam's transgressions that we have to deal with this devil's jurisdiction and choose what we will do, according to our situations. We all must still have the free agency to choose who we will serve.

At the Tower of Babel, all mankind spoke the same language, and the planet where the God's dwelled, or in mythical terms, Mount Olympus, hovered just above the earth, and the earth was still one landmass(joined together). The magnetic pull of the planet of the Gods on the water made a giant pillar of water stand up toward the planet, making it appear as if Atlas were holding up the world. This was where Nimrod got the wild idea that he, and everyone in the land of his kingdom of Shinar, were going to build a great tower that would reach up to Heaven. The "Sons of God" would not participate in such an event, but because of this problem, and to take advantage of this situation, God determined to scatter the people abroad to occupy the world/His "Vineyard". (See the parable/riddle of the vineyard).

And **the whole earth was of one language**, and **of one speech**. And it came to pass, as they journeyed from the east[Mountains of Arrarat-in Turkey, that they found a plain in the land of Shinar[Iraq]; and they dwelt there. And they said one to another, Go to, let us make brick, and burn them throughly, and they had brick for stone, and slime had they for morter. And they said, Go to, let us build us a city and **a tower, whose top may reach unto heaven**; and let us make us a name, lest we be scattered abroad upon the face of the whole earth. And the Lord came down to see the city and the tower that the children of men builded. And the Lord said, Behold, the people is one, and they have all one language; and this they begin to do: and now nothing will be restrained from them, which they have imagined to do. Go to, let us go down, and there confound their language, that they may not understand one another's speech. So **the Lord scattered them abroad** [including the Jaredites who came to the Americas] from thence **upon the face of all the earth**: and they left off to build the city. Therefore is the name of it called Babel; because the Lord did there confound the language of all the earth: and from thence did the Lord scatter them abroad upon the face of all the earth. (Genesis 11:1–9, KJV)

It was in these days that Japheth and Shem's posterity was also growing on the face of the earth. Shem had a son called Eber, who had a son named Peleg. And it was in Nimrod's day when the language of the people, because of the Tower of Babel, was confounded, and the people were scattered to different parts of the earth. It wasn't until the days of Peleg that the earth was divided. "And unto Eber were born two sons: the name of one was **Peleg**; for **in his days was the earth divided**; and his brother's name was Joktan" (Genesis 10:25, KJV).

The timing of the confounding of the language of the people and the time when the heavens fled away were closely coordinated. Revelation mentioned the heavens fleeing away. "Then I saw a great white throne, and him that sat on it, from whose face **the earth and the heaven fled away**; and there was found no place for them" *(Revelation 20:11, KJV)*.

So after the language of the people was confounded, the people gathered into groups and went to different parts of the world to be alone with the ones they could understand. Later then, the planet where the Gods dwelled, left, breaking the magnetic pull on the watery pillar and returning the water to the earth, making the water level higher, thus dividing the earth into continents and into islands. Remember, before, it was one solid landmass. God led the Jaredites to the promised land via the "GREAT DEEP", as there was much water, but it just was not quite so deep. Later, led other groups out of certain countries, and they were instructed to build ships or barges at various times, whatever the case might be, and flee persecution, such as the Pilgrims, with the promise of prosperity and peace if they would obey the commandments of the Lord.

It is amazing to witness just how wise and great God is. We all started out as one family, regardless of color, speaking the same language for generations up to the time of the Tower of Babel. God then confounded the languages, thus dividing the people into areas of the earth and then sending the earth away from before Him and dividing the landmass with water. Now in these latter days, we can see how the people are beginning to return to speaking the same language again.

The ability to get around the world and come together is so much faster, and the speed and ability to obtain knowledge through the internet and to communicate worldwide is so fantastic. Knowledge does flow over the earth like a flood. "For **the earth shall be filled with the knowledge of the glory of the Lord**, as the waters cover the sea" (Habakkuk 2:14, KJV).

It is literally at our fingertips. I am going to do my best to show in the next chapter the timeline from the Tower of Babel, when God confounded the Language of the people, and the scattering of them throughout His vineyard, to bring about His wonderful purposes. This Work is dedicated to showing that the Book of Mormon is True, because if it is true, then everything that Joseph Smith did and said is true also, at the same time, exposing the lies and what is meant by the meaning of Lehi's vision of the "***Mists of Darkness***". It is just as simple as that.

Chapter 2

The Genealogy and Generations of Adam

To get a timeline of when Peleg, who was the king of Babylon then, actually lived, one needs to understand a little genealogy, and how everyone relates to one another. Adam, the first man was placed here on this earth, which pretty much started from the year of finished creation, or 6,000 years, which includes those B.C., and A.D., as to the beginning, and the finishing of man kinds existence. Anytime predating the existence of Christs' presence on this earth, is a given that this period was "Before Christ" or "BC". *"Thus the heavens and the earth were finished, and all the host of them.""and on the seventh day God ended his work which he had made; and he rested on the seventh day,, from all his work which he had made."(Genesis 2:1-2, KJV)*

Adam lived 930 years which was almost 1,000 years by himself, but Adam had sons and daughters within this 930 years, each one living to almost 1,000 years also. The timeline from the creation, and when Adam became a living soul on this earth, as he was placed here, was around 6,000+ years ago. Adam then died 930 years later, as the length of his life. Christ, who came in the "Meridian of Time", or the year "0". is when time started all over, at his birth, and every civilization began reckoning their calendars here.(see Tower of Babel Wikipedia; https://en.m.wikipedia.org>wiki March 9, 2012). Then from the time of Christ to our present time, has been 2023 years, give or take a few years, making a total of around, 6,000+ years from the time Adam was placed on the earth.

There have been many researchers who have struggled to pinpoint the perfect dates, concerning what a generation would be, but it is almost impossible to do, due to the many variables, and debatable issues. Examples of these for instance, such as some generations are larger than the ones we see now, and there are a wide range of years in earlier generations, gaps in generations due to deaths, overlapping generations, birth rites, the reckoning of times, etc.. Most historians are ultimately close to the same time frames, based upon the facts that we do know, and based upon facts gathered from the Bible, and other pertinent scriptures, etc..

One of the most important issues and tools for determining the timelines, is by reference to the term: *"generation"* See Oxford Dictionary; **generation**(gen.er.a.tion). "1. All of the people born and living at about the same time, regarded collectively, i.e. peer groups, age, and age group." See also "Black's Law Dictionary", fourth Edition: *"generation"* May mean either a degree of removal in computing descents, or a single succession of living beings in *natural descent.* McMillan v. School Committee, 107 N.C. 609, 12 S.E. 330, 10 L.R.A. 823.

Today we see a generation described as, the average period, usually about 20-30 years, during which children are born, grow up, become adults, begin to marry, and plan their own families. Thus begin another generation. Today children by law, are considered as adults at the age of 18, and are very sexually active, and wanting to begin families. Then by 45-years old, the children of the preceding generation are grown, out of school, working, and are already thinking of marrying. For the parents to live to 100-years is quite a feat.

From the time of Adam, who lived to be 930-years, and then reared his first son, Cain. Cain turned out to be a liar and a murderer from the beginning, and followed after Satan, and was united with him. Cain was never mentioned as one of the generations of Adam, especially after he killed his brother Abel through collaboration, with Satan, to get riches and power. Cain was the devil's own, and was never mentioned as the head of a generation, nor of inheriting any birthright from Adam. Abel also, was not named as a son and head of a generation, because his life was ended prematurely, by Cain.

The Bible tells us that from the time of Adam to Noah was 10-generations. *"This is the book of the generations of Adam, in the day that God created man, in the likeness of God made he him;"*...(Genesis 5: 1-32, KJV).

His first generation is Seth, having begotten him at the age of 130-years, Adam then lived 930 years rearing other sons and daughters. Only Seth was mentioned as the first generation from Adam. Seth was a son of God, having also received blessings of inheritance, including the birthright from among all of his other brothers and sisters. Seth then lived 105 years before he begat the next obedient son of God, through Enos. Seth then lived 912 years and begat other sons and daughters before he died.

Likewise, Enos lived 90-years and begat Cainan, then lived a total of 905 years before he died. Cainan's first generation began at being 70-years old before he begat Mahallaleel, and then lived to the ripe old age of 910 years before he died, also having other sons and daughters. Mahallaleel at 65 years begat Jared, and then died at the age of 895 years. Jared lived 162 years before he begat Enoch, then continued having other sons and daughters to the age of 962 years, then he died.

Enoch lived 65 years and begat Methusaleh, then lived until he was 365 years when, because of him being an obedient "son of God", and perfect, was taken up to be with God, while he was alive in the flesh. Methusaleh was 187 years old before he begat Lamech, then continued having other sons and daughters up to the age of 969 years. After 182 years, Lamech begat Noah, then before he died, lived to the age of 770 years. Noah in turn lived 500 years then begat three sons; Shem, Ham and Japheth. Each son was counted in the same generation. Noah then lived after the flood, to the age of 950 years old. Shem, Ham and Japheth were each around 100 years old before entering the Ark, then were on the Ark a whole year, and while on the Ark, they had no children.

It appears that a generation varies, and begins in the Bible from the age of the man to his first son having the birthright as a "son of God", throughout the period as other children are conceived and born. For instance, From Adam to Seth was 130 years to that generation, but that generation included Cain and Able, and any other sons and daughters that may have been born, from the time Adam chose to father children, up to the time of his death. It also shows how God rewards those who diligently seek Him, and who obeys His commandments.

Now, if you take the 10-generations of Adam, then add them all together and then divide by the number of generations(10), the number of years between generations averages out to 105 years between Adam and Noah. Each generation then extended over 900 years, which included other sons and daughters in that generational group.

Noah was 500 years old to the time he began begetting Shem, Ham, and Japheth. He was 600 years old by the time he, with his family entered the Ark, which included only eight. Noah with his wife, and Shem, Ham, and Japheth, with each one of their wives, making a total of eight people. Shem, Ham, and Japheth, by this time were each at least 100 years old, and neither one had any children before they entered the Ark, and had no children during the year they were on the Ark, and the same exited the Ark without any children.

From the time then, that Adam was placed on the earth and commanded to multiply and replenish the earth, to the time that Noah and his family exited the Ark, we have a pretty sound knowledge that 1592 years went by. This brings us to about 3,385 years B.C.. After leaving the Ark, the life span of men was greatly reduced from over and around, 900 years, to only half of that proven through the lives of Shem, Ham and Japheth, also drastically reducing the generation spans, of father to son down, to around 30 years.

"Now these are the generations of Shem: Shem was an hundred years old, and begat Arphaxad two years after the flood:""And Shem lived after he begat Arphaxad five hundred years, and begat sons and daughters.""And Arphaxad lived five and thirty years[35], and begat Salah:""And Arphaxad lived after he begat Salah four hundred and three years[438], and begat sons and daughters.""And Salah lived thirty years[30], and begat Eber:""And Salah lived after he begat Eber four hundred and three years[433], and begat sons and daughters.""And Eber lived four hundred and thirty years, and begat Peleg:""And Eber lived after he begat Peleg four hundred and thirty years[Eber, the father of Peleg, lived to 860 years old], and begat sons and daughters.""And Peleg lived thirty years and begat Reu:""And Peleg lived after he begat Reu two hundred and nine years[239], and begat sons and daughters.""And Reu lived two and thirty years[23] , and begat Serug:""And Reu lived after he begat Serug two hundred and seven years[230

yrs], and begat sons and daughters.""And Serug lived thirty years and begat Nahor:""And Serug lived after he begat Nahor two hundred years[230], and begat sons and daughters.""And Nahor lived nine and twenty years[29], and begat Terah:""And Nahor lived after he begat Terah an hundred and nineteen years[148]], and begat sons and daughters.""And Terah lived seventy years, and begat Abram, Nahor, and Haran.".....(Genesis 11:10-26, KJV).

The reader can clearly see that Shem and his wife started having children two years after they left the Ark, after the flood, and that Shem was already 100 years old at least. Chances are that Shem, being the oldest of three, was probably 1-3 years older than his other two younger brothers, unless they were triplets or there was a set of twins. That means, if Shem was a 100 years old then his younger brothers were 99(Japheth) and 97(Ham) at best. Through Shem stemmed the "sons of God".

Noah, his father, had lived after the flood to be 950 years old, whereas, Shem only lived to be 600 years old before he died. From then on up through Eber, with the exception of **Peleg's** father, Eber, who lived to be **860** years old. Other than Eber, the men were only living in excess of four hundred years. The longevity dropped in half from Noah to Shem in that same generation, then from Shem to Eber(Eber lived twice as long as Shem almost) in just four generations. From Peleg through Serug half again as long, to the total of 200 years, which had dropped drastically within 3 generations. Then from the posterity of Serug, beginning with Nahor the life span dropped to just under a 120 years, just as God said it would in Genesis. This shows how age varied even down through the generations, and they were large and mighty men.

> *"And it came to pass, when men began to multiply on the face of the earth, and daughters were born unto them,""That the sons of God [men of the gospel covenant]saw the daughters of men[women of the world]that they were fair; and they took them wives of all which they chose.""And the Lord said, My spirit shall not always strive with man, for that he also is flesh:* **yet his days shall be an hundred and twenty years.** *"(Genesis 6:1-3, KJV)*

Shem was 100 years old when he entered the Ark with his family. When the Ark settled in the Mountains of Ararat, and he was 101 years old when he left the Ark, and in another year he begat Arphaxad. Shem then lived a total of 500 years and begat other sons and daughters, many of which became men of "renown. Some of which included Elam: who became the *Father of the Persians.* Another is Asshur: *Father of the Assyrians;* Lud, *Father of the Lydians;* Aram: *the Father of the Syrians;* And Arphaxad: *Father of the Chaldeans.*

Another clear fact that is evident, is that from Adam to Noah the generations averaged 105 years for the young man to mature, to when they actually began raising families. Even for Shem to have his first son, Arphaxad, took 102 years at least. Arphaxad then only took 35 years, for him to begin his family when he begat Salah who took only 30 years to begat Eber. Eber had his first generation after 430 years with his posterity beginning with Peleg. Eber, then lived another 430 years after Peleg: "in whose days the earth was divided", as described in *(Genesis 11:1-9, KJV).* Peleg was also the *Father and founder as the first King of Babylon.* Peleg had a wife whose name was *"Sinaar".* The Tower of Babel was built on the *"Plain of Shinar"[named after the wife of Peleg possibly]* by the people of Nimrod, the mighty hunter.

This means that Eber had other sons and daughters, one of which was named Joktan, as we are told in *(Genesis 10:25, KJV),* as to Peleg having a younger brother. Eber, Peleg's father, was still alive after Peleg died by 101 years. Eber was alive long enough to see his grandson, Reu, grow and begin his family, with the birth of his great grandson, Serug. This also means that genes through Eber, and his posterity to live long lives, outside the normal age-group was astounding.

Peleg in turn began his first generation in 30 years by begetting Reu, and from Reu to his son, Serug was 32 years. From Serug to his first generation was 30 years with Nahor, and likewise from Nahor to Terah, the father of Abraham, was 29 years. Then Terah to Abraham was 70 years, and from Abraham to his first son, not counting Ishmael, but Isaac, a son of God, and future father of Jacob and Esau, was 81 years.

Abraham was told by the Lord, after making covenant with Abraham, that his posterity would be as numerous as the stars in the night sky. The Lord also promised Abraham that his posterity would go into bondage for four hundred years, and that after four generations, would be led out of bondage as a nation, and his posterity would be rewarded and receive the land as their inheritance forever.

"And when the sun was going down, a deep sleep fell upon Abraham; and, lo, an horror of great darkness fell upon him.""And he said unto Abram, know of a surety that thy seed shall be a stranger in a land that is not theirs, and shall serve them; and they shall afflict them **four hundred years;"***"And also that nation, whom thou shall serve, will I judge: and afterward shall they come out with great substance.""And thou shalt go to thy fathers in peace; thou shalt be buried in a good old age.""But in the* **fourth generation** *they shall come hither again: for the iniquity of the Amorites is not yet full."(Genesis 15:12-16, KJV)*

The Lord reckoned the generations of Abram's seed while in bondage to be 100 years, and as they truly were in Egypt 400 years, this was construed as 4-generations. In this sense, God used a generation as a form of measurement of a life time. Joseph, while in Egypt, saw his sons children, and their children's children up to the third generation, himself dying at the age of 110 years old. Thus, it was expected that each generation would live to be around 100 years old.

"And Joseph dwelt in Egypt, he, and his father's house: and Joseph lived an **hundred and ten years**.*""And Joseph saw Ephraim's children of the* **third generation:** *the children also of Machir the son of Manasseh were brought up upon Joseph's knees.""And Joseph said unto his brethren, I die: and God will surely visit you, and bring you out of this land unto the land which he sware to Abraham, to Isaac, and to Jacob.""And Joseph took an oath of the children of Israel, saying, God will surely visit you, and ye shall carry up my bones from hence.""So Joseph died, being an* **hundred and ten** *years old: and they embalmed him, and he was put in a coffin in Egypt."(Genesis 50:22-26, KJV)*

God also used this same lifetime measurement of a generation when he created the earth and everything in it, and on it, in six days/6,000-years, and resting the seventh.*(Genesis 2:4-5, KJV)*. A generation in the beginning was considered by God as one day/1000 years, because that was how God reckoned time, and including the fact: that from the time of Adam to Noah(ten generations), almost all were living past 900-years.

From the time of Adam to Noah, the generation was measured from son of birthright, to son of birthright, which averaged a little over 100 years, as shown earlier. Then adding to that, the Israelites in Egypt were there 4 generations, or 400-years, as each male was expected to live 100 years, We must be practical when we talk about generations. A man who is only going to live to be 100, cannot wait till they are 100 to begin having children, unless they don't want to leave a posterity.

From the time of Shem to Abraham, the average generation was 30-36 years. King David tells us that in his day the life-span was only 80 years at best, if not only 70-years. *"The days of our years are **three score years and ten**; and if by reason of strength they be **fourscore years**; yet is their strength labour and sorrow; for it is soon cut off, and we fly away."(Psalms 90:10, KJV)*

Here are the 42 generations from Abraham to Jesus Christ. *"...17"So all the generations from Abraham to David are **fourteen generations;** and from David until the carrying away into Babylon[11th year of the reign of King Zedekiah] are **fourteen generations;** and from [Zedekiah] the carrying away into Babylon unto Christ are **fourteen generations."** (Matthew 1:1-17, KJV).*

The reader can plainly see how the lengths of generations vary from time to time. There are many extenuating circumstances that influence the life-span of the generations. In Adam's day to Noah the people were shielded from exposure to the sun, and only had to harvest their food, and lived beyond 900 years, and took over 100 years between generations. Whereas, from Noah to Shem, now having exposure from the suns rays, and having to work hard to grow and harvest their food, they were living up close to 500 years, then from Shem to Eber, 450 years, and they took up to 50 years between child rearing. Then from Eber, to Peleg, to Serug, 200 years, and were rearing children at 30 years. Then even more-so from Serug to Nahor, 120 years, and from Nahor to Abraham, 100 years and holding throughout the slave camps of Egypt and the reign of King David, to the time of Christ.

The Stress through the wars and bondage, hard work, and exposure, will shorten the life of any people. The generations averaged from Jacob to Joseph, 40-years, from Joshua to King David 40-years, from David to his son Solomon, 40-years and from Solomon to Christ 40-years. 40-years was the length of time for the "children of Israel" to die out in the desert/wilderness, before they could be led across the River Jordan to occupy the land.

> *"Harden not your hearts, as in the provocation, in the day of temptation in the wilderness:""When your fathers tempted me, proved me, and saw my works **forty years**.""Wherefore I was grieved with that **generation**, and said, they do always err in their heart; and they have not known my ways.""So I sware in my wrath, They shall not enter into my rest.""Take heed, brethren, lest there be in any of you an **evil heart of unbelief**, in departing from the living God."…15 "While it is said, Today if ye will hear his voice, harden not your hearts, as in the provocation."For some, when they had heard did provoke: howbeit not all that came out of Egypt by Moses." "But with whom was he grieved **forty years**? Was it not with them that had sinned, whose carcases fell in the wilderness?""And to whom sware he that they should not enter into his rest, but to them that believed not?""So we see that they **could not enter in because of unbelief**."(Hebrews 3:8-12, 15-19, KJV).*

Forty years was the length of time it took for the unbelieving generation of the children of Israel to die out, before the next generation could cross over the River Jordan, who were ready and were exercising their belief and faith in Christ. They were anxious to receive the blessings promised and reserved for them, and ready to pay the price and do whatever was needed, in order to accomplish their tasks. Because of their unbelief, the blessings of the Everlasting Priesthood Covenant and the New and Everlasting Covenant of Marriage was not extended to them except for just a few, like Moses, Joshua, Caleb, Phinehas, etc., until Christ changed it when He died on the cross.

We are now in the last dispensation, the dispensation of the *"fulness of times"*. The talk about years, and generations and dispensations carry with them a measurement of time, before Christ comes back to redeem His people. The days of mankind on this earth are numbered, and this is the reason that God keeps track of the number of years, and talks about generations, as to when he rests again from His labors on this earth, before His judgments come.

Here is how it looks from the eyes of the author:

From: Adam to Noah is 10 -- generations, including down to Shem: 1650 years – 2333 B.C.

From: Shem to Abraham 10 -- generations, age shortened by half: 910 years

From: Abraham to King David –14 generations, age shortened again: 560 years

From King David to 11th year King Zedekiah-14 generations average: 560 years

From King Zedekiah to Jesus Christ – 14 generations, average 40: 560 years

From Jesus Christ to our present day: 2023 years A.D.

Total years from Adam being first, placed on earth to multiply, to now: **6263** years.

We are actually into the **Millenium** talked about, where On the seventh day God finished His labor, then he rested from all of His work. *"Thus the heavens and the earth were finished, and all the host of them.""And on the seventh day God ended his work which he had made; and he rested on the seventh day from all his work which he had made.""And God blessed the seventh day, and sanctified it: because in it he had rested from all his work which God created and made."(Genesis 1:1-3, KJV)*

This earth is alive, because if it was dead, it would not be able to support life itself. It has fulfilled the purpose of It's creation, and because of this will also receive it's Celestial Glory. The days are numbered for all of God's creations, worlds without end. The author cannot say for sure how many years this earth has seen, but he knows that unless mankind repents of their sins and calls upon their only true creator, that when he comes, which could be any day, He will catch them unaware.

Those experts who think to use terms *"prehistoric", "stone age",* or in any way, thinking to discredit God, or that this creation of man on this earth was 120 or 130 million years ago, are going to wish the rocks would fall upon them to hide them from the piercing gaze of an indignant God, knowing they didn't change when they knew better. Accordingly, they can predate rocks all they want, chances are they were here infinitely, not just for 120 to 130+ million years ago. Suppose that, by the term creation, God took the materials that already existed and formed this world, rocks and all into what is now this earth. It would take the wind out of the sails of these Atheist/Evolutionists, wouldn't it. Or suppose that the inhabitants of this earth, before we began, failed to live up to their covenants, and were cleansed from off the face of this earth, and God started again, worlds without end. God laughs at the wisdom of man, and has already beaten them at their own game.

> *"In the beginning God created the heavens and the earth.""**And the earth was without form, and void**; and darkness was upon the face of the deep. And the Spirit of God moved upon the face of the waters."…"And God said, Let the waters under the heaven be **gathered together unto one place, and let the dry land appear: and it was so.**"…(Genesis 1:1-2, 9, KJV)*

> *"But only an <u>account of this earth, and the inhabitants thereof, give I unto you,</u>. For behold, **<u>there are many worlds that have passed away by the word of my power. And there are many that now stand, and innumerable are they unto man;</u>** but all things are numbered unto me, <u>for they are mine and I know them.</u>" (Moses section: 1:35, Doctrine and Covenants}*

It was after the earth was formed that he placed every plant, animal, and human upon the earth to also fulfill the purposes of their creation. *"These are the generations of the heavens and of the earth when they were created, in the day that the Lord God made the earth and the heavens.""**And every plant of the field before it was in the earth, and every herb of the field before it grew:** for the Lord God had not caused it to rain upon the earth, **and there was not a man to till the ground."**…"And the Lord God planted a garden eastward in Eden; and there **he put the man whom he had formed.**"(Genesis 2:4-5. 8, KJV)*

God does have a plan for this earth, and in his mercy and good grace, and kindness, is limitless upon everyone and everything that fulfills the measure of their creation. This goes for all of His people within this earthly vineyard, wherever He places them as they diligently seek Him. This brings us to the people who were led to the Americas during the time of the Tower of Babel.

Chapter 3

The Jaredites/Olmecs Beginning & Journey from Tower of Babel

The Jaredites/Olmecs Journey
From The Tower of Babel [Iraq] to America

We are now going to focus on "the days of Peleg", when God confounded the languages of the people and divided the earth, by water. The confounding of the languages was done because of one, namely, Nimrod, who in the days of Peleg: Father of Babylon, conspired to build a tower for the purpose of ascending up to Heaven where the Gods were, on Mount Olympus. The plain of Shinar was in the Kingdom of Babylon, what we know today as the country of Iraq.

> *"These are the families of the sons of Noah, after their generations,*
> *in their nations: and by these were the nations divided in the earth after*
> *the flood."(Genesis 10:32, KJV)*

> *"And it came to pass, when men began to multiply on the face of the earth,*
> *and daughters were born unto them, that the sons of God[those who kept the*
> *commandments of God] saw the daughters of men that they were **fair,** and*
> *they took them **wives** of all which they chose."(Genesis 6:1-4, KJV)* Make
no mistake, but the "sons of God" are those who received the "fulness of the gospel" of Jesus Christ, and the "natural man" of the world, are those who don't. The sons of God were through the lineage of Noah

through Shem, through Peleg, through Abraham etc., receiving the birth-rite by obeying the commandments of God, and receiving the fullness of the gospel, through the priesthood covenant.

The "daughters of men" referred to here, were from the lineage of Japheth, who is the father of the orientals. Japheth's sons are Magog, the father of the Scythians, or, north of the Black Sea in Russia]; Gomer, the beginning of the Gallatians (Galls), who are the French- the Francum, dwelling in the land of Franza, by the river Franza, and by the river Senah. Japheth is also the father of Madai – the Medes; also Javan, the father of the Grecians; also **Tubal**, the father of Iberes/ Spain, those who dwell in the land of Tuskanah, by the river Pashniah; **daughters of Tubal** _were the fairest women in all the earth._ From among these women were who the 'sons of God" chose as their wives. They were from among the Orientals, the French, the Scythians/ Russians, the Spanish, because of their beauty. Other sons of Japheth: Meshech, the father of the Cappadocians; and Tiras, the father of the Tracians; the Rushnash/Russia; the Cushni; and the Ongolis/ Mongols, dwelling by the sea Jabus, by the river Cura, which empties into the river Tragan.

This is the one reason you will find Oriental DNA in Ancient America. (See Genealogy from Adam to the 12 Tribes. By John Paul Pratt). The Book of Ether gives a basic genealogy of the beginning, and even several of the names prevalent in the oriental culture and civilizations, for example: "Kim", as well as names derived through the lineage of "Shem".

> *"And the whole earth was of one language, and of one speech.""And it came to pass, as they journeyed from the east, that they found a plain in the land of Shinar[desert plain]: and they dwelt there.""And they said one to another, Go to, let us make brick, and burn them throughly. And they had brick for stone, and slime had they for mortar.""And they said, Go to, let us build us a city and a tower, whose top may reach unto heaven; and let us make us a name, lest we be **scattered abroad upon the face of the whole earth**.""And the Lord came down to see the city and the tower, which the children of men builded.""And the Lord said, Behold, the people is one, and they have **all one language**; and this they begin to do: and now nothing*

*will be restrained from them, which they have imagined to do.""Go to, let us go down, and there **confound their language**, that they may not understand one another's speech.""So the Lord scattered them abroad from thence upon the face of all the earth: and they left off to build the city.""Therefore is the name of it called Babel; because the Lord did there confound the language of all the earth: and from thence did the Lord scatter them abroad upon the face of all the earth."(Genesis 11:1-9, KJV) https://www.youtube.com/watch?v=otOfeaJB1DU*

So long to Prehistoric. Some researchers and historians have the creation placed around 4,359 years B.C., but my calculations are, when Adam was placed in the Garden of Eden, when time for man actually began, and is a more precise, and practical starting point. The author's belief is that man was placed here on this earth 3978 years B.C., and having the flood happening around 2,333 years B.C.. We all know these events transpired somewhere in this time frame, before the coming of Christ. We should be counting from the time man was first placed on the earth instead. This earth took 6-days/6,000 years, with everything in it, to create, including animals, water, plants, organizing the universe, the rotation of the planets and stars, etc.. He then rested within the 7th-day/1000 years, from all of this work, before placing man/Adam and Eve upon the earth.

Everything already preexisted, or was created before it was placed on earth: *"These are the generations of the heavens and of the earth when they were created, in the day the Lord God made the earth and the heavens""**And every plant of the field before it was in the earth, and every herb of the field before it grew: for the Lord God had not caused it to rain upon the earth, and there was not a man to till the** ground."(Genesis 2:4-5, KJV)*

The author's goal is to place the years and dates as close to the times as to help the reader understand when the civilizations of America took place, from where they originated, why they came here, who they were, how they got here, where they went, and why they were destroyed.

First of all, B.C. means "Before Christ" and A.D. Doesn't mean after death, as that would be impossible, because this term began being used in calculating calendars in all civilizations at the birth of Jesus Christ. Christ lived at least 33-years before he was crucified upon the cross, in Jerusalem. Therefore, "A.D." stands for "Anno Domino", a Latin term on the Julian, or Gregorian Calendar, meaning *"In the year of the Lord"*. Maybe it might be simpler to calculate time instead of "Before Christ"(B.C.), to using the term, "After Creation"(A.C.), therefore making it unnecessary to count back in time to arrive at the nearest possible time that the ancient civilizations began in America.

However, using the term Before Christ, helps us to understand how many years this earth is given before it too receives it's celestial glory, as it is also a living soul, and is fulfilling it's purpose of creation. So, if the author's calculations are correct, 4,240 years passed away before the birth of Christ, and then to date: 2023 years have passed away since the birth of Christ, equaling exactly 6,263 years. That means that <u>Christ is set to come very soon, any year now</u>, give or take a few years, if any, especially judging by the things going on in the world, and the evilness in the hearts of mankind.

It is the goal of the author to show that the earlier civilizations that were already here, and those that went before, and when the Pilgrims came here to America, etc., are the same as the Aztecs, Mayans, Incans, Olmecs, and Toltecs, who all of which did exist here, and many of which still do, and were greatly blessed of the Lord at one time. The sad thing is that the people on this land are headed in the same direction today, as when two civilizations earlier, quit calling upon God. They allowed "secret societies" to corrupt their governments. Everyone is striving for riches, power, control, and is joining themselves to the beast/corporation. They want their ease and comfort, and want to exercise their lusts, and are seeking possessions, without having an eye single to the glory of Almighty God.

Noah, being already 600 years old, and his three young sons spent their growing up period for 100 years preparing the Ark, and meanwhile preaching the gospel of Jesus Christ to the people round about. Now if correct, this earth is only allotted 6,000 years before the millennium of another 1,000 years, after which, it receives it's "paradisiacal glory". This information dates Noah to approximately 2,333 years B.C.(Before Christ), and just before he entered the ark with his family of eight. This is a pretty accurate, but not perfect reckoning, as there are many variables.

From the time of Adam being placed on the earth, to the time after the flood was approximately 1651 years. Nimrod and the people around, began work on the Tower of Babel 700 years after the flood, and spent 107 years approximately, building such a huge structure, and were not even close to finishing it. They had to have a lot of people to do this, because it took much man power. First off, it took skill in laying bricks, it meant making a solid foundation, baking bricks, collecting mortar, etc..107 years though, was not nearly long enough to complete this monumental task and would have been, and in reality was a waste of time, as it provoked God to anger, because of the audacity and nerve of man to think that they could invade the heavens and become like God without obeying his commandments. This knowledge brings us to about 3,983 years B.C.. The Heavens overhead were much further away than meets the eye, and secondly, God wasn't going to let it happen, and He didn't let it happen.

So, if from the time of placing Adam on earth to now, 2023 A.D., places us over 6,263 years to the beginning, when God placed Adam and Eve on the earth, and commanding them to multiply and replenish the earth. To rehearse the calculations, we must first, add the generations of man up to the time of Christ, then subtract 4240 years B.C. from 6000, equaling 1760 years B.C. Now subtract 1760 years from our current time, 2023 then you would have approximately 263 years into the 7,000th year, even into the Millenium. It is debatable whether or not, the author is off in his calculations by a few years, give or take, because of variables, as discussed earlier, as it is almost impossible to be perfect in every detail.

The days of Peleg were 239 years, in fact, Peleg was born in 2221 B.C., and he died in 1982 B.C., and as the scripture says: *"And unto Eber were born two sons: the name of one was* **Peleg***; for in his days was the earth divided; and his brother's name was Joktan."(Genesis 10:25, KJV)* **"And Peleg lived after he begat Reu 209 years, and begat sons and daughters."** *(Genesis 11:19, KJV)*

Obviously **Reu** was only one of the sons and daughters of Peleg: King of Babylon. Reu was born 2192 B.C., and died: 1953 B.C.

B.C. Now you can see according to the author's figures and information that he is just about right on, and Peleg lived exactly 239 years, as did his son, Reu, as he also lived to be 239 years..

Peleg's father, Eber was born in 2255 B.C., 64 years, before Nimrod. Nimrod was born in 2070 B.C. and he died in 1855 B.C., but he lived during the days of Peleg, 88 years. These were the days when the earth was divided, and God came down and confounded the language of the people.

Eber, also lived before he fathered Peleg, 430 years. He then lived after Peleg another 430 years, having other sons and daughters. *"And Eber lived four hundred and thirty years, and begat Peleg:""And Eber lived after he begat Peleg four hundred and thirty years, and begat sons and daughters."(Genesis 11:16-17, KJV)*. Eber, lived to be 860 years old. He outlived his own son, Peleg, by 191 years. From this stock, came forth the **"Giants/Olmecs"** into the Americas, between the years 2070 B.C. To 1982 B.C., when not only was Nimrod alive at the time, by 88 years, but also, Peleg's father by 191 years.

It therefore, is my educated opinion that **Jared of the Book of Ether, in** the Book of Mormon is a direct descendant, along with his brother, whose name is **"Mohanri Moriancumr"**, **both** came out during the days of Peleg, being direct descendants of Peleg, or, through Eber, his father, before the languages were confounded. **They were large and mighty men**, as they were living in those days to exceed 200 years, some of which were still living in excess of 800 years, almost 900 years still. They kept their records from the time of Adam, through their forefathers, the same as the people in the Bible kept theirs'.

*"Therefore I do not write those things which transpired from the days of Adam until that time; but they are had upon the plates; and whoso findeth them, the same will have power that he may get the full account.""But behold, I give not the full account, but a part of the account I give, from the **tower***[of Babel] *down until they were destroyed.""And on this wise do I give the account. He that wrote this record was Ether, and he was a descendant of Coriantor.""Coriantor was the son of Moron.""Moron was the son of Ethem.""Ethem was the son of Ahah.""And Ahah was the son of Seth.""And Seth was the son of Shiblon.""And Shiblon was the son of Com.""And Com was the son of Coriantum.""And Coriantum was the son of Amnigaddah.""And Amnigaddah was the son of Aaron.""And Aaron was a descendant of*

*Heth, who was the son of Hearthom.""And Hearthom was the son of Lib.""And Lib was the son of Kish.""And Kish was the son of Corom.""And Corom was the son of Levi.""And Levi was the son of Kim.""And Kim was the son of Morianton.""And Morianton was a descendant of Riplakish.""And Riplikish was the son of Shez.""And Shez was the son of Heth.""And Heth was the son of Com.""And Com was the son of Coriantum.""And Coriantum was the son of Emer.""And Emer was the son of Omer.""And Omer was the son of Shule.""And Shule was the son of Kib.""And Kib was the son of Orihah, who was the son of **Jared;**"*

"Which Jared came forth with his brother[Mohanri Moriancumr] and their families, with some others and their families, <u>from the great tower, at the time the Lord confounded the language of the people</u>, and swore in his wrath that they should be scattered upon all the face of the earth; and according to the word of the Lord the people were scattered." "The brother of <u>Jared[Mohanri Moriancumr] being a large and mighty man,</u> and <u>a man highly favored of the Lord</u>, Jared, his brother, said unto him: Cry unto the Lord, that he may not **confound us that we may not understand our words.***(Ether 1:4-34, Book of Mormon) https://reasons.org/explore/blogs/voices/does-the-tower-of-babel-confirm-genealogical-gaps-in-genesis-11*

The Lord led the families of Jared and his brother to this land we know as America, and received it as an inheritance long before any other people came. They left the Tower at the confounding of the language of all the people, and because they were faithful in calling upon God, they were blessed with The America's as their inheritance. They left the tower between the death of Nimrod and the birth of Peleg. This was between 1908 B.C. to 1996 B.C., giving a window of 88 years.

Nimrod was already 151 years old, he, being the reason for the provocation, when Peleg was born, and lived to 127 years after Peleg died, so Jared and his brother left within the period that both Nimrod and Peleg were alive at the same time, which was 88 years. This gave the Jaredites/Olmecs plenty of time to prepare their families, gather their flocks and herds, gather their honey bees, put away seeds etc., that was going to go with them as the Lord led them. We must take the whole life of Peleg, meaning his whole 239 years, as the days of Peleg. Many things happened during the days of Peleg, to be able to come to the knowledge that the Bible is true, and understand that other things added to why these things came to pass in the days of Peleg.

And the Lord commanded the brother of Jared/Mohanri Moriancumr: *"Go to and gather together thy flocks, both male and female, of every kind; and also of the seed of the earth of every kind; and thy families; also Jared thy brother and his family; and also thy friends and their families, and the friends of Jared and their families.""And thou shalt go at the head of them down into the valley which is northward. And there will I meet thee, and I will go before thee into a land which is choice above all the lands of the earth."...(Ether 1:41-42, Book of Mormon).*Archaeological and Historical Evidence – The Geographical Location of the Jaredites (supportingevidences.net)

This time-frame is the perfect date, and tells beyond any shadow of a doubt who the "Olmecs" are, the name which, the alleged experts/ scientists use, to discredit Joseph Smith and the Book of Mormon. They use the term "Olmecs" when trying to explain who the civilization was that predated every other civilization. They know the empty cities exist, the people at one time being blessed by God, but they don't know where they came from, or where they went, but they predated the Toltecs, the Incas, the Mayans and the Aztecs, and whatever else they can come up with to make it appear, they know what they are talking about . There are giants in the land described by their ruins as being **"Olmecs",** the name given by the natives of central America; meaning *"rubber people".*(See Mohanri Moriancumr and His Brother Named Jared by Dan R. Hender).

The experts try to explain the ancient predecessors religious beliefs, always as some pagan forms of worship. Their buildings are still standing, almost intact, but no one to inhabit them. This is what happens to people who were once greatly blessed by God, then turn about and worship other gods and fail to call upon the only true God, and they sin against such great light and knowledge. These people of Central America, and throughout North America, were large and mighty men. They were giants compared to us, as they lived to be

200 to 300 plus years old, some maybe more, when they first came here from the Great Tower. All of the skeletons found, from the west to the east coasts, and from north to the south, all varied in heighth,. They measured anywhere from 7-25 feet tall, to maybe in some instances 30 feet tall. The taller having indications as living longer.(see i.e. Teotihuacan, and the City of Tula in southern central Mexico)

*"And it came to pass that[Mohanri Moriancumr] the brother of Jared, (now the number of the vessels which had been prepared was eight) went forth unto the mount , which they called Shelem, because of its exceeding height, and did molten out of the rock sixteen small stones; and they were white and clear, even as transparent glass; and he did carry them in his hands upon the top of the mount, and cried again unto the Lord saying:""O Lord, thou hast said that we must be encompassed about by the floods....""And it came to pass that when[Mohanri Moriancumr] the brother of Jared had said these words, behold, the Lord stretched forth his hand and touched the stones one by one with his finger. And the veil was taken from off the eyes of [Mohanri Moriancumr] the brother of Jared, and he **saw the finger of the Lord; and it was as the finger of a man, like unto flesh and blood; and the brother of Jared fell down before the Lord, for he was struck with fear.**""And the Lord saw that[Mohanri Moriancumr] the brother of Jared had fallen to the earth; and the Lord said unto him: Arise, why hast thou fallen?""And he said unto the Lord: **I saw the finger of the Lord**, and I feared lest he should smite me; for I knew not that the **Lord had flesh and blood. "**(Ether 3:1-2, 6-8, Book of Mormon).*

Two additional stones were touched by the finger of the Lord, called **"Seer Stones"**, of which were used by Joseph Smith later to translate the Book of Mormon from the gold plates of Nephi. *These are the same stones that King Mosiah* used, in translating the records of the Jaredites into their language then.

"And it came to pass that the Lord said unto[Mohanri Moriancumr] the brother of Jared: Behold, thou shalt not suffer these things which ye have seen and heard to go forth unto the world, until the time

*cometh that I shall glorify my name in the flesh; wherefore, ye shall treasure up the things which ye have seen and heard, and show it to no man.""And behold, when ye shall come unto me, ye shall write them and shall seal them up, that no one can interpret them; for ye shall write them **in a language that cannot be read.**""And behold, these **two stones** will I give thee, and ye shall seal them up also with the things which ye shall write.""For behold, the language which ye shall write I have confounded; wherefore I will cause in my own due time that these **stones** shall magnify to the eyes of men these things which ye shall write.""And it came to pass that the Lord commanded him that he should seal up the **two stones** which he had received, and show them not, until the Lord should show them unto the children of men."(Ether 3:21-24, 28, Book of Mormon)*

The easiest way to calculate time "Before Christ"(B.C.) is by calculating backwards, with the lowest number being the most recent, or closer to the birth of Christ. The larger numbers are closer to the days of Peleg, as to the date closest to the time of the Jaredite migration from the Tower of Babel. Or easier yet, is to subtract 2023 A.D. From 6,263 years given for this earth before the Millenium, and remembering we are 263 years into the millennium already, then subtracting everything else from there, is all before Christ, being 4,240 years, from when Adam was placed in the garden.

Jared and his brother and all the families that came with them, built , what they called barges. There were eight of them, and a stone that was touched by the Lord, was placed in each end to give them light. The Lord gave the brother of Jared two extra stones that were placed in a bow frame and attached there , to look like what we call glasses today. They wanted light in their barges as they were driven by the wind upon the ocean, and often submerged beneath the waves. After entering their barges, The winds arose and they were blown upon the waters, first through the Red Sea, then through the Indian Ocean, down into the Atlantic Ocean, up the east coast of South America, and landing off the coast of Central America.

They were on the ocean almost a year, 344 days to be exact. There were 22 families who came with them, and they were a large people. Mohanri Moriancumr, the brother of Jared, was a Godly man. He was a prophet and a large and mighty man, as the scripture describes him. (Ether 1:34, Book of Mormon).

Even though Peleg lived to be 239 years, his fathers were living to over 400 years, and had time to become quite large. Even at 200 years, a child could become quite large. Even during their wars at the end, when they exterminated their whole civilization, they were still mentioned after 1000 years, as being large and mighty men. Anyone wishing to know more about these "giants", need to read the "Book of Ether in the Book of Mormon, because it truly does give a true history about many of those cities today in Central America that are still intact but are completely empty. It describes where the people came from, how our Great God prospered them, and what happened to them when they quit calling upon Him, and how it happened.

The Jaredites/Olmecs had much prosperity when they were keeping the commandments of God. They prospered greatly when they remembered God first, and then lifted their neighbors up. They were blessed with riches. They had all manner of fruit, livestock, etc.. They had all manner of work animals, including horses, asses, and elephants, etc.. However, good and just men are human, and they get old, and are replaced by other generations, who are ungrateful for the sacrifices their fathers made before them, for the welfare, and blessings for generations to come. The sacrifices made by their forefathers, are taken for granted, and forgotten as the next generations inherits a life of ease and riches, and quickly forget to remember that God who prospered their parents.

*"And the Lord began again to take the curse from off the land, and the house of Emer did prosper exceedingly under the reign of Emer; and in the space of sixty years they had become exceedingly strong, insomuch that they became exceedingly rich---""Having all manner of fruit, and of grain, and of silks, and of fine linen, and of gold, and of silver, and of precious things;""And also all manner of cattle, of oxen, and cows, and of sheep, and of swine, and of goats, and also many other kinds of animals which were useful for the food of man.""And they also had horses, and asses, and there were **elephants**, and cureloms and cumoms.""And thus the Lord did pour out his blessings upon this land, which was choice above all other lands; and he*

commanded that whoso should possess the land should possess it unto the Lord, or they should be destroyed *when they were ripened in iniquity; for upon such, saith the Lord: I will pour out the fulness of my wrath." (Ether 9:16-20, Book of Mormon). https://www.zenger. news/2022/08/09/pic-refile-newly-found-mammoth-butchering-site-proves-humans-were-in-north-america-much-earlier/*

Take into account that much of what is said on these websites, when evolutionists, or liberal speak about the times, and how long they lived before they found the skeletons is their opinions, but still knowing that the life on this earth was not more than 7,000 years at the most, otherwise, to believe anything more than this is an attempt to make God out to be a liar. That is absolutely impossible, or God would cease to be God, and would fall like lightning, even as Satan fell, with a third of the hosts of Heaven, and were cast down to earth.

200 Mammoth Skeletons Found Buried Beneath Mexico Airport Site (businessinsider.com)
butchered Mammoth https://shepherdexpress.com/news/features/unearthing-wisconsins-lost-history/
https://shepherdsexpress.com
https://gizmodo.com/butchered-mammoth-bones-new-mexico-1849365357
https://www.nationalgeographic.com/animals/article/151007-woolly-mammoth-michigan-extinction-humans-science
https://gizmodo.com/Butchered Mammoth: by Isaac Schultz-search
Hebior Mammoth-Milwaukee WI: photo by Timothy Rour-University of Texas@Austin

*"And Emer did execute judgment in righteousness all his days, and he begat many sons and daughters; and he begat Coriantum, and he anointed Coriantum to reign in his stead.""And after he had anointed Coriantum to reign in his stead he lived four years, and he saw peace in the land; yea, and he even saw **the Son of Righteousness**[Jesus Christ], and did rejoice and glory in his day; and he died in peace.""And it came to pass that Coriantum did walk in the steps of his father, **and did build many mighty cities,** and did administer that which was good unto his people in all his days. And*

it came to pass that he had no children even until he was exceedingly old."(Ether 9:21-23. Book of Mormon).

These people were highly favored of the Lord, and were blessed and prospered when they kept the commandments of God, and always remembered to call upon Him. When they quit doing so, then Satan took possession of their hearts. There is no such thing as keeping religion separate from state or separation of Church and State. One master or the other is going to rule in our hearts, in our laws, and in our minds. It was not long after Coriantum's day that they, the people, went backwards to their vomit, which was in just a generation or two. It is a wonder how people who were once greatly blessed and favored by the Lord, can become so wicked so quickly. The people were seeking for power over one another, they wanted riches at any cost, they wanted benefits, titles of nobility, they had become hard and selfish, and they quit seeking the will of the Lord. The Jaredites/Olmecs had possessed this land as a gift from God for well over1,000-years before they destroyed their civilization out of selfishness. One battle to another, worrying only about their own selfish ambitions, wanting complete domination. That sounds like Hitler wanting everyone to believe he is God, when compared to what God has created, and looking down to our little planet, and laughing, not even hearing a muffled squeek, from where God is sitting.

*"But behold, the **Spirit of the lord had ceased striving with them**, and Satan had full power over the hearts of the people; for they were given up unto the hardness of their hearts, and the blindness of their minds that they might be destroyed; wherefore they went again to battle.""And it came to pass that they fought all that day, and when the night came they slept upon their swords.""And on the morrow they fought even until the night came.""And when the night came they were drunken with anger, even as a man who is drunken with wine; and they slept again upon their swords.""And on the morrow they fought again; and when the night came they had all fallen by the sword save it were **fifty and two** of the people of Coriantumr, and **sixty and nine** of the people of Shiz.""And they slept upon their swords that night, and on the morrow they fought again, and they contended in their might*

with their swords and with their shields, all that day.""And when the night came there were **thirty and two** *of the people of Shiz, and* **twenty and seven** *of the people of Coriantumr.""And it came to pass that they ate and slept, and prepared for death on the morrow.* **And they were large and mighty men as to the strength of men.""***And it came to pass that they fought for the space of three hours, and they fainted with the loss of blood.""And it came to pass that when the men of Coriantumr had received sufficient strength that they could walk, they were about to flee for their lives; but behold Shiz arose, and also his men, and he swore in his wrath that he would slay Coriantumr or he would perish by the sword.""Wherefore, he did pursue them, and on the morrow he did overtake them; and they fought again with the sword. And it came to pass that when they had all fallen by the sword,* **save it were Coriantumr and Shiz***, behold Shiz had fainted with the loss of blood.""And it came to pass that when Coriantumr had leaned upon his sword, that he rested a little,* **he smote off the head of Shiz***.""And it came to pass that after he had smitten off the head of Shiz, that Shiz raised up on his hands and fell; and after that he had struggled for breath, he died.""And it came to pass that Coriantumr fell to the earth, and became as if he had no life.""And the Lord spake unto Ether, and said unto him: Go forth. And he went forth, and beheld that the words of the Lord had all been fulfilled; and he finished his record; (and the hundredth part I have not written) and he hid them in a manner that the people of Limhi[Mulekites[Toltecs], later to join with the Nephites[Mayans] did find them.""Now the last words which are written by Ether are these:Whether the Lord will that I be translated, or that I suffer the will of the Lord in the flesh, it mattereth not, if it so be that I am saved in* **the kingdom of God. Amen.***"(Ether 15:19-34, Book of Mormon).*

https://youtu.be/WHn2GWjlK9Q *Giants in the Ozarks Mountains of Missouri[Jaredites]*

https://youtu.be/sVmOnwng6gs *Giants Emerging Everywhere: Texas, Nevada, Mexico, etc.*

https://youtu.be/I5GMVmsxKdY *Bone Cave in Tennessee[Jaredites] more of Goshen Tunnel MA*

Giants in West Virginiahttps://www.thearchaeologist.org/blog and other places[Jaredites]

Moroni is the one who is abridging the records of these Jaredites/ Olmecs, before he is forced to continue to flee from the Lamanites/ Aztecs after the Nephites/Mayans have lost their last great battle in the destruction of their civilization, of which Moroni is part of, and witness to. These records of the Jaredites/Olmecs were found on 24 gold tablets, translated By King Mosiah, then stored, and now abridged by Moroni to come forth by Joseph Smith, in 1830. Speaking now of the Jaredites/Olmecs by Moroni, as he explains the dark reason both civilizations were destroyed:

*"And now I, Moroni, do not write the manner of their oaths and combinations[secret orders], for it hath been made known unto me that they **are had among all people,** and they are had among the Lamanites[Aztecs].""And they have caused the destruction of this people[Jaredites/Olmecs] of whom I am now speaking, and also the destruction of the people of Nephi[Mayans].""And whatsoever nation shall uphold such **secret combinations[secret orders/catholic orders/satanic orders]** to get power and gain, until they shall spread over the nation, behold, <u>they shall be destroyed</u>; for the Lord will not suffer that the blood of his saints, which shall be shed by them, shall always cry unto him from the ground for vengeance upon them and yet he avenge them not.""Wherefore, **O ye Gentiles[talking about us/you and I], it is wisdom in God that these things should be shown unto you,** that thereby ye may repent[change] of your sins, and suffer not these <u>**murderous combinations[secret orders]** shall get above you, which are built up to get power and gain---and the work, yea, even the work of destruction come upon you, yea, even the sword of <u>the justice of the Eternal God</u> shall fall upon you, to your <u>overthrow and destruction if ye shall suffer these things to be,</u>""Wherefore the Lord commandeth you, **when ye shall see these things come among you [liberals/democrats/communists/ liars] that ye shall <u>awake to a sense of your awful situation, because of this secret combination[secret orders/catholic orders]</u>** which shall be among you; or wo be unto it, because of the blood of them[**abortions, just men and women, etc.**] who have been slain; for*

they cry from the dust for vengeance upon it, and also upon those[liberals, democrats, communists, etc.] who built it up."**"For it cometh to pass that whosoever buildeth it up seeketh to <u>overthrow the freedom of all lands, nations, and countries; and it bringeth to pass the destruction of all people, for it is built up by the devil[and his minions], who is the father of all lies;</u>** *even that same **liar** who beguiled our first parents, yea, even that same liar who hath caused man to commit murder from the beginning; who hath hardened the hearts of men that they have murdered the prophets, and stoned them, and cast them out from the beginning."(Ether 8:20-25, Book of Mormon)*

Nephitehttps://play.google.com/store/audiobooks/details/ Richard_J_Dewhurst_The_Ancient_Giants_Who_Ruled_ Am?id=AQAAAEDM_ky-kM

https://www.amazon.com/Ancient-Giants-Americas-Suppressed-Evidence/ dp/163265069X/ref=asc_df_163265069X/?tag=hyprod-20&li nkCode=df0&hvadid=312115051380&hvpos=&hvnetw=g&hvr and=10018220811465073705&hvpone=&hvptwo=&hvqmt=& hvdev=m&hvdvcmdl=&hvlocint=&hvlocphy=9019241&hvtargid =pla-492212775551&psc=1#immersive-view_1667172686138 Northwest shore of Yukatan Penn

To read the Book of Mormon, gives a true understanding of these ancient people and are not far removed from our own present situation. America is on the road to destroying themselves, if they don't change and call upon God. It was the hand of the Lord that swept the Jaredites/"Olmecs", from the face of the earth. The so called experts are ignorant themselves, and reject the truth/Spirit of God and are left to guessing what happened. They even admit in many cases, that they don't know. In these instances, they are right, they don't know, and they are just guessing and trying to appear intelligent. Is all they need to do is read the Book of Mormon, and they will find that it makes a lot of sense. It will help put all of the puzzle pieces together. How can a historian or anyone claiming to be intelligent, fail to at least read the record already written that is testifying of the truth?

They lean upon their own learning and understanding, wanting the masses to believe they are wise. "O that cunning plan of the evil one! O the vainness, and the frailties, and the foolishness of men! **When they are learned they think they are _wise_, and they hearken not unto the counsel of God, for they set it aside, supposing they know of themselves, wherefore their _wisdom is foolishness_, and it profiteth them not. And they shall Perish.** *"""But to be learned is good "if" they hearken unto the counsels of God."""But wo unto the rich, who are rich as to the things of the world. For because they are rich they despise the poor, and they persecute the meek, and their hearts are upon their treasures; wherefore, their treasures is their god. And behold, their treasure shall perish with them also."""And wo unto the **deaf that will not hear**; for they shall perish."""Wo unto the **blind that will not see; for they shall perish also.**"(2 Nephi 9:28-32, Book of Mormon)*

Thus, they are ignorant on purpose, proven by their rejection of knowledge. *"Knowing this first, that there shall come* **in the last days _scoffers_, walking after their own lusts,** *"""And saying, Where is the promise of his coming? For since the fathers fell asleep, all things continue as they were from the beginning of the creation."""***For this they _willingly are ignorant of_,** *that by the word of God the heavens were of old, and the earth standing out of the water and in the water:"""Whereby the world that then was,* **_being overflowed with water_**, *perished."""But the heavens and the earth, which are now, by the same word are kept in store,* **reserved unto fire against the day of judgment _and perdition of ungodly men._** *"""But, beloved, be* **not ignorant of this one thing**, *that one day is with the Lord as a thousand years, and a thousand years as one day."(2 Peter 3:3-8, KJV)*

The Jaredites/Olmecs, came to this land prior to the Nephites/Mayans, by approximately 1500 years. They left the Tower of Babel between the years 1996 B.C. to 1908 B.C., and were brought to the Americas in barges, they made themselves, as they were instructed by the Lord, long before Columbus was even a sparkle in his daddy's eye. What we do know pretty sure, is when the destruction of the Jaredites/Olmecs took place, and why. As said earlier, they traveled in barges in the water and were driven by the wind, and they washed up onto the beaches in Central/Southern Mexico. From there they overspread the

Americas, and were a blessed people until they destroyed their own civilization.

There Were Giants on the Earth, by Manuel Ortiz Sepulveda; https://www.academia.edu

https://m.central.edu The Ancient Giants Who Ruled America: July 15, 2022

https://youtu.be/sSiNhBhuBOU Giant Bones in Minnesota

The Jaredites/Olmecs were almost done with the process of destroying their civilization, by the first year of the reign, of King Zedekiah, king of Judah, in the Bible. Their wars were still ongoing, unknown to the whole world, here in the Americas, clear up to the time of the 11th and final year of King Zedekiah's reign. The Jaredite/Olmec civilization lasted about 1000 years. To about 600 B.C., when they were discovered by Zarahemla, leader of the Mulekites. Zarahemla is the one that found a record written on stone tablets, and the surviving leader/giant of the Jaredites/Olmecs and nursed him for 9 months/9 moons, before he died.

Richard J. Dewhurst, narrated by Nick McDougal; The Ancient Giants Who Ruled America; The missing Skeletons and the Great Smithsonian Cover-up.

Ancient Giants of the Americas: Suppressed Evidence and the Hidden History of a Lost Race by the Smithsonian Institute: by Xaviant Haze

Zarahemla is the leader of the People of the Mulekites/Toltecs, of whom the land of Zarahemla is named after. Later, as will be told, a man named Limhi delivered 24 tablets of gold, to an Ammon, who in turn delivered to prophet and King, Mosiah, of the people of Nephi/Mayans. King Mosiah in turn, translated them, and then, the plates were later abridged by Moroni. Moroni is this same son of Mormon, after the last battle of the Nepite/Mayan people, to hide these plates in the **Hill Cumorah**, to come forth today as the book of Ether, being translated from the gold plates, by the prophet Joseph Smith, delivered to him by Moroni, to ultimately become the "Book of Mormon".

The Mulekites left Jerusalem at the 11th and final year of the reign of King Zedekiah, king of Jerusalem, Mulek being the son of Zedekiah. This all happened just before Jerusalem was destroyed, ransacked, and Daniel, Shadrack, Meshack, and Abednego, were carried away captive as young men, into Babylon/Iraq. The Jaredite/Olmecs, final war had taken place at the hill, called Shim, The hill Shim is on the west side of the country we know today as Guatemala. Their burial sites, because of carnage and serious amount of people killed, were dumped into mass graves.

https://youtu.be/bq01lRiY1UY : 3000 giants in one grave, one of many graves throughout the wars of the Jaredites[Olmecs]. https://youtu.be/lSO-bFwMx2I : Olmec/Jaredite Legacy.

https://youtu.be/LMpRuL6sRQY :Ancient Fossils guarded by the Smithsonian

3000 giants found in one grave. https://youtu.be/KrpG1N0gf-M :https://youtube.com/shorts/ZeRFGy6o27Y?feature=share : Giants in Nevada

https://youtube.com/shorts/ZziGQjQMD5g?feature=share:Giants in Lake Delvan, Wisconsin.

Make no mistake about it, we are related to these giants, who just happened to live 200 to as high as just under a 1,000 years. We all carry the same Genes, and as far as the six fingers and toes on each hand and foot, we also carry those genes as well. Just like anything else God has done and foreseen thousands of years in advance, he makes available ways of confounding the wisdom of of the learned, and proving the foolishness of men. The ability to form as the need arises, such as teeth in the mouth, the healing of the body, and in this case, as the body grows and the need arises to have an extra finger on each hand, in order to compensate the work burden, and/or in carrying heavy loads put upon them, or toe on each foot, necessary for balance is built in. Finding these giants with 6-fingers or 6-toes on each limb is understandable, because in that size of man like the Kandahar Giant of Afghanistan, he was 18-feet tall, and he had six toes on each foot and 6-fingers on each hand. This giant was killed there in just 2003-2005, by our own U.S. Military, but it has even been covered up.

I can promise you this, that God has reserved this world for his children, appointed to this world, and no other is able to come here and interfere with our world. No fallen angels, no aliens etc.. God knows before hand, the thoughts of your hearts. It was like he said to Cain, who killed Abel his brother. You can imagine anything you want in your minds, but the all seeing, and all powerful, Almighty God wouldn't let that happen. If anything, any abnormalities would come through the abominations, and filthiness of man, who violate the commandments of God. The beastiality, the inbreeding, the homosexuality, the witchcrafts, the sicknesses, and diseases, the cutting and operations of experimentations, caused by the depravity of mankind from the beginning. When a people after knowing of the ways of God, and having such great light, and then turn their backs on him after being so blessed and favored of the Lord, they will be destroyed. He will turn this land over to another people, and it is happening, even as we breathe.

Chapter 4

The Origin, journeyings, arrival of Lehi's Family/Mayans to South America

The Origin and The Journeyings of the people of Lehi from Jerusalem

600 B.C.

Lehi and his family, who is really the father of what we know today, as the Mayans, & the Aztecs, traveling together as a family, along with one other family, named: Ishmael, and one servant of Laban, named Zoram. They fled Jerusalem, all being of the tribe of Joseph, led by the hand of God, beginning in the first year of the reign of King Zedekiah, king of Judah. Zedekiah, previously called Mattaniah, was replacing King Jahoiakim, by Nebuchadnezzar II, King of Babylon. The kings of Judah at this time were in their positions at the whims of Nebuchadnezzar. It was because of the disobedience of Gods commandments, by the people of Jerusalem and all of Israel, that they were put into this position. Zedekiah was simply a puppet king, taking orders from the King of Babylon. If they got out of order they were simply replaced, one way or another. *http://www. supportingevidences.net/lehi-traveling-from-jerusalem/*

Zedekiah, began his reign within the 6th century B.C., being about 600 B.C.. He was allowed to be there for 11-years, before he displeased the King of Babylon for rebellion, and Jerusalem was to be attacked, destroyed and ransacked, and many prisoners were carried off to Babylon/Iraq. Before the 11th year, or final year of the reign of King Zedekiah, another group were told to depart from Jerusalem, we understand to be Mulekites/Toltecs, or from the family of Mulek, also out of Jerusalem, and the son of King Zedekiah, king of Judah. In fact he arrived in Central America just a few years earlier than Lehi and his family, who had landed off the coast of northern Chile, and he found the last man standing, of the civilization of the giants, king of the Jaredites/Olmecs.

The Mulekites/Toltecs, found the remaining survivor of the Giants, and took care of him for 9-**Moons/9-**months, until he died. His name was Coriantumr. This was before Lehi and his group landed off the coast of Chile, in 589 B.C. It was 30-years later, that the Nephites divided from the Lamanites, and made their way north-westerly, to northern Peru, and establishing the land of Nephi. The land of Nephi was still at a higher elevation, being higher up in the Andes Mountains. The land of Nephi encompassed Northern Peru, Ecuador, parts of western Brazil, and southwestern Colombia. The Land of Nephi bordered on the headwaters of the Sidon River/Rio Magdalena.

It wasn't until after 320 years, from the time the Nephites/Mayans landed in northern Chile to the time King Mosiah was told by the Lord to move further north where they ended up, and there found the narrow neck of land that borders the sea on the East, and the sea on the West, as we will soon see. In fact, after the Nephite/Mayans separated themselves from the Lamanites/Aztecs, gave the Nephites/Mayans time to build up great cities, whereas, the Lamanites/Aztecs became a bloodthirsty, and idolatrous people, hunting only meat in the wilderness. They were a continuous scourge and nuisance to the Nephites/Mayans, by always stealing their property if they could, and always going to pick a fight with the Nephites/Mayans, even if they came out holding the empty sack. The Nephites/Mayans were continually repelling them and slaughtering thousands in the process, even though against great odds.

So you see, the Jaredites lasted until they quit calling upon God, then God replaced them with the next civilization, by giving the land to another people. Later you will understand how the Mulekites/ Toltecs meet and join with the Nephites to become one people under the title of Nephites/Mayans. You will also understand the break off of these same people into another group called Lamanites/Aztecs. It took Lehi and his families 11 years before they arrived off the coast of Chile, South America, via ship they had built, as they did so, being instructed of the Lord. At this same-time the Mulekites/Toltecs were en-route, and landing at the same time off the coast of Central America.

Lehi, and his families, came up along the western coastline of South America, whereas, the Mulekites came up along the east Coastline of Central America, landing where the Jaredites/Olmecs landed. This is why they stumbled into the ruins of the Jaredites/Olmecs ahead of the Nephites/Mayans. It was 320 years later when the Nephites/Mayans eventually made their way north to Colombia and joined with the Mulekites/Toltecs. They all eventually met up in Central America, but the Nephites/Mayans continued in the land of Zarahemla, in the area of what we know today, as northern Colombia, and then both the Mulekites/Toltecs, and the Nephites/Mayans joined for survival, educational and religious purposes.

Lehi was told by the Lord in the first(1st)-year of King Zedekiah's reign, to leave his home in Jerusalem, because the Lord had shown him the destruction of Jerusalem, which was imminent, in the very near future. Mulek, and his family group, left just before the destruction of Jerusalem in the eleventh(11th)-year, last and final year of Zedekiah's reign, just before Nebuchadnezzar besieged Jerusalem, to destroy it. Lehi also was shown ahead of time, what was to happen, if he stayed. He was shown in a vision to take his family and one other family, to go, and being a true believer and a "son of God", he was obedient, and he left. I am going to attempt to let you see the facts from Nephi's point of view.

This book is about the inhabitants of the Ancient American people including: Indians in North America(Sioux, Chippewa, Ojibwa, Iroquois Apache Cheyenne, ,, Incas, Aztecs, Mayans, Tetonics, Toltecs, and the Olmecs etc.. You will see that we have not, nor ever have been told the true history of our country when we were in school, but there truly is a cover-up going on to blind the eyes of our children to the things of God. This book's purpose is to get the people to think, as many people are saying and getting evidence of history that the God haters, liberals, communists, evolutionists, and many other

Anti-God-Atheists groups and people etc., are discrediting God, and covering up. Now they are saying the same things: "What we are being told about our history in America is proven to be untrue."(see Scott Wolter, America Unearthed). There is proof of ancient inhabitants before Columbus, all over America. Thus, my purpose in writing this book is to put the puzzle pieces together, and <u>ultimately prove the Book of Mormon is **true**</u>. Now if the Spirit of Truth doesn't work in you, during and while reading this book, and seeing all of the proof that makes sense, then probably the Spirit of God is not in you, or anywhere around you, but you are influenced by another spirit.

Because the Book of Mormon is true, then everything the Prophet Joseph Smith has done in bringing forth the Book of Mormon is true, and because it is true, then he truly is a Prophet of God, because everything he has done and said, and written is true also. We then need to pay attention in order to enable ourselves to understand the Word of God, because without believing he is a Prophet, hinders all people, in this last dispensation, from entering into the highest Kingdom(Celestial), and being in the presence of Almighty God, our Father in Heaven, even the Ancient of Days, even Adam.

This book is based upon facts, and as I sit here writing, I testify that these things are true about the ancient inhabitants of the Americas, and I know without any shadow of a doubt that Joseph Smith is a true prophet of God, and we must understand why it is so important to know these things, or we can in no wise go back into the presence of God Almighty. This story about the Nephites/Mayans, and the Lamanites/Aztecs begins, around 600 B.C., at the beginning of the first year of the reign of King Zedekiah, king of Judah:

> "For it came to pass in the commencement of the first year of the reign of Zedekiah, king of Judah, (my father, Lehi, having dwelt at Jerusalem in all his days); and in that same year there came **many prophets, prophesying** unto the people that they must repent, or the great city **Jerusalem must be destroyed.**"(1 Nephi 1:4, Book of Mormon).

Nephi was a young man, growing up in Jerusalem during a time of conflict, as Jerusalem was in subjection to Nebechadnezzar II, King of Babylon. Nebuchadnezzar had just put down the previous king of Judah, Jehoiakim, and replaced him with King Zedekiah, his real name being: Mattaniah. This was the first year of the reign of Zedekiah, King of Judah, who was a puppet king, allowed there by the King of Babylon. Judah was considered as a province by the King of Babylon, and allowed certain liberties to his subjects, within limits.

Nephi's father, Lehi, grew up in Jerusalem his whole life, and was schooled and educated in the languages of Hebrew, Egyptian, as well as the Babylonian language. He understood what was going on, and as a father, he educated his children, and always talked openly with his children, and his whole family about God, and his ways. He talked about government, current events, including political and government issues, and signs of the times. He also taught them to obey the commandments of God early on. He was well educated in the ways of the Hebrew, and the Egyptian, and more. He was very successful in business, and was considered as pretty well off, never wanting for anything. He was probably in the highest middle class to lower elite class bracket of society, and a leader among his peers.

*"I Nephi, having been born of goodly parents, therefore I was taught somewhat in all the learning of my father; and having seen many afflictions in the course of my days, nevertheless, having been highly favored of the Lord in all my days; yea, having had a **great knowledge** of the goodness and the **mysteries of God**, therefore I make a record of my proceedings in my days.""Yea, I make a record in the **language of my father, which consists of the learning of the Jews and the language of the Egyptians.**"(1 Nephi 1:1-2, Book of Mormon)*

Nephi was a strong young man, tall and stout, and deliberate in his beliefs and knowledge. He watched growing up, as many wise men/prophets, came speaking and prophesying with great power. And knowledge, telling the people what they were doing wrong, in not supporting the truth and obeying the commandments. He listened to the prophets who came among them, warning them that if they didn't change and do what is right before God, then ultimately, Jerusalem would be destroyed, and they would lose all of their freedom. Nephi was acquainted with what a system of freedom, versus a system of force was. He therefore, prayed to God continually, watching and waiting for the people to obey God, and change from their evil ways. He prayed that the people would be valiant and diligent in their government. If the people didn't change and get involved, he knew they were on their way into total subjection. Like it is today with us in America, in 2023. We are on the same road of self destruction if we don't change/repent.

Nephi was very sensitive to the truth, and he loved, and believed his father, when his father told him stories about God, and how his forefathers came out of bondage from Egypt about 100 years or so, prior to crossing the Red Sea on dry ground. He loved to hear these stories of great faith and he wanted to believe and experience, mighty miracles, because of his faith, just like Caleb and Joshua, past leaders of the Children of Israel.

Nephi knew that the time in his present situation was 600 B.C., and that The Messiah, Jesus Christ, would come in the flesh, a Redeemer, and King of kings, a Savior of the world, and would come as prophesied for thousands of years in advance. So Israel and the people were in a countdown of great expectations for a Savior to come as prophesied by their prophets long ago. Nephi knew that his forefathers were in slavery to the Egyptians for 400-years, and it grieved him to know that they were headed for slavery again to the Kingdom of Babylon. He just didn't know at his present time how long the tribes of Israel would be in bondage to Babylon, but it was proven that they were slaves to Babylon for 70 years. Nephi didn't know this, because his life was about to change drastically for ever, for his good, because he loved God.

Nephi had three-brothers older than him. The youngest of these three, was Sam, who had a strong conservative nature like himself, and was easily entreated to do good, and believe in God. His older brothers were liberal by nature, and they were very rebellious, and didn't want to hear the truth, but were content in doing what they wanted, and had no mind for God. They were obnoxious, demanding, selfish, and disobedient, and because of these things, they were ignorant of the things of God. Nephi knew that this was the nature of people who were once free, were now more corruptible and easily led into bondage, because of their ignorance.

Nephi's father, Lehi, was a good man, but in certain times exhibited weakness, like anyone does in times of severe hardship, uncertainty, grief and stress. Lehi gave great attention to the things of God, and always made his mind clear to the people he came in contact with, about how he felt about God, and what he could see coming for his nation, if the people didn't change and support freedom. Lehi constantly prayed to God, and taught his family the best he could, to those who would listen. He constantly sought knowledge for his family's sake and his own. He constantly meditated on the words of God, wanting to know how he stood before God, when one day, he received by vision, in full daylight, what he was to do.

Lehi was very proactive in teaching the people, and telling them of their faults, and that they would be destroyed if they didn't change. There were many people who didn't want to hear, and didn't like being told they were wrong, and so, to shut him up, they were planning on killing him. Lehi didn't know this until he was traveling to and fro, out and about calling the people to change, as he was fulfilling his work by commandment of the Lord, when a pillar of fire came and dwelt on a rock; probably an angel of the Lord, and from this, he saw and heard much being told him.

"Wherefore it came to pass that my father, Lehi, as he went forth prayed unto the Lord, yea, even with all his heart, in behalf of his people""And it came to pass as he prayed unto the Lord, there came a **pillar and dwelt upon a rock before him; and he saw and heard much**; *and because of the things he saw and heard* **he did quake and tremble exceedingly**.*"(1 Nephi 1:5-6, Book of Mormon).*

After he saw this, and because of what he learned, he returned home with the Spirit of God upon him, and was carried away, as it were, into a vision concerning Jerusalem, it's wickedness of the people, and their pending destruction. He had also seen many other great and wonderful things which he later taught to those who would listen to him, and believe him.

"Wherefore, I would that ye should know, that after the Lord had shown so many marvelous things unto my father, Lehi, yea, concerning the **destruction of Jerusalem***, behold he went forth among the people, and began to prophesy and to declare unto them concerning the things which he had both seen and heard.""And it came to pass that the Jews did mock him because of the things which he testified of them; for he truly testified of their wickedness and their abominations; and he testified that the things which he saw and heard, and also the things which he read in the book, manifested plainly of the coming of a* **Messiah***, and also the redemption of the world.""And when the Jews heard these things they were angry with him; yea, even as with the prophets of old, whom they had cast out, and stoned, and slain; and they also sought his life, that they might take it away. But behold, I, Nephi, will show unto you that the tender mercies of the Lord are over all those whom he hath chosen, because of their* **faith***, to make them mighty even unto the power of deliverance."(1 Nephi 1:18-20, Book of Mormon).*

"Zedekiah was one and twenty years old when he began to reign, and he reigned eleven years in Jerusalem, and his mother's name was Hamutal the daughter of Jeremiah of Libnah.""And he did that which was evil in the eyes of the Lord, according to all that Jehoiakim had done.""For through the anger of the Lord it came to pass in Jerusalem and Judah, till he had cast them out from his presence, that **Zedekiah rebelled against the King of Babylon.""And it came to pass in the ninth year of his reign, in the tenth month, in the tenth day of the month, that Nebuchadnezzar king of Babylon came,** *he and his whole army, against Jerusalem, and pitched against it, and built forts against it round about.""So the city was* **besieged unto the eleventh year of king Zedekiah.***"(Jeremiah 52:1-5, KJV).https:// www.youtube.com/watch?v=tHtkTpXUK0g*

Lehi wasn't long in getting his family together, and preparing to leave Jerusalem because of what he was told. Unbeknownst to Lehi, the destruction of Jerusalem came 9-years later, by Nebuchadnezzar, king of Babylon, who utterly destroyed Jerusalem, tearing the walls down, and carrying the poorer class of the people captive, back to Babylon/Iraq. This included Daniel, Meshak, Shadrack, and Abednego. The wealthier class were utterly destroyed by the sword. https://bookofmormoncentral.org/blog/watch-compelling-book-of-mormon-evidence-for-lehi-s-journey-through-arabia

After declaring unto the people what would happen to them if they didn't change, they wanted to kill him, the same as they had done in the past to Holy men, and prophets before him. *"For behold, it came to pass that the Lord spake unto my father, yea, even in a dream, and said unto him: Blessed art thou Lehi, because of the things which thou hast done; and because thou hast been faithful and declared unto this people the things which I commanded thee, behold, they seek to take away thy life.""And it came to pass that the Lord commanded my father, even in a dream, that he should take his family and depart into the wilderness.""And it came to pass that he was obedient unto the word of the Lord, wherefore he did as the Lord commanded him.""And it came to pass that he departed into the wilderness. And he left his house, and the land of his inheritance, and his gold, and his silver, and his precious things, and took nothing with him, save it were his family, and provisions, and tents, and departed into the wilderness."*(1 Nephi 2:1-4, Book of Mormon).

Nephi obeyed and believed, and supported his father. He helped get the family together, and leave the area. Nephi was a huge asset to his family, and he was irreplaceable to his father. The family consisted of Nephi, Sam, Laman, Lemuel, Lehi and his wife Sariah. The servant of Laban: called Zoram and the family of Ishmael came later to join them, as they set out on their journey to a promised land. Lehi had access to a book given him by 12 disciples, who came down from heaven, and he, Lehi, was told to read. And as he read the book, it plainly testified of the destruction of Jerusalem, and it also testified of Christ to come in the future. The record of the children of Israel up to that time consisted of at least, the Five Books of Moses, up to the time of Zedekiah king of Judah, and all records were kept by one who was holy, in this case it was Jeremiah, and considered as a prophet of God, as he was accurate in his accounts of the people because of what they were doing. *Archaeological and Historical Evidence - Lehi Traveling from Jerusalem to the Red Sea (supportingevidences.net)*

Lehi and his family left Jerusalem and went south to just before the red sea, and crossed over the river that emptied out of the sea of

Galilee, and came also into a valley, where they paused and camped for a while. Then from there they traveled south along the shore of the Red Sea in Arabia.

"*And he also spake unto Lemuel: O that thou mightest be like unto this valley, firm and steadfast, and immovable in keeping the commandments of the Lord!*"*"Now this he spake **because of the stiffneckedness of Laman and Lemuel[fathers of the Aztecs]; for they did murmur in many things against their father,** because he was a visionary man, and had led them out of the land of Jerusalem, to leave the land of their inheritance**, and their gold, and their silver, and their precious things, to perish in the wilderness.** And this they said he had done because of the foolish imaginations of his heart.*"*"And thus **Laman and Lemuel**[Fathers of the Aztecs**] being the eldest, did murmur because they knew not the dealings of that God who had created them.**"*"...And it came to pass that the Lord spake unto me, saying: Blessed art thou, Nephi, because of thy faith, for thou hast sought me diligently, with lowliness of heart.*"*"And inasmuch as ye shall keep **my commandments, ye shall prosper,_ and shall be led to a land of promise; yea, even a land which I have prepared for you; yea, a land which is choice above all other lands**[The Americas].*"*"And inasmuch as thy **brethren shall rebel against thee, they shall be cut off from the presence of the Lord.**"*"...For behold, in that day that they shall rebel against me, I will **curse, them even with a sore curse,** and they shall have no power over thy seed **except they shall rebel also.**"*"**And if it so be that they rebel against me, they shall be a scourge unto thy seed, to stir them up in the ways of remembrance.**(1 Nephi 2:10-13,19-21, 23-24, Book of Mormon)*

The Lord had told the people from the very beginning what he was doing, what he was planning, and what was going to happen, if they didn't do what he expected of them, after they received such great blessings. Nephi was very careful to search the scriptures himself, to know what his father knew and saw, and he delighted in the things of God. When his father said it was time to leave Jerusalem. Nephi was in prompt support with what his father said, because he too had the Spirit of Revelation, and knew for himself. He was quick to gather his family and provisions, including weapons in which to obtain food in the country, because they were taking a journey, and not coming back.

"And he came down by the borders near the shore of the Red Sea; and he traveled in the wilderness in the borders which are nearer the Red Sea; and he did travel in the wilderness with his family, which consisted of my mother, Sariah, and my elder brothers, who were Laman and Lemuel, and Sam. (1 Nephi 2:5, Book of Mormon)

God provided Lehi and his family with direction, and where to go on their journey. He even provided them with a **compass**, that worked for them as long as they were doing as they were directed.

There was something missing however. Then after 3-days after they were out in the wilds of Israel, God told Lehi they needed to return to get some records, of their families history, genealogy, and promises to the children of Israel and , written on plates of Brass, otherwise, they would go backwards into ignorance, and in so doing, would rapidly, forget the ways of God. Actually, the "Plates of Brass", was the "Old Testament", of the Bible, as we know it today, up to the time of King Zedekiah.***https://bookofmormoncentral.org/blog/archaeological-evidence-for-7-locations-on-lehi-s-journey-to-the-promised-land***

*"And it came to pass that I, Nephi, returned from speaking with the Lord, to the tent of my father." "And it came to pass that he spake unto me, saying: Behold I have dreamed a dream, in the which the Lord hath commanded me that thou and thy brethren shall return to Jerusalem." "For behold, Laban hath the **record of the Jews and also a genealogy of my forefathers, and they are engraven upon plates of brass.**" "Wherefore, the Lord hath commanded me that thou and thy brothers should go unto the house of Laban, and **seek the records**, and bring them down hither into the wilderness." "And now, thy brothers murmur, saying it is a hard thing which I have required of them; but behold I have not required it of them, **but it is a commandment of the Lord.**"(1 Nephi 3:1-5, Book of Mormon).*

Lehi, knowing Nephi was of sound understanding in the ways of the Lord, knew also that he could count on his youngest son to get the job done. Nephi, led his 3-brothers back to Jerusalem, on the mission of getting the "Plates of Brass", the record of their people. He did this at the request of his father, Lehi. The Plates of Brass were held by a relative of Lehi's, who having a liberal mindset, was very obstinate, and foreign to the things of God. Therefore, Nephi was obliged to kill Laban, in order to fulfill the commandment of God, and obtain these necessary records for the preservation of the people when they reached the Americas later on, which came about 11-years later. Nephi, therefore, understood the importance of these records, and why the Lord told him that he would prepare a way for him to accomplish the things that the Lord had commanded, and Nephi did. Nephi was put in the position of being a leader and a teacher to his older brothers. It was Nephi, that the Lord spoke through, when he sent them back to Jerusalem several times.

It was also to Nephi, saying: *"that inasmuch as thou shalt keep my commandments. thou shalt be made a ruler and a teacher over thy brethren.""For behold, in that day that **they[Laman and Lemuel] shall <u>rebel</u>** against Me[the Lord], **I will curse them even with a sore curse, and they shall have no power over thy seed[the Mayans] except they[Mayans] shall <u>rebel</u> against me[the Lord] also.""And if it shall be that they[the Mayans] <u>rebel</u>** against me, they**[the Aztecs] shall be a <u>scourge</u> unto thy seed, to stir them up in the ways of remembrance."**(1 Nephi 2:21-23, Book of Mormon)*

So you see, the Mayans and the Aztecs, started out as one family. Through disagreements, pride, selfishness, greed, and vindictiveness, and jealousy, the families divided later on and fought each others families throughout the centuries, to the Nephites/Mayans utter destruction, because they, in the end, after receiving so many blessings of the Lord, did exactly what the Lord warned Nephi about early on. The Nephites/Mayans ceased to obey the commandments of God, and ceased to acknowledge him in all things. This is the way our civilization is headed now, and we will have our scourges(Democrats, and secret societies), bite America in the backside, if we don't change. Even America will be destroyed if the inhabitants don't turn to God.

Nephi was a valiant leader, and got the records contained upon the plates of brass, that he was commanded to get, even though he had to kill Laban to do it. He then impersonated Laban, after donning the clothing and armor of Laban, and successfully fooled Laban's servant, Zoram. Nephi commanded Zoram, in the voice of Laban, telling him to get the records contained on the plates of brass, then telling him to follow him out to his brethren outside the city, carrying the plates of brass. When Nephi came to where his brothers were, he called to them, which frightened Zoram, because he now knew he had been fooled, and was about to run away. Nephi, however, was a large young man, and restrained/took hold of Zoram, to keep him from running. He could not afford to let Zoram get away alive, otherwise it would give away Lehi's family's position in the wilderness, and soldiers would be sent to kill them.

Nephi did the next best, merciful thing, under the circumstances. He promised Zoram he could live, if he agreed to go with them, and promising him his freedom. *"And now I, Nephi, being a man **large in stature**, and also having received much strength of the Lord, therefore I did seize upon the servant of Laban, and held him, that he should not flee.""And it came to pass that I spake with him, that if he would hearken unto my words, as the Lord liveth, and as I live, even so that if he would hearken unto our words, we should spare his life."..."Now we were desirous that he should tarry with us for this cause, that the **Jews might not know our flight into the wilderness**, lest they should pursue us and destroy us."(1 Nephi 4:31-32, 36, Book of Mormon).*

Zoram readily accepted this tradeoff, since he didn't want to die. He had everything to gain in this bargain, including his **freedom.** The four brothers, along with Zoram, set off to reunite with Lehi and Sariah in the wilderness. They were commanded to return again later to ask another family to go with them on their journey. This family had predominantly girls, whereas, Lehi's family was all boys. So the reader, might be able to see the predicament if not rectified early on. Nephi and his brothers returned to Jerusalem to get the family of Ishmael. Ishmael loved the things of God and so, came down into the wilderness heading for the Americas with the family of Lehi. Lehi was waiting to continue their journeying when Nephi and the rest returned from their trip to Jerusalem. Lehi was shown that if they had not left Jerusalem themselves, and if they had stayed after being warned of the Lord, that they also would have been destroyed or carried away into Babylon. Most likely destroyed, because the upper class was all destroyed, because they were highly educated, and would be the most problematic. Whereas the poorer class was more teachable, and were carried captive into Babylon.

All throughout these family trials, Nephi's older brothers, Laman and Lemuel, demonstrated the rebellious, liberal mindset. They wanted what felt good to them. They loved money, and power, but the truth was not what they wanted to hear, because it made them feel guilty, and when they heard the Truth/the voice of God, they wanted to rebel. Many times, Laman and Lemuel wanted to take Nephi's life, in order to shut him up. They resented the fact that their youngest brother was their teacher and example, and the thought that he was trying to rule over them, or may in the future rule over them, was too much to take.

A good example of this, is when, the brothers had all returned to Jerusalem the first time, to get the Brass Plates. Laman and Lemuel were fearful and wanted to jump ship at the first hurdle, but Nephi kept them going, and wouldn't let them quit. Nephi is the type of character who listened to his father, Lehi. Nephi believed that his father was leading by the Spirit of God. He asked God himself if Lehi, his father was right, and desired to know and understand what his father had seen and heard. Because of Neph's faith, God blessed him and gave him much more knowledge, as he exercised what he already knew.

Laman, (first future Aztec king), didn't want to trek back to Jerusalem with Nephi, (first future Mayan king), but he went because he felt obliged to go, as he did not want to be out done by his younger brother, and therefore, went. Even then, they were fighting, and Laman and Lemuel conspired to kill Nephi. They were always trying to discredit him, and bring him down. Just like any liberal, who is a scourge to freedom.

Nephi endured great tribulation, both in mind and body, but he persevered because he loved God first, then his family was blessed. Nephi's first duty was to God, to accomplish what God told him to do. If Nephi hadn't have been there, the rest of the family would have had a much harder time. Nephi had the gift of leadership. He had a deliberateness, and stubborn resolve. He was nobody's floor-mat, and having the knowledge and the love of God in himself, made him a stand up pillar, and the best friend anyone could ever have. He greatly respected his father, and wanted to see his father succeed, and even gave his father loving advice from time to time, as necessary.

Nephi, even though he had the ability to receive knowledge for himself, went out of his way to ask his father's advice on important issues, concerning the things of God. His father then always went to his Father in Heaven. Thus, a chain of command/authority was established for the flow of knowledge and revelation, which blessed Lehi and his family, and friends, including Zoram.

Lehi was informed by the Lord at this time to leave Jerusalem, and who else would willingly go, at the same time, keeping silent as to what they were wanting to accomplish. They needed to take great care to keep this knowledge within the family circle and very close friends, including Zoram, or else this mission would have been in danger of failing, and they would not have been able to achieve what they were commanded to do by the Lord.

The Lord provided them with a compass that guided them through the wilderness and upon the great deep, as long as they were obedient and were calling upon God. They also carried many seeds, honey bees, food, provisions, and weapons, by which to obtain meat, and by which to defend themselves, if needed. They took with them whatever was essential for the preservation of their civilization.

"And now I, Nephi [first Mayan king], proceed to give an account upon these plates of my proceedings, and my **reign and ministry;** *wherefore, to proceed with mine account, I must speak somewhat of the things of my father, and also my brethren.""For behold, it came to pass after my father had made an end of speaking the words of his dream, and also exhorting them to all diligence, he spake unto them concerning the Jews---""That after they should be destroyed, even that great city* **Jerusalem,** *and* **many be carried away captive into Babylon,** *according to the own due time of the Lord, they should return again, yea, even be brought back out of captivity they should possess again the land of their inheritance.""***Yea, even <u>six hundred</u>**

years from the time that my father left Jerusalem, a prophet would the Lord God raise up among the Jews—even a Messiah, or, in other words, a <u>Savior of the world.</u>" (1 Nephi 10:1-4, Book of Mormon).

It is not hard for the reader to understand in this scripture that Lehi, and his family, Ishmael and his family, and Zoram, all left Jerusalem, heading for the Americas, 600 years before Christ. This group is who today, the experts label as the **Mayans and the Aztecs.** Even though Lehi and his families left Jerusalem in 600 B.C., in the first year of King Zedekiah, they took longer to get to the Americas, and they traveled inland from the coast of northern Chile. After 320 years, they moved into southern Colombia, Ecuador, and northern Peru and parts of Brazil as the "Land of Nephi.", and were then later told by God to move to northern Colombia, and control the narrow neck of land at Panama, and where they encountered, and joined with the Mulekites/ Toltecs, led by their leader/king, Zarahemla.

The Mulekites/Toltecs had left Jerusalem 11 years after Lehi/ Mayans/Aztecs had left Jerusalem, but yet they got to Central America also 320 years sooner than the Nephites, and were inhabiting the vacant cities of the Jaredites/Olmecs, when the Nephites finally arrived overland. This is the same area where the Mulekites found the last surviving Giant/Jaredite/Olmec; King Coriantumr. The final battle ground for the Jaredites/Olmecs, was the hill Shim, located in southern Mexico area, close to the Yucatan Peninsula, and northern border of Guatemala.

The origin of the "Mayans" and the "Aztecs", as the term used by the alleged experts, actually came from Jerusalem as one family at first, then divided after they got to their promised land, not long after landing and beginning their habitation on the coast of northern Chile, South America. Most accounts of this are so close together, and the 320 years it took the Nephites/Mayans to meet the people of Zarahemla/Toltecs, was that they landed off of the coast of northern Chile, then went inland, and began farming. Later, after 30-years, for the necessity of safety and self preservation, divided from the Lamanites/Aztecs, moving north to the land of Nephi/northern Peru, Ecuador, Colombia etc.. Thus, continues the story about the travels of the family of Lehi, including Lehi's wife, Sariah, their four sons, Nephi, Sam. Laman and Lemuel, Ishamael and his several sons and daughters, and Zoram, the servant of Laban.

They left Jerusalem 600 B.C., having to stop from time to time, as God directed, to get first, the Brass Plates, from Laban, then having to return another time to get Ishmael and his family. When they first left Jerusalem, God provided Lehi with a compass, that only worked for them as long as they were obeying the commandments of God. They went southwesterly towards the Red Sea, and along it through Arabia, to the location called Bountiful.

> "And it came to pass that we did again take our journey in the wilderness; and we did travel **nearly eastward from that time forth. A**nd we did travel and wade through much affliction in the wilderness; **and our women did bear children in the wilderness.**" "And so great were the blessings of the Lord upon us, that while **we did live upon raw meat in the wilderness, our women did give plenty of suck for their children, and were strong, yea, even like unto the men; and they began to bear their journeyings without murmurings.**"
> "And thus we see that the commandments of God **must be fulfilled**. And if so be that the children of men keep the commandments of God he doth nourish them, and strengthen them, and provide means whereby **they can accomplish the thing which he has commanded them;** wherefore he did provide means for us while we did sojourn in the wilderness[wilds of Arabia, along the shores of the Red Sea]."
> "And we did sojourn[travel and subsist] for the space of **many years, yea, even eight years in the wilderness**[in the wilds of Arabia]."
> "And we did come **to the land which we called Bountiful, because** of its much fruit and also wild honey; and all these things were prepared of the Lord that we might not perish. And we beheld **the sea, which we called Irreantum, which being interpreted, is many waters.**"(1 Nephi 17:2-5, Book of Mormon)

(see http://www.supportingevidences.net/lehi-traveling-from-jerusalem/) also (see https://bookofmormoncentral.org/blog/archaeological-evidence-for-7-locations-on-lehi-s-journey-to-the-promised-land).

Here at Bountiful, is where God instructed Nephi; future Mayan King, to build a ship. Nephi asks Laman; future king of the Aztecs, to give him help to build this ship. Laman and Lemuel rebelled against Nephi when they went to get the Plates of Brass from Laban, and again, when they went back to get the family of Ishmael, and they whined and moaned when Nephi broke his steel bow, thinking they were going to starve, and they now refused to give Nephi help in building the ship that was to bring them here to the Americas. Nephi continually had to be an example to them and teach them the ways of God. From here on out, the older brothers were very jealous and several times tried to take Nephi's life. One prior time, is when Nephi broke his steel bow, leaving the family in question of what was to become of them. The next time, was while they were on the ship they had built, while heading to the promised land.

While they were traveling through the wilderness, carrying their burdens, God strengthened them in their toils through their faith that even their women folk, were strong like the men in carrying their burdens. Many times, to avoid having to build fires to cook their meat, which would have alerted their enemies, they chose instead, to eat their meat raw. Amid many great tribulations, including, child bearing, conflicts among themselves, sometimes hunger, nevertheless, they were led South to the Shores of the Indian Ocean, and Where Nephi called the land, Bountiful.

> "And it came to pass that we did pitch our tents by the seashore; and notwithstanding [despite what] we had suffered many afflictions and much difficulty, yea, even so much that _we cannot write them all, we were exceedingly rejoiced when we came to the seashore; and we called the place **Bountiful, because of its much fruit.**_" "(1 Nephi 17:6, Book of Mormon) https://knowhy.bookofmormoncentral.org/knowhy/has-the-location-of-nephis-bountiful-been-discovered ; http://bmaf.org/node/628

Here the family rested while the brothers built the ship, the Lord was directing them to build. They also gathered honey bees, seeds of every kind, animals that would help them sustain life, like the goat and the sheep. Lehi's family was from the elite-class. They were very learned and educated and successful in their vocations. They were among the high-middle class, if not the Rich. They were respected among their peers. They knew how to conduct business, and could both speak and write Hebrew and Egyptian languages. They were not poor, but very well to do. They knew how to farm, build, and they worked very hard, and were an industrious people. Further, they were blessed by God because of their willingness to listen to his commandments.

Nephi was humble, and easily entreated, as well as his older brother Sam. They both were favored of God because of their obedience. They definitely were not party to things they knew were not right, but only sought the truth, after searching out what Nephi's father said. Nephi always went to God himself, so that he could know for himself if what his father said, or saw, was true. He always asked for the explanation, and always received an answer from God, because of his diligence in wanting to know for himself.

Nephi was not blind when following his father's words, because he was able to see. Therefore, he cared not about having to leave their property, or friends, or their much wealth that they had up to the time they gave it away to get the Brass Plates from Laban. Nephi was instructed by God, while in Bountiful, how to build a ship. He employed the help of his brothers to do so. Nephi was shown how, even the same, as when God instructed Noah how to build the Ark. The ship was well-built, and able to withstand the pounding of the waves from the turbulent ocean.

> "And it came to pass that after I, Nephi, had been in the land of **Bountiful** for the space of many days, the voice of the Lord came unto me, saying: Arise, and get thee into the mountain. And it came to pass that I arose and went up into the mountain, and cried unto the Lord.""And it came to pass that the Lord spake unto me, saying: Thou **shalt construct a ship**, after the manner which I shall show thee, that I may **carry thy people across these waters.**""And I said: Lord, whither shall I go that I may find **ore to molten, that I may make tools** to construct the ship after the manner which **thou hast shown unto me?**""And it came to pass that the Lord told me whither I should go to find ore, **that I might make tools.**""And

*it came to pass that I, Nephi, did make **a bellows**, wherewith to blow the fire, of the skins of beasts; and after I had made a **bellows**, that I might have wherewith to blow the fire, I did **smite** two stones together that I might make a fire."" For the Lord had not hitherto suffered that we should make much fire, as we journeyed in the wilderness; for he said: I will make thy food become sweet, that ye cook it not."…"Yea, and the Lord said also that: After ye have arrived in the promised land, ye shall know that I, the Lord, am God: and that I the Lord, did deliver you from destruction; yea that I did bring you out of the **land of Jerusalem.**""Wherefore I, Nephi, did strive to keep the commandments of the Lord, and I did exhort my brethren to faithfulness and diligence.""And it came to pass that I **did make tools** of the ore which I did **molten out of rock.*** (1 Nephi 17:7-12, 14-16, Book of Mormon)*

When they finally set sail, they followed the instructions given them from God as was shown on a compass, called the Liahona. From time to time, Lehi could read a writing on the ball of the compass, instructing him in the way they should go. They sailed south into the Gulf of Aden, past the mouth of the Red Sea, then west into the Indian Ocean, following a favorable southwest wind, probably the same direction the Mulekites took, and were sailing along very well for a time. If they had stayed on this course, they surely would have traveled up the east coast of South America, and would have landed where the Jaredites, or the Mulekites before them had landed. However, Laman and Lemuel began rebelling, and because of this, their compass ceased to work. The Lord changed the direction of the wind and began blowing them off course, and as the scriptures say: They were blown back four days, and were threatened with destruction if they didn't repent.

*"And it came to pass that they did worship the Lord, and did go forth with me[Nephi]; and we did **work timbers of curious workmanship**. And the Lord did show me from time to time after what manner I should **work the timbers of the ship.**" "Now I Nephi, did not work the timbers after the manner which was learned by men, neither did I build the ship after the manner*

of men; but I did build it after the manner which the <u>Lord had</u> <u>shown unto me; wherefore, it was not after the manner of</u> men."

"And I, Nephi, did go into the mount oft, and I did **pray oft unto the Lord**; *wherefore the* **Lord showed unto me** <u>great things</u>." *"And it came to pass that after I[Nephi] had finished* **the ship**, *according to the* **word of the Lord**, *my brethren* **beheld that it was** **good**, *and that the* <u>workmanship thereof was exceedingly fine</u>; *wherefore, they did humble themselves again before the Lord." "And it came to pass that the voice of the Lord came unto my father[Lehi], that we should arise and go down into the* **ship**." *"And it came to pass that on the morrow, after we had prepared all things,* **much fruits and meat from the** **wilderness, and honey in abundance, and provisions according to** **that which the <u>Lord</u> had commanded us,** *we did go down* **into the** **ship**, *with all our loading and our* **seeds,** *and whatsoever thing we had brought with us, every one according to his age; wherefore, we did all go down* **into the ship, with our wives and our children.**" *"And now, my father had begat two sons in the wilderness; the elder was called Jacob and the younger Joseph." "And it came to pass after we had all* **gone down into the ship**, *and had taken with us our provisions and things which had been commanded us,* **we did put forth into the** **sea and were driven forth before the wind towards the <u>promised</u>** **<u>land</u>**[the Americas]." " *(1 Nephi 18:1-8, Book of Mormon)*

The scriptures tell us, that they sailed several days on a favorable course, but then Laman and Lemuel began disrespecting God, and the members of their family who were observing the commandments of God, including Nephi, and their father Lehi. Therefore, the compass quit working for them, and they knew not where to steer their ship. It is the author's opinion, that Lehi had sailed down, and around the Cape of Hope of Africa, then toward the east coast of South America, following the wind pattern and the natural ocean currents, but because of Laman and Lemuel, God got angry and began to drive them off course. The Lord knew their thoughts, and what they were planning, and unless they change now, he might as well drown them in the ocean.

"And after we had been **driven forth before the wind for the** **space of <u>many days</u>,** *behold, my brethren and the sons of Ishmael and*

*also their wives began to make themselves merry[drink strong drink], insomuch that they began to dance, and to sing, and to speak with much rudeness, yea, **even that they did forget by what <u>power</u> they had been brought thither**; yea, they were lifted up unto exceeding rudeness." "And I, Nephi[first Mayan King], began to fear exceedingly lest the **Lord** should smite us because of our iniquity, that we should be swallowed up in the depths of the sea; wherefore, I, Nephi, began to speak to them with much soberness; but behold they[future Aztec kings] were angry with me, saying: **We will not that our younger brother shall be a ruler over us.**" "And it came to pass that Laman[First future Aztec king] and Lemuel did take me and bind me with cords, and they did treat me with much harshness; nevertheless. The **Lord did suffer it** that he might show forth **his power**, unto the fulfilling of his **word** which he had spoken concerning the wicked." "And it came to pass that after they had bound me insomuch that I could not move, <u>the compass which had been prepared of the Lord, did cease to work.</u>" (1 Nephi 18:9-12, Book of Mormon)*

The scriptures say, that they were blown back several days, and were about to be sunken in the depths of the ocean, and receive a watery grave. The Author's opinion, is that they were blown back to the southern tip of South America, where the Indian, the Atlantic, and the Pacific Oceans meet, which is the graveyard of many ships, because of the great turbulence of the water at this point. However, because of the threat of being destroyed, Laman and Lemuel, repented and released Nephi, and asked for forgiveness, and Nephi once again led them on their way, but now went up the western coast of South America, and eventually landed just off the coast of northern Chile. **Some believe they landed at the 30**[th] **south latitude.** This theory makes much sense, and is parallel with many other facts, included in this book. (see http://nephicode.blogspot.com/2010/07/where-lehi-landed-30-south-latitude-in.html

*"Wherefore they knew not whither they **should steer the ship**, insomuch **that there arose a <u>great storm, yea, a great and terrible tempest, and were driven back upon the waters for the space of three days;</u>** and they began to be frightened exceedingly lest*

*they should be drowned in the sea; nevertheless they did not loose me[Nephi]." "**And on the fourth day which we had been driven back, the tempest began to be exceedingly sore**." "And it came to pass that we were about to be swallowed up in the depths of the sea. And after we had been **driven back upon the waters for the space of four days,** my brethren began to see that the judgments of God were upon them, and that they must perish save that they should repent of their iniquities; wherefore, they came unto me, and loosed the bands which were upon my wrists, and behold they had swollen exceedingly; and also mine ankles were much swollen, and great was the soreness thereof." "...And it came to pass after they had loosed me, behold I took **the compass, and it did work whither I desired it.** And it came to pass that **I prayed unto the Lord**; and after I had prayed the winds did cease and there was a **great calm.**" "And it came to pass that I, Nephi, **did guide the ship, that we sailed** again **towards the promised land**[the Americas]." "And it came to pass that **after we had sailed for the space of many days we did arrive at the promised land**[South America]; and we went forth upon the land, and did pitch our tents; and we did call it the promised land."(1 Nephi 18:13-16,21-23, Book of Mormon)*

This is why the Mulekites/Toltecs, who left 11-years after the Nephites/Mayans and Aztecs, to get to the Americas, arrived at least eleven years earlier, to inhabit the empty cities of the Jaredites/Olmecs, and found the last surviving Jaredite/Olmec, who lived with them for nine moons/9-months, after they arrived. His name was Coriantumr, and he lived long enough to intermarry with the Mulekites/Toltecs and still have offspring. Coriantumr's descendants appeared as dissenting Nephites/Mayans, now a Lamanite/Aztec general, leading a huge army of Lamanites/Aztecs straight into the heart of Zarahemla. His name too, was Coriantumr, and is described as a large and mighty man. More will be said about this Coriantumr towards the end of this book.

Nephi and Sam had conflict at every turn with Laman and Lemuel, their older brothers. When Lehi and his group first left Jerusalem, Laman and Lemuel never stopped complaining and lamenting leaving their money, their ease and comfort, and their carefree way of life there. They didn't care about God or the truth, just their own selfish ambitions, and they weren't about to let their youngest brother be their teacher and rule over them. They rebelled when they went with Nephi to get the Plates of Brass, when they went again to get the family of Ishmael, when they were afraid of starving because Nephi broke his steel bow, and especially groaned and complained when they were asked to help Nephi build a ship. They hated to have to depend on Nephi to teach them the things of God, to be told about their sins.

Yet, the Liahona/compass only worked for Nephi. It was Nephi they depended on to feed them in the wilderness, and it was Nephi/ Father of the Mayan civilization, who got them to the promised land. It was also Nephi/first king of the Mayans, who taught them to farm when they landed off the coast of Chile, to work with all manner of metal, making tools etc.. So, you can imagine that Laman and Lemuel were desperate to destroy Nephi, and his family, in order to make themselves look better. Just like liberals/Democrats/socialist, brats. They would rather destroy their own freedom, burning their own cities down under their feet, because someone was doing something right and they weren't. They so quickly forgot the words of the Lord before they ever came to the Americas. It is the same thing the Democrats/ Socialists/libtards, are doing to our beloved Donald Trump, to keep him from doing good for our country of America.

> "Yea, and the Lord said also that: After ye have arrived in the promised land[The Americas], ye **shall know that I, the Lord, am God; and that I, the Lord, did deliver you from destruction; yea, that I did bring you out of the land of Jerusalem.**" "Wherefore, I, Nephi, did strive to keep the commandments of the Lord, and I did exhort my brethren to faithfulness and diligence." (1 Nephi 17:14-15, Book of Mormon)

The continuous disrespect, the unwillingness to cooperate and obey the commandments of God persisted. It was so very easy for them to forget the many blessings they enjoyed from God, through their brother, Nephi, and were brushed aside, because of their vain ambitions, their lust for riches, their lust for power, their pride, jealousy, and their selfishness, became a stumbling block to them. What Laman and Lemuel didn't understand, was that Nephi was driven by his knowledge of what the Lord had shown to him that was to come upon the people later. Nephi had a sense of responsibility that he could not avoid. Nephi had a duty to God that he was determined to carry out. Wicked people can never understand this, because they are going continuously away from the light. Nephi saw in visions, the future of the Americas.

> *"And it came to pass that the angel said unto me: Look, and behold thy seed, and also the seed of thy brethren. And I looked and beheld the* **land of promise***[the Americas]; and I beheld multitudes of people, yea, even as it were in number as many as the sand of the sea."* *"And it came to pass that I beheld multitudes gathered together to battle, one against the other; and I beheld wars, and rumors of wars, and great slaughters with the sword among my people."* *"And it came to pass that I beheld many generations pass away, after the manner of wars and contentions in the land[Americas]; and I beheld many cities, yea, even that I did not number them."* *"And it came to pass that I saw a* **mist of darkness***[disinformation/lies] on the face of the* **land of promise***[the Americas]; and I saw lightnings, and I heard thunderings, and earthquakes, and all manner of tumultuous noises; and I saw the earth and the rocks, and they rent; and I saw the mountains tumbling into pieces; and I saw the plains of the earth, that they were broken up; and I saw many cities that they* **were sunk***[i.e. Mocum/ Rock Lake, WI]; and I saw many that they were burned with fire; and I saw many that did tumble to the earth, because of the quaking thereof."* *"And it came to pass after I saw these things, I saw the vapor of darkness[the lies of Satan], that it passed from off the face of the earth; and behold,* **I saw multitudes who had not fallen** *because of the great and terrible judgments of the Lord."* **"And I saw the heavens open, and the Lamb of God descending out of heaven; and he came down and showed himself unto them."** *"**And I also saw and bear record that the Holy Ghost fell upon twelve others; and they were ordained of God, and chosen."***... (1 Nephi 12:1-7, Book of Mormon)

When they landed off the coast of Chile, South America, there was no mention, or record of anyone being there already ahead of them.

The only other people we have a record of being there ahead of the family of Lehi/Mayans/Aztecs, are those inhabitants mentioned earlier as the Mulekites/Toltecs and the Jaredites/Olmecs, as recorded in the Book of Ether, in the Book of Mormon. However, these peoples were predominantly in Central America at the time.

When Lehi and his family set their feet on solid land again, they immediately went to work farming, as anyone would, knowing they needed to feed their families. As the scriptures records: They planted all the seeds for food that they had brought with them. The brothers of Nephi, and their families expected to be fed also.

> *"And it came to pass that after we had sailed for the space of many days* **we *did arrive at the promised land***[Americas]*; and we went forth upon the land, and did call it the **promised land**." "And it came to pass that we did begin to till the earth, and we began to **plant seeds;** yea, we did put all our seeds into the earth, which we had brought **from the land of Jerusalem***. And it came to pass that they did grow exceedingly; wherefore, we were **blessed in abundance**." "And it did come to pass that we did find upon the **land of promise**[the Americas], as we journeyed in the wilderness, that there were beasts in the forests of every kind, **both the cow and the ox, and the ass and the horse and the goat and the wild goat,** and all manner of wild animals, which were for the use of men. And we did find **all manner of ore, both of gold, and of silver, and of copper**."(1 Nephi 18:23-25, Book of Mormon)*

It wasn't long after landing, that Lehi gathered his family around him to bless them, and explain to them the importance of keeping the commandments of God, and stressed the importance of looking to God for their blessings. *"And now my sons, I would that ye should look to the great Mediator, and hearken unto his great commandments; and be faithful unto his words,* **and choose eternal life** *according to the **will of his Holy Spirit;**" "And not choose **eternal death**, according to the **will of the flesh and the evil which is therein, which giveth the spirit of the devil power to captivate, to bring you down to hell, that he may reign over you in his own kingdom.***"(2 Nephi 2:28-29, Book of Mormon)*

Lehi also recounted the many blessings that God had given them. He also rehearsed to Laman and Lemuel, the goodness of God in blessing them because of their youngest brother, Nephi. He encouraged them to listen to Nephi, because he always sought the will of God in making his decisions. Then it records that Lehi, their father died, and was buried.

"And it came to pass after my father, Lehi, had spoken unto all his household, according to the feelings of his heart and the Spirit of the Lord which was in him, he waxed old. And it came to pass that he died, and was buried." "And it came to pass that not many days after his death, Laman and Lemuel and the sons of Ishmael were angry with me because of the admonitions of the Lord." (2 Nephi 4:12-13, Book of Mormon)

Here, Nephi, Sam, Laman, Lemuel, the younger brothers that were born to Lehi and Sariah , while on the ship, Jacob and Joseph, and the ex-servant of Laban, Zoram, also a very good friend of Nephi, and the sons of Ishmael, all of which had wives, began to multiply upon the land. This was the family of Lehi and Ishmael, the source of the **beginning of the Mayan and Aztec civilizations**. Nephi made and kept records of his people on metal plates, and maybe, some were stone, but him being blessed of God, him being a son of God, used metal, whether gold or brass, or silver, it doesn't matter. What we do know is, gold lasts longer, and the records received by Joseph Smith, were gold plates, from which were translated the *Book of Mormon*.

*"And after I had made these plates by way of commandment, I, Nephi, received a commandment that the ministry and the prophecies, the more plain and precious parts of them, should be written upon these plates; and that the things which were written should be kept for the instruction of my people, who should possess the land, and also for **other wise purposes**, which purposes are known unto the Lord." "Wherefore, I, Nephi, did make a record upon other plates, which gives an account, or which gives a greater account of the **wars and contentions and destructions of my people.**" "And this have I done, and commanded my people what they should do after I was*

gone; and that these plates should be handed down from one generation to another, or from one <u>prophet to another</u>, until further commandments of the Lord."(1 Nephi 19:3-4, Book of Mormon)

Nephi talks several times about Christ, 33-years after his birth, and 600 years after they have left Jerusalem, visiting the Americas. Nephi talks about the death of Christ and the destruction of cities and how they will be destroyed. He mentions 3-days of darkness, and the earthquakes, tempests, and many other destructions to come at his death. He also mentions how Christ is hung upon the cross for the sins of the world.

*"And behold he cometh, according to the words of the angel, in **six hundred years from the time my father left Jerusalem.** " "And the **world**, because of their iniquity, shall judge him to be a thing of naught; wherefore they scourge him, and he suffereth it; and they smite him, and he suffereth it.Yea, they spit upon him, and he suffereth it, **because of his loving kindness** and his **long-suffering** towards the children of men." "And the God of our fathers, who were led out of Egypt, out of bondage, and also were preserved in the wilderness by him, yea, the God of Abraham, and of Isaac, and the God of Jacob, yieldeth himself according to the words of the angel, as a man, into the hands of wicked men, to be **lifted up**, according to the words of Zenock, and to be **crucified**, according to the words of Neum, and to be **buried in a sepulchre**, according to the words of Zenos, which he spake concerning **the three days of darkness,** which would be a sign given of his death unto those who should inhabit the Isles of the sea, **more especially those who are of the house of Israel.** " "For thus spake the prophet: The Lord God shall visit **all the house of Israel at that day,** <u>some with his voice, because of their righteousness,</u> <u>unto their great joy and salvation,</u> and others with the thunderings and the lightnings of his power, by **tempest, by fire, and by smoke, and vapor of darkness, and by the opening of the earth, and by mountains which shall be carried up."**(1 Nephi 19:8-11, Book of Mormon)*

Nephi also, while filled with the Spirit of revelation and prophesy, tells of the destruction of the wicked when Christ dies on the cross.

He tells how wicked cities will be sunken in the ocean, and sunken in the earth, having earth cover them up. Also cities being sunken in the earth and having water cover their wickedness. He also mentions how some will be burned with fire, including their capital city of Zarahemla, and talks about cities being shaken by earthquakes until the buildings collapse and destroy the wicked within them. Nephi also talks about the end times, and bringing back the children of Israel to a knowledge of the truth, and that great and "abominable church' shall be destroyed. Now that's *"Global Warming"* folks, no question about it.

*"For behold, saith the prophet, the time cometh speedily that **Satan shall have no more power** over the hearts of the children of men; for the day soon cometh that all the **proud and they who do wickedly shall be as stubble; and the day cometh that they must be burned.** "* *"For the time soon cometh that the fulness of the wrath of God shall be poured out upon all the children of men; **for he will not suffer that the wicked shall destroy the righteous.** " "Wherefore, he will preserve **the righteous by his power,** even if it so be that the fulness of his wrath must come, and the righteous be preserved, even unto the destruction of their **enemies by fire. Wherefore, the righteous need not fear;** for thus saith the prophet, **they shall be saved even if it so be as by fire.***(1 Nephi 22:15-17, Book of Mormon)*

Chapter 5

Division of the Nephites/Mayans & Lamanites/Aztecs From Lehi's Family

Lehi prepares to die, he blesses his sons, and tells them of their lineage encourages them to follow Nephi as their leader

Before their father, Lehi, died however, he talked to each son and admonished each one to be faithful, and obey the commandments of God. He told them about visions he had concerning all of them, and got personal visions concerning each one individually. He informed them of the blessings God has granted unto them thus far, because they have received a land of promise. Lehi their father, also informed them that Jerusalem had now been destroyed, just as God said it would, and they should be thankful and grateful to God for bringing them to this land that was choice above all others. He also emphasized, that if they had not left when they were told by God to do so, that they also would have been destroyed.

*"For, behold, said he, I have seen a vision, in which I know that **Jerusalem is destroyed;** and had we remained in **Jerusalem** we should also have perished." "But, said he, notwithstanding our afflictions, we have obtained **a land of promise**[Americas], **a land which is choice above all other lands;** a land which the Lord God hath covenanted with me should be a land for the inheritance of my seed[the Mayans and the Aztecs]. Yea, the Lord hath covenanted*

*this land unto me, and to my children forever, and also all those who should be led **out of other countries by the hand of the Lord.** (2 Nephi 1:4-5, Book of Mormon)*

Before Lehi dies, he specifically cautions Laman and Lemuel, and those he knows support his two older sons, to keep the commandments of God, and if they do these things, the land will always be to them *"a land of liberty"*. This was Lehi's last caution before he died, to hopefully reach through and perhaps change the course of what he knew was going to happen to his posterity in the future of the Americas. If they neglected to keep the commandments then the land **shall be cursed because of them.**

*"Wherefore, this land is consecrated unto him whom he shall bring. And if it so be that they shall **serve him** according to the commandments which he hath given, **it shall be a land of liberty unto them;** wherefore, they shall **never be brought down into captivity;** if so, it shall be because of **iniquity;** for if **iniquity shall abound cursed shall be the land** for their sakes, but unto the <u>righteous it shall be blessed forever.</u>" (2 Nephi 1:7, Book of Mormon)*

*"But behold, when the time cometh that they shall dwindle in unbelief, after they have received so great blessings from the hand of the Lord---**having a knowledge** of the creation of the earth, and marvelous works of the Lord from the creation of the world; **having power given them**[Priesthood Covenant] to do all things by faith; **having all the commandments** from the beginning, and having been brought by his infinite goodness into this **precious land of promise---** behold, I say, if the day shall come that they **will reject the Holy One of Israel**, the true Messiah, their Redeemer and their God, behold, the judgments of him that is just shall rest upon them." "Yea, he will bring **other nations** unto them, and he will give unto them power, and he will **take away** from them the **lands of their possessions**, and he will cause them to be **scattered and smitten.**" "Yea, as one generation passeth to another there shall be **bloodsheds, and great visitations among them:** wherefore, my sons, I would that ye would remember; yea, I would that ye would hearken unto my words." "**O that ye**</i>*

would awake; awake from a deep sleep, yea, even from the sleep of hell[the world], and shake off the awful chains[contracts, lies, love of money, temptations etc.] by which ye are bound, which are the chains which bind the children of men, that they are carried away captive down to the eternal gulf of misery and woe." (2 Nephi 1:10-13, Book of Mormon)

*"Awake and arise from the dust, and hear the words of a trembling parent, whose limbs ye must soon lay down in the cold and silent grave, from whence no traveler can return; a few more days and I go the way of all the earth." "But behold, **the Lord hath redeemed my soul from hell; I have beheld his glory, and I am encircled about eternally in the <u>arms of his love</u>.**" "And I desire that ye should **remember** to observe the statutes and the judgments of the Lord; behold, this hath been the <u>anxiety of my soul from the beginning</u>." "My heart hath been weighed down with sorrow from time to time, for I have feared, lest for the hardness of your hearts the Lord your God should come out in the fullness of his wrath upon you, that ye be cut off and destroyed forever;" "Or, that a cursing should come upon you for the space of many generations; and ye are visited by sword, and by famine, and are hated, and are led according to the will and captivity of the devil."* (2 Nephi 1:14-18, Book of Mormon)

As Lehi continues talking to the future of his posterity, Laman and Lemuel/the Aztecs, They have not been cursed with the dark skin as of yet, but Lehi has foreseen what was going to happen to them because of their childishness/selfishness, and unbelief, but he still cautions them, as a good parent would. *"O my sons, that these things might not come upon you, but that ye **might be a choice and favored** people of the Lord. **But behold, his will be done; for his ways are righteousness forever.**" "And he hath said that: Inasmuch as ye shall keep my commandments ye shall prosper in the land; but inasmuch as ye will not keep my commandments ye shall be cut off from my presence."*(2 Nephi 1:19-20, Book of Mormon)

*"Rebel no more against your brother[Nephi: first Mayan Leader], **whose views have been glorious,** and who hath kept the commandments from the time that **we left Jerusalem;** and who hath*

been an instrument in the hands of God, in bringing us forth into **the land of promise**[The Americas]; for **were it not for him, we must have perished with hunger in the wilderness;** *nevertheless, ye sought to take away his life; yea, and he hath suffered much sorrow because of you." "And I exceedingly fear and tremble because of you, lest he shall suffer again; for behold, ye have accused him that he sought power and authority over you; but I know that he hath not sought for power nor authority over you, but he hath sought the glory of God, and your own eternal welfare."(2 Nephi 1:24, Book of Mormon)*

"And now my son, Laman[first king of the Aztecs]*, and also Lemuel and Sam, and also my sons who are the sons of Ishmael, behold, if ye will hearken unto the voice of Nephi*[first Mayan king] *ye shall not perish. And if ye <u>hearken unto him I leave unto you a blessing, yea, even my first blessing.</u>" "But if ye will not hearken unto him*[Nephi] *I take away my first blessing, yea, even my blessing, and it shall rest upon him*[Nephi]*." "And now, Zoram, I speak unto you: Behold, thou art the servant of Laban; nevertheless, thou hast been brought out of the* **land of Jerusalem,** *and I know that thou art a true friend unto my son, Nephi, forever." "Wherefore, because thou hast been faithful thy seed shall be blessed with his seed,…"(2 Nephi 1:28-31, Book of Mormon)*

Obviously, Nephi has already been chosen as the first leader and example/role model for Lehi's family, by Lehi, before Lehi is gone. As mentioned earlier, Lehi and Sariah, had two more sons, Jacob and Joseph, of which he included them in his blessing. Lehi, their father, encouraged them to listen to their older brother, Nephi, and in the end, if they do this, they will inherit the Kingdom of God. To Joseph, he is telling him that he is named after Joseph who was sold into Egypt by his own brethren, and that he is a direct descendant of this Joseph. He tells him of the great covenants and promises the Lord had made with Joseph, because of Joseph's faithfulness, and that this same Joseph did truly see his, Lehi's day. We are talking about the origination of the Mayans and Aztecs here, as they are from the **Tribe of Joseph**, that same Joseph who was sold into Egypt by his older brothers.

*"And now, **Joseph,** my last-born, whom I have brought out of the wilderness of mine afflictions, may the Lord bless thee forever, for thy seed shall not utterly be destroyed." "For behold, thou art the fruit of my loins; and I am a descendant of **Joseph who was carried captive into Egypt.** And great were the covenants of the Lord which he made with **Joseph**." "Wherefore, <u>**Joseph truly saw our**</u> day. And he obtained a promise of the Lord, that out of the fruit of his loins the Lord God would raise up a **righteous branch** unto the house of Israel; not the Messiah, but a branch which was to be broken off, nevertheless, to be remembered in the covenants of the Lord that the Messiah should be made manifest unto them in the **latter days,** in the spirit of power, unto the bringing of them out of **darkness** unto light---yea, out of hidden darkness and out of **captivity unto freedom.**" "For Joseph truly testified, saying,: A seer[Joseph Smith] shall the Lord **my God raise up, who shall be a choice seer unto the fruit of my loins." "Yea, Joseph** truly said: Thus saith the Lord unto me: A choice seer will I raise up out of the fruit of thy loins; and he shall be esteemed highly among the fruit of thy loins. And unto him[Joseph Smith] will I give commandment that he shall do a work for the fruit of thy loins, his brethren, which shall be of great worth unto them, even to the bringing of them to the knowledge of the covenants which I have made with thy fathers." (2 Nephi 3:3-7, Book of Mormon)*

*"And I will give unto him[Joseph Smith] a commandment that he shall do none other work, save the work which I shall command him. And I will make him great in mine eyes; for he[Joseph Smith] shall do my work." "And he[Joseph Smith] shall be great like unto **Moses,** whom I have said I would raise up unto you, to deliver thy people, O house of Israel." "And Moses will I raise up, to deliver thy people out of the land of Egypt." "But a seer[Joseph Smith] will I raise up out of the fruit of thy loins; and unto him[Joseph Smith] will I give power[the priesthoods] to bring forth my word unto the seed of thy loins---and not to the bringing forth my word only, saith the Lord, but to the **convincing** them of my word, which will have gone forth among them." "Wherefore the fruit of thy loins shall write; and the fruit of the loins of Judah shall write; and that which shall be written by the fruit of thy loins, and also that which shall be written by the fruit of the loins of*

Judah, **shall grow together, unto the confounding of false doctrine** *and laying down of contentions,* <u>and establishing peace</u> *among the fruit of thy loins, and bringing them to the* **knowledge of their fathers in the latter days,** *and also to the knowledge of my covenants[Priesthood and Marriage covenanats], saith the Lord." (2 Nephi 3:8-12, Book of Mormon)*

"And out of weakness he[Joseph Smith] shall be made strong, in that day when my work [the translation of the plates of Nephi and restoring the fullness of the gospel of Jesus Christ] shall commence among all my people, unto the restoring thee, O house of Israel, saith the Lord." "And thus prophesied Joseph, saying: Behold, that seer[Joseph Smith] will the Lord bless; and they that seek to destroy him shall be confounded; for this promise, which I have obtained of the Lord, of the fruit of thy loins, **shall be fulfilled.** *Behold,* <u>**I am sure of the fulfilling of this promise;**</u> *"* <u>**"And his name shall be called after me; and it shall be after the name of his father.**</u> *And he[Joseph smith]* **shall be like unto me; for the thing, which the Lord shall bring forth by his**[Joseph Smith's] **hand, by the power of the Lord shall bring my people unto** *salvation." "Yea, thus prophesied Joseph:* <u>**I am sure of this thing, even as I am sure of the promise of Moses; for the Lord hath said unto me, I will preserve thy seed forever.**</u>*"(2 Nephi 3:13-16, Book of Mormon)*

"And the Lord hath said: **I will raise up a Moses; and I will give power unto him in a rod; and I will give judgment unto him in** <u>**writing. Yet I will not loose his tongue, that he**[Joseph Smith] **shall speak much, for I will not make him mighty in speaking.**</u> *But I will write unto him my law, by the finger of mine own hand; and I will make a spokesman for him[Oliver Cowdrey]." "And the Lord said unto me also: I will raise up unto the fruit of thy loins; and I will make for him[Joseph Smith] a spokesman[Oliver Cowdrey]. And I, behold, I will give unto him that he[Oliver Cowdrey] shall* **write the writing**[take dictation/transcribe] *of the fruit of thy loins; and the spokesman[Oliver Cowdrey] shall declare[witness and testify of] it." "And the words which he shall write shall be the words which are expedient in my wisdom should go forth unto the fruit of thy loins.*

And it shall be as if the fruit of thy loins had cried unto them from the dust; for I know their faith." (2 Nephi 3:17-19, Book of Mormon)

Lehi died shortly after blessing and admonishing each son, but before this happened, he called Laman and Lemuel, his rebellious sons to his side one last time. Lehi foresees them rebelling against their brother Nephi, and pleads with them as a loving, caring parent, not wanting to see his children cut off from the presence of the Lord. He pleads to them to keep the commandments of God, knowing they are going to rebel anyway. It grieves their father knowing that, because of their teachings, and knowledge, they still will stray and be lost forever from the presence of the Lord. He is attempting to make them understand how important it is for them to listen to the Holy One of Israel, and delight in the truth. He is attempting to bless their posterity because they will be brought up in ignorance, but yet sheds hope that their descendants, through the **Gentiles/**us, will receive the gospel of Jesus Christ, and many yet will be saved in the Kingdom of God in the Latter-Days.

*"And it came to pass after my father, Lehi, had spoken unto all his household, according to the feelings of his heart and the Spirit of the Lord which was in him, he waxed old. And it came to pass that he **died, and was buried**." "And it came to pass that not many days after his death, **Laman and Lemuel and the sons of Ishmael were angry with me[Nephi]** because of the admonitions of the Lord." "For I, Nephi, was constrained to speak unto them, according to his word; for I had spoken many things unto them, and also my father, before his death; many of which sayings are written upon mine other plates; for a more history part are written upon mine other plates." (2 Nephi 4:12-14, Book of Mormon)*

Lehi died soon after, and now that their father and mother were now dead, and buried there in Chile, South America, Laman and Lemuel now felt they no longer needed to keep loyalties for their father and mother's sake, and now began to scheme how they were going to kill their younger brother, to prevent him from being a ruler over them. Thus, **the beginning of the Mayan and Aztec**

civilizations, as the experts want to call them. At least, I must be a better expert on the Mayans, the Aztecs, the Toltecs, and the Olmecs, because, I, at least know that none of them are prehistoric, for all had records, and I at least know where they came from, who they were, how they got here and where they went. This is through the Spirit of revelation, and the Spirit of God/ the truth that tells me and testifies of these things, taking into consideration all of the facts relevant to past, present, and future, and myself, knowing firsthand, of the mercies and revelations of God.

Now that Laman and Lemuel's father was dead and buried, they now felt all common ground was ended with their younger brother, and those who stood with him, Nephi. They found it much easier to dislike Nephi to the point of wanting to kill him. Like any liberal, they think completely opposite to the truth, in fact they hate the truth, because they don't want to be made to feel guilty while disobeying the commandments of God. This is what happens to all people who love money, and power. They just can't get enough unless they control it all. Therefore, they were listening to that evil spirit that causes discord, greed, jealousy, lust, fear and envy, and because they were rejecting the truth, they were now headed into outer darkness. Next, they began to make plans to satisfy their lust for riches, power, and control over one another, even if they have to kill, as Cain did Able, so it was in this case.

*"Behold, it came to pass that I, Nephi[Mayan king/prophet], did cry much unto the Lord my God, because of the anger of my brethren," "But behold, **their anger did increase against me, insomuch that they did seek to take away my life.** " "Yea, they did murmur against me, saying: Our younger brother thinks to rule over us; and we have had much trial because of him; wherefore, now let us **slay him,** that we may not be afflicted by his words. For behold, __we will not have him to be our ruler; for it belongs unto us, who are the elder brethren, to rule over this people.__ " "Now I do not write upon these plates all the words which they murmured against me. But it sufficeth me to say, __that they did seek to take away my life.__ " "And it came to pass that the Lord __did warn me, that I, Nephi, should depart from them and flee into the wilderness, and all those who would go with me.__ "*

'*Wherefore, it came to pass that* **I, Nephi, did take my family, and also Zoram and his family, and Sam, mine elder brother and his family, and Jacob and Joseph, my younger brethren, and also my sisters, and all those who would go with me were those who believed in the warnings and the revelations of God;** *wherefore, they did hearken unto my words." "And we did take our tents and whatsoever things were possible for us, and did journey in the wilderness for the* **space of many days.** *And after we had journeyed for the space of many days we did pitch our tents." "And my people would that we should call the name of the* **place Nephi; wherefore we did call it Nephi.** *" "And all those who were with me did take upon them to call themselves the* **people of Nephi**[*as the experts say Mayans*](*2 Nephi 5:1-9, Book of Mormon*)

Nephi, the First King of the Nephites/Mayans, as they were called by his people, because they revered him for being a man of God, and being a great blessing to those who love the Lord. **This Nephi, being the first king of the Nephites/Mayans.** Thus, the separation of the Mayans and the Aztecs. Nephi had no other choice, but to gather his families, and those who would go with him into the wilderness, including Zoram, Sam, Jacob, and Joseph, and all their wives, and leave. They went many days, before they settled down into the wilderness of South America, to start over. Nephi, in his wisdom brought all of the records available to them, including the Plates of Brass, and the sword of Laban, and Laban's armor, he acquired when he slew Laban. They, the Nephites/Mayans, went further north to the land in northern Peru and Ecuador, western Colombia, northern Bolivia, and even into northwestern Brazil's rain forest, and they called it the land of Nephi.

He brought the Liahona/compass, used to bring them out of Jerusalem, through the wilderness and across the oceans, by ship, and also all of their possessions that they could possibly carry, in order to preserve their lives and get a fresh start in another place. In order to keep from having to retaliate against Laman and Lemuel, they willingly left their homes and what property they couldn't take with them, to the murderers and would be thieves, and those who didn't want to work, and they only left by commandment of the Lord. If there was going to be bloodshed, then Nephi's brethren, Laman and Lemuel, had to be the ones to commit the first offense, at which time the people of Nephi were justified in defending themselves.

They, the Nephites/Mayans prospered greatly in this new land, that they named after their leader, the *"Land of Nephi"*, but knowing that Laman and Lemuel/the Aztecs, and their supporters, were hostile to them, they knew that they needed to be prepared, and therefore, arm themselves against an attack by the Lamanites/Aztecs. The people who followed Laman, took upon themselves the name, **Lamanites, or people of Laman/Aztecs,** and the followers of Nephi, took upon themselves the name of **Nephites, or the people of Nephi/ Mayans.** These people were blessed of God because they took upon themselves the gospel of Jesus Christ, and obeyed his commandments, and they kept records of their civilization. Where is the neanderthal or the prehistoric in all of this?

> *"And I, Nephi, did take the **sword of Laban, and after the manner of it did make many swords,** lest by any means the people who were now called **Lamanites[Aztecs] should come upon us and destroy us;** For I knew their hatred towards me and my children and those who were called my people." "And I did teach **my people**[Mayans] **to build buildings, and to work in all manner of wood, and of iron, and of copper, and of brass, and of steel, and of gold, and of silver, and of precious ores, which were in great abundance."* "And I Nephi[Mayan king] **did build a temple; and I did construct it after the manner of the temple of Solomon** save it were not built of so many precious things; for they were not to be found upon the land, wherefore, it could not be built like unto Soloman's temple. But the **manner of the construction was like unto the temple of Solomon; and the workmanship thereof was exceedingly fine."* "And it came to pass that I, Nephi, did cause my people to be industrious, and to labor with their hands." "And it came to pass that they would that I should be their king. **But I, Nephi, was desirous** that they should have no king; **nevertheless, I did for them according to that which was in my power."**(2 Nephi 5:14- 18, Book of Mormon)*

Because of the rebelliousness, and the disobedience of Nephi's brothers, to the commandments of God, they received a cursing from God, just as the Lord promised would happen if they were to become a scourge to their brethren. Now their skins were changed from a fair white skin, and replaced with a skin of blackness/darkness, to come upon them. They were lazy, shiftless, and continually seeking to attack the Nephites/Mayans whenever, wherever they could. They didn't work, but sought to make their living from hunting wild beasts in the forest. They became a loathsome, and a blood thirsty, and wild people.

"And behold, the words of the Lord had been fulfilled unto my brethren, which he spake concerning them, <u>that I should be their ruler and their teacher. Wherefore, I had been their ruler and their teacher,</u> according to the commandments of the Lord, <u>until the time they sought to take away my life.</u>" "Wherefore, the word of the Lord was fulfilled which he spake unto me, saying that: Inasmuch as they will not hearken[listen] to thy words they shall be cut off from the presence of the Lord. And behold, they were cut off from his presence." "And he had caused the **cursing to come upon them, yea, even a sore cursing, because of their iniquity. For behold, They had hardened their hearts against him, that they had become like flint; wherefore, <u>as they were white, and exceedingly fair and delightsome,</u> that they might not be enticing unto my people[Nephites/Mayans] the Lord God did cause a <u>skin of blackness</u> to come upon them."** *"And thus saith the Lord God: I will cause that they shall be* **loathsome unto thy people,** *save they shall repent of their iniquities." "And cursed shall be the seed of him that* **mixeth with their seed; for they shall be cursed even with the same cursing.** *" "And the Lord spake it, and it was done." (2 Nephi 5:19-23, Book of Mormon)*

"And because of their cursing which was upon them they did become an idle people, full of mischief and subtlety, and did seek in the <u>wilderness for beasts of prey</u>." *"And the Lord said unto me:* <u>**They[the Lamanites/Aztecs] shall be a scourge unto thy seed[Nephites/Mayans], to stir them up in remembrance of me; and inasmuch as they will not remember me, and hearken unto my words, they[Aztecs] shall scourge them[Mayans] even**</u>

unto destruction." *"(2 Nephi 5:24-25, Book of Mormon)* NOW
570 B.C.

The people of Nephi had not yet heard of the narrow neck of
Land west of the country we know today as Colombia, or Panama.
When the people of Nephi went many days from their relatives, the
Lamanites, into the wilderness, they basically went up northward into
the northern tip of Chile, Bolivia, all of Peru and Ecuador, and even
into Brazil's Amazon. These parts became the **Land of Nephi** for
a very long time, for approximately 290-years. They were 30-years,
before they were commanded to separate from Laman and Lemuel.
The temple that Nephi had built, was in the City of **Shilom**, which
is in northern Peru, in the land of Nephi. These are the people who
built the road system all throughout western South America. They
built buildings, worked fine workmanship in all manner of ores. It
is not the people living there today, who are responsible for this fine
workmanship.

The Nephites/Mayans, including what is known as Incas, are the
same, and they were educated and blessed of the Lord. They built
ships, they farmed with tools made from steel, also made weapons of
war made from fine steel. They were experts in building, and experts in
cement, obviously that is true, because their buildings are still standing
today. They had such amazing technology, that they could carve
road systems out of sheer sides of rock cliffs, and fit stones together of
oblong shapes and sizes, and cement them together, with cement like
glue, and still be level on top like they were poured from a cement
mixer. Actually, this was workings of their expertise in cement. They
could make cement appear as stones of all sizes and shapes, that were
so perfectly fit together, that a knife blade or a credit card couldn't fit
between, anywhere, and yet was perfectly level on top, like they were
poured from a cement mixer and formed, and actually, they were.
Where is the caveman, or stone age, or bronze age, like evolutionists
want you to believe, in that?

(see *A Map of Mormon Geological Theology (kottke.org)***24/part 2
summaries of models.pdf**

Also: https://youtu.be/i-N3NYOL0c0 This video confirms the
link just above, which is evidence of the map proving the settling

of the Americas by the people of Lehi. This is a 25,000 mile road system from northern Chile,throughout Peru, Bolivia and Ecuador, to Colombia.

From then on the Lamanites/Aztecs, inhabited South America, except for the time-being, the people of Nephi stayed in the land of Nephi for 290-years, before they saw the need to migrate further north into what is today called Northern Colombia, South America. This is where the land of Zarahemla was located. https://geology. com/world/colombia-satellite-image.shtml ; The Nephites/Mayans settled here in northern Colombia, being just south of the narrow neck of land, separating the north country from the south country. Any good general, always plans strategically, an escape route in case of trouble, and this point made it easier to defend against attack by the Lamanites/Aztecs. It was like putting your backs to the wall, in order to not be surrounded by your enemies, and having a back door to escape through if need be.

The land of Zarahemla/Colombia, was divided strategically by high ground, like a canyon, making it difficult for the enemy to attack from the south, because the canyon had a river that flowed through it going north. It was the only river that flowed from this narrow strip of wilderness/ high ground/mountainous area, north to the sea, which emptied out into the Carribbean. At the same time, they could defend the land north. This was the river Sidon. This is the only river that flowed north with enough water, and was straight enough, to carry dead bodies to the sea as spoken of by Alma, later in this text.
*(see   https://en.wikipedia.org/wiki/Magdalena_River#/media/File:Rio_
     Magdalena_Delta_landsat.jpg*
*https://en.wikipedia.org/wiki/Magdalena_River#/media/File:Rio_
     Magdalena River .*

Chapter 6

Geographical Facts of the Mayans & Aztecs; Where they Roamed

Division of Nepites/Mayans and the Lamanites/Aztecs in The Land of Nephi/Colombia

For the time being, the Nephites/Mayans were at peace in the land of Nephi/Peru and vicinity, and they set about raising their food, and flocks, and spreading out upon the land, at the same time watching and guarding against the day the Lamanites/Aztecs would come upon them, and you know they will, because the mindset of a liberal/democrat/socialist, scumbag can't get enough control or possessions, because they want it all. The Lamanites/Aztecs were doing the same thing further south, populating and spreading out upon the land. Little by little the Nephites/Mayans were spreading out by migrating northward into what we know today as North America, and Canada.

https://www.mapquest.com/travel/7-ancient-ruins-of-central-america

The Lamanites/Aztecs had become a very idle people, and instead of being industrious, they chose instead, to live by always hunting and killing their food. The Lamanites/Aztecs had become an idolatrous, a vicious and a blood thirsty people. *"And because of their **cursing which was upon them** they did become an **idle people**, full of mischief and subtlety, and did seek in the wilderness for beasts of prey."(2 Nephi 5:24, Book of Mormon)*

Yet the Lamanites/Aztecs were to remain a scourge unto the Nephites/Mayans, just as the Lord had told them would happen, if the Nephites ever went backwards and forgot their God, after receiving so many blessings. *"And the Lord God said unto me: **They shall be a <u>scourge unto thy seed, to stir them up in remembrance of me; and inasmuch as they will not remember me, and hearken unto my words, they shall scourge them even unto destruction.</u>"***(2 Nephi 5:25, Book of Mormon)

Nephi continued keeping their records upon the plates he had started, from the time they had landed in the promised land, which were made upon plates of gold, because there was much gold to be had there, and gold would keep indefinitely, and was easily formed and written upon. From the time the people of Nephi/Mayans had separated themselves from the Lamanites/Aztecs, **forty years** had went by, and there already had been many wars and contentions with the Lamanites/Aztecs. The Lamanites/Aztecs, were just like the liberals/communists today, who are always seeking power and control, always seeking free benefits, because they didn't want to work. **<u>Now 560 B.C.</u>**

*"And it sufficeth me to say that <u>forty years</u>**[560 B.C.]***<u>had passed away, and we already had wars and contentions with our brethren.</u> (2 Nephi 5:34, Book of Mormon)*

Throughout the records, Nephi, the first Mayan king was keeping, was in observance of the commandment of God to do so, for the purpose of preserving the history and genealogy to be handed down to his posterity from generation to generation. This was to fulfill the promises made by God to Joseph, who was sold into Egypt, that Joseph's posterity should never perish as long as the earth was still standing. These same plates, were to be be handed down to Joseph's posterity to be brought forth and translated, as Joseph's posterity "was speaking from the dust". These are the records that were passed to Joseph Smith, in 1830, being a direct descendant of Joseph, who was sold into Egypt, to be translated by him, by the gift and power of God. Joseph Smith received the abridgment of the plates of Nephi, by Mormon through Mormon's son, Moroni at the last, as you will soon see.

"Wherefore, for this cause hath the Lord God promised unto me that these things which I write shall be kept and preserved, and handed down **unto my seed**, *from generation to generation, that the promise may be fulfilled unto* **Joseph,** *that his seed should never perish as long as the earth should stand." "Wherefore, these things shall go from generation to generation as long as the earth shall stand; and they shall go according to the will and pleasure of God;* **and the nations who shall possess them shall be judged of them according to the words which are written.***"(2 Nephi 25:21-22, Book of Mormon)*

Nephi/Mayan king, stops to explain, and encourage those who read the record he is writing, and admonishes them to not take these writings lightly. He explains that Joseph Smith, truly is a descendant of that same Joseph who was sold into Egypt, who will in the latter-days, be the instrument in bringing this people of whom he is writing to light, as if a voice is speaking from the dust, and calling the world to repentance.

"And it shall come to pass that the Lord God shall bring forth unto you the words of a book, and they shall be the words **of them which have slumbered."** *And behold the book shall be sealed; and in the book shall be a revelation from God, from the beginning of the world to the ending thereof." "Wherefore, because of the things which are sealed up, the things which are sealed shall not be delivered in the day of the* **wickedness and abominations of the people.** *Wherefore the book shall be kept from them."* ***"But the book shall be delivered unto a man*** *[Joseph Smith],* **and he shall deliver the words of the book,** *which are the words of those who have slumbered in the dust, and he shall deliver these words* **unto another** *[Martin Harris];" "But the words which are sealed he shall not deliver, neither shall he deliver the book. For the book shall be sealed by the power of God, and the revelation which was sealed shall be kept in the book until the own due time of the Lord, that they may come forth; for behold, they* **reveal all things from the foundation of the world unto the end thereof."** *(2 Nephi 27:6-10, Book of Mormon)*

"And the day cometh that the words of the book which were sealed shall be read upon the house tops;[sins of the guilty will be shouted from the housetops] and they shall be read by the **power of Christ; and all things shall be revealed** *unto the children of men which ever have been among the children of men, and which ever will be even unto the end of the earth."* *"Wherefore, at that day when the book[Plates of Nephi/gold plates]. Shall be delivered unto the man[Joseph Smith] of whom I have spoken, the* **book[gold plates of Nephi] shall be hid from the eyes of the world,** *that the eyes of none shall behold it* **save it be that three witnesses[Oliver Cowdrey, David Whitmore, Martin Harris] shall behold it, by the power of God, besides him[Joseph Smith] to whom the book shall be delivered; and they shall testify to the truth of the book and the things therein."** *"And there is none other which shall view it, save it* **be a few**[11 other witnesses] **according to the will of God, to bear testimony of his word** *unto the children of men; for the Lord God hath said that the words of the faithful should speak as if it were from the dead."* *"Wherefore, the Lord God will proceed to bring forth the words of the book[***Book of Mormon***]; and in the mouth of as many witnesses as seemeth him good will he establish his word;* **and wo be unto him that rejecteth the word of God!".** *(2 Nephi 27:10-14, Book of Mormon)*

"But behold, it shall come to pass that the Lord God shall say unto him[Joseph Smith] to whom he shall deliver the book: **Take these words which are not sealed and deliver them to another[Martin Harris], that he may show them unto the learned, saying: Read this, I pray thee. And the learned shall say: Bring hither the book, and I will read them."** *"And now because of the glory of the* **world and to get gain will they say this, and not for the glory of God."** *"And the man[Martin Harris] shall say: I cannot* **bring the book[gold plates], for it is sealed."** **"Then shall the learned[professor] say: I cannot read it."** *"Wherefore it shall come to pass, that the Lord God will deliver again the book[Plates of Nephi/ gold plates] and the words thereof to him[Joseph Smith] that is not learned; and the man that is not learned shall say:* **I am not learned."** *"Then shall the Lord God say unto him: The learned shall not read*

them, *for they have rejected them, and I am able to do mine own work; wherefore thou[Joseph Smith] shall read the words which I shall give unto thee.*" "*Touch not the things which are sealed, for I will bring them forth in mine own due time; for I will show unto the children of men that I am able to do mine own work.*" "*Wherefore, when thou[Joseph Smith] hast read[translated] the words which I have commanded thee, and obtained the witnesses[Oliver Cowdrey, David Whitmore, Martin Harris, & eleven others] which I have promised unto thee, then shalt* **thou seal up the book [Plates of Nephi] again, and hide it up unto me, that I may preserve the words which thou hast not read, until I shall see fit in mine own wisdom to reveal all things unto the children of men.**" *(2 Nephi 27:15-22, Book of Mormon)*

"*For behold, I am God; and I am a God of miracles; and I will show unto the* **world** *that I am the same yesterday, today, and forever; and I will work not among the children of* **men** **save it be according to their faith.**" "*And again it shall come to pass that the Lord shall say unto him[Joseph Smith] that shall read[translate] the words that shall be delivered to him:*" "*Forasmuch as this people draw* **near unto me with their mouths, and with their lips do honor me, but have removed their hearts far from me, and their** **fear towards me is taught by the precepts of men---**" *(2 Nephi 27:23-25, Book of Mormon)*

"*Stay yourselves, and wonder; cry ye out, and cry: they are drunken, but not with strong drink.*" "*For the Lord hath poured out upon you the spirit of* **deep sleep, and hath closed your eyes: the prophets and your rulers, the seers hath he covered.**" "*And the vision of all is become unto you as the* **words of** **a book that is sealed, which men deliver to one that is learned, saying Read this , I pray thee: and he saith, I cannot; for it is sealed:**" "*And the book is delivered to* **him that is not learned, saying, Read this, I pray thee: and he saith, I am not learned.**" "*Wherefore the Lord said, Forasmuch as this people draw near me with their mouth, and with their lips do honour me, and their* **fear toward me is taught by the precept of men:**" "*Therefore, behold, I will proceed to do a marvelous work among this* *people, even a marvelous work and a wonder; **for the wisdom of their wise men shall perish, and the understanding of their prudent men shall be hid**." (see Isaiah 29:9-14, KJV)*

He is warning the Gentiles/us, in 2023, and those who support **secret orders,** who destroy their country, and destroy the saints of God. He tells them that the book he is writing will "cry from the ground" because of the blood of the Saints that is shed by the "world", demanding justice for those who knew the truth, but never listened to the Spirit of God, thus, injuring their brother/neighbor. This includes all of the churches who lie to their people and teach false doctrine, practice false policies, and uphold false laws. They are the ones who cause the people of God to **err, and therefore the people are left in hell because they won't search the scriptures for themselves and instead, allow themselves to be deceived.**

> *"Yea, and there shall be many which shall teach after this manner, false and vain and foolish doctrines, and shall be puffed up in their hearts, and shall seek deep to hide their counsels from the Lord; and **their works shall be in the dark**." "And the blood of the saints shall cry from the ground against them." "Yea, <u>they have all gone out of the way; they have become corrupted.</u>" "Because of the pride, and because of **false teachers, and false doctrine, their churches are lifted up; because of pride they are puffed up.**" "They rob the poor because of their fine sanctuaries; they rob the poor because of their fine clothing; and they persecute the meek and the poor in heart, because in their pride they are lifted up." "They wear stiff necks and high heads; yea, and because of **pride and wickedness and abominations, and whoredoms, they have all gone astray save it be <u>a few, who are the humble followers of Christ</u>; nevertheless, they are led, that in many instances they do err because they are taught the precepts of men.**" (2 Nephi 28:9-14, Book of Mormon)*

There are many who will reject the plates of Nephi/the Book of Mormon, especially these alleged experts, seeking for mysteries of ancient cultures and writings, but won't believe the truth, when the truth is right in front of them. They will reject the idea that Joseph

Smith brought forth the record of the Mayans and the Aztecs, the Toltecs, and the Olmecs, and translated it by the power of God, and it stands as a second witness to the record of the Jews/the Bible, and a second witness of the gospel of Jesus Christ.

"And because my words shall hiss forth---many of the **Gentiles** *shall say: A Bible! A Bible!We have got a Bible, and there cannot be any more Bible." "But thus saith the Lord God: O fools, they shall have a Bible; and it shall proceed forth from the Jews, mine ancient covenant people. And what thank they the Jews for the Bible which they receive from them?Yea, what do the Gentiles mean? Do they remember the travails, and the labors, and the pains of the Jews, and the diligence unto me, in bringing forth* **salvation unto the Gentiles?"** *"O ye Gentiles, have ye remembered the* **Jews, mine ancient covenant people?** *Nay; but ye have cursed them, and have hated them, and have not sought to recover them. But behold, I will return all these things upon your own heads;* **for I the Lord have not forgotten my people.** *"(2 Nephi 29:3-5, Book of Mormon)*

"Thou fool, that shall say: **A Bible, we have got a Bible, and we need no more Bible.** *Have ye obtained a Bible save it were by the Jews?" "Know ye not that there are more nations than one? Know ye not* **that I, the Lord God, have created all men, and that I remember those who are upon the isles of the sea; and that I rule in the heavens above and in the earth beneath; and I bring forth my word unto the children of men, yea, even upon all the nations of the earth?"** *"Wherefore murmur ye, because that ye shall receive* **more of my word? Know ye not that the testimony of two nations is a witness unto you that I am God, that I remember one nation like unto another? Wherefore, I speak the same words unto one nation like unto another. And when the two nations shall run together the testimony of the two nations shall run together also."** *"(2 Nephi 29:6-8, Book of Mormon)*

*"**And I do this that I may prove unto many that I am the same yesterday, today, and forever; and that I speak forth my words according to mine own pleasure.** And because that I have*

spoken one word ye need not suppose that I cannot speak another; *for my work is not yet finished; neither shall it be until the end of man, neither from that time henceforth and forever."* **"Wherefore, because that ye have a Bible ye need not suppose that I have not caused more to be written."***(2 Nephi 29:9-10, Book of Mormon)*

It is after the plates of Nephi/gold plates/abridgment of Mormon, are brought forth in the latter-day. They will then be taken to the Lamanites/Aztecs and to the Jews, and then sealed up again to the Lord, just as it happened. It happened after Joseph Smith finished the translation of the plates of Nephi, as the Book of Mormon.

"And now, I would prophesy somewhat more concerning the Jews and the Gentiles. For after the book[Book of Mormon] of which I have spoken shall come forth, and be written unto the Gentiles, and sealed up again unto the Lord, there shall be many which shall believe the words which are written; and they shall carry them forth unto the remnant of our seed." "And then shall the remnant of our seed know concerning us, how that we came <u>**out of Jerusalem, and that they are descendants of the Jews.**</u>*" "And the gospel of Jesus Christ shall be declared among them; wherefore, they shall be restored unto the knowledge of their fathers, and also to the knowledge* **of Jesus Christ, which was had among their fathers."***(2 Nephi 30:3-5, Book of Mormon)*

As we watch and witness the issues today, ramping up, such as pro-life vs. abortion, liberal vs. conservative, voter fraud vs. honest elections, and God vs. Satanism, a person cannot help noticing the great division unveiling itself. *"For the time speedily cometh that the Lord God shall* **cause a great division among the people, and the wicked will he destroy; and he will spare his people, yea, even if it so be that he must destroy the wicked by fire."***(2 Nephi 30:10, Book of Mormon)*

"When the **Son of man shall come in his glory,** *and all the holy angels with him, then shall he sit upon the throne of his glory." "And* <u>before him shall be gathered</u> **<u>all nations;</u>** <u>and he shall separate them one from another, as a shepherd divideth his</u> **<u>sheep from the goats.</u>***"*

*"And **he shall set the sheep on his right hand,** but the **goats on the left.** " "**Then shall the King say unto them on his right hand, Come, ye blessed of my Father, inherit the kingdom prepared for you from the foundation of the world:** " "Then shall he say also unto them on the* left hand, **Depart from me, ye cursed, into everlasting fire, prepared for the devil and his angels:** " *"Then shall he answer them, saying,* **Verily I say unto you, Inasmuch as ye did it not to one of the least of these, ye did it not to me.** " "**And these shall go away into everlasting punishment:** but the righteous into life eternal.* "*(compare Matthew 25:31-34,41,45, KJV).*

Christ is so close to returning and destroying the wicked as foretold by the ancient prophets of the Book of Mormon and the Bible. Throughout all of the generations of the Nephite people/ Mayan people, the Lamanites/Aztecs from the land south or South America, consistently vexed the people of Nephi/Mayans and kept them reminded of the commandments of the Lord. The Lamanites/ Aztecs were continually contentious, and willing to war and steal from the Nephites/Mayans, even if it meant killing them in order to enrich themselves. They were constantly trying to bring the Nephites/ Mayans into bondage and subjection. The Lamanites/Aztecs wanted their Democracy, as long as it benefited them. Doesn't that sound familiar, when you recall the words of Pelosi, or Biden, or Clinton, etc. just to name a few?

The Lamanites/Aztecs became Idolaters, and worshipping the Sun god, Ashtoroth, and others. They thought completely opposite to the people of Nephi/Mayans, who were sons and daughters of God. The Aztecs turned to Satan and practiced the sacrificing of children, and anyone taken prisoner in battle. The "children of the sun" in Peru, disclosed to be "Incas", according to the experts, but are in actuality, one of the many dissenting groups from the Nephites/ Mayans, practicing their own brand of worshipping Satan. The South American Lamanites/Aztecs were divided into kingdoms, and very often fought among themselves, and made slaves of lower kingdoms, all belonging to a liberal system of force.

Whereas, the Nephites/Mayans were divided into districts/lands, ruled by a good and holy man acting as their leader/king, who also was their prophet and teacher, who talked directly to God. Later during King Mosiah's reign, it was changed to being under a panel of "Judges" with there being one chief judge. From then on, the system was under the rule of law, and time was kept by calculating how many years from the time of the **"Reign of the Judges over the people of Nephi"**. This is like our system today, under the Constitution, where everyone has equality under the law. Everything was established by the **by the voice of the people**.

Just like now, so it was then, there were liberals, called "King-men", who sought to alter the law to benefit their supposed, noble birth/elitism, because of their riches, and high learning. It was the same back during the Nephite/Mayan period, where our southern border is a shambles, Liberals/Democrats/Kingmen/Gadianton Robbers/Socialists/Communists, take your pick, are a scourge to the freedom of our American-Republic.

> *"And it came to pass that many means were devised to reclaim and restore the Lamanites[Aztecs] to the knowledge of the truth; but it all was vain, for they delighted in wars and bloodshed, and they had an eternal hatred against **us[Nephites/Mayans]**, their brethren. **And they sought by the power of their arms to destroy us** continually."*
> *"Wherefore, the people of Nephi[Mayans] did fortify against them with their arms, and with all their might, trusting in the God and rock of their salvation; wherefore, they became as yet, **conquerors of their enemies.**" (Jacob 7:24-25, Book of Mormon)*

The Nephites/Mayans were conscientious and concerned about preserving their records, to be able to have them shown to the Lamanites/Aztecs later, if by any chance the Nephites/Mayans failed to do as God wanted them to do, by living up to their covenants. The Lamanites/Aztecs took on a culture of wildness. They were ferocious, and blood thirsty, and they wore animal skins, and they dwelled in tents.

> *"And I bear record that the people of Nephi[Mayans] did seek diligently to restore the Lamanites[Aztecs] **unto the true faith in God**. But our labors were in vain; **their hatred was fixed, and they***

were led by their <u>evil nature that they became wild, and ferocious,</u>
<u>and a blood-thirsty people, full of idolatry and filthiness; feeding</u>
<u>upon beasts of prey; dwelling in tents, and wandering about in</u>
<u>the wilderness with a short skin girdle about their loins and</u>
<u>their heads shaven; and their skill was in the bow, and in the</u>
<u>cimeter, and the ax, And many of them did eat nothing save</u>
<u>it was raw meat; and they were continually seeking to destroy</u>
<u>us.</u>"(Enos 1:20, Book of Mormon)

It was now over **320** years from the time that Lehi first left Jerusalem with his family to the promised land/the Americas. The Plates of Nephi/the Mayan record had been passed down from prophet to prophet, from generation to generation, just as the first Nephi/Mayan king desired, when he first started them. The record continued about the people of Nephi, through Jacob, Enos, Jarom, Omni, Amaron, Chemish to Aminidab. All accounts by each man who kept the record mention the wars they were involved in, while defending their people from the Lamanites/Aztecs. The Lamanites/Aztecs were constantly stalking and fighting the Nephites/Mayans, trying to get an advantage over them for this whole **320** years, thus far. The records were then handed down to Abinadom, who wrote a few words, then passed them to his son, Amaleki. **280 B.C.**

Chapter 7

Lehi's Family's Journeys through Saudi Arabia to Bountiful Shipyard

The Reign of King Mosiah

Amaleki witnessed and wrote concerning Mosiah, who was made king over the Land of Nephi at first, then later the people of Zarahemla joined with them, after discovering them, beyond the narrow neck of land, from Northern Colombia.   At this time, the people of Nephi/Mayans were still occupying the land of Nephi in which consisted of , Peru, South America, under the rule of King Mosiah. They soon had to migrate northward again to the land called Zarahemla, divided by the Rio Magdalena River that flowed north into the Carribean. The Mayans were constantly having to guard against attack from the Lamanites/Aztecs, because there were so many directions from which the Lamanites/Aztecs could come upon them. Therefore, the Lord warned Mosiah, king of the Nephites/Mayans, to move out of there with whomsoever would go with him, out of the land of Nephi, which they inhabited.

They now went northeast, into the area, now called northern Colombia, South America. This area they, the Nephites/Mayans called the Land of Zarahemla, after discovering another people also from Jerusalem, called the Mulekites/Toltecs. These people had left Jerusalem on a ship 11 years after Lehi and his followers left Jerusalem, into the wilderness of Arabia. The Nephites/Mayans, upon discovering, the people of Zarahemla/Toltecs, the people of Zarahemla/Toltrecs wanted to join with the Nephites/Mayans under the rule of King Mosiah, to be numbered with the Nephites/Mayans. The Land now settled by the people of Nephi/Mayans would bear the name, Land of Zarahemla. They then were able to control the Lamanites/Aztecs from overrunning them from the land southward .

Not all of the people of Nephi/Mayans left with King Mosiah. Some insisted on staying and hanging onto their possessions in the Land of Nephi/Peru, but they quickly went into bondage to the Lamanites/Aztecs because of their decisions. We will come back to these remaining people who didn't go with King Mosiah, king of the Mayans, when he joined with the people of Zarahemla/Toltecs, later on.

*"Behold. I am Amaleki, the son of Abinadom. Behold, I will speak unto you somewhat concerning Mosiah, **who was made king over the land of Zarahemla; for behold he being warned of the Lord that he should flee out of the land of Nephi, and as many as would hearken unto the voice of the Lord should also depart out of the land with him, into the wilderness---"** "And it came to pass that he did according as the Lord had commanded him. And they departed out of the land into the wilderness, as many as would hearken unto the voice of the Lord; and **they were led by many preachings and prophesyings. And they were admonished continually by the word of God; and they were led by the power of his arm, through the wilderness until they <u>came down into the land which is called the land of Zarahemla.</u>" "And they <u>discovered a people called the people of</u> Zarahemla[Toltecs]. <u>Now, there was great rejoicing among the people of Zarahemla[Toltecs]</u>; and also Zarahemla[King of Toltecs] did rejoice exceedingly, because the Lord had sent the people of Mosiah[Mayans] with the <u>plates of brass which contained the record of the Jews.</u>" "Behold, it came to pass that Mosish discovered that the people of Zarahemla[Toltecs] came out from <u>Jerusalem at the time that Zedekiah, king of Judah, was carried away captive into Babylon.</u>" "And they journeyed in the wilderness, and were brought by the hand of the Lord across the great waters, into the land where Mosiah discovered them; and they had dwelt there from that time forth." "** (Omni 1:12-16, Book of Mormon)*

"And at the time Mosiah discovered them[Toltecs], they had become exceedingly numerous. Nevertheless, they had had many wars and serious contentions, and had fallen by the sword from time to time; and their language had become corrupted; and they had brought no records with them; and they denied the being of their creator; and Mosiah, nor the people of Mosiah could understand them." "But it came to pass that Mosiah caused that they should be taught in his language. And it came to pass that after they were taught in the language of Mosiah[Hebrew/Mayan language], *Zarahemla[king of Toltecs] gave a genealogy of his fathers, according to his memory; and they are written, but not in these plates."* "And it came to pass that the *people of Zarahemla[Toltecs], and of Mosiah[Mayans], did unite together; and Mosiah was appointed to be their king.*" (Omni 1:17-19, Book of Mormon)

★*"And it came to pass in the days of Mosiah, there was a large stone brought unto him with engravings on it; and he did interpret the engravings by the gift and power of God."* "And they gave an account of one *Coriantumr* and the slain of his people[Olmecs]. And *Coriantumr was discovered by the people of Zarahemla[Toltecs]; and he[Coriantumr] dwelt with them for the space of nine moons."* "It also spake a few words concerning his fathers. And his first parents came out from *the tower, at the time the Lord confounded the language of the people;* and the severity of the Lord fell upon them according to his judgments, which are just; *and their bones lay scattered in the land northward[Yukatan/ Southern Mexico]."* "(Omni 1:20-22, Book of Mormon)

"Behold, I, Amaleki, was born in the days of Mosiah[king of the Mayans]; and I lived to see his death; and Benjamin, his son, did reign in his stead." "And behold, I have seen , in the days of king Benjamin, *a serious war and much bloodshed between the Nephites[Mayans] and the Lamanites[Aztecs].* But behold, the Nephites[Mayans] did obtain much advantage over them; yea, insomuch that King Benjamin did drive them[Lamanites/Aztecs] out of the land of Zarahemla." (Omni 1:23-24, Book of Mormon)

This was when King Mosiah/king of the Mayans learned of another people known as the Jaredites/Olmecs, who were here in North America before Zarahemla, a descendant of Mulek/Toltecs, son of King Zedekiah, who left Jerusalem 589 B.C.. Mulek left Jerusalem in the last year of the reign of King Zedekiah, before the destruction of Jerusalem by Nebuchadnezzar II, King of Babylon. This was mentioned in an earlier chapter, and now has come around, full circle, where all three periods, or peoples are joined together. The Nephites/Mayans, Mulekites/Toltecs, and Jaredites/ Olmecs/giants, were all fair skinned/white people.

The people of Zarahemla/Toltecs had become quite numerous previous to the time when King Mosiah/Mayan king, encountered them, but because the people of Zarahemla/Toltecs didn't bring any records with them, and had no way of teaching their children the language they were speaking, the language began to be corrupted. They didn't have any history or genealogy to go by, in remembrance of who they were, and the commandments they were to keep.

Zarahemla provided King Mosiah/Mayan king, a stone with engravings on it by the Jaredites/Olmecs, of which, Zarahemla and his people were now occupying their empty houses.

If it took the Nephites/Mayans over 320 years to find their way to the Land of Zarahemla, then it was almost that long, that the people of Zarahemla occupied the buildings built by the Jaredites/Olmecs-giants. It was the Mulekites/Toltecs who first discovered the empty cities of the Jaredites/Olmecs, and nursed the last remaining giant of a man for 9-moons/9-months, before he died. Coriantumr was the last survivor of the large and mighty men of the Jaredites/Olmecs. He must have been a brute of a man, as he was the last man standing, and also 9-months is long enough to still marry and have a start of an offspring. This will be seen later that it indeed did happen.

https://www.mapquest.com/travel/7-ancient-ruins-of-central-america/

Zarahemla asked King Mosiah if he knew anyone who could interpret the engravings on the stone, written by the Jaredites/Olmecs, that the prophet Ether had recorded and left in a way it could be found by the people who occupied their cities, and it happened to be the Mulekites who found it, and it was delivered by Zarahemla to King Mosiah to interpret it. *(see: Book of Ether, Book of Mormon)*

King Mosiah of the Nephites/Mayans, did take and interpret/translate the records of the Jaredites/Olmecs, but considering the secret orders among their people, he never brought it forth among his people, because of how they would be tempted to bring back the evilness of the Jaredites, by practicing what they had been destroyed for. He understood the nature of man, therefore, he hid up the record until the destruction of his people, after which, Moroni brought forth the record, before he had to flee for his life, after their last great battle. He was pointing out that the Jaredites/Olmecs were destroyed by the workings of secret orders/Jesuits/Illuminati/socialists/liberals, all of which are conspiring to destroy our government in 2023, even now the **deep state** is collaborating to bring President Trump down to keep him from running for President of our Republic. This is the very same thing that destroyed the Nephites/Mulekites/Mayans & Toltecs, 1000- years later.

America is on the very same road to destroying herself also, by letting the liberals/Democrats destroy and alter our laws. We are being overrun by the Lamanites/Aztecs, the same as the Nephites/Mayans,Toltecs allowed to happen to themselves. Our Republic is being transformed into a communist nation because the people's lack of knowledge, and the wherewithal to stand against tyranny. The people who are taking credit for the amazing architecture, are not the ones who actually did the work. The people who did the work were blessed of God when they were obeying the commandments. The ones who sit there and try to take credit for the work, are actually descendants of the ones who were set there as a scourge to the Nephites/Mayans, if they didn't keep their covenants they had made to God.

Chapter 8

The Battles of the Great Nephite/Mayan General—Moroni

The geographical facts about the Mayans and Aztecs

From the time that King Mosiah and the Nephites/Mayans joined with the people of Zarahemla/Toltecs, almost 400 years had gone by from the time Lehi and his people left Jerusalem. Amaleki, who was born during the days of King Mosiah, saw the death of Mosiah, and saw the days of King Benjamin, king of the Nephites/Mayans. Amaleki had no son to keep the records of his people in his stead, so he handed them to King Benjamin, who continued in keeping the records of the Nephites/Mayans.(Omni 1:25, Book of Mormon)

> *"And I began to be old; and, having no seed, and knowing king Benjamin[king of the Mayans/Toltecs]to be a just man before the Lord, wherefore I shall deliver up **these plates** unto him, exhorting all men to come unto God, the Holy One of Israel, and believe in prophesying, and in revelations, and in the ministering of angels, and in the gift of speaking with tongues, and in the **gift of interpreting languages,** and in all things which are good; **for there is nothing good save it comes from the Lord:** and that which is evil cometh from the devil."(Omni 1:25, Book of Mormon)*

Amaleki witnessed during the days of King Benjamin, the wars between the Nephites/Mayans and the Lamanites/Aztecs. He witnessed the Nephites/Mayans driving the Lamanites/Aztecs out of the Land of Zarahemla again. King Benjamin drove the Lamanites/Aztecs back, killing many of them in a bloody slaughter, causing them to fear going to war for several years, in which, the Nephites/Mayans had peace. Also, during the days of King Benjamin, the Lamanites/Aztecs, used the land of Nephi as their staging area, from where they organized to attack the Nephites/Mayans, now in the Land of Zarahemla.

It was at this time that a certain number of men decided to return back to the Land of Nephi. This group of men who wanted to go, wanted to find out what had happened to the people left behind, when king Mosiah and his people left, and they were wanting to know how they fared. They, themselves, wanted to know if they could go back to the land of their first inheritance to reclaim their land, they once held before they were forced to leave, because of the threat of the Lamanites/Aztecs.

"And now I would speak somewhat concerning a certain number who went up into the wilderness to **return to the Land of Nephi***; for there was a large number who were desirous to possess the land of their inheritance." "Wherefore, they* **went up into the wilderness***[Andes of Peru, and Ecuador]. And their leader being a strong and mighty man, and a stiffnecked man, wherefore he caused a contention among them; and they were all slain, save fifty, in the wilderness[Andes Mountains], and they returned again to the land of Zarahemla." "And it came to pass that they also* **took others to a considerable number***, and* **took their journey again into the wilderness***[up into the mountains]." "And I, Amaleki, had a brother who also went with them; and I have not since known concerning them. And I am about to lie down in my grave;* **And these plates are full***. And I make an end of my speaking." (***Omni** *1:27-30, Book of Mormon)*

Every time the Lamanites/Aztecs attacked the Nephites/Mayans, they lost many warriors, into the thousands, which cured their desire to come back right away, and many times they came because they were forced to by their wicked kings.

"And it came to pass also that the armies of the Lamanites/Aztecs **came down out of the land of Nephi,** <u>to battle against his people, but behold, king Benjamin</u> *gathered* <u>together his armies, and he did stand against them; and he did fight with the strength of his own arm, with the sword of Laban.</u> *" "And in the* <u>strength of the Lord</u> *they did contend against their enemies, until* <u>they[the Nephites/Mayans]</u> **had slain many thousands of the Lamanites[Aztecs] until they had driven them out of all the lands of their inheritance.** *"(Words of Mormon 13-14, Book of Mormon)*

Before Lehi left Jerusalem with his family, they were all taught in the language of the Hebrew and the Egyptian languages. They could read and write Egyptian and Hebrew, therefore teaching these things unto their children was very important, as King Mosiah did. To be educated makes it much easier to understand the mysteries of God. On the other hand, having all of this knowledge and understanding the mysteries of God, and receiving the **covenants they made with God, the more is expected from them.** If they keep the commandments of God, they become highly favored of God, but if highly favored people turn their backs on God, they will be destroyed.

"And now there was no more contention in all the land of Zarahemla, among all the people who belonged to king Benjamin[Nephites/Mayans], so that king Benjamin had <u>continual peace</u> *all the remainder of his days." "And it came to pass that he had three sons; and he called their names* **Mosiah, and Helorum, and Helaman.** *And he* <u>caused</u> **that they should be taught in all the language of his fathers, that thereby they might become men of understanding; and that they might know concerning the prophecies which had been spoken by the mouths of their fathers, which were delivered them by the hand of the Lord.** *" "And he also taught them concerning* <u>their record which were engraven upon the plates of brass,saying:</u> **My sons, I would that ye should remember that were it not for these plates, which contain these records and these commandments, we must have suffered in ignorance, even at this present time , not knowing the mysteries of** <u>God.</u> *" "It were not possible that our father,* **Lehi,** *could have remembered all these things, to have* <u>taught them to his</u>*

*children, except it were for the help of these plates; **for he having been
taught in the language of the Egyptians therefore he could read
these engravings, and teach them to his children, that thereby
they could teach them to their children, and so fulfilling the
commandments of God, even down to this present time.***"(Mosiah
1:1-4, Book of Mormon)*

King Benjamin wanted to address his people before he gave up his
duty as king, to his son, Mosiah. He had the people gather round the
Temple in the land of Bountiful. Bountiful is just northeast of the land
of Zarahemla, both located in Northern Colombia, at the beginning of
the narrow neck of land, bordering Panama. It was at Bountiful, that
Teancum headed Coriantumr, general of Ammoron, who so brazenly,
marched down into Zarahemla unexpectedly, then dared to march
north thinking to secure the Narrow Neck of land, but had to march
by Bountiful. This war will be talked about later, but right now the
Nephites/Mayans are at peace.

> *"And it came to pass that when they came up to the **temple**,
> they pitched their tents round about, every man according to his family,
> consisting **of his wife, and his sons, and his daughters, and their
> sons, and their daughters,** from the eldest down to the youngest,
> every family being separate one from another." "And they pitched their
> **tents round about the temple**, every man having his tent with the
> door thereof towards **the temple**, that thereby they might remain in
> their tents and hear the words which king Benjamin should speak unto
> them;" "For the **multitude being so great** that king Benjamin could
> not teach them all within the walls of the **temple,** therefore he caused
> **a tower to be erected,** that thereby his people[Mayans] might hear
> the words which he should speak unto them."(Mosiah 2:5-7, Book
> of Mormon) https://upload.wikimedia.org/wikipedia/commons/e/
> e7/BRM3458-Weston-Map-of-Ancient-America_Mormon-1899_
> lowres-1888x3000.jpg*

The group of men who returned to the Land of Nephi, in Peru
in the Andes Mountains, having the purpose, of finding out what
had happened to the Nephites/Mayans who didn't leave with King

Mosiah. They were the ones who insisted on staying there, not wanting to give up their possessions and start over, they also were never heard from again. King Mosiah then dispatched 16 strong men, with the charge of returning to the land of Nephi/Ecuador/Peru, to find out what happened to his fellow Nephites/Mayans. The Land of Nephi was just south of the borders of the land of Zarahemla, in the mountains of Ecuador and Peru, and bordering the Lamanites/Aztecs territory on the south and to the east.

"And now, it came to pass that after king Mosiah had had continual peace for the space of three years, he was desirous to know concerning the people who **went up** *to dwell in the* **land of Lehi-Nephi,** *or in the* **city of Lehi-Nephi;** *for his people had heard nothing from them from the time they left the land of Zarahemla; therefore, they wearied him with their teasings." "And it came to pass that king Mosiah granted that sixteen of their strong men might go* **up to the land of Lehi-Nephi**, *to inquire concerning their brethren."(Mosiah 7:1-2, Book of Mormon)* **Now 124 B.C.**

Ammon and his men wandered for 40-days, not knowing the exact course or location of the land, but eventually ran into the king of the land, himself, and were immediately arrested. The Nephites/Mayans had carved out quite a maze of road system out of the Andes Mountains for the last 480-years, and trying to find the right valley among the Andes is hard for us to imagine.

"And when they had wandered forty days they came to a hill, which is north of the land **of Shilom**, *and there they pitched their tents." "And* **Ammon** *took three of his brethren, and their names were Amaleki, Helem, and Hem, and they* **went down** *into the land of* **Nephi**." "And behold, they met the king of the people who were in the land of Nephi, and in the land of Shilom; and they were surrounded by the king's guard, and were taken, and were bound, and were committed to prison." "And it came to pass when they had been in prison two days they were brought before the king, and their bands were loosed; and they stood before the king, and were permitted, or rather commanded, that they should answer the questions which he should ask them." (Mosiah 7:5-8, Book of Mormon)*

"And he said unto them: Behold, I **am Limhi, the son of Noah**, *who was the son of Zeniff, who* <u>**came up out of the land of Zarahemla**</u> *to inherit this land, which was the land of their fathers, who was made a king* <u>*by the voice of the people.*</u>*" "And now I desire to know the cause whereby ye were so bold as to come near the walls of the city, when I, myself, was with my guards without the gate?" "And now, when Ammon saw that he was permitted to speak, he went forth and bowed himself before the king; and rising again he said: O king, I am very thankful before God this day that I am yet alive, and I am permitted to speak; and I will endeavor to speak with boldness;" "For I am assured that if ye had known me ye would not have suffered that I should have worn these bands. For I am Ammon, and am a descendant of* **Zarahemla**, *and have come* **up** *out of the land of Zarahemla to inquire concerning our brethren, whom Zeniff brought* **up out of that** *land." (Mosiah 7:9-10, 12-13, Book o,f Mormon)*

"And now, It came to pass that after Limhi had heard the words of Ammon, he was exceedingly glad, and **said: Now I know of a surety that my brethren who were in the land of Zarahemla are yet alive.** *And now, I will rejoice; and on the morrow I will cause that my people shall rejoice also." "For behold, we* **are in bondage to the Lamanites[Aztec], and are** taxed<u>**with a tax which is grievous to be** borne.</u> *And now, behold our brethren will deliver us out of our* **bondage**, *or out of the hands of the Lamanites[Aztecs/ liberals], and we will be* **their slaves**: *for it is better that we be* **slaves to the Nephites[***Mayans***] than to pay** **tribute** *to the king of the Lamanites[Aztecs/Liberals]." "...to the* <u>**amount of one half of our corn, and our barley, and even all our grain of every kind, and one half of the increase of our flocks and our herds; and even one half of all we have or possess the king of the Lamanites[Aztecs] doth exact from us, or our lives.**</u>*" (***Mosiah** *7:14-15, 22, Book o,f Mormon)*

It turns out that King Limhi and his people were in bondage to the Lamanites/Aztecs, and were sure glad that the people of Zarahemla/ Mayans still existed. Knowing this, gave them more hope of freedom. They were at this time paying tribute to the Lamanites/Aztecs. They were an Iniquitous people, and this is why they had gone into bondage and were slaves to the Lamanites/Aztecs. It was from the the king of of this land now, Limhi, that Ammon received 24-plates in gold, written by the prophet Ether about the destruction of the Jaredites/Olmecs. Ammon then took the plates to King Mosiah, who translated them, but it wasn't until just before the Nephites/Mayans last battle, that Mormon abridged them, and included them into the Gold Plates, that Joseph Smith translated, who brought them forth for all to read in 1830.

*"And the king said unto him: Being grieved for the afflictions of my people, I caused that forty and three of my people should take a journey into the wilderness, that thereby they might find the **land of Zarahemla**, that we might appeal unto our brethren to deliver us out of bondage." "And they were lost in the wilderness for the space of many days, yet they were diligent, and found not the land of Zarahemla but returned to this land , having traveled in a land among many waters, **having discovered a land which was <u>covered with bones of men[the Jaredites[Olmecs], and of beasts, and was also covered with ruins of buildings of every kind,</u>** having discovered a **<u>land which had been peopled with a people who were as numerous as the hosts of Israel.</u>** (Mosiah 8:7-8, Book o,f Mormon)

*"And for a testimony that the things that they had said are true **<u>they have brought twenty-four plates which are filled with engravings, and they are of pure gold.</u>"** "And behold, also, they have brought **<u>breastplates, which are large, and they are of brass and of copper, and are perfectly sound.</u>"** "And again, they have brought swords, the hilts thereof have perished, and the blades thereof were cankered with rust; and is there one in the land that is able to interpret the language or the engravings that are on the plates. Therefore I said unto thee: Canst thou **translate?"** **"Now Ammon said unto him: I can assuredly tell thee , O king, of a man that can translate the records;** for he has wherewith **<u>that he can look, and translate all records that are of ancient date; and it is a gift from God. And the things are called interpreters, and no man can look in them except he be commanded, lest he should look</u>**

for that he ought not and he should perish. And whosoever is commanded to look in them, the same is called a seer ." (Mosiah 8:9-11, 13, Book o,f Mormon)

*"Now king Limhi had sent, previous to the coming of Ammon, a small number of men to **search for the land of Zarahemla**; but they could not find it, and they were lost in the wilderness." "Nevertheless, they did find a **land which had been peopled; yea, a land which was <u>covered with dry bones; yea, a land which had been peopled and which had been destroyed;</u>** and they, having supposed it to be the land of Zarahemla, returned to the land of Nephi, having arrived in the borders of the land not many days before the coming of Ammon." "**<u>And they brought a record with them, even a record of the people whose bones they had found; and it was engraven on plates of ore[gold]."</u>** (Mosiah 21:25-27, Book of Mormon)*

On America Unearthed , Scott Wolter, does a You tube video talking about the Warlike, Montezuma, king of the Aztecs, and that he was known to go as far as into the northern U.S. To fight and pillage. The Lamanites/Aztecs were like the liberals/Democrats are today. If they can get something without working for it, or by producing it, they will. So it is with these Lamanites/Aztecs at this time, as it is throughout history when liberals/Democrats get into power. They were using the people of Limhi as slaves to grow the food, then took it from them at the edge of the sword, when it was harvested and ready to use.

*"Therefore it came to pass, that after we had dwelt in the land[Nephi] for the space of twelve years that king Laman[Aztec king] began to grow uneasy, lest by any means my people[Incas] should wax strong in the land, and that they could not overpower them and bring them into bondage." "Now they[the Aztecs] were a lazy and idolatrous people; therefore they were desirous to bring us into bondage, that they[liberals] might **glut themselves with the labors of our hands;** yea, that they might feast themselves upon the flocks of our fields." "Therefore it came to pass that king Laman began to stir up his people[Aztecs] that they should contend with my people; therefore*

there began to be wars and contentions in the land." "And God did hear our cries[prayers] and did answer our prayers; and we did go forth in his might; yea, we did go forth against the Lamanites[Aztecs], and in one day and a night we did slay three thousand and forty-three; we did slay them even until we had driven them out of our land." "And I, myself, with mine own hands, did help to bury their dead. And behold, to our great sorrow and lamentation, two hundred and seventy-nine of our brethren were slain." (Mosiah 9:11-13, 18-19, Book of Mormon)

The Lamanites/Aztecs were a continual scourge to the Nephites/Mayans. They were always trying to rob, or take advantage of the people of Nephi/Mayans any way they could. Look at our border crisis today, illegals have come across our borders by the millions. Is it going to stop, when they have illegally overrun our country? I honestly don't think so. The Lamanites/Aztecs were taught by their fathers to always hate the white man. Even on the indian reservations today, most are unwilling to work and be productive, but instead, hold their hands out for free government grants, that others have to pay for. On the other hand, the liberals/Democrats, want to use the protected classes to their advantage, for the purpose of getting and maintaining power, and to launder their money. What you are witnessing is racketeering, and a steady destruction of the country from within.

*"They were a **wild, and ferocious, and a blood-thirsty people, believing in the tradition of their fathers, which is this---** Believing that they were driven out of the land of **Jerusalem** because of the iniquities of their fathers, and that they were wronged in the wilderness by their brethren, and they were also wronged while crossing the sea;" "And again, that they were wronged while in the land of their first inheritance[in Chile], after they had crossed the sea, and all this because that Nephi was more faithful in keeping the commandments of the Lord---therefore he was favored of the Lord, for the Lord heard his prayers and answered them, and he took the lead of their journey in the wilderness." "And thus they have taught their children that they should hate them, and that they should murder them, and that they should rob and plunder them, and do all they could to destroy*

them; therefore they have an eternal hatred towards the children of Nephi[Mayans]"(Mosiah 10:12-13, 17, Book of Mormon)

When the liberals/Democrats/communists, in this case the, Lamanites/Aztecs, When they can't find anyone to fight, deceive, enslave, or control, they will most assuredly turn on their own, until they successfully destroy their own families, communities, and countries. This was the state that Ammon found the people of Limhi in, abject slavery.

*"Now they[the Aztecs] durst not slay them[the Mayans], because of the oath which their king had made unto Limhi; but they[Aztecs] would smite them[Mayans] on their cheeks, and exercise **authority over them; and began to put heavy burdens on their backs, and drive them as they would a dumb ass---**" "Yea, all this was done that the word of the Lord might be fulfilled." "and now the afflictions were great, and there was no way that they could deliver themselves out of their hands, for the Lamanites[Aztecs] had surrounded them on every side." "And it came to pass that the people began to murmur with the king because of their afflictions; and they began to be desirous to go against them[Aztecs] to battle. And they[Mayans] did afflict the king sorely with their complaints; therefore he granted unto them that they should do according to their desires." "And they gathered themselves together again, and put on their armor, and went forth against the Lamanites[Aztecs] to drive them out of their land." "And it came to pass that the Lamanites[Aztecs] did beat them, and drove them back, and slew many of them." "Yea, they went again even the third time, and suffered in the like manner; and those that were not slain returned again to the city of Nephi." "And they did humble themselves even to the dust, subjecting themselves to the **yoke of bondage, submitting themselves to be smitten, and to be driven to and fro, and burdened, according to the desires of their enemies."** "And now the Lord was slow to hear their cry because **of their iniquities;** nevertheless the Lord did hear their cries and began to soften the hearts of the Lamanites[Aztecs] that they began to ease their burdens; yet the Lord did not see fit to deliver them out of bondage."(Mosiah 21:3-8,12-13,15, Book of Mormon)*

The Lamanites/Aztecs, were divided into many kingdoms throughout South America. The Incas[Tetonics] are just one of those groups, being all related and here at the same time. It talks throughout the Book of Mormon, of the many kingdoms among the Lamanites/ Aztecs, and how they treated each other. They were always warring among themselves, just as the North American Indians, not too long in the past, have done.

It is true, that God laughs at the men and women who are learned, who then think they are wise. They rely on their own understandings, but yet they can't understand where the Olmecs/Giants, and the Mayans, and the Aztecs, came from, they can't understand why there are so many massive cities which used to be populated with thousands, and even tens of thousands of inhabitants, but yet the cities are standing intact, and vacant and they don't know where the people went. The same having much learning in construction, irrigation, etc., and were so intelligent, blessed by God, but yet they are gone, and these experts don't have any idea of where they went , and why. https://www.youtube.com/watch?v=lMfumtWOsWU

Chapter 9

The Nephites/Mayans North American Migration

Geographical Facts about the Land of Nephi[Mayans]
and the land of Zarahemla, and battles waged by Alma

A quick **recap of events up to this time, by King Mosiah, to let the people know just how great were the blessings the Lord had bestowed upon them,** being facts about the civilization of the Mayans and Aztecs are these: They left Jerusalem at the year 600B.C. and they consisted of two families: the family of Lehi and the family of Ishmael, and a single man named Zoram. Lehi's family were all boys: Laman, Lemuel, Sam, Nephi, Jacob and Joseph and the friend of Nephi: Zoram. The family of Ishmael was predominantly girls, who paired off with the sons of Lehi and Zoram, and they all became one family. Lehi had two more sons before they got to the Americas: Jacob and Joseph. Jacob and Joseph probably married into the family of Zoram later on, as they were the ones who were not directly related to the rest, until then.

They started out from the southern tip of Arabia after having traveled for 8 years south to the tip of Saudi Arabia, to a valley called Bountiful, because of it's much fruit, honey bees, and wood for making lumber. Here Nephi was instructed to build a ship, which probably took 2-3 more years there. Lehi and his family, left Arabia, from the Strait of Oden, sailing from the Mouth of the Red Sea, out into the Indian Ocean, around the Southern tip of Africa, following the natural winds and current that not only the Jaredites/Olmecs followed, but the Mulekites/Toltecs followed 11-years later.

Lehi and his family, the future Mayans & Aztecs, were close to the South American coast, after having sailed for many days. It was then that the sons of Lehi: Laman and Lemuel rebelled again against the commandments of the Lord. Their compass stopped working, and the winds began blowing them backwards, into the Magellan Strait, and around the southern tip of South America. By the time their compass started working again, the family was on the west coast of South America, heading north. They landed off the coast of Chile, at the 30th degree Latitude, being Northern Chile.

*"Woe to the land **shadowing with wings[north and south America look like wings on a map]**, which is beyond the rivers of Ethiopia[Africa]:" "That sendeth **ambassadors by the sea, even in vessels of bulrushes[Jaredites/ Olmecs in their eight barges] upon the waters, Go, ye swift messengers, to a nation scattered and peeled, to a people terrible from their beginning hitherto; a nation meted out[judged and found wanting] and trodden down[destroyed civilizations], whose land the rivers have spoiled!" "All ye inhabitants of the world, and dwellers on the earth, see ye, when he lifteth up an ensign on the mountains; and when he bloweth a trumpet, hear ye."(Isaiah 18:1-3, KJV)*

Here they began to farm, planting all of the seeds they had brought with them, hunting, and raising livestock that was available on the land. Here their families began spreading out upon the land. Then Lehi and Sariah, the parents of Laman, Lemuel, Sam, and Nephi, died. Up to now Laman and Lemuel, had continually been rebelling against the Lord because of their younger brother Nephi, who for the greater part was responsible for bringing them successfully to the Americas. Laman and Lemuel were jealous, selfish, and envious of their younger brother because of his standing with their father, and he was much more faithful and knowledgeable to the things of God.

After their father died, Laman and Lemuel planned to kill their younger brother, because they didn't want him to be a ruler over them. This is the start of the Aztecs, and because of their rebellions, God cursed them with the dark skin, so that they would be known readily for who they were. God knew that their posterity would grow up in ignorance because of their fathers sins, therefore, He was merciful to them, that if they received the gospel of His Son, Jesus Christ, that they could be redeemed. God also used them as a scourge to the Nephites/Mayans to remind the people of Nephi/Mayans of their covenants. The people who followed after Nephi, since Nephi's father, Lehi, was now dead, were called after his son, Nephites.

Because of the plan to kill their younger brother, Nephi, God told Nephi to leave his brothers, and take anyone who would go with him and depart into the wilderness. They took their families, the compass, the sword of Laban, the Brass Plates, and the records Nephi was now making, and whatever else they could carry in the way of provisions, and left. Thus, the birth of the **_Mayans_** and the **_Aztecs_**.

The account is, that the people of Nephi/[Mayans traveled north many days, then began again to till the earth, raise flocks and herds, and multiply. Many days could be weeks, and then could only mean just a few. Anyway, they moved into the extreme northern regions of Chile, Peru, Ecuador, and probably even further inland into parts of Bolivia and Brazil. By the time the Nephites/Mayans left the land of Nephi, 320 years had went by before they even found the people of Zarahemla. Their migration further north came after all of the wars and consistent attacks, and by being continually surrounded by the Lamanites/Aztecs, it became a necessity for them to move to preserve the safety of their families. When King Mosiah was told by the Lord to take his people and move again, he understood, and obeyed immediately.

★*"And now king Mosiah caused that all the people should be gathered together."* *"Now there were not so many of the children of* **Nephi[Mayans],** *or so many of those who were descendants of Nephi, as there were of the people of Zarahemla* **[Toltecs]**, *who was a descendant of Mulek, and those who came with him into the wilderness."* *"And there were not so many of the people of Nephi[Mayans] and of the people of Zarahemla[Toltecs] as there were of the Lamanites* **[Aztecs];** *Yea,* **_they were not half so numerous._** *"And now all the people of Nephi[Mayans] were assembled together, and also all the people of Zarahemla[Toltecs], and they were gathered together* **in two bodies.** *"And it came to pass that Mosiah* _did read, and caused to be read, the records of Zeniff,_ *from the time they left the land of Zarahemla until they* **returned again.** *"And he also read the account of Alma and* *his brethren, and all their afflictions, from the time they left the land of Zarahemla until the time they returned again." "And now, when Mosiah had made an end of reading the records, his people who tarried in the land were* **struck with wonder and amazement."...** *"And again, when they thought of the immediate* **goodness of God, and his power in delivering Alma and his brethren** *out of the hands of the Lamanites[Aztecs] and out of bondage, they* **did raise their voices and give** **thanks to God.** *(Mosiah 25:1-8,10, Book of Mormon)*

It is now **91 B.C.,** and king Mosiah wanted to do something great for his people upon stepping down from his throne. None of his sons wanted to become king, and unless king Mosiah did something to protect their freedom, because to have an outsider become king, he knew could, and would be catastrophic, as it was with the Jaredites/Olmecs. He set them up a system that the *"voice of the people"* should carry the responsibility of their own government. He lectured to them and described the disadvantages of having a king. Mosiah encourages the people to do everything by the voice of the people, but admonishes them, that they must be diligent and call always on God for their guidance, because when the time comes that the voice of the people are more for wickedness than the way of God, then the people will be destroyed, and it is only them to blame for their own destruction.

"And behold, now I say unto you, **ye cannot dethrone an iniquitous king save it be through much contention, and the shedding of much blood.** *" "For behold, he has his friends in iniquity[secret orders], and he keepeth his guards[military] about him; and he teareth up the laws of those who have reigned in righteousness before him; and he trampleth under his feet the commandments of God;" "And he* **enacteth laws, and sendeth them forth among his people**[executive orders], yea, laws after the manner of his own wickedness; *and whosoever doth not obey* **his** *laws he causeth to be destroyed; and whosoever doth rebel against him he will send his armies against them to war, and if he can he will destroy them; and thus an unrighteous king[or President]* **doth** pervert **the ways of all righteousness.** *"(Mosiah 29:21-23, Book of Mormon)*

***"*Therefore, **choose you by the voice of this people,** judges[supreme court judges as well and not appointed by wicked presidents etc.], that ye may be judged according to the **laws which have been given you by our fathers, which are correct, and which are given them by the hand <u>of the Lord</u>.*" "*Now it is not common that the <u>voice of the people</u> desireth anything <u>contrary to that which is right;</u> but it is common for the <u>lesser part of the people to desire that which is not right</u>; therefore this **shall ye observe and make it your law---to do your business by the voice of the people.**"* "*And if the time comes that the **voice of the people** <u>doth choose</u> <u>**iniquity,**</u> [by silence also, sitting on the fence as lukewarm] **then is the time that the judgments of God will come upon you; yea, then is the time he will visit you with great destruction even as he has hitherto visited this land.**[destruction of the Jaredites/Olmecs]."* "*And now if ye have judges, and they do not judge you according to the law which has been given, <u>ye can cause that they be judged</u> of a higher judge**[appeal]**.*" "*If your higher judges do not judge righteous judgments, ye shall cause that **<u>a small number of your lower judges</u>** should be gathered together, and **<u>they shall judge your higher judges</u>**, **<u>according to the voice of the people.</u>**"*(Mosiah 29:25-29, Book of Mormon)

***"*And **<u>I command you</u>** to do these things **in the fear of the Lord;** and I command you to do these things, and **that ye have no <u>king;</u>** that if these people commit sins and iniquities <u>they shall be answered upon their own heads.</u>*" "*For behold I say unto you, the sins of many people have been caused <u>by the iniquities of their kings;</u> therefore their iniquities are answered upon the heads of their kings.*" "*And I desire that **this inequality should be no more in this land, <u>especially among this my people; but I desire that this land be a land of liberty, and every man may enjoy his rights and privileges alike, so long as the Lord sees fit that we may live and inherit the land,</u>** yea even as long as any of our posterity remains upon the face of the land.*" (Mosiah 29:30-32, Book of Mormon)

The Nephites/Mayans traveled many days heading in a north-easterly direction, until they came to a land where they had a natural barrier on their south being a mountainous wilderness strip from east to west, and a river that flowed northward to the sea, and to the northwest was a narrow neck of land, bordered by a sea on the west and a sea on the east. This is where they spread out and began again to farm and worship God and raise their families. They named this land of their inheritance: The Land of Zarahemla. Some historians and archaeologists using science, want to argue that the most obvious route of travel was based upon ocean currents, summer and winter, but we need to realize the Jaredites/Olmecs and the Mulekites/Toltecs, followed these ocean currents. We also need to realize that the Nephites/Mayans and Aztecs, were blown back for several days.

This is the only location that makes sense, as it is the only river that flows northward into the sea, in the area of the Caribbean, as will be proven as the account of their battles and wars show. The Rio Grande de la Magdalena River, is the only major river in this part of the country, that begins from the mountains south and flows north to the sea. The Name of this river was called Sidon, by the Nephites/Mayans. This is the same river that the Nephites/Mayans used, to throw the bodies of the slain Lamanites/Aztecs into and used to cross the river to fight on both sides as the enemy came in on the boundaries of their land. The river had enough current as it cascaded from the mountains, and was deep enough, and straight enough to the sea, that it could sweep the numerous dead corpses away, yet, it was shallow enough that the Nephite/Mayan armies could go from side to side to defend their land. It was also shallow enough, that in order to get across, if enough bodies were piled in fast enough, men could use the corpses as a bridge to cross.

They sojourned this way now, since they left Jerusalem, and landing in Chile, for around 320 years, as they slowly migrated north, into northern Colombia. Meanwhile, the Mulekites/Toltecs, just north of the narrow neck of land were inhabiting the cities of the Jaredites/Olmecs, in the Land of Desolation, known today as Panama, Nicaragua, Yukatan, Guatemala, and beyond the narrow neck of land into southern Mexico. It would be impossible for the Mississippi River to be this Sidon River, because the Mississippi is to big and deep, and flows south and not north. To cross the Mississippi River, crossing over on the bodies of the slain, would be impossible, unless you had a speed boat, because of how deep and wide, the river is, proven by what Alma and his armies did with the Magdalena River/Sidon River, in Colombia, South America.

"And this Amlici had, **by his cunning**[lies, disinformation, promises of riches and positions of power], drawn away much people after him; <u>even so much that they began to be **very** powerful; that they began to endeavor to establish Amlici to be a **king** over the people.</u>" "Now this was alarming to the people of the church, and also to all those who had not been drawn away after the persuasions of Amlici; for they knew **<u>that according to their law[Constitution] that such things must be established by the voice of the people.</u>**" "Therefore, if it were possible that Amlici should gain the voice of the people, he, being a wicked man, <u>would deprive them of their rights[Bill of Rights] and privileges of the church;</u> **for it was his intent to <u>destroy</u> the church of God.**" "And it came to pass that the people assembled themselves together throughout all the land, every man according to his mind, whether it were for or against Amlici, in separate bodies, having much dispute[debate] and wonderful contentions one with another." "And thus they did assemble themselves together to cast in their voices[vote] concerning the matter; and they were laid before the judges[Supreme Court]." "And it came to pass that the voice of the people came against[didn't want] Amlici, that he was not made king over the people." "Now this did cause much joy in the hearts of those who were against him; but Amlici did stir up those who were in his favor to anger[insurrection] against those who were not in his favor." "And it came to pass that they gathered themselves together, and did consecrate Amlici to be their king." "Now when Amlici was made king over them he commanded them that they should take up arms against their brethren;[Revolt] and this he did that he might subject them to him." (Alma 2:2-10, Book of Mormon)

"And it came to pass that the **Amlicites**[Mayan dissenters] came up on the hill **Amnihu,** which was **east of the river Sidon**[Rio Magdalena], **which ran by the land of Zarahemla,** and there they began to make **war** with the Nephites[Mayans]." "Now Alma, Being <u>the chief judge and the governor of the people of Nephi[Mayans]</u>, therefore he went up *with his people, yea even with his captains, and chief captains, **yea, at the head of his armies, against the Amlicites**[dissenters] **to battle.***" *"And they began to **slay the Amlicites**[Mayan dissenters] upon the hill **east of Sidon**. And the Amlicites[dissenters/insurrectionists] did contend with the Nephites[Mayans] with great strength. Insomuch that many of the Nephites[Mayans] did fall before the Amlicites[dissenters/ insurrectionists]."* (Alma 2:15-17, Book of Mormon)

*"Nevertheless the Lord did strengthen the hand of the Nephites[Mayans], **that they slew the Amlicites**[dissenters/ insurrectionists] **with great slaughter**, that they began to flee before them."* *"And it came to pass that the Nephites[Mayans] did pursue the Amlicites[dissenters/liberals] all that day, and did slay them with much slaughter, insomuch that there were slain of the Amlicites[dissenters/ liberals] twelve thousand five hundred thirty and two souls; and there were slain of the Nephites[Mayans] six thousand five hundred sixty and two souls."* *"And it came to pass that when Alma could pursue the Amlicites[Mayan dissenters/liberals] no longer he caused that his people should pitch their tents in the **valley of Gideon**[just SE of Zarahemla], the valley being called after that Gideon who was slain by the hand of Nehor with the sword; and in this valley the Nepites[Mayans] did pitch their tents for the night."* *"And Alma sent spies to follow the remnant of the the Amlicites[dissenters/liberals/ democrats], that he might know of their plans and their plots, whereby he might guard himself against them, that he might preserve his people from being destroyed."* (Alma 2:18-21, Book of Mormon)

"Now those whom he had sent to watch the camp of the Amlicites[Mayan dissenters] were called Zeram, and Amnor, and Manti, and Limher; these were they who went out with their men to watch the camp of the Amlicites[Mayan dissenters/liberals]." *"And it came to pass that on the morrow they returned in **great haste**, being greatly astonished, and struck with much fear, saying:"* *"Behold, we followed the camp of the Amlicites[Mayan dissenters/liberals], and to our great astonishment, in the land of Minon[south of Gideon], above the land of Zarahemla, in the course of the land of Nephi[on the road back to land of Nephi], we saw a numerous host of the*

Lamanites[Aztecs]; and behold, the Amlicites[Mayan dissenters/ liberals] have joined them;" "And they are upon our brethren in that land; and they are fleeing before them with their flocks, and their wives, and their children towards our **city[Zarahemla]** *and except we make haste they obtain possession of our city[Zarahemla], and our fathers, and our wives, and our children be slain." "And it came to pass that the people of Nephi[Mayans] took their tents, and departed out of the land of Gideon[northwest] towards their city, which was the city of Zarahemla." **(Alma** 2:22-26, Book of Mormon)*

"And behold, as they were <u>crossing the river</u> **Sidon***[Rio Magdalena], the Lamanites[Aztecs] and the Amlicites[Mayan dissenters/liberals], being as* **numerous almost, as it were, as the sands of the sea,** *came upon them." "Nevertheless, the Nephites[Mayans] being* **strengthened by the hand of the Lord, having prayed mightily to him that he would deliver them out of the hands of their enemies, therefore the Lord did hear their cries, and did strengthen them, and the** <u>**Lamanites[Aztecs]**</u> **and the** <u>**Amlicites[dissenters/liberals]**</u> **did** <u>**fall before them.**</u>*" "And it came to pass that Alma[Donald Trump] fought with Amlici[Joe Biden] with the sword* <u>face to face;</u> *and they did contend mightily, one with another." "And it came to pass that Alma[Donald Trump] being a man of God, being exercised with much faith, cried, saying[I will never stop fighting, I will never concede, I will never give up, and]: O Lord, have mercy and spare my life, that I may be an instrument in thy hands to save and preserve this people." "Now when Alma[President Donald Trump] had said these words he contended again with Amlici[Imposter Joe Biden]; and being strengthened, insomuch that he* <u>slew Amlici with the sword.</u>*" "And he also contended with the* **king of the Lamanites***[Aztecs]; but the king of the Lamanites[Aztecs]* <u>fled</u> *back from before Alma[President Donald J. Trump] and sent his guards[liberal prosecuting attorney] to contend with Alma[Donald J. Trump]."(Alma 2:27-32 , Book of Mormon)*

"But Alma[Donald J. Trump], with his guards, contended with the guards[evil democrat deepstate] of the king of the Lamanites[Aztecs] until he slew and drove them back." "And thus **he cleared the ground, or rather the bank, which was on the west of the river** <u>*Sidon,*</u>

throwing the bodies of the Lamanites[Aztecs] who had been slain into the waters of Sidon[Rio Magdalena], that thereby his people[Nephites/Mayans] might have room to cross and contend with the Lamanites[Aztecs] and the Amlicites[dissenters/liberals, Bidenites] on the west side of the river Sidon[Rio Magdalena]."
"And it came to pass that when they[All of the Mayan soldiers] had all crossed the river **Sidon** *that the Lamanites[Aztecs] and the Amlicites[disenters/liberals] began to flee before them, notwithstanding they were so numerous that they could not be numbered." "And they fled before the Nephites[Mayans] towards the wilderness which was west and north, away from the borders of the land; and the Nephites[Mayans] did pursue them with their might, and did slay them." "Yea, they were met on every hand, and slain and driven, until they were scattered on the west, and on the north, until they reached the wilderness,* **which was called Hermounts;** *and it was that part of the wilderness which was* **infested by wild and ravenous beasts.**" "*And it came to pass that many died in the wilderness of their wounds, and were devoured by those beasts and also the vultures of the air; and their bones have been found, and have been heaped up on the earth."* **(Alma 2:33-37, Book of Mormon)**

Hermounts is in Central Colombia, in the strip of wilderness, east, and beyond the River Sidon, into the jungles of Brazil?, etc. There are some tribes of natives still there that are very seldom seen, or heard of to this day, in the wilds along the Amazon River. The Seminole Indians/natives, from the wilds of the Florida everglades are a prime example of this. The beasts that are there today, are lizards, huge snakes, Alligators, crocodiles, big cats, wart hogs, etc.. There are even stories surfacing about dinosaurs living in the swamps of Brazil.

After fighting the Amlicites, who were traitors to the Nephites/Mayans, comprised of the Priests of Noah and numerous hosts of the Lamanites/Aztecs who were slain by the thousands, the Nephites/Mayans threw the bodies of the dead enemy into the Sidon River/Magdalena River, and then they were taken and dumped into the sea at the Caribbean, the Gulf Coast area. Zarahemla is described as being on the west side of the Sidon/Magdalena River, and the land of Nephi was south of the land of Zarahemla, into Ecuador and Peru, Bolivia, and maybe a part of Brazil. https://upload.wikimedia.org/wikipedia/ commons/9/9a/Book_of_Mormon_Lands_and_Sites2.jpg

That narrow neck of land began at the land Bountiful, where their main temple was, and acted as a strategic defense area for the people of Nephi/Mayan people, as it proved to be when Teancum headed the armies of the Lamanites/Aztecs under their wicked kings: Amlici and Ammaron,. If Zarahemla had have been in the North, then the Nephites would have been surrounded by their enemies constantly on all sides, and the land north would already have been overrun.

"And now as many of the Lamanites[Aztecs] and the Amlicites[dissenters/liberals] who had been slain upon the bank of the **river Sidon were cast into the waters of Sidon**[Rio Magdalena]; and behold their bones are in the depths of the sea, and they are many.*"* *"And the Amlicites[liberals/communists] were distinguished from the Nephites[Mayans], for they had marked themselves with* **red in their foreheads after the manner of the Lamanites;** *nevertheless they had not* **shorn their heads** *like unto the Lamanites[Aztecs]."* *"Now the heads of the Lamanites[Aztecs] were* **shorn;** *and they were* **naked, save it were** **skin which was girded about their loins, and also their armor, which was girded about them,** *and their bows and their arrows, and their stones, and their slings, and so forth."* *"And* **the skins of the Lamanites**[Aztecs] **were dark,** *according to the mark which was set upon their fathers,* **which was a curse upon them because of their transgression** *and their rebellion against their brethren, who consisted of Nephi, Jacob, and Joseph, and Sam, who were just and holy men."(Alma 3:3-6, Book of Mormon)*

"And their brethren sought to **destroy** *them, therefore they were* **cursed;** *and the Lord God* **set a mark upon them, yea, upon Laman and Lemuel, and also the sons of Ishmael, and Ishmaelitish women."** *"And this was done that their* **seed might be distinguished** *from the seed of their brethren, that thereby the Lord God might preserve his people, that they might not* **mix and believe in incorrect traditions which would prove their destruction.***"* *"And it came to pass that* **whosoever did mingle his seed with that of the Lamanites[Aztecs]** *did bring the same curse upon his*

*seed." "Therefore, whosoever suffered himself to be led away by the Lamanites[Aztecs] was called <u>under that head, and there **was a mark set upon him.**</u>" "(**Alma** 3:7-10, Book of Mormon)*

*"And in one year were thousands and tens of thousands of souls sent to the eternal world, that they might reap the rewards **according to their works**, whether they were **good or bad,** to reap eternal **happiness or eternal misery**, according to the **spirit which they listed to obey,** whether it be a **good spirit or a bad one.**" "<u>**For every man receiveth wages of him whom he listeth to obey, and this according to the words of the spirit of prophecy; therefore let it be according to the truth. And thus endeth the fifth year of the reign of the judges.**</u>"(Alma 3:26-27, Book of Mormon)* **Now 89 B.C.**

Many Nephites/Mayans united to the Church of God In this same year, because they mourned the loss of those killed during the war with the Lamanites/Aztecs, believing it was the judgments of God upon them because of their own wickedness. About three thousand five hundred souls united themselves to the Church of God in **87 B.C..** However, in **81 B.C.,** Alma noticed a great wickedness in the Church of God, even to exceed that of those out of the church. Like it is today, in 2023 It began to fail in it's progress and became a great stumbling block.

*"And thus, in the eighth year of the <u>reign of the judges</u>[81 B.C.], there began to be **great contentions** among the people of the church; yea, there were envyings, and **strife, and malice, and persecutions, and pride,** even to exceed the pride of those who did not belong to the church of God."And thus ended the eighth year of the reign of the judges; and the <u>**wickedness of the church was a great stumbling-block to those who did not belong to the church; and thus the church began to fail in its progress.**</u>" "And it came to pass in the commencement of the ninth year[80 B.C.], Alma saw the <u>wickedness of the church,</u> and he saw also that the **example of the church** began to lead those who were unbelievers on from one piece of iniquity to another, thus bringing on the **destruction of the people.**"(Alma 4:9-11, Book of Mormon)***Now 80 B.C.**

https://whc.unesco.org/en/list/414/ Teotihuacan : Is an ancient city that was already standing, but empty when the Mulekites came to the Americas in 587-589 B.C. They were inhabiting the ruins of the Jaredites/Olmecs when King Mosiah and his people discovered the Mulekites, 320-years later. At that time, the Mulekites were being led by a man named Zarahemla. The Mulekites, when they arrived in the Ameicas, also befriended the last survivor of the Jaredite civilization. The name, *"Nephites"*, stayed with the people of Nephi, and was taken by the people of Zarahemla when they joined with the people of Nephi, at this time.

https://sites.google.com/site/bomgeography/internal-map/new-world-commentary/d/desolation

https://www.mapquest.com/travel/7-ancient-ruins-of-central-america/

The Book of Mormon is no myth! For anyone to think that, makes them just as ignorant as these so called experts who strive at relying on their own wisdom, and it is because they won't open their own eyes and see what is in front of them,. Anyone can see the marvelous architectures of the ancient peoples, even to excel the abilities in several instances, of our modern day technology. These people were not *"Pre-Christian"* nor were they *"Pre-historic"*, as they kept their covenants to the Lord better than we as Christians do today. There were many saved in the kingdom of God by the thousands if not the 100's of thousands, maybe into the millions, and practiced Christianity as we do today, and they kept their records very efficiently and precisely under commandment of the Lord Jesus Christ.

Many people don't want to accept the facts that all of these civilizations started here in the South and Central American areas, because they want to think that North America should have the glory, but we must remember that Christ loved all of the people, and blessed and prospered them greatly when they were observing his commandments. It was only when they quit calling upon His name, is when they fell, because they chose the master they preferred to serve, based upon their own selfish desires. As the Nephites/Mayans, now comprised of the People of Zarahemla and the People of Nephi, protected their borders in the land of Zarahemla, the people spread into the north country, as the Book of Mormon, explains.

The seat of the Nephite government was in South America, beginning in the earlier period, in the Land of Nephi for 320-years, in Peru, and Ecuador. Then from the land/City of Zarahemla, in Northern Colombia. The people spread into the north country, even building of ships and sailing off to inhabit other areas, to never return. https://www.youtube.com/watch?v=hvqANniyRzI

The three civilizations: Jaredites/Olmecs; Mulekites/Toltecs; and the Nephites/Mayans, all ended up in central America, some sooner than others, but they were there. The Jaredites/Olmecs were just ending their civilization to be replaced by the Mulekites/Toltecs, around 589 B.C.. The Mulekites and the Nephites/Mayans joined about 320 years later, when the Nephites/Mayans worked their way northward as the Lord directed them, to the area just south of the narrow neck of land, and found the people of Zarahemla. This would be a round 280 B.C.. Meanwhile, The Nephites/Mayans had to watch and protect their borders from the Lamanites/Aztecs and drive them back from time to time, sometimes with a great slaughter.

As long as the Nephites/Mayans were mindful of God and observing His commandments, The Nephites/Mayans prospered and were blessed exceedingly. They had laws that were by the voice of the people, and nothing was done save it was done by the voice of the people. There is in every period, in every civilization, liberal/ Democrats, who undermine the freedom of mankind in all ages, desiring control of all people, worlds without end, as it was in the war that had just ended. It was started by those rich, who wanted power and authority, who wanted to have a king put over them. Amlici wanted to be this king, despite what the majority of the people wanted. Surely the rich and supposed elite know what is the best for the people, as the liberals want to believe. This thinking is called a Democracy, where the rich rule, and it's presidents are appointed by the rich, in the forms of kings, dictators, generals, with the jurisdiction of force. This is how slaves are made, and tyranny moves in upon the people.

There are so many uninhabited cities in Mexico, central America, and South America, not to mention ruins in every part of the North American continent. Cities like Cancun, Calakmul, Teotihuacan, Playa Del Carmen, Riviera Maya, Cozumel, Tulum, Rock Lake Wisconsin[Mocum], and many others. There is evidence of other civilizations all over the Americas, that is screaming the truth from the roof tops. For all of these uninhabited cities, liberal thinking people, so called experts, historians, and professors, put a name on a culture, seeming to forget about Almighty God, themselves.

They don't want to give credit to Him, and recognize that He could lead groups out of the old world, fleeing bondage and persecution. They instead, are unsure and undecided, always learning, but never willing to take a stand and come to a knowledge of the truth, therefore discrediting Almighty God. There is so much disinformation and lies that exist and so many people willing to spread them. Unless one understands this, and is/are *free thinkers* themselves, they would never come to a knowledge of the truth.

All of theses cities were beautifully built, the construction was so magnificently contrived by such an intelligent civilization, by a people who seemingly were blessed with great knowledge, but yet miraculously have vanished without a trace or record. These people predated, what the alleged experts call, a ie. *"bronze age"* or *"prehistoric"* period, trying to describe a period, of the people who actually lived at the time. What does "prehistoric" mean? This word is simply a bunch of nonsense, as the term implies that God is Prehistoric. There, however, is a long rich history of God, as recorded in the Bible and Book of Mormon. There is also a record of the ancient civilizations that inhabited the Americas, from the Tower of Babel, to the Mayans and Aztecs, make no mistake.

Both the Bible, and the Book of Mormon, are records of people long ago, and are truly words of them, as those speaking from the dust, as explained in the words of Isaiah. *"And thou shalt be brought down, and shalt* **speak out of the ground, and thy speech shall be low out of the dust, and thy voice shall be, as one that hath a familiar spirit, out of the ground, and thy speech shall <u>whisper out of the dust.</u>"** *(Isaiah 29:4, KJV)*

> *"And now , my beloved brethren, all those who are of the* **house of Israel,** *and all ye ends of the earth,* <u>*I speak unto you as the* **voice of one crying from the dust:*** *Farewell until that great day shall come."*</u> *(2 Nephi 33:13, Book of Mormon)*

The people who now remain, and are inhabiting these areas, are considered as a "Normal Culture". This culture you see of these people is not a culture "synonymous" with a people blessed by the Lord. The culture lacks the ear marks of a people who worship Almighty God. Instead, it is a culture indicative of one whose people worship and rely on Satan himself, through their symbols, traditions, sacrifices and culture. They are not blessed with great intelligence, as was their predecessors, who once inhabited the land. Is all that is shown, is what once was.

They are remnants of a people once blessed by the Lord, but are now proof of how backward they have become. Yes, the Mayans/ Nephites and Aztecs/Lamanites did it to themselves, because they turned their backs on God, and out of rebellion, began their own pagan practices. Each town took on habits and practices in opposition to what they knew to be right with God. Therefore, God quit working with these people, and they, like many nations before and after them, dwindled in unbelief and ignorance. They were left to depend on their own imaginations and strength. This kind of mentality breeds selfishness.

Wars erupted, and ultimately the people left their cities, for fear of the women and children being offered up as sacrifices to the Lamanite/ Aztec gods and idols. The Aztecs were at one time as believing in Almighty God as the Mayans, and maybe more genuine in their beliefs, than the Mayans at one time. However, the Nephites/Mayans were judged more harshly, for they were given more, and therefore, more was expected from them. Thus, they were swept off the face of the earth without a trace, letting the people wonder and guess as to their demise.

Christ, Himself, visited the Ancient Americas, and he touched down in the land of Bountiful, and He stood personally at the temple, located just south of the narrow neck of land, and bordering the land of Zarahemla on the south, all of which is in Northern Colombia, South America. (See map of the Lands of the Nephites)

After the Lamanites/Aztecs overran the lands of the Nephites/ Mayans, they left in their wake in North America, the American Indians/Native Americans, consisting of tribes, such as the Navajo, Apache, Sioux, Cherokee, Cheyenne, Arapaho, Chippewa, Seminole,

Utes, and many more. Many of these tribes came from those dissenters, from the Nephites/Mayans, and those who joined the Lamanites/ Aztecs to keep from being slaughtered at the last.

No alleged expert is needed to take a DNA sample, nor is a liberal wanted to spread their disinformation and lies, as is the case by the Smithsonian Institute, as they cover up and hide information and artifacts, and discoveries and evidence that show the truth of these things mentioned herein. Liberals do this in the attempt to discredit Joseph Smith's work of bringing forth the Book of Mormon. It is not discrediting just Joseph Smith, but it is actually discrediting God. More about the facts of these ancient civilizations will be told in the next chapter. We truly live in a time where there is great *"mists of darkness"*, where, without knowledge people would let go of the *"rod of iron"*, and lose their way.

The war against God is so prevalent, the lies are so blatant, that liberal institutions, professors in colleges, because of their degrees of learning, are listened to by our youth, as experts. These professors/ alleged experts override and are **replacements for** *good common sense and decency*. God laughs at the wisdom of men, and the lies they tell in order to get praise of the world.

When Christopher Columbus first sailed to the Americas, he discovered an island off of the coast of South America, inhabited by an all white community of natives/Mayan Indians. Since the fall of the Mayan civilization, the people of Nephi/Mayans had been steadily hunted and destroyed when found, and it was amazing to find this last group, who had survived on this isolated island. The island's name is Tayasal, which shortly after, was overrun by Spaniards under the direction of the Roman Catholic Church.

1492 marked the beginning of the Spanish coming against the Lamanites/Aztecs with their Catholicism, and finally forcing their will and religion upon the people. America is on the same track to destroying their own civilization, and having God hand our country over to another, because the people of God have turned away from obeying His simple, but basic commandments. Everyone wants to get rich without producing anything. They break the very first commandment and fail to honor God in everything they say and do. They fail to teach their children to do what is right. They uphold evil laws that violate freedom. Actually, God is justified right now in judging America harshly, and he will, because they have dwindled in unbelief.

> ★ *"For he that diligently seeketh shall find; **and the mysteries of God shall be unfolded** unto them, by the power of the Holy Ghost, as well in these times as in times of old, and as well in times of old as in times to come; wherefore the course of the Lord is one eternal round."(1 Nephi 10:19, Book of Mormon)*

God told the people thousands of years before 1830 A.D., about the Book of Mormon/records of the Nephites/Mayans, and the Jaredites/ Olmecs, that were to come forth. He foretold the Latter-Days, and that they would come forth from a descendant of the tribe of Joseph. He worked through Moroni, knowing Joseph Smith, at a young age was going to be in the New York area. Yes, Joseph smith was truly called of God to do this thing. Moroni was told where to hide up the Plates of Nephi, written on Gold Plates in the Hill Cumorah. We know today as the State of New York, around the area of Palmyra, as the home place of this 14 year old boy. Was this accidental that everything came together like clock work? There is no way that this could be an accident.

Joseph Smith was only a boy of 14-years old. He was still very naive, but yet very sober even as General Mormon who at 16 led the armies of the Nephites/Mayans up to the time they were destroyed. Joseph Smith was in the place he was in for a specific purpose, and it happened to be in the area/place of the Hill Cumorah, where the plates of Nephi were buried. He couldn't have had the ability to get to Central America to the Hill Shim to get any plates, and make it all of the way back to New York without being in grave danger at every turn. We all know how Satan set out to sabotage his mission from the beginning. On top of all that, he was told to come back every year for 4-years to receive further instruction from Moroni, before he was entrusted with the plates physically. It would have been impossible for him to do that otherwise. It had to be as convenient as possible for a boy of 14.

He was visited by Moroni, and he did get those plates out of the Hill Cumorah, and he did translate the plates of Nephi from the gold plates, and they do give a history of the ancient Nephites/Mayans and Lamanites/Aztecs. I also believe that he did see the vault where there were countless records, just as Mormon described. The brother of Jared had a similar experience, as well as the first Nephi who was taken up into a high mountain. God makes the program, and sees fit to make sure his will is carried out. Do ignorant people really think that things happen by accident. Moroni was the messenger who was qualified to do what he did to notify Joseph Smith of the gold plates, because Moroni buried them there, and he was an angel of God.

God is no respecter of persons: *"Therefore, __when they are out of the world they neither marry nor are given in marriage; but are appointed "angels in heaven," which angels are ministering servants for those who are worthy of a far more, and exceeding, and eternal weight of glory."__ __"For these angels did not abide my law; therefore, they cannot be enlarged, but remain separately and singly, "without exaltation, in their saved condition, to all eternity; and from henceforth are not gods, but are "angels of God forever and ever."__ (Section 132:16-17, Doctrine and Covenants)*

Moroni was now fleeing for his life, and having traveled to New York, as we know it today, but Moroni called it the Land of Cumorah. The hill where he hid the records for the last time before Joseph Smith received charge of them. This was the same hill where Mormon gathered his people in by the millions as the last stand of the Nephites/Mayans. Moroni and his ten thousand soldiers were mowed down, along with millions more of his countrymen, including men women and children. They watched in terror as the numberless hosts of the Lamanite/Aztecs fell upon them with the sword, the ax, and countless weapons of destruction.

Even as God foretold the coming of the Messiah, His Son as the Savior of the world, where he would be born, when he would be born, who his parents would be, the circumstances leading up to it, the miraculous signs to be given, and many more. Every detail was foretold and also was carried out exactly as described, even though his mother had to ride 90 miles on a donkey to get to Bethlehem, to be born in a barn. Does anyone really believe this was an accident, and that all of those witnesses about this same thing was an accident?

Looking at it very closely, the same thing happened in the case of Joseph Smith. Every detail about what he did was foretold thousands of years ago, and it all happened even though it was Moroni, who had to bury the plates of gold in a hill, close to where this young boy of 14 was able to get them. God made sure that His own words, and plan was fulfilled. Other examples are the Children of Israel going into bondage for 400-years, the destruction of Jerusalem, the Flood. God is in charge consistently and just throws us in where he wants us to be, to see if we will live up to his commandments.

There are many more examples of the deliberateness of God, such as God raising up a Moses, and when Pharoah wanted to kill all of the baby boys, God still outsmarted the Egyptians by having his enemies raise Moses themselves. He was right under their noses, this great future leader of the children of Israel, being reared, and educated, given power and prestige, groomed to be the next Pharoah of Egypt. My great Father in Heaven, does these things to show that he is deliberate, and will do as he says, and to let the people of the world know, that He/God is always in control. He wrote the play, he narrates it, and he has, and will fulfill his word.

Chapter 10

Nephite/Mayan Wars Leading up to the Birth of Christ

Alma the Chief Judge and Prophet Sets the Church back in order

All of the **Alters** found in the ruins of these ancient cities, were used for offering blood offerings of unblemished sheep, goats, calves, etc. as a commandment by God, as the Children of Israel were still keeping the **Law of Moses,** and the Nephites/Mayans, the Lamanites/Aztecs, and the Mulekites/Toltecs, were all remnants of the tribe of Joseph. They were also still under the obligation *to continue in observing the Law of Moses, until Christ was resurrected*. When king Benjamin called the people together to announce his son, Mosiah, as the new king, there were countless people with their families attending. All of them brought with them firstlings of their flocks and herds to offer as sacrifices, as they were still obligated to live the law of Moses. Imagine how many blood sacrifices and burnt offerings were completed that day at the temple in Bountiful.

> *"Therefore, after Alma having established the church at Sidom, seeing a great check, yea, seeing that the people were checked as to the pride of their hearts, and began to humble <u>themselves before God, and</u> <u>began to assemble themselves together at their sanctuaries to worship</u> <u>God before the alter, watching and praying continually, that they might</u>*

be delivered from Satan, and from death, and from destruction---
"(Alma 15:17, Book of Mormon)

All of these **Mounds** found today are **burial mounds**, for when, after a big battle, they heaped the bodies up and carried dirt and threw it on the dead, to keep them from stinking, and also from polluting their water supply. *"Nevertheless, after many days, their dead bodies were heaped up upon the face of the earth, and they were **covered with a shallow covering**. And now so great was the scent thereof that the people did not go in to possess the land of **Ammonihah for many years**. And it was called Desolation of Nehors[liberal minded, power hungry people]; for they were of the profession of Nehor, who were slain; and their lands remained desolate."(Alma 16:11, Book of Mormon)* **Now 80 B.C.**

It was prophesied many years in advance that Christ would appear to his other sheep that were not of the same fold as the the people in Jerusalem, and that they too were of the House of Israel. Many of the people, both Nephites/Mayans, and Lamanites/Aztecs inquired where the **Son of God** would come after his resurrection, and were promised that **Christ would appear to them.** Many Priests and teachers went among the people admonishing them to keep the commandments of God.

*"Holding forth things which must shortly come; yea, holding **forth the coming of the Son of God**, his sufferings and death, and also the resurrection of the dead." "And many of the people did inquire concerning the **place where the Son of God should come**; and they were taught **that he would appear unto them after his resurrection; and this the people did hear with great joy and gladness.**" "And now after the church had been established[put in order] throughout all the land[of the Nephites/Mayans]---having got the **victory over the devil, and the word of God being preached in its purity in all the land,** and the Lord pouring out his blessings upon the people---thus ended the fourteenth year of the reign of the judges **over the people of Nephi[Mayans]." (Alma 16:19-21, Book of Mormon)***

Now 77 B.C. Through studying the scriptures, the sons of Mosiah/Mayan missionaries, having gone up to the Land of Nephi, to teach the Lamanites the error of their ways, described how they received the *"Spirit of Revelation and Prophecy"*, and they were able to teach with authority, as they had gained a knowledge of the **Truth**.

> *"Now these sons of Mosiah were with Alma at the time the <u>angel</u> first appeared unto him; therefore Alma did rejoice exceedingly to see his brethren; and what added more to his joy, they were still his brethren; and <u>in the Lord;</u> yea, and they had **waxed strong in the knowledge of the truth; for they were men of a sound understanding and they had searched the scriptures diligently, that they might know the word of God.**" "But this is not all; **they had given themselves to much prayer, and fasting; therefore they had the spirit of prophecy, and the spirit of revelation, and when they taught they taught with power and authority from God.**" (Alma 17:2-3, Book of Mormon)*

The sons of Mosiah/Mayan king, had great success in converting many Lamanites/Aztecs and bringing them to the knowledge of God. They went out with courage up to the Land of Nephi, now occupied by the Lamanites, to teach them what had been revealed to them through their diligent prayer and searching of the scriptures. They became humble and **valiant in the testimony of the Truth.** They were unafraid of what man could do to them, and they were willing to lay their lives down for their brethren, the Lamanites/Aztecs. What greater love for Christ could anyone have?

> *"Now, these are they who were <u>converted unto the Lord:</u>" "The people of the Lamanites[Aztecs] who were in the <u>land of</u> Ishmael;" "And also of the people of the Lamanites[Aztecs] in the <u>land of Middoni;</u>" "And also of the people of the Lamanites[Aztecs] who were in the <u>city of</u> Nephi;" "And also of the people of the Lamanites[Aztecs] who were in the <u>land of Shilom,</u> and who were in the <u>land of Shemlon,</u> and in the <u>city of Shimnilom</u>." " And these are the names of the cities of the **Lamanites[**Aztecs] **that were converted unto the Lord;** and these are they that **laid down the weapons of their rebellion, yea, all their weapons of war; and they were all** Lamanites[not dissenters]." "(Alma 23:8-14, Book of Mormon)*

Out of all of the Lamanites/Aztecs converted, there was only one dissenter that was converted back to the truth. The rest conspired and made plans to go up and kill the newly converted Christians, and force them to recant their decisions to follow Christ. Many Lamanites/Aztecs united with the Nephites/Mayans, and they covenanted to never take up their weapons of war against their fellow man again, ever. In fact, when a Lamanite/Aztec gained the knowledge of the truth/voice of Christ, they never varied from what they knew to be true.

"Now there was <u>not one soul among all the people[Aztecs] who had been converted unto the Lord that would take up arms against their</u> brethren; nay, they would not even make <u>any</u> preparations for war; yea, and also their <u>king</u> commanded them that <u>they should not."</u>
"Now, these are the words which he said unto the people concerning the matter: <u>I thank my God, my beloved people, that our great God has in goodness sent these our brethren, the Nephites[Mayans], to</u> preach unto us, and to convince us of the <u>traditions of our</u> wicked fathers." *"And behold, I thank my great God that he has given us a portion of his **Spirit** to soften our hearts, that we have <u>opened a correspondence with these brethren, the Nephites[Mayans]."</u> "And behold, I also thank my <u>God,</u> that by opening this correspondence we have <u>been convinced of our sins, and of the many murders which we have committed."</u> "And I also thank my God, yea, my great God, that he hath<u> granted unto us that we might **repent**</u> of these things, and also that he hath <u>forgiven us of our many sins and murders which we have committed, **and taken away the guilt from our hearts, through the merits of his Son."**</u>*
*"And now behold, my brethren, since it has been all that we could do, (as we were the <u>most lost of all mankind)</u> to repent of all our sins and the many murders which we have committed, and to get God to take them away <u>from our hearts, **for it was all that we could do to repent sufficiently before God that he would take away our stain---"**</u> "Now, my best beloved brethren, since God <u>hath taken away our **stains, and our swords have become bright, then let us stain our swords no more with the blood of our brethren."**</u> (Alma 24:6-12, Book of Mormon)*

These Lamanites/Aztecs were all pure descendants of Laman and Lemuel, the first Aztec kings, that joined themselves with the people of God, the Nephites/Mayans. Once they understood the truth they never turned back, and were willing to be killed. rather than take the risk of being turned away from God's kingdom, through more murders of their brethren.

"*Now when the Lamanites[Aztecs] saw that their brethren **would not flee from the sword, neither would they turn aside to the right hand or to the left, but that they would lie down and perish, and praise God even in the very act of perishing under the sword---***" "*Now when the Lamanites[Aztecs] saw this they did forbear from slaying them; and there were many whose hearts had swollen in them for those of their brethren who had fallen under the sword, **for they repented** of the things which they had done.*" "*And it came to pass that they threw down their weapons of war, and they would not take them again, **for they were stung for the murders which they had committed;** and they came down even as their brethren, relying upon the mercies of those whose arms were lifted to slay them.*" "*And it came to pass that the people of God were joined that **day by more than the number who had been slain;** and those who had been slain; were righteous people, therefore we have no reason to doubt but what they were saved.*" *(Alma 24:23-26, Book of Mormon)*

"*Now the greatest number of those of the Lamanites[Aztecs] who slew[murdered] so many of their brethren were **Amalekites** and **Amulonites,** the greatest number of whom were after the order of the **Nehors**[liberals/communists/Democrats].*" "*Now, among those who joined the people of the Lord, **there were none who were Amalekites or Amulonites, or who were of the order of Nehor, but they were actual descendants of Laman and Lemuel**[the first Aztec kings].*" "*And thus we can plainly see that **after a people have been enlightened by the Spirit of God, and have had a great knowledge of things pertaining to righteousness, and they have fallen away into sin and transgression, they become more hardened, and thus their state becomes worse than though they had never known these things.**"(Alma 24:28-30, Book of Mormon)*

*"Behold, how many thousands of our brethren **has he loosed from the pains of hell;** and they are brought to <u>sing redeeming love,</u> and this because of the **power of his**[Christ's] **word which is in us,** <u>therefore have we not great reason to rejoice?"</u> "Yea, we have reason <u>to praise him forever, for he is</u> **the Most High God**, and <u>has loosed our brethren from</u> **the chains of hell."**(Alma 26:13-14, Book of Mormon)*

*★"Yea, **he that repenteth and exerciseth faith, and bringeth forth good works, and prayeth continually without ceasing---** <u>unto such is given to know the mysteries of God; yea, unto such it shall be given to reveal things which never have been revealed; yea, and it shall be given unto such to bring thousands of souls to repentance, even as it has been given unto us to bring these our brethren</u>[Aztecs] <u>to repentance.</u>"(Alma 26:22, Book of Mormon)*

The Lamanites/Aztecs who joined with the Nephites/Mayans, because they came to know God, once having this knowledge, never took up arms again, against one another, but would rather lay down and be killed themselves, than take up their swords against their brothers. No greater love hath a man, than he that will lay down his life for a friend.

*"For behold, they had rather sacrifice their own lives than even to take the life of their enemy; and they have buried their weapons of war deep in the earth, **because of their love towards their brethren."** "And now behold I say unto you, **has there been so great love in all the land?** Behold, I say unto you, Nay there has not, **even among the Nephites/**Mayans."(Alma 26:32-33, Book of Mormon)*

Dissenters of the Nephites/Mayans, who went over to join with the Lamanites/Aztecs, stirred the Lamanites/Aztecs up to anger against those who believed now in God, to war against them. Rather than fight back against their brothers, they prostrated themselves upon the ground and allowed themselves to be killed, rather than kill. Through this means, many more Lamanites/Aztecs were brought to a knowledge of the truth, and joined with the people of God. Because of the dissenting

NephitesMayans, lying to them, to get them to kill their own, they went on a war path and sought out and hunted the Amulonites, and killed as many as they found, and also went over to the land of the Nephites/Mayans, and destroyed the evil city of Ammonihah, the same city that was infested with liberals and Democrats, who were studying and planning to destroy the freedom of the people.

"*And behold, now it came to pass that those Lamanites[Aztecs] were more angry because they had slain their brethren; therefore they swore vengeance upon the Nephites[Mayans]; and they did no more attempt to slay the people of Anti-Nephi-Lehi at that time.*" "*But they took their armies and went over into the borders of the land of Zarahemla, and fell upon the people[Nephites/Mayans] who were in the **land of Ammonihah** and destroyed them.*"*(Alma 25:1-2, Book of Mormon)*

The Nephites/Mayans welcomed the "born again" Lamanites/Aztecs, and gave them an inheritance among themselves, in the "Land of Jershon". This land was just south of Bountiful, and northeast of Zarahemla, by the seashore, of the east sea.(see map of the land of the Nephites/Mayans)These people were called the, people of Ammon.

"*And it came to pass that the chief judge sent a proclamation throughout all the land, desiring the **voice of the people concerning the admitting their brethren,** who were the people[Lamanites/Aztecs] of Anti-Nephi-Lehi.*" "*And it came to pass that the **voice of the people** came, saying: Behold, we will give up the land **of Jershon**, which is on the east by the sea, which joins the land Bountiful, which is on the south of the land Bountiful; and this land Jershon is the land which we will give unto our brethren[the Lamanites/Aztecs] for an inheritance.*" "*And it came to pass that it did cause great joy among them. And they[Children of Ammon/Aztecs] went down into the land of Jershon, and took possession of the land Jershon; and they were called by the Nephites[Mayans] the people of Ammon; therefore they were distinguished by that name ever after.*"*(Alma 27:21-22, 26, Book of Mormon)*

*"And they did look upon the shedding of blood of their brethren with the greatest abhorrence; and they never could be prevailed upon to <u>take up arms against their brethren;</u> and they never did look upon death with any <u>degree of terror, for their hope and views of Christ and the resurrection;</u> therefore, <u>death was swallowed up to them</u> **by the victory of Christ over it.**" "Therefore, they would suffer death in the most aggravating and distressing manner which could be inflicted by their brethren, before they would take the sword or cimeter to smite them." "And thus they were a <u>zealous and beloved people,</u> **a highly favored people of the Lord.**"* (Alma 27:28-30 Book of Mormon)

It was now **76 B.C.**, and 15-years had gone by since the beginning of the Reign of the Judges. Alma, himself, was obliged to take up his sword from time to time in the defense of his country, and the Nephite/Mayan way of life. He mentions, that because of the number of the slain, how they heaped up the bodies, and buried them by heaping dirt over them. Who then would want to go in and dig up a bunch of dead people, except archaeologists, who think that they are uncovering a bunch of mysteries, when the truth can be read.

*Now 75 B.C. *"And from the first year to the fifteenth has brought to pass the destruction of <u>many thousand lives; yea, it has brought to pass an awful scene of bloodshed.</u>" "And the bodies of many thousands are laid low in the earth, while the **bodies of many thousands are moldering in <u>heaps</u> upon the face of the** earth; yea, and many thousands are mourning for the loss of their kindred, because they have <u>reason to fear,</u> according to the promises of the Lord, that they are <u>consigned to a state of endless</u> wo." "While many thousands of others truly mourn for the loss of their kindred, yet they rejoice and <u>exult in the hope, and even know, according to the promises of the Lord, **that they are raised to dwell at the right hand of God, in a state of never ending happiness.**</u>" "And thus we see **how great the inequality of man is because of sin and transgression, and the power of the** <u>devil,</u>which comes by the cunning plans which he hath **devised to ensnare the hearts of men.**" "And thus we see **the great call of diligence of men to labor in the vineyards of the Lord;** and <u>thus we see the great reason of sorrow, and **also of rejoicing**---sorrow</u>*

*because of **death and destruction among men, and joy because of the light of Christ unto life.**" (Alma 28:10-14, Book of Mormon)*

Alma is remorseful, and remembers what he has gone through, and the rebellious nature of man in general. He remembers his success in bringing many to a knowledge of God, and also, he understands the easiness, in which man can turn to serving Satan. Alma is speaking from experience, as he once was a wayward youth himself. He understands how **dangerous it is to procrastinate the day of repentance/ change.**

> ★*"O That I **were an angel, and could have the wish of my heart**, that I might go forth and **speak with the trump of God, with a voice to shake the earth,** and cry repentance unto **every people!**"* *"Yea, I would declare unto every soul, as with the **voice of thunder, repentance and the plan of redemption,** that they should repent and come unto our God, that there might not be more sorrow upon all the earth." "But behold, I am a man, and do sin in my wish; for I ought to be content with the things which the Lord hath alotted unto me." "I ought not to harrow[rationalize] up in my **desires**, the firm decree of a just God, for I know that he granteth unto men **according to their desire,** whether it be unto **death** or unto **life; yea,** I know that he allotteth unto men, yea, **decreeth unto them decrees which are unalterable, according to their wills, whether they be unto salvation or unto** destruction." "Yea, **I know that good and evil have come before all men**; he that knoweth not good from evil is **blameless**; but he that knoweth good and evil, to him it is given according to his desires, whether he desireth good or evil, life or death, joy or remorse **of conscience.**"(Alma 29:1-5, Book of Mormon)*

Every time it looked as though the Nephites/Mayans were at peace and beginning to prosper, some group; in this case Zoramites/liberals/ woke, were studying to destroy the freedom of the people, and began dissenting over to the Lamanites/Aztecs, and threatening the security of the Nephites/Mayans. It seems as though every city; in this case, Antionum, would get wild ideas that would corrupt their beliefs in how they were to worship God. They would get vain imaginations of what they pictured in their own minds, that they wanted to believe, rather than go according to facts as laid down by the Lord.

*"Now it came to pass that after the end of Korihor, Alma having received tidings that the **Zoramites**[woke community] **were perverting the ways of the Lord,** and that **Zoram**, who was their leader, <u>was leading the hearts of the people</u> [convincing them through vanity] <u>to bow down to **dumb idols,**</u> his <u>heart began to **sicken** because of the iniquity of the people,</u>" "For it was the cause of great sorrow to Alma to know of iniquity among his people[the Mayans]; therefore his heart was exceedingly sorrowful because of the separation of the **Zoramites** from the **Nephites**[Mayans]." "Now the Zoramites had gathered themselves together in a land which **was called Antionum, <u>which was east of the land of Zarahemla</u>**, which lay nearly bordering upon the seashore, which was south of the land Jershon, which also bordered upon the wilderness south, which wilderness was full of the **Lamanites**[Aztecs]." "Now the Nephites[Mayans] greatly feared that the Zoramites would enter into a correspondence with the Lamanites[Aztecs], <u>and that it would be the **means of great loss on the part of the Nephites**</u>[Mayans]." "Now the Zoramites were **dissenters** from the Nephites[Mayans]; therefore <u>they had had the word of God preached unto them</u>[they were without excuse]." "But they had fallen <u>into great errors, for they would not observe to keep the commandments of God</u>, and his statues, **<u>according to the law of Moses.</u>**"(Alma 31:1-4,8, Book of Mormon)*

Many Nephite/Mayan cities had ways of corrupting themselves, and their beliefs in God. They remind me of the many denominations, each of which, get a wild idea of what makes them the true church. Despite the simple differences that each one uses to set themselves apart from the others as the true church, when the truth is, what all Christian churches teach, is the gospel of Jesus Christ, putting them on equal ground, despite their fact or fiction differences. Because they have received the gospel of Jesus Christ, makes them heirs to redemption, as was promised by Christ, recorded several times in all scriptures. Alma however, was surprised to witness, to what degree the Zoramites went to, in the imaginations of their hearts, as he and others arrived in their land to do some serious missionary work.

*"Now, when they had come into the land, behold, <u>to their</u> <u>astonishment,</u> they found that the Zoramites had <u>built synagogues,</u> <u>and that they did gather themselves together on one day of the week,</u> **<u>which day they did call the day of the Lord;</u>** and they did worship <u>after a manner</u> which Alma and his brethren had never beheld;" "For they had a place <u>built up in the center of their synagogue, a place for</u> <u>standing, which was high above the head; and the top thereof</u> **would** **only admit one person.**" "Therefore, whosoever desired to <u>worship</u> <u>must go forth and stand upon the top thereof, and stretch forth his</u> <u>hands towards heaven, and cry with a loud voice, saying:"</u> **"Holy, holy God; we believe that thou art God, and we believe that thou art holy, and that thou wast a spirit, and that thou art a spirit, and that thou wilt be a spirit forever.**" "Holy God, we believe that thou hast separated us from our brethren; and we do not believe in the **tradition of our brethren, which was handed down to them by the childishness of their fathers; but we believe that thou hast elected us to be thy holy children; and also thou hast made it known unto us that there shall be <u>no Christ.</u>**" "But thou art the same yesterday, today, and forever; **and thou hast elected us that we shall be saved <u>whilst all around us are elected to be cast by thy wrath</u> <u>down to hell; for the which holiness, O God, we thank thee; and</u> <u>we also thank thee that thou has elected us, that we may not be</u> <u>led after the foolish traditions of our brethren, which doth bind</u> <u>them down to a belief of Christ,</u>** which doth lead their hearts to wander **far from thee, our God.**" "And again we thank thee, O God, **<u>that we are a chosen and a holy people. Amen.</u>**" (Alma 31:12-18, Book of Mormon)*

*"And it came to pass that they[Alma and other Mayan brethren] did go forth, and began to preach the **<u>word of God</u>** unto the people[Zoramite/Mayans], entering into their synagogues, and into their houses; yea, and even they did preach the word in their streets."* *"And it came to pass that after much labor among them, they began to have **<u>success among the poor class of people</u>**[Mayans]<u>;</u> for behold, they were cast out of the synagogues because of the **<u>coarseness of their</u> <u>apparel---</u>**" "Therefore they were not permitted to enter into their synagogues to worship God, <u>being esteemed as filthiness; therefore they</u>*

were poor; yea, they were esteemed by their brethren as dross; therefore they were poor as to things of the world; and also they were poor in heart." "Now as Alma was teaching...there came a great multitude unto him, who were those of whom we have been speaking. of whom were the poor in heart, because of their poverty as to the things of the world." "I say unto you, it is well that ye are cast out of your synagogues, that ye **may be humble, and that ye may learn wisdom;** *for it is necessary that ye should learn wisdom' for it is because that ye are cast out, that ye are despised of your brethren because of your exceeding poverty, that ye are brought to a lowliness of heart; for ye are necessarily brought to be humble." (Alma 32:1-4, 12 Book of Mormon)*

This is what a **Democracy** does to a people. It separates them into classes, and the rich rule, and are appointed into positions of power and not elected by we the people. In a Democracy, only the rich rule. This is a communist system of government, where the people are treated as chattel. A **Republic** is the democratic form of government where all people are equal; poor or rich, male or female, black or white, and are all treated equally under the law.

The Nephites/Mayans were very diligent at one time in teaching the gospel among themselves and also among the Lamanites/Aztecs. They all, like us, have had many of the same weaknesses that plague our own society, and that we ourselves, need to guard against today. Alma even had to chastise his own sons at times, and help them to understand, the truth, even while in the mission field.

★*"And this is not all, my son. Thou didst do that which was grievous unto me; for thou didst forsake the ministry, and go over into the land of Siron among the borders of the Lamanites[Aztecs], after the harlot Isabel." "Yea, she did steal away the hearts of many;* **but this was no excuse for thee, my son. Thou shouldst have tended to the ministry wherewith thou was entrusted.** *"Know ye not, my son, that these* **things are an abomination in the sight of the Lord; yea, most abominable above all sins save it be the shedding of innocent blood or denying the Holy Ghost?"** *"For behold, if ye* **deny the Holy Ghost when once has had a place in you, and ye know that ye deny it, behold, this is a sin which is unpardonable;**

yea, and whosoever murdereth against the light and knowledge of God, it is not easy for him to obtain forgiveness; yea, I say unto you my son, that it is not easy for him to obtain forgiveness." "And now, my son, I would to God that ye had not been guilty of so great a crime. I would not dwell upon your crimes, to harrow up your soul, if it were not for your good." "But behold, ye cannot hide your crimes from God; and except ye repent they will stand as a testimony against you at the last day." "Now my son, I would that ye should repent and forsake your sins, and go no more after the lusts of your eyes, but cross yourself in all these things; for except ye do this ye can in nowise inherit the kingdom of God. Oh, remember, and take it upon you, and cross yourself in these things.(Alma 39:3-9, Book of Mormon)

"Suffer not yourself to be led away by any vain or foolish thing; suffer not the devil to lead away your heart again after those wicked harlots[whores]. Behold, O my son, how great iniquity ye brought upon the Zoramites; for when they saw your conduct they would not believe in my words." "And now the Spirit of the Lord doth say unto me: Command thy children to do good, lest they lead away the hearts of many people to destruction; therefore I command you, my son, in the fear of God, that ye refrain from your iniquities;" "That ye turn to the Lord with all your mind, might, and strength; that ye lead away the hearts of no more to do wickedly; but rather return unto them, and acknowledge your faults and that wrong which ye have done." " Seek not after riches nor the vain things of this world; for behold, you cannot carry them with you."(Alma 39:11-14, Book of Mormon)

The Church of God among the Nephites/Mayans was prospering greatly, and God at different times sent his prophets among them testifying of the coming of Christ, who was to come in the very near future, to redeem his people.

"And now, my son, I would say somewhat unto you concerning the coming of Christ. Behold, I say unto you, that it is he that surely shall come to take away the sins of the world; yea, he cometh to declare glad tidings of salvation unto his people." "And now

my son, this was the ministry unto which ye were called, to declare these glad tidings unto this people, to prepare their minds; or rather that salvation might come unto them, that they prepare the minds of their children to hear the word at the time of his coming." "And now I will ease your mind somewhat on this subject. Behold, you marvel why these things should be known so long beforehand. Behold, I say unto you, **is not a soul at this time as precious unto God as a soul will be at the time of his coming?"** **"Is it not necessary that the plan of redemption should be made known unto this people as well as unto their children? Is it not as easy at this time for the Lord to send his angel to declare these glad tidings unto us as unto our children, or as after the time of his coming?"** *(Alma 39:15-19, Book of Mormon)*

"Now my son, here is somewhat more I would say unto thee; for I perceive that thy mind is worried concerning the **resurrection of the dead.**" *"Behold, I say unto you, that there is no resurrection---... until* **after the coming of Christ.**" *"Behold,* **he bringeth to pass the resurrection of the dead.** *But behold, my son, the resurrection is not yet. Now, I unfold unto you a* **mystery;...But I show unto you one thing** *which I have inquired diligently of God that I might know---that is concerning the* **resurrection.**" *"Behold, there is a time appointed that* **all** *shall come forth from the dead. Now when this time cometh no one knows; but* **God knoweth the time which is appointed.**" *"Now, whether there shall be one time, or a second time, or a third time, that men shall come forth from the dead, it mattereth not; for God knoweth all these things; and it sufficeth me to know that this is the case---that there is a time appointed that all shall rise from the dead."* *"Now there must be a* **space betwixt the time of death and the time of the resurrection."** *(Alma 40:1-6, Book of Mormon)*

"Now concerning the state of the soul between death and the resurrection---Behold, it has been made known unto me **by an angel, that the spirits of all men, as soon as they are departed from this mortal body, yea, the spirits of all men, whether they be good or evil, are taken home to that God who gave them life."** *"And then shall it come to pass,* **that the spirits of those who are righteous are**

received into a state of happiness, which is called paradise, a state of rest from all their troubles and from all care, and sorrow." "And then it shall come to pass, that the **spirits of the wicked, yea, who are evil---for behold, they have no part nor portion of the Spirit of the Lord;** for behold, they chose evil works rather than good; **therefore the spirit of the devil did enter into them, and take possession of their house---**and these shall be cast into outer darkness; there shall be weeping, and wailing, and gnashing of teeth, and this because of their own iniquity, **being led captive by the will of the devil." "** *(Alma 40:11-13, Book of Mormon)*

"Now my son, I do not say that their resurrection cometh at the resurrection of Christ; but behold, I give it as my opinion, that the souls and the bodies are reunited, **of the righteous, at the resurrection of Christ, and his ascension into heaven."** "Yea, this bringeth about the restoration of those things of which has been spoken by the mouths of the prophets," **"The soul shall be restored to the body, and the body to the soul; yea, every limb and joint shall be restored to its body; yea, even a hair of the head shall not be lost; but all things shall be restored to their proper and perfect frame."** "(Alma 40:20, 22-23, Book of Mormon)

"I say unto thee, my son, **that the plan of restoration is requisite**[required] **with the justice of God;** for it is requisite that all things should be restored to their proper order. Behold, it is requisite and **just** according to the **power and resurrection of Christ,** that the soul of man should be restored to its body, and that every part of the body should be restored to itself." "And it is requisite[mandatory] with the **justice of God that men should be judged according to their works;** and if their works were good in this life, and the **desires of their hearts were good**, that they should also, at the last day, be restored unto that which is good."(Alma 41:2-3, Book of Mormon)

Now 73 B.C. There were more liberal/communists/kingmen versus Conservatives/republicans/freemen, among the Zoramites at this time. Anyone who was converted among them, who chose to follow Christ, was thrown out of their midst. The majority of the

Zoramaites dissented over to the Lamanites/Aztecs, comparable of today's liberals/Democrats. For gain, they became "foreign agents" to China, and Russia. It really is morbid, to watch the ignorance of these liberal, ignorant, experts, with their archaeologist crews, digging through the skeletons of the dead, looking for artifacts, and clues as to the way they lived, and their religions.

*"For behold, it came to pass that the Zoramites[dissenting Mayans] became Lamanites[Aztecs]; therefore, in the commencement of the eighteenth year[73 B.C.] the people of the Nephites[Mayans] saw that the Lamanites[Aztecs]were coming upon them; therefore they made **preparations for war;** yea, they gathered their <u>armies in the land of Jershon.</u>" "And it came to pass that the Lamanites[Aztecs] came with their <u>thousands</u>; and they came into the land of the Zoramites; and a man by the name of <u>Zarahemnah</u> was their leader." "And now, as the <u>Amalekites</u>[Mayan dissenters/traitors]<u> were of a more wicked and murderous disposition</u> than the Lamanites[Aztecs] were, in and of themselves, therefore, Zarahemnah appointed <u>chief captains over the Lamanites[Aztecs],</u> **and they were all Amalekites and Zoramites**[dissenters/liberals]." "Now this he did that he <u>might preserve</u> **hatred** <u>towards the Nephites[Mayans],</u> that he might bring them into **subjection to the accomplishment of his designs.**" (Alma 43:4-7, Book of Mormon)*

*"And now the design of the <u>Nephites[Mayans] was to support their lands, and their houses, and their wives, and their children, that they might preserve them from the hands of their enemies; and also that they might **preserve their rights and their priviledges, yea, and also their liberty, that they might worship God according to their desires.**</u>" "For they knew that if they should fall into the hands of the Lamanites[Aztecs/liberals], that whosoever should **worship God in spirit and in truth, the true and living God,** <u>the Lamanites[Aztecs/liberals] would destroy.</u>" "Yea, and they also knew the **extreme hatred** of the Lamanites[Aztecs] towards their brethren, who were the people of Anti-Nephi-Lehi, who were called the people of Ammon[Lamamites/Aztecs in Jershon]---and they would not take up arms, yea, they had entered into a covenant and they would not break it---therefore, if they should fall into*

the hands of the Lamanites[Aztecs] they would be destroyed. (Alma 43:9-10, Book of Mormon)

"And the Nephites[Mayans] would not suffer that they should be destroyed; therefore they gave them lands for their inheritance." "And the people of Ammon[born again Aztecs] did give unto the Nephites[Mayans] a large portion of their substance to support their armies; and thus the Nephites[Mayans] were compelled, alone, to withstand against the Lamanites[Aztecs], who were a compound of Laman and Lemuel, and the sons of Ishmael, and all <u>*those who had dissented from the Nephites[Mayans], who were Amalekites and Zoramites, and the descendants of the priests of Noah.*</u>*" "Now those descendants*<u>*were as numerous, nearly as the Nephites[Mayans];*</u>* and thus the Nephites[Mayans] were obliged to contend with their brethren, even unto bloodshed.* *"(Alma 43:12-14, Book of Mormon)*

This year is 73 years before Christ was to be born, and in it brought many traitors to their country, and countrymen. Liberal traitors, looking for self-gain, power, control, and they wanted to forget about God in order to justify their sins. The Lamanites/Aztecs were lazy and didn't want to work, and they always had their hands out wanting to take from those who did work. Therefore, all of these Liberal, selfish groups, to feel justified, wanted to either subject God's people, or destroy them entirely, but as long as the Nephites/Mayans remembered to call upon God, the Nephites/Mayans were made strong, regardless of the odds. In this year a new Nephite/Mayan general takes the reins of leadership, and his name is **Moroni.**

Chapter 11

The Birth of Christ & The Change in the Reckoning of Time

MORONI
The great Nephite/Mayan general

Moroni the great Nephite/Mayan general, at the age of 25-years old, was called into the service of his country to defend the people of Ammon, the Lamanites/Aztecs, who joined with the Nephites/Mayans, and were given the land of Jershon. Moroni was a true son of God, believing deeply in the scriptures and was a man of great faith.

> *"And **Moroni took all the command, and the government of their wars. And he was only twenty and five years old, when he was appointed** <u>**chief captain over the armies of the Nephites**</u>[Mayans]."*
> *"And it came to pass that he met the Lamanites[Aztecs] in the borders of Jershon, and his people were armed with swords, and with cimeters, and all manner of weapons of war." "And when the armies of the Lamanites[Aztecs] saw that **Moroni, had prepared his people with** <u>**breastplates and with arm-shields, yea, and also shields to defend their heads, and also they were dressed with thick clothing---**</u>"*
> *"Now the army of Zarahemnah[Aztecs] was not prepared with any such thing; they <u>had only their swords and their cimeters, their bows and their arrows, their stones and their slings; and they were naked, save it were a skin which was girded about their loins;</u> yea, all were*

*naked, save it were the **Zoramites** and the **Amalekites**;" "But they were not armed with breastplates, nor shields---therefore they <u>were exceedingly afraid of the armies of the Nephites</u>[Mayans] <u>because of their armor,</u> notwithstanding their number **being so much greater than the Nephites**[Mayans](Alma 43:17-21, Book of Mormon)*

Zarahemnah, therefore decided he wouldn't attack with his Lamanite/Aztec armies there, but conspired to go somewhere else that might be easier to conquer. Moroni and the Nephites/Mayans were ahead of the Lamanites/Aztecs at every turn, because he inquired of the prophet of God, Alma, who went to God for answers. Moroni got word from Alma, of where the Lamanites/Aztecs were entering the Land of the Nephites/Mayans, and he set a plan in motion to stop them. He planned his defense and attack around a Hill Riplah, which was east of the River Sidon /Rio Magdalena, in Northern Colombia. This war ended the 18th-year reign of the Judges, being, at the end of the year **73 B.C.**

*"And now, as Moroni knew the intention of the Lamanites[Aztecs], that it <u>was their intention to destroy their brethren, or to subject them</u> <u>and bring them into bondage that they might establish a kingdom unto</u> <u>themselves over the land;</u>" "And he also knowing that it was the <u>only</u> <u>desire of the Nephites[Mayans]to preserve their lands, and their</u> **liberty, and their church,** <u>therefore he thought it no sin that he should defend</u> <u>them by stratagem; therefore , he found by his spies which course the</u> <u>Lamanites[Aztecs] were to take.</u>" "Therefore, he divided his army and brought a part over into the valley, and concealed them on the **east, and on the south of the hill Riplah;**" "And the remainder he concealed in the west **valley, on the west of the river Sidon**[Rio Madalena], and so down into the borders of the **land Manti.**" "And thus having placed his army according to his desire, he was prepared to meet them." "And it came to pass that the Lamanites[Aztecs] came up on the north of the hill, where a part of the army of Moroni[Mayan army] was concealed'" "And as the Lamanites[Aztecs] had passed the **hill Riplah** and came into the valley, and began to cross the river **Sidon** [Rio Magdalena], the army which was concealed on the **south of the hill,** which was led by a man whose name was **Lehi, <u>and he led his</u>***

army forth and encircled the Lamanites[Aztecs] about on the east in their rear." "*And it came to pass that the Lamanites[Aztecs], when they saw the Nephites[Mayans] coming upon them in their rear, turned them about and began to contend with the army of Lehi[Mayans].*" (Alma 43:29-36, Book of Mormon)

"*And the work of death commenced on both sides, but it was more dreadful on the part of the Lamanites[Aztecs], for their nakedness was exposed to the heavy blows of the Nephites[Mayans] with their swords and their cimeters,* **which brought death almost at every stroke.** " "*While on the other hand, there was now and then a man fell among the Nephites[Mayans] by their swords and the loss of blood, they being shielded from the more vital parts of the body, or the more vital parts of the body being shielded from the strokes of the Lamanites[Aztecs], by their breatplates, and their armshields, and their head-plates; and thus the Nephites[Mayans]* **did carry on the work of death among the Lamanites[Aztecs].**" "*And it came to pass that the Lamanites[Aztecs] became frightened, because of the great destruction among them, even until they began to* **flee** *towards the river* **Sidon**[Rio Magdalena].*" "*And they were pursued by* **Lehi and his men**; *and they were driven by* **Lehi into the waters of Sidon**[Rio Magdalena]. And **Lehi retained his armies upon the bank of the river Sidon**[Rio Magdalena] *that they should not cross.*" (Alma 43:37-40, Book of Mormon)

"*And it came to pass* **Moroni and his army met the Lamanites[Aztecs] in the valley, on the other**[west] **side of the river Sidon**[Rio Magdalena], *and began to fall upon them and to slay them.*" "*And the Lamanites[Aztecs] did* **flee** *again before them, towards* **the land of Manti**; *and they were met again by the armies of Moroni.*" "*Now in this case the Lamanites[Aztecs] did fight exceedingly; yea, never had the Lamanites[Aztecs] been known to fight with such exceedingly great courage, no, not even from the beginning.*" "*And they were inspired by the Zoramites and the Amalekites, who were their chief captains and leaders, and by Zarahemnah, who was their chief captain, or their chief leader and commander;* **yea, they did fight like dragons**, *and many of the Nephites[Mayans[were slain by* *their hands, yea, for they did smite in two many of their head-plates, and they did pierce many of their breastplates, and they did smite off many of their arms; and thus the Lamanites[Aztecs] did smite in their fierce anger."* "Nevertheless, the Nephites[Mayans] *were inspired by a better cause,* **for they were not fighting for monarchy or power but they were fighting for their homes and their liberties, and their wives and their children, and their all, yea, for their rites of worship and their church."** *(Alma 43:41-45, Book of Mormon)*

★*"And they were doing that which they felt was the duty which they owed to their God; for the Lord had said unto them, and also unto their fathers, that:* **Inasmuch as ye are not guilty of the first offense, neither the second, ye shall not suffer yourselves to be slain by the hands of your enemies."** *"And again, the Lord has said that:* **Ye shall defend your families even unto** *bloodshed. Therefore for this cause were the Nephites[Mayans] contending with the Lamanites[Aztecs], to defend themselves, and their families, and their lands, their country, and their rights, and their religion." "And it came to pass that when the men of Moroni saw the fierceness and the anger of the Lamanites[Aztecs], they were about to shrink and flee from them.* **And Moroni, perceiving their intent, sent forth and inspired their hearts with these thoughts---yea, the thoughts of their lands, their liberty, yea, their freedom from bondage."** *"And it came to pass that they turned upon the Lamanites[Aztecs], and they cried with one voice unto the Lord their God,* **for their liberty and their freedom from bondage."** *"And they began to stand against the Lamanites[Aztecs] with power;* **and in that selfsame hour that they cried unto the Lord for their freedom, the Lamanites[Aztecs] began to flee before them;** *and they fled[west] even to the* **waters of Sidon** *[Rio Magdalena]." "Now, the Lamanites[Aztecs] were more numerous, yea, by* **more than double the number of the Nephites**[Mayans]; *nevertheless, they were driven insomuch that they were gathered together in one body in the* **valley, upon the bank by the river Sidon** *[Rio Magdalena]." "Therefore the armies of Moroni[Mayan armies] encircled them about, yea, even on both sides of the river, for behold,* **on the east were the men of Lehi."** *"Therefore when Zarahemnah[lamanite/Aztec general] saw the men of* **Lehi on**

the east of the river Sidon [Rio Magdalena], and the armies of Moroni on the west of the river Sidon [Rio Magdalena], that they were encircled about by the Nephites [Mayans], **they were struck with terror.**" "Now Moroni, when he saw their terror, commanded his men to stop shedding their [Aztecs] blood."(Alma 43:46-54 Book of Mormon)

"And it came to pass that they did stop and withdrew a pace from them. And Moroni said unto Zarahemnah: **Behold, Zarahemnah, that we do not desire to be men of blood.**" "**Behold, we have not come out to battle against you that we might shed your blood for power; neither do we desire to bring you into bondage. But this is the very cause for which ye have come against us; yea, and ye are angry with us because of our religion.**" "But now, ye behold that the Lord is with us; and ye behold that he has delivered you into our hands. And now I would that ye should understand that this is done unto us because of our religion and our faith in Christ. And now ye see that ye cannot destroy this our faith." "Now ye see that this is the true faith of God; yea, ye see that God will support, and keep, and preserve us, so long as we are faithful unto him, and unto our faith, and our religion; and never will the Lord suffer that we shall be destroyed except we should fall into transgression and deny our faith." "(Alma 44:1-4, Book of Mormon)

"And now, Zarahemnah, I command you, in the name of that all powerful God, who has strengthened our arms that we have gained power over you, by our faith, by our religion, and by our rites of worship, and by our church, and by the sacred support which we owe to our wives and our children, **by that liberty which binds us to our lands and our country; yea, and also by the maintenance of the sacred word of God, to which we owe all our happiness; and by all that is most dear unto us---**" "Yea, and this is not all; **I command you by all the desires which ye have for life, that ye deliver your weapons of war unto us, and we will seek not your blood, but we will spare your lives, if ye will go your way and come not again to war against us.**" "And now, if ye will not do this, behold, ye are in our hands, <u>and **I will command my men that they shall fall upon you, and inflict the wounds of death in your bodies, that ye may become extinct; and then we will see who shall have power over this people; yea, we will see who shall be brought into bondage.**</u>" *(Alma 44:5-7,Book of Mormon)*

"*And now it came to pass that when Zarahemnah had heard these sayings he came forth and delivered up his sword and his cimeter, and his bow into the hands of Moroni, and said unto him:* <u>Behold, here are our weapons of war; we will deliver them up unto you, but we will not suffer ourselves to take an oath unto you, which we know we shall break, and also our children; but take our weapons of war, and suffer that we may depart into the wilderness ; otherwise we will retain our swords, and we will perish or conquer.</u>" "*Behold, we are not of your faith;*<u>we do not believe that it is God that has delivered us into your hands; but we believe that it is your cunning that has preserved you.</u>" "*And now when Zarahemnah had made an end of speaking these words, Moroni returned the sword and the weapons of war, which he had received, unto Zarahemnah, saying:* **Behold, we will end the conflict.**" *(Alma 44:8-10, Book of Mormon)*

"*Now I cannot recall the words which I have spoken, therefore* **as the Lord liveth, ye shall not depart except ye depart with an oath** <u>**that ye shall not return again against us to war.**</u> **Now as ye are in our hands** <u>**we will spill your blood upon the ground, or ye shall submit to the conditions I have proposed.**</u>" "*And now when Moroni had said these words, Zarahemnah retained his sword, and he was angry with Moroni, and he rushed forward that he might slay Moroni; but as he raised his sword, behold,* <u>one of Moroni's soldiers smote it even to the earth, and it broke by the hilt; and he also smote Zarahemnah that he took off his scalp and it fell to the earth. And Zarahemnah withdrew from before them into the midst of his soldiers[Aztecs].</u>" "*And it came to pass that the [Mayan]soldier who stood by, who smote off the scalp, took it from off the ground by* <u>the hair, and laid it upon the point of his sword, and stretched it forth unto them, saying unto them with a loud voice:</u>" " **Even as this scalp has fallen to the earth, which is the scalp of <u>your chief</u>, so shall ye fall to the** *earth except ye will deliver up your weapons of war and depart with a <u>covenant of peace.</u>"* "Now there were <u>many, when they heard these words and saw the scalp which was upon the sword that they were struck with fear; and many came forth and threw down their weapons of war at the feet of Moroni, and</u> **entered into a covenant of peace.** And as many as entered into a covenant they suffered to depart into the wilderness.*"(Alma 44:11-15, Book of Mormon)*

"Now it came to pass that Zarahemnah was exceedingly wroth, and he did stir up the remainder of his [Lamanite/Aztec] soldiers to anger, to contend more powerfully against the Nephites[Mayans]." "And now Moroni was angry, because of the stubbornness of the Lamanites[Aztecs]; therefore he <u>commanded his people that they should fall upon them and slay them. And it came to pass that they began to slay them; yea, and the Lamanites[Aztecs] did contend with their swords and their might.</u>" "But behold, their <u>naked skins and their bare heads were exposed to the sharp swords of the Nephites[Mayans];</u> yea, behold they were pierced and smitten, yea, and did <u>fall exceedingly fast before the swords of the Nephites[Mayans]; and they began to be swept down, even as the soldier of Moroni had prophesied.</u>" "Now Zarahemnah, when he saw that they were about to be destroyed, cried mightily unto Moroni, promising that he would covenant and also his people[Aztec soldiers] with them, if they would spare their lives, that they **never would come to war again against them.**" *(Alma 44:16-19, Book of Mormon)*

"And it came to pass that Moroni caused that the <u>work of death</u> should cease again among the people. And he took the weapons of war from the Lamanites[Aztec soldiers]; and after they had entered into a covenant with him of peace they were suffered to depart into the wilderness." "Now the <u>number of their[Aztecs] dead was not numbered because of the greatness of the number; yea, the number of</u> their dead was **exceedingly great, both on the Nephites [Mayans] and on the Lamanites [Aztecs].**" "And it came to pass that they did cast their[Aztecs soldiers] dead into the **waters of Sidon**[Rio Magdalena], and they have **gone forth and are buried in the depths of the** sea. [Atlantic Ocean/Carribean]." "And the armies *of the Nephites [Mayans], or of Moroni, returned and came to their houses and their lands." "And thus **ended the eighteenth year of the reign of the judges over the people of Nephi[Mayans].** And thus ended the record of Alma, <u>which was written upon the plates of Nephi.</u>"(Alma 44:20-24, Book of Mormon)*

From the time that Lehi and his family had left Jerusalem, to travel and live in the Americas, and be known as Nephites/Mayans, had now been 528-years, now **72 B.C.**. Alma, the Nephite/Mayan prophet having journeyed towards the land of Melek, had now been taken up to God, like Moses, and has been joined with the Church of the Firstborn in Heaven, beyond the veil.

*"And it came to pass in the nineteenth year of the judges over the people of Nephi[Mayans], that Alma came unto his son Helaman and said unto him: **Believest thou the words which I spake unto thee concerning those records which have been kept?" "And Helaman said unto him: yea, I believe.** " "And Alma said again: **Believest thou in <u>Jesus Christ, who shall come?</u>** " "And he said: **Yea, I believe all the words which thou hast** spoken." "And Alma said unto him again: **Will ye keep my commandments?** " "And he said: **Yea, I will keep thy commandments with all my heart.** " "Then Alma said unto him: **Blessed art thou; and the Lord shall prosper thee in this** land." "**But behold, I have somewhat to prophesy unto thee; but what I prophesy unto thee ye shall not make known; yea, what I prophesy unto thee shall not be made known, even until the prophesy is fulfilled; therefore write the words which I shall say.** " "And these are the words: <u>**Behold, I perceive that this very people, the Nephites**</u> [Mayan people],<u>**according to the spirit of revelation which is in me, in four hundred years from the time that Jesus Christ shall manifest himself unto them, shall dwindle in unbelief.**</u> " "Yea, **and then shall they see wars and pestilences, yea, famines and bloodshed, even until the people of <u>Nephi</u>**[Mayan people]<u>** shall become extinct---**</u> " "(Alma 45:2-11, Book of Mormon)*

★*"Yea, and this because they shall dwindle in unbelief and fall into the <u>works of darkness, and lasciviousness, and all manner of iniquities; yea, I say unto you, that because they shall sin against so great light and knowledge, yea, I say unto you, that from that day, even the fourth generation shall not pass away before this great iniquity shall come.</u>" "And when that great day cometh, **behold, the time very soon cometh that those who are now, or the seed of those who are now numbered among the people of Nephi**[people of Mayans], **shall no more be numbered among the people of Nephi.**" "But whosoever remaineth, <u>and is not destroyed in that great and dreadful day, shall be numbered among the Lamanites</u>[Aztecs], **and shall become like unto them, all, save it be a few who shall be called the disciples of the Lord; <u>and them shall the Lamanites</u>**[Aztecs] **pursue even until they shall become extinct.**" "And <u>now, because of iniquity, this prophesy shall be fulfilled.</u>" (Alma 45:12-14, Book of Mormon)

Even the native American Indians look differently from tribe to tribe. Some have more distinguished features, that if they weren't brown skinned, would look identical to a friend or relative. Even in Mexico today, there are some that have very prominent features. The extinction of the Nephites/Mayans, foretold over 400-years before it happened, as Alma, the Nephite prophet foretells, and explains that there is a cursing or a blessing unto every nation upon this land of the Americas.

★★★*"And now it came to pass that after Alma had said these things to Helaman, he blessed him, and also his other sons; and he also blessed the earth <u>for the righteous sake.</u>" "And he said: **<u>Thus saith the Lord God---Cursed shall be the land, yea, this land, unto every nation, kindred, tongue, and people, unto destruction, which do wickedly, when they are fully ripe; and as I have said so shall it be; for this is the cursing and the blessing of God upon the land, for the Lord cannot look upon sin with the least degree of allowance.</u>**" "And now when Alma had said these words he blessed the church, yea **all those who should stand fast in the faith from that time henceforth.**" "And when Alma had done this he departed *out of the land of Zarahemla, as if to go into the land of* **Melek. And it came to pass that he was** <u>never heard of more; as to his death or burial we know not of</u>*."* *"Behold,* <u>this we know, that he was a righteous man;</u> **and the saying went abroad in the church that he was taken up by the Spirit, or buried by the hand of the Lord, even as Moses. But behold, the scriptures saith the Lord took Moses unto himself;** *and we suppose that he has also received Alma in the spirit, unto himself; therefore, for this cause we know nothing concerning the death and burial."(Alma 45:15-19, Book of Mormon)*

Helaman, the son of Alma became Chief Judge of the Nephites/ Mayans, and began once again to establish the Church of Jesus Christ, and he talks about how quickly through periods of prosperity, how people are so quick to be lifted up because of their riches. They think that they are blessed and favored of God because of their riches and their high learning. What they forget so easily is, that God gives them these special blessings and gifts so that they can help their neighbors, and to see what they will do with their special gifts.

Chapter 12

Secret Societies/Communists Infesting the Mayans & Aztecs

Moroni's war against Amalekiah, the dissenter from the Nephites/Mayans Who conspired to dethrone the Lamanite/Aztec King

"For behold, because of their wars with the Lamanites[Aztecs] and the many little dissensions and disturbances which had been among the people, it became expedient that the <u>word of God should be declared among them,</u> yea, and that a <u>regulation should be made throughout the church.</u>" "Therefore, [Mayan/Nephite prophet] Helaman and his brethren went forth to establish the church again in all the land, yea, in every city throughout all the land which was possessed by the people of Nephi [the Mayans]. And it came to pass that they did appoint <u>priests and teachers throughout all the land, over all the churches."</u> "And now it came to pass that after Helaman and his brethren had appointed priests and teachers over the churches <u>that there arose a dissension[controversy] among them, and they would not give heed to the words of Helaman and his</u> brethren;" "But they[priests and teachers]<u>grew proud, being lifted up in their hearts, because of their exceedingly great riches;</u> therefore they grew rich in their own eyes, and would not give heed to their[Helaman's] words, to walk uprightly before God."(Alma 45:21-24, Book of Mormon)

The people who had gained much through commerce/business, and their higher education believe that they are more entitled to being the elite-class, and begin to conspire to alter the laws to have a king over the people. They turn to a system of force, very like Democracy. Amalickiah was their leader from among the rich, thinking to destroy the Liberty of the people. They remind me of the Democrats today with their Secret Orders, i.e. Illuminatti, Jesuits etc. everyone wants to be rich to the things of the world.

> *"Now the leader of those who were wroth against their brethren was a large and a strong man; and his name was Amalickiah." "And Amalickiah was desirous that he should be their king; and they were the greater[majority] part of them the lower judges of the land, and they were seeking for power." "And they had been led by the flatteries of Amalickiah, that if they would support him and establish him to be their king that he would make them rulers over the people." "Thus they were led away by Amalickiah to dissensions, notwithstanding the preaching of Helaman and his brethren, yea, notwithstanding their exceedingly great care over the church, for they were high priests over the church." "And there were many in the church who believed in the flattering words of Amalickiah, therefore they dissented even from the church; and thus were the affairs of the people of Nephi[Mayans] exceedingly precarious and dangerous, notwithstanding their great victory which they had had over the Lamanites[Aztecs], and their great rejoicings which they had had because of their deliverance by the hand of the Lord." "Thus we see how quick the children of men do forget the Lord their God, yea, how quick to do iniquity, and to be led away by the evil one." (Alma 46:3-8, Book of Mormon)*

> *"Yea, we see that Amalickiah[Mitt Romney]/[Harry Reed]/ [Barack Obama]/[Mike Pence], etc.], because he was a man of cunning device and a man of many flattering words, that he led away the hearts of many people to do wickedly; yea, and to seek to destroy the church of God, **and to destroy the foundation of liberty which God had granted unto them**, or which blessing God had sent upon the face of the land for the righteous sake." "And now it came to pass **when Moroni, who was the chief commander of the armies of the**

Nephites[Mayans], *had heard of these dissensions, he was angry with Amalickiah."(Alma 46:10-11, Book of Mormon)*

Moroni. General of the Nephite/Mayan armies raised up a **Standard of Liberty**, to be raised up on every tower, like our **Flag** over this country. We love our **Star Spangled Banner** in America, And we are firmly against anyone who disrespects it, and seeks to alter our laws, and violate their oaths of office, as we see many people do. Our Constitution is only as strong as those who are entrusted to protect the law, and by keeping their oaths of office.

★★★*"And it came to pass that he[Moroni] rent his coat; and he took a piece thereof, and wrote upon it---**In memory of our God, our religion, and freedom, and our peace, our wives, and our children---and he fastened it upon the end of a pole." "And he fastened on his headplate, and his breatplate, and his shields, and girded on his armor about his loins; and he took the pole, which had on the end thereof his rent coat, (and he called it the title of liberty) and he bowed himself to the earth, and he prayed mightily unto his God for the blessings of liberty to rest upon his brethren, so long as there should be a band of Christians remaining to possess the land---" "For thus were all the true believers of Christ, who belonged to the church of God, called by those who did not belong to the church." "And those who did belong to the church were faithful; yea, all those who were true believers in Christ took upon them, gladly, the name of Christ, or Christians as they were called, because of their belief in Christ who should come." "And therefore, all this time, Moroni prayed that the cause of the Christians, and the freedom of the land might be favored." "And it came to pass that when he had poured out his soul to God, he named all the land which was south of the land Desolation, yea, and in fine, all the land both on the north and on the south---A chosen land, and the land of liberty."* ` (Alma 46:12-17, Book of Mormon)

★★★*"And when Moroni had said these words, he went forth among the people, waving the rent part of his garment in the air, that all might see the writing which he had written upon the rent part, and crying with a loud voice, saying:" "Behold, whosoever will maintain this title upon the land, let them come forth in the strength of the Lord, and enter into a covenant that they will maintain their rights, and their religion, that the Lord God may bless them.*" "*And it came to pass that when Moroni had proclaimed these words, behold, the people came running together with their armor girded about their loins, rending their garments in token, or as a covenant, that they would not forsake the Lord their God; or, in other words, if they should transgress the commandments of God, or fall into transgression, and be ashamed to take upon them the name of Christ, the Lord should rend them even as they had rent their garments.*"(Alma 46:19-21, Book of Mormon)

"*And it came to pass that when Amalickiah saw that the people of Moroni were more numerous than the Amalikiahites---and he also saw that his people were doubtful concerning the justice of the cause in which they had undertaken---therefore, fearing that he should not gain the point, he took those of his people who would and departed into the land of Nephi[Ecuador, Peru].*" "*Now Moroni thought it was not expedient that the Lamanites[Aztecs] should have any more strength; therefore he thought to cut off the people of Amalickiah, or to take them and bring them back, and put Amalickiah to death[for insurrection/ treason]; yea, for he knew that he would stir up the Lamanites[Aztecs] to anger against them, and cause them to come to battle against them; and this he knew that Amalickiah would do that he might obtain his purposes.*"(Alma 46:29-30, Book of Mormon)

In order for liberals/communists to achieve their evil purposes, they stoop to sedition and treason. The freedom of a people is as strong, as those who are elected for this fiduciary position of public-trust, who take their oath of office seriously, when they uphold the Supreme Law of the Land. They covenant to defend it against all enemies, foreign and domestic, instead of taking advantage of the people they are entrusted to protect.

★"*And it came to pass that Amalickiah fled with a small number of his men, and the remainder were delivered up into the hands of Moroni and were taken back into the land of Zarahemla[for military* *tribunal]." "Now, Moroni being a man who was appointed by the chief judges <u>and the voice of the people[elected], therefore</u> he had power[admiralty jurisdiction] according to his will with the <u>armies of the Nephites[Mayans], to establish and to exercise authority over them."</u> "And it came to pass that whosoever of the Amalickiahites that would not enter into a covenant to support the <u>cause of **freedom, that they might maintain a free government,** he caused to be **put to death**</u>. (Alma 46:33-35, Book of Mormon)*

Moroni, upon learning of the situation involving these Kingmen/ liberals. communists, immediately rectified the situation by marching on Zarahemla, to put down the Sedition, as now they were facing an imminent security risk, because they threatened to join with their enemies, the Lamanites[Aztecs]. Those who wouldn't support Freedom, were put to death. Therefore, the people were obliged to hoist upon every tower in the land, the title of Liberty[Flag]. Thus ended the year of **72 B.C.**

*"And it came to pass also, that he[Moroni] caused the **title of liberty**[flag] <u>to be hoisted upon every tower which was in the land, which was possessed by the Nephites[Mayans]; and thus **Moroni planted the standard of liberty among the Nephites**[Mayans]."</u> "And they began to have **peace again in the land;** and thus they did maintain peace in the land until nearly the **end of the nineteenth year**[72 B.C.] **of the reign of the judges."**(Alma 46:36-37, Book of Mormon)*

Communists/Liberals commit treachery among themselves for profit, to get power and riches, even if they have to kill each other to accomplish their evil tasks. Just look upon what is going on in our own government in 2023, in the United States of America. As Solomon says: *"There is nothing new under the sun"*.

"Now we will return in our record to <u>Amalickiah</u> and those who had fled with him into the wilderness; for, behold, <u>he had taken those who went with him, and went up into the land of Nephi among the Lamanites</u>[Aztecs], and did stir up the Lamanites[Aztecs], to anger

*against the people of Nephi[Mayans], insomuch that the king of the Lamanites[Aztecs] sent a <u>proclamation</u> throughout all the land, among his people, that they should gather themselves together again to go to battle against the Nephites[Mayans]." "And it came to pass that when the <u>proclamation</u> had gone forth among them they were <u>exceedingly afraid; yea, they feared to displease the king, and they also feared to go to battle against the Nephites[Mayans]</u> **lest they should <u>lose their lives.</u>** And it came to pass that they would not, or the more part of them would not, obey the commandments of the king." "And now it came to pass that the king was wroth because of their disobedience; therefore <u>he gave Amalickiah the command of that[woke] part of his army which was obedient unto his commands, and commanded him that he should go forth **and compel them to arms.**</u>" "Now behold, this was the desire of Amalickiah; for he being a very **subtle man to do evil** therefore he laid the plan in his heart to <u>dethrone the king of the Lamanites[Aztecs].</u>" "And now he had got the command of those parts of the Lamanites[Aztecs] who were in favor of the king[fellow liberals]; and he sought to gain favor of those who were not obedient; therefore he went forward to the place which was **<u>Onidah</u>**, for thither had all the Lamanites[Aztecs] fled; for they discovered the army coming, and supposing that they were coming to destroy them, therefore they fled to Onidah, to the <u>place of arms.</u>" (Alma 47:1-5, Book of Mormon)*

To a Communist/Liberal, treason was common-place, and to be expected, as Satan is their god, as it was to Amalickiah in the place of arms at Antipas. This was where the Lamanites/Aztecs were gathered to resist the king's woke military, that was wanting to force them to lay down their lives for this unjust cause, of fighting the Nephites/Mayans for no apparent good reason. They knew to go against the Nephites/ Mayans in this situation, was an almost 100% guarantee that they would lose their lives, whereas, they had a better chance of survival if they resisted the orders of a dictatorial/liberal king.

"And they had appointed a man to be their king and a leader over them, being <u>fixed in their minds with a determined resolution that they would not be subjected to go against the Nephites[Mayans].</u>" "And it came to pass that they had gathered themselves together upon the

top of the mount which was called <u>Antipas,</u> in preparation to battle." "Now it was not Amalickiah's intention to give them battle according to the commandments of the king; but behold, it was his intention to gain favor with the armies of the Lamanites[Aztecs], that he might place himself at the head and dethrone the king and take possession of the kingdom." "And behold, it came to pass that he caused his army to pitch their tents in the valley which was near the <u>mount Antipas.</u>" "And when it was night he sent a <u>secret embassy</u> into the mount Antipas, desiring that the leader of those who were upon the mount, whose name was <u>Lehonti</u>, that he should come down to the foot of the mount, for he desired to speak with him."(Alma 47:6-10, Book of Mormon)

"And it came to pass that when Lehonti received the message he durst not go down to the foot of the mount. And it came to pass that Amalickiah sent again the second time, desiring him to come down. And it came to pass that Lehonti would not; and he sent again the third time." "And it came to pass that when Amalickiah found that he could not get Lehonti to come down from off the mount, he went up into the mount, nearly to Lehonti's camp, and he sent again the fourth time his message unto Lehonti, desiring that he would come down, and that he would bring his guards with him." "And it came to pass that when Lehonti had come down with his guards to Amalickiah, that Amalickiah desired him to come down with his army in the night-time, and surround those men in their camps over whom the king had given him command, and that he would deliver them up into Lehonti's hands, <u>if he would make him (Amalickiah) a second leader over the whole army.</u>" "(Alma :47:11-13, Book of Mormon)

"And it came to pass that Lehonti came down with his men and surrounded the men of Amalickiah, so that before they awoke at the dawn of day they were surrounded by the armies of Lehonti." "And it came to pass that when they saw that they were surrounded, they plead with Amaleckiah that he would suffer them to fall in with their brethren, that they might not be destroyed. Now this was the very thing which Amaleckiah desired, that he might accomplish his designs in <u>dethroning the king</u>" "And now it was the custom among the Lamanites[Aztecs],

if their chief leader was killed, to appoint <u>the second leader to be their chief leader.</u>" "And it came to pass that Amalickiah caused that one of his servants should <u>administer poison by degrees to Lehonti, that he died</u>." "Now, when Lehonti was dead, the Lamanites[Aztecs] appointed Amalickiah to be their <u>leader and chief commander</u>." "And it came to pass that Amalickiah, marched with his armies(for he had gained his desires) to the land of Nephi, to the city of Nephi, which was the chief city." (Alma 47:14-20, Book of Mormon)

"And the king[of the Lamanites/Aztecs] came out to meet him with his guards, for he supposed that Amalickiah had fulfilled his commands, and that Amalickiah had gathered together so great an army to go against the Nephites[Mayans] to battle." "But behold, as the king came out to meet him Amalickiah caused that his servants should go forth to meet the king, <u>as if to reverence him because of his greatness.</u>" "And it came to pass that the king put forth his hand to raise them, as was the custom with the Lamanites[Aztecs], as a token of peace, which <u>custom they had taken from the Nephites[Mayans].</u>" "And it came to pass that when he had raised the first from the ground, <u>behold he stabbed the king to the heart;</u> and he fell to the earth." "Now the servants of the <u>king fled;</u> and the servants of Amalickiah raised a cry, saying:" " Behold, the <u>servants of the king have stabbed him to the heart, and he has fallen and they have fled; behold, come and see.</u>"(Alma 47:21-26, Book of Mormon)

"And it came to pass that Amalickiah commanded that his armies should march forth and see what had happened to the king; and when they had come to the spot, and found the king <u>lying in his gore</u>, Amalickiah pretended to be wroth, and said:<u>whosoever loved the king, let him go forth, and pursue his servants that they may be slain.</u>" "And it came to pass that all they who loved the king, when they heard these words, came forth and pursued after the servants of the king." "Now when the servants of the king saw an army pursuing after them, they were frightened again, and fled into the wilderness, and came over into the <u>land of Zarahemla and joined the people of Ammon.</u>" "And the army which pursued after them returned, having pursued after them in vain; <u>and thus Amalickiah, **by his fraud, gained the hearts of**</u>

the people." "*And it came to pass on the morrow he entered the city Nephi with his armies, and took possession of the city.*"*(Alma 47:27-31, Book of Mormon)*

"*And now it came to pass that the <u>queen,</u> when she had heard that the king was slain---for Amalickiah had sent an embassy <u>to the queen informing her that the king had been slain by his servants, that he had pursued them with his army, but it was in vain, and they had made their escape---</u>*" "*Therefore, when the queen had received this message she sent unto Amalickiah, desiring that he would spare the people of the city; and she also desired him that he should come in unto her; and she <u>also desired him that he should bring witnesses with him to testify concerning the death of the king.</u>*" "*And it came to pass that Amalickiah took the <u>same servant that slew the king, and all them who were with him</u>[his bunch of Democrat liars], and went in unto the queen, unto the place where she sat; and they all testified[lied under oath] unto her that the king was slain by his own servants; and they said also: They have fled; does this not testify against them? And thus they <u>satisfied the queen concerning the death of the king.</u>*" "*And it came to pass that Amalickiah sought the favor of the queen, <u>and took her unto him to wife;</u> **and thus by his fraud,** <u>and by the assistance of his cunning servants,</u> **he obtained the kingdom**<u>; yea, he was acknowledged king throughout the land, among the people of the Lamanites</u>[Aztecs], who were composed of the Lamanites and the Lemuelites and the Ishmaelites, and all the **dissenters** of the Nephites[Mayans], from the reign of Nephi[first Mayan king]down to the present time.*" *(Alma 47:32-35, Book of Mormon)*

"*Now these dissenters, having the same instruction and the same information of the Nephites[Mayans], yea, having been instructed in the same knowledge of the Lord, nevertheless, it is strange to relate, not long after their dissensions they became **more hardened and impenitent, and more wild, wicked and ferocious than the Lamanites[Aztecs]-** --drinking in with the traditions of the Lamanites[Aztecs]; giving way <u>to indolence, and all manner of lasciviousness; yea, entirely forgetting the Lord their God.</u>*"*(Alma 47:36, Book of Mormon)*

Now doesn't this sound just like what took place in the election of 2020? It is not enough for a Communist/Liberal to have just a little power, but a Communist/liberal can never get enough power or money. They are unrestrained as to the means of acquiring their ambitions, because they ignore God and his commandments. They would rather go backwards into outer darkness, than go towards the truth. It amazes me that Anti-Christian mentalities can be so stupid as to think that all of the power that can be had by them, still is owned by that God who gave them life. When they die, they surely cannot take their power and possessions with them.

> *"And thus he[Amalickiah] did inspire their hearts against the Nephites[Mayans], insomuch that in the latter end of the <u>nineteenth year of the reign of the judges,</u> he having accomplished his designs thus far, yea, having been made king over the Lamanites[Aztecs], he[Amalickiah] sought also to reign <u>over all the land, yea, and all the people who were in the land, the Nephites</u>[Mayans] as well as the Lamanites[Aztecs]." "Therefore he had accomplished his **design,** for he had hardened the hearts of the Lamanites[Aztecs] and **blinded their minds,** and stirred them up to anger, insomuch that he had gathered together a numerous host to go to battle[for no provocation] against the Nephites[Mayans]." "For he was determined, because of the greatness of the number of his people, to overpower the Nephites[Mayans] and to bring them into **bondage.**" "Now it came to pass that while Amalickiah **<u>had thus been obtaining power by fraud and deceit, Moroni on the other hand, had been preparing the minds of the people to be faithful unto the Lord their God.</u>"**(Alma 48:2-4, 7,, Book of Mormon)*

Moroni was a man who loved his God, his country, and his fellow man. He was up and preparing his fortifications, and staying upon God, and obeying his commandments. Who do you think in a situation such as this, will God bless and preserve. God is real, and he is going to favor his people to show the world that he can and will favor those who rely upon him despite the odds against them.

***"And Moroni **was a strong and mighty man;** *he was a man of perfect understanding; yea, a man that did not delight in bloodshed;* **a man whose soul did joy in the liberty and the freedom of his country, and his brethren from bondage and slavery;**" "*Yea, a man whose heart did swell with thanksgiving to his God, for the many privileges and blessings which he bestowed upon his people; a man who did labor for the welfare and* **safety of his people.**" "*Yea, and he was a man who was firm* **in the faith of Christ, and he had sworn with an oath to defend his** *people[against all enemies, foreign and domestic],* **his rights, and his country, and his religion, even to the loss of his blood.**" "*Now the Nephites[Mayans] were taught to defend* *themselves against their enemies, even to the shedding of blood if necessary; yea, and they were also taught never to give an offense, yea, and never to raise the sword except it were against an enemy, except it were to preserve their lives.*" "*And thus was their faith, that by so doing* **God would prosper them in the land,** *or in other words, if they were faithful in keeping the commandments of God that he would prosper them in the land; yea, warn them to flee, or to prepare for war, according to their danger;*"… "*Yea, verily, verily I say unto you,* **if all men had been, and were, and ever would be, like unto Moroni, behold, the very powers of hell would have been shaken forever; yea, the devil would never have power over the hearts of the children of men.**" **(Alma** *48: 11-15, 17, Book of Mormon)*

Moroni caused his men and anyone who could, and would help, to fortify the Nephite/Mayan cities, in order to more easily be defended. He caused earth to be heaped up around about them. For all of these reasons, arrogant, Amalickiah swore to drink Moroni's blood. Amalickiah, himself used to be Christian, and at one time had tasted the tender mercies of God himself, but he can't pursue his vain ambitions for power and riches in good conscience while he is a Christian. He has to defy God, and take it out on Moroni, he supposes.

*"Behold, I said that the city of **Ammonihah** had been rebuilt. I say unto you, yea, that it was in part rebuilt; and because the Lamanites[Aztecs] had destroyed it once because of the iniquity of the people, they supposed that it would be an easy prey for them."*

*"But behold, how great was their disappointment; for behold, the Nephites[Mayans] had dug up a <u>ridge of earth round about them, which was so high that the Lamanites[Aztecs] could not cast their stones and their arrows at them that they might take effect, neither could they come upon them save it was by their place of entrance.</u>" "Now at this time the chief captains of the Lamanite[Aztecs] were astonished exceedingly, because of the **wisdom of the Nephites**[Mayans] in preparing their places of security." "Now the leaders of the Lamanites[Aztecs] had supposed, because of the greatness of their numbers, yea, they supposed that they should be privileged to come[waltz in] upon them as they had hitherto done; yea, and they had also prepared themselves with shields, and with breastplates;and they had prepared themselves with garments of skins, yea, very thick garments to cover their nakedness."(Alma 49:3-6, Book of Mormon)*

*"And being thus prepared they supposed that they should easily overpower and subject their brethren to the <u>yoke of bondage, or slay and massacre them according to their pleasure.</u>." "But behold, to their uttermost astonishment, they were prepared for them, in a manner which never had been known among the children of Lehi. Now they were prepared for the Lamanites[Aztecs], to battle after <u>the manner of the instructions of Moroni.</u>" "And it came to pass that the Lamanites[Aztecs], or the Amalickiahites, were exceedingly astonished at their manner of preparation for war." "Now, if king Amalickiah had come **down** out of the land of Nephi, at the head of his army, perhaps he would have caused the Lamanites[Aztecs] to have attacked the Nephites[Mayans] at the city of Ammonihah; for behold, <u>he did care not for the blood of his people[the means justifies the end to a communist].</u>" (Alma 49:7-10, Book of Mormon)*

*"But behold, Amalickiah did not come down himself to battle. And behold, his chief captains durst not attack the Nephites[Mayans] at the city of Ammonihah, <u>for Moroni had altered the management of affairs among the Nephites[Mayans], insomuch that the Lamanites[Aztecs] were disappointed in their places of retreat and they could not come upon them.</u>" "Therefore they retreated into the wilderness, and took their camp and marched towards the **land of Noah**, supposing that to*

be the next best place for them to come against the Nephites[Mayans]." "For they knew not that Moroni had fortified, or had built forts of security, for every city in all the land round about; therefore, they marched forward to the land of Noah with a firm determination; yea, their chief captains came forward and took an oath that they would destroy the people of that city." "But behold, to their astonishment, the city of **Noah**, which had hitherto been a weak place, had now, by the means of Moroni, become strong, yea, even to exceed the strength of the city of Ammonihah." "And now, behold, this was wisdom in Moroni; for he had supposed that they would be frightened at the city of Ammonihah; and as the city of **Noah** had hitherto been the weakest part of the land, therefore they would march thither to battle; and thus it was according to his desires...."(Alma 49:11-15, Book of Mormon)

"Now behold, the Lamanites[Aztecs] could not get into their forts of security by any other way save by the entrance, because of the highness of the bank which had been thrown up, and the depth of the ditch which had been dug round about, save it were by the entrance." "And thus were the Nephites[Mayans] prepared to destroy all such as should attempt to climb up to enter the fort by any other way, by casting over stones and arrows at them." "Thus they were prepared, yea, a body of their strongest men, with their swords and their slings, to smite down all who should attempt to come into their place of security by the place of entrance; and thus they were prepared to defend themselves against the Lamanites[Aztecs]." (Alma 49:18-20, Book of Mormon)

"Now when they found that they could not obtain power over the Nephites[Mayans] by the pass, they began to dig down their banks of earth that they might obtain a pass to their armies, that they might have an equal chance to fight; but behold, **in these attempts they were swept off by the stones and arrows which were thrown at them;** instead of filling up their ditches by pulling down the banks of earth, they were filled up in measure with their dead and wounded bodies." "Thus the Nephites[Mayans] had all power over their enemies;and thus the Lamanites[Aztecs] did attempt to destroy the Nephites[Mayans] until their chief captains were all slain; yea, and more than a thousand of the Lamanites[Aztecs]were slain; while on the other hand, **not one single** *soul of the Nephites[Mayans] which was slain." "There were about fifty who were wounded, who had been exposed to the arrows of the Lamanites[Aztecs]through the pass, but they were shielded by their shields, and their breatplates, and their head-plates, insomuch that <u>their wounds were upon their legs, many of which were very severe." "(Alma 49: 22-24,Book of Mormon)*

*"And it came to pass, that when the Lamanites[Aztecs] saw that their chief captains were all slain they fled into the wilderness. And it came to pass that <u>they returned to the land of Nephi, to inform their king, Amalickiah,</u> **who was a Nephite[Mayan]** by birth, concerning their great loss." "And it came to pass that he was exceedingly angry with his people, because he had not obtained his desire over the Nephites[Mayans]; **he had not subjected them to the yoke of bondage."** "Yea, he was exceedingly wroth **, and he did curse God, and also Moroni, swearing with an oath that he would drink his blood; and this because Moroni had kept the commandments of God in preparing for the safety of his** people." "And it came to pass, that on the other hand, **the people of Nephi**[Mayan people] did thank the Lord their God, because **of his matchless power in delivering them from the hands of their enemies."(Alma 49:25-28, Book of Mormon)*

Moroni made more preparations by heaping up more earth around all vulnerable cities, and had built upon the mounds, breastworks. He knew it was inevitable that Amalickiah would try again to subject his people, so he was diligent in his preparedness.

"And it came to pass that Moroni did not stop making preparations for war, or to defend his people[the Mayans] against the Lamanites[Aztecs]; for he caused that his armies should commence in the <u>commencement of the twentieth year of the reign of the judges,</u> that they should commence in digging up heaps of earth round about all the cities, throughout all the land which was possessed by the Nephites[Mayans]." "And upon the top of these <u>ridges of earth he caused that there should be timbers, yea, works of timbers built up to the height of a man,</u> round about the cities." "And he caused that upon those works of timbers there should be a frame of pickets built upon

the timbers round about; and they were <u>strong and high.</u>" "And he caused <u>towers to be erected that overlooked those works of pickets, and he caused places of security to be built upon those towers, that the stones and the arrows of the Lamanites</u>[Aztecs] could not hurt them." "And they were prepared that they could cast stones from the <u>top thereof, according to their pleasure and their strength, and slay him who should attempt to approach near the walls of the city.</u>" "Thus Moroni did prepare strongholds against the coming of their enemies, round about every city in all the land."(Alma 50:1-6, Book of Mormon)

Moroni then made any encroaching Lamanites/Aztecs, get back into the borders of their own lands, and back into their south country, for security reasons, as now the Nephites/Mayans were at war with the Lamanites/Aztecs. This ended the 21st year of the reign of the Judges. Thus, ended the year of **70 B.C.**

*"And it came to pass that Moroni caused that his armies should go forth into the **east wilderness; yea, and they went forth and <u>drove all the Lamanites</u>**[Aztecs]<u> who were in the east wilderness into their own lands,</u> **which were south of the land of Zarahemla**." "And the land of Nephi did run in a <u>straight course from the sea east to the sea west.</u>" "And it came to pass that when Moroni had driven all the Lamanites[Aztecs] out of the east wilderness, which was north of the lands of their own possessions , he caused that the inhabitants who were in the land of Zarahemla and in the land round about should go forth into the east wilderness, even to the borders by the seashore, and possess the land. " "And he also placed armies on the south, in the borders of their possessions, and caused them to erect fortifications that they might secure their armies and their people from the hands of their enemies." "And thus he cut off all the strongholds of the Lamanites[Aztecs] in the east wilderness, yea, and also on the west,fortifying the line between the Nephites[Mayans] and the Lamanites[Aztecs] between the land of **Zarahemla** and the land of Nephi, from the **west sea**, running by the head of the **river Sidon**[Rio Magdalena]---the Nephites[Mayans] possessing all the **land northward of the land Bountiful,** <u>according to their pleasure.</u>" (Alma 50:7-11, Book of Mormon)*

Thus Moroni, with his [Mayan]armies, which did increase daily because of the assurance of protection which his works did bring forth unto them, <u>did seek to cut off the strength and the power of the Lamanites[Aztecs]</u> from off the lands of their possessions, that they should have no power upon the lands of their possession." "And the Nephites[Mayans] began the foundation of a city, and <u>they called the name of the city</u> **Moroni***; and it was by the east sea; and it was on the south by the line of the possessions of the Lamanites[Aztecs]." "And they also began a foundation for a city between the city of* **Moroni** *and the city of* **Aaron***, joining the borders of Aaron and Moroni; and they called the name of the city, or the* **land, Nephihah.***" "And they also began in that same year to <u>build many cities on the north, one in a particular manner which they called</u>* **Lehi,** *<u>which was in the north by the borders of the seashore.</u>" "And thus ended the* **twentieth year***." "And in these* **prosperous circumstances were the people of Nephi[Mayans] in the commencement of the twenty and first year of the reign of the judges over the people of Nehi***[Mayans]."(Alma 50:12-17, Book of Mormon)*

The next 4-years was dedicated by Moroni and the military in establishing new cities, as strategically placed bastions, or forts for growth and defensive purposes. Thus passed **67 B.C.**, Then liberals had to rear their evil, selfish, ugly heads, in the need of more power, riches and control, thus bringing on more war and bloodshed, and misery.

"And it came to pass that in the <u>commencement of the twenty and fourth year of the reign of the judges</u>, there would also have been peace among the people of Nephi[Mayan people] had it not been for a <u>contention</u> which took place among them concerning <u>the land of Lehi, and the land of Morianton,</u> which joined upon the borders of Lehi; both of which were on the borders by the seashore." "For behold, the people who possessed the land of **Morianton** *did claim a part of the land of Lehi; therefore there began to be a <u>warm contention</u> between them, insomuch that the people of Morianton <u>took up arms</u> against their brethren, and they were determined by the sword to slay them." "But behold, the people who possessed the land of Lehi fled to the*

*camp of Moroni, and appealed unto him for assistance; **for behold they were not in the wrong.**" "And it came to pass that when the people of Morianton, who were led by a man whose name was Morianton, found that the people of Lehi had fled to the camp of Moroni, they were exceedingly fearful the army of Moroni should come upon them and destroy them." "Therefore, Morianton put it into the their hearts that they should flee to the **land which was northward** [North America], **which was covered with large bodies of water, and take possession of the land which was northward.**" "And behold, they would have carried this plan into effect, (which would have been a cause to have been lamented) but behold, Morianton being a man of much passion[had a very hot temper], therefore he was angry with one of his maid servants, and he fell upon her and beat her much." (Alma 50:25-32, Book of Mormon)*

*"And it came to pass that she fled, and came over to the [Mayan general's] **camp of Moroni, ,** and told Moroni all things concerning the matter, **and also concerning their intentions to flee into the land northward.**" "Now behold, the people who were in the land **Bountiful, or rather, Moroni,** feared that they would hearken to the words of Morianton and unite with his people, **and thus he would obtain possession of those parts of the land, which would lay a foundation for serious consequences among the people of Nephi**[Mayans], **yea, which consequences would lead to the overthrow of their**[the Mayan people's] **liberty.**" "Therefore Moroni sent an army, with their camp, to head the people of Morianton, to stop their flight **into the land northward.**" "And it came to pass that they did not head them[intercept] until they had come to the borders of the **land Desolation; and there they did head them, by the narrow pass which led by the sea into the land northward, yea, by the sea, on the west, and on the east.**" "And it came to pass that the army which was sent by Moroni, which was led by a man whose name was **Teancum,** did meet the people of **Morianton;** and so stubborn were the people of Morianton, (being inspired by his flattering words) that a battle commenced between them, in the which Teancum did slay Morianton and defeat his army, and took them prisoners, and returned to the camp of Moroni. **And thus ended the twenty and fourth***

year of the judges over the people of Nephi*[Mayan people]." (Alma 50:33-35, Book of Mormon)* Now **the end of <u>67 B.C.,</u>**

As it is in our day, for everyone who is placed or elected into a position of public trust, to covenant with an *"oath of affirmation"* to protect their countries laws, from the common notary republic, the military, state and local government officials, including judges, all the way up to the President of the United States, so it was with the Nephites/Mayans. Their judges took an oath of office to uphold their laws and defend their freedom, from <u>all enemies foreign and domestic</u>. The ten commandments were embodied into their laws, even as our laws embody the true principle on how to judge and protect each other, under the Constitution. The Nephites/Mayans had and practiced <u>Common-Law,</u> plain and simple, and they stood by it.

What has happened to our American-Republic? Why do we have so many foreign and domestic enemies walking our streets? Why isn't Joe Biden etc., upholding their oaths of office to defend our liberty? Why didn't Mike Pence defend our liberty, after him swearing an oath to defend the Constitution from "...all enemies foreign and domestic...", then give our communist enemies access to the government without so much as an argument? If he was keeping his oath he would have done anything, but allow the liberals to destroy our country. He had it in his power, but he dropped the ball.

> *"Behold, it came to pass that the <u>son of Nephihah was appointed to fill the judgment-seat, in the stead of his father; yea, he was appointed</u>* ***chief judge and governor over the people*** *[Mayans],* ***with an oath and sacred ordinance to judge righteously, and to keep the peace and the freedom of the people, and to grant unto them their sacred privileges to worship the Lord their God, yea, to support and maintain the cause of God in all his days, and to bring the wicked to justice according to their crime."*** *"Now behold, his name was* **Pahoran** *[chief Mayan judge]......"(Alma 50:39-40, Book of Mormon)*

All public servants, and the laws of the government, were all voted on, and upheld by the voice of the people. All government employees, elected or appointed, must swear to uphold the Constitution as their first contract, and to honor and protect it against all enemies foreign and domestic. Most of our enemies in this country are domestic, especially those Democrats/liberals, and others who all must take the oath, and have it filed in the county where they are employed, with the clerk of the Recorder's office, all the way down to the Public Notary. The sad thing is, that many of these public servants are the ones who are stretching that fine thread by violating their oaths of office, and violating the rights of the people they are supposed to protect. You can see it every day, or read about in the papers, about police brutality, Crooked officials in all levels are getting rich at the expense of their employers, we the people. Examples are too innumerable to mention, and ongoing.

"Therefore, those who were desirous that the law should be altered were angry with him[Pahoran/Donald J. Trump], and desired that he should no longer be chief judge over the land; therefore there arose a warm dispute concerning the matter, but not unto bloodshed." "And it came to pass that those who were desirous that Pahoran[Donald J. Trump] should be dethroned from the judgment-seat were called __king-men[Democrats]__, for they were desirous that the __law should be altered in a manner to overthrow the free government and to establish a king over the land.__" "And those who were desirous that Pahoran[Donald J. Trump] __should remain chief judge over the land took upon them the name of freemen[Conservatives];__ and thus was the division among them, for the freemen[conservatives/sons and daughters of God] had sworn or covenanted to maintain their rights[common-law] and the privileges of their religion[1st Amendment] by a free government[Republic]." "And it came to pass that this matter of their contention was __settled by the voice of the people.__ And it came to pass that the voice of the people came in favor of the freemen, and Pahoran[Donald J. Trump] retained the judgment-seat, which caused much rejoicing among the brethren of Pahoran and also __many of the people of liberty,__ who also put the king-men[Democrats/liberals/communists/goats] to silence, that they durst not oppose but were obliged to maintain __the cause of freedom.__" "Now those who were in favor of kings __were those of high birth[rich],__ and they sought to be kings[with titles of nobility]; and

*they were supported by those who sought **power and authority over the people.**" (Alma 51:4-8, Book of Mormon)*

Communists/liberals think they are the elite and of high birth, and think to alter the laws of the land, in order to achieve their purpose of control, and to get rich. They call their system "Democracy", and back then, was the same as it is today, just different terms, or names. The liberals during the Nephite/Mayan and Lamanite/Aztec days are exactly the same as it was then, except bloodshed was spilled at the point of a sword, whereas today, the liberals/Communists actually have made greater headway in the form of altering the laws under Uniform Commercial Codes.

"But behold, This was a **critical time for such contentions to be among the [Mayan] people of Nephi;** for behold, [communist/liberal] Amalickiah had again stirred up the hearts of the **Lamanites**[Aztecs] against the **people of the** Nephites[Mayans], and he was gathering together soldiers from all parts of his land, and arming them , and preparing them, and preparing for war with all diligence; **for he had sworn to drink the blood of Moroni.**" "But behold, **we shall see that his promise which he made** was **rash;** nevertheless, he did prepare himself and his armies to come to battle against the [Mayans] Nephites." "Now his armies were not so great as they had hitherto been, because of the many thousands[of Aztecs] who had been **slain by the hand of the Nephites[Mayans];** but notwithstanding[despite] their great loss, Amalickiah had gathered a wonderfully great army. Insomuch that he feared not to come **down to the land of Zarahemla**[out of Ecuador, Peru. Southern Colombia, Bolivia/land of Nephi]." "Yea, even Amalickiah did himself **come down,** at the head of the **Lamanites**[Aztecs]. And it was in the twenty and fifth year**[66 B.C.]** of the reign of the judges;and it was at the same time that they had begun to settle the affairs of their contentions concerning the chief judge, Pahoran."(Alma 51:9-12, Book of Mormon)

***"And it came to pass that when the men **who were called king-men** [liberals/Democrats/communist-bastards] had heard that the **Lamanites**[Aztecs] **were coming down to battle**[invading] they *were glad in their hearts; and would not take up arms, for they were wroth with the chief judge, and also **with the people[loyal to freedom] of liberty**, that they would not take up arms to **defend their country.**" "And it came to pass that **when Moroni saw** this, and also that the Lamanites[Aztecs] were coming into the borders of the land, he was exceedingly wroth because of the stubbornness of those people whom he had labored with so much diligence to preserve; yea, he was exceedingly wroth[disgusted]; his soul was filled with anger against them." "And it came to pass that he[Moroni] sent a **petition, with the voice of the people, unto the governor of the land,** desiring that he should read it, and give him(Moroni) power to compel those dissenters[seditionists/rebels] **to defend their country or to put them to death.**" "**For it was his first care to put an end to such contentions and dissensions among the people; for behold, this had been hitherto a cause of all their destruction. And it came to pass that it was granted according to the voice of the people.**"(Alma 51:13-16, Book of Mormon)*

***"And it came to pass that **Moroni commanded that his army should go against those king-men, to pull down their pride and their "nobility", and level them with the earth, or they should take up arms and support the cause of liberty**." "And it came to pass that the **armies did march forth against them; and they did pull down their pride and their "nobility", insomuch that as they did lift their weapons of war to fight against the men of Moroni they were hewn down and leveled to the earth.**" "And it came to pass that there were **four thousand of those dissenters who were** hewn[chopped] down by the sword; and those of their **leaders who were** not slain in battle were taken **and cast into prison,** for there was no time for **their trials at this period.**"(Alma 51:17-19, Book of Mormon)*

Military law or Admiralty Law was used for bringing those who commit Sedition, and Treason, to justice and as a means of compelling such to change or be destroyed(hung, executed any way whatsoever etc.) because of the "security risks to the country if such high crimes were not addressed. In cases of law of the Sea, "Merchant Law"upon the high seas, the captain, commodore, admiral etc. has absolute jurisdiction to enforce this system of judgment upon the high seas of commerce, and in the military. As does the President of the United States, who has jurisdiction of Maritime Law in Washington D.C., and all territories of the United States, Corporation.

"And the remainder of those **dissenters[seditionists], rather than be **smitten down to the earth by the sword, yielded to the standard of liberty, and were compelled to hoist the title of liberty upon their towers, and in their cities, and to take up arms in defence of their country.**" "And thus **Moroni put an end to those king-men**[liberal/communist-bastards], **that were not any known by the apellation of king-men;** and thus he put an end to the stubbornness and the pride **of those people**[Mayans] **who professed the blood of nobility;** but they were brought down to humble themselves like unto their brethren, and to fight valiantly for their **freedom** from bondage." **(Alma** 51:20-21, Book of Mormon)

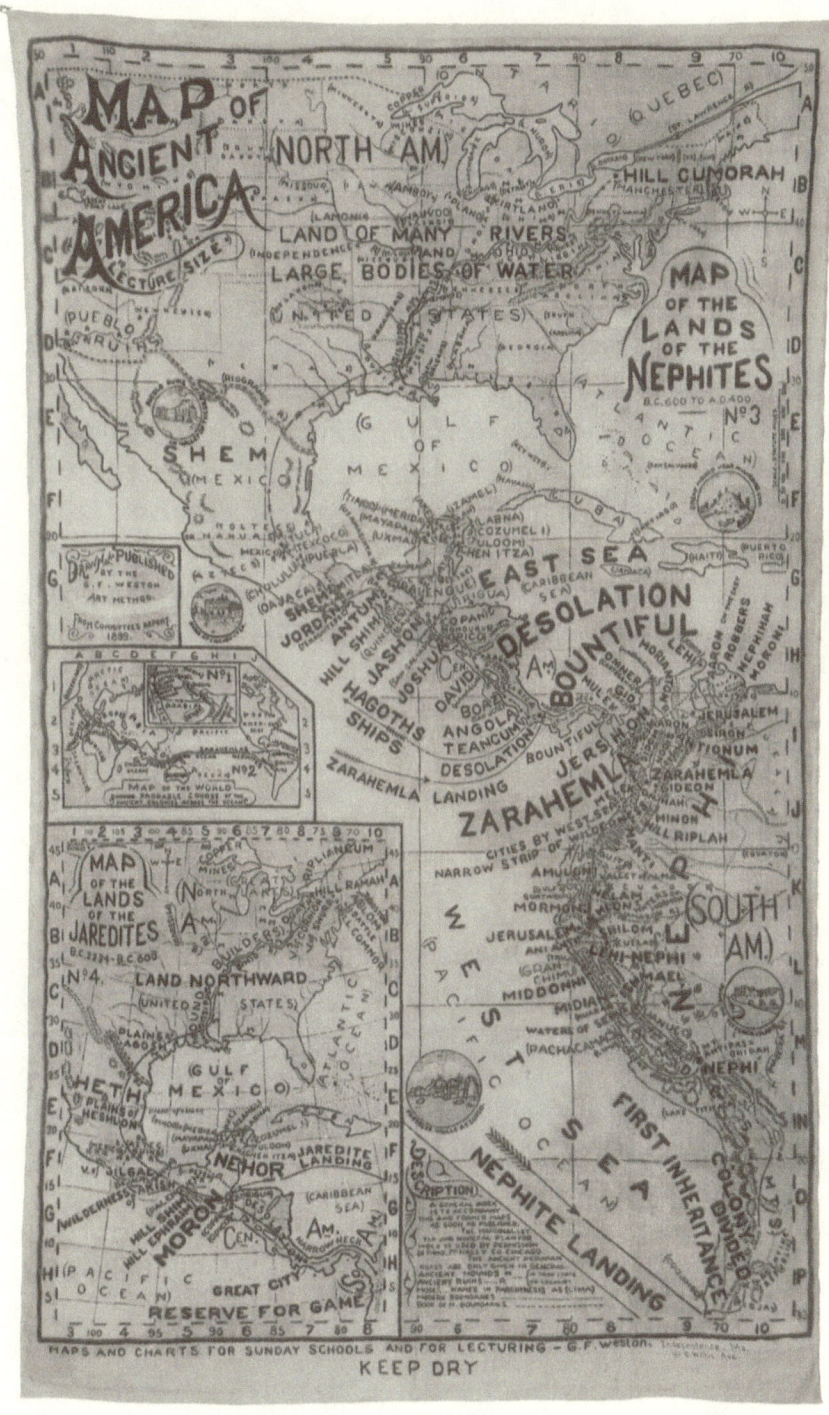

There were more wars between the Nephites/Mayans and the Lamanites/Aztecs, as Amaleckiah and his people dissented over to the Lamanites/Aztecs looking for revenge, and wanting to bring the Nephites/Mayans into subjection. He devises a plan to get control of the whole kingdom of the Lamanites/Aztecs, by having the king killed and then marrying the Queen. When he achieved his goals, he then returned to make war with his own people, the Nephites/Mayans.

*"And it came to pass that the Nephites[Mayans] were not sufficiently strong in the city of **Moroni**; therefore Amalickiah[Lamanite/ Aztecs] did drive them[the Nephites/Mayans], **slaying many.** And it came to pass that Amalickiah <u>took possession of all their fortifications.</u>" "And those who fled out of the city of **Moroni** came to the city of **Nephihah;** and also the people of the city of **Lehi** gathered themselves together, and made preparations and **were ready to receive the <u>Lamanites</u>[Aztecs] <u>to battle.</u>**" "And it came to pass that <u>Amalickiah</u> would not suffer the <u>Lamanites</u>[Aztecs] to go against the city of <u>Nephihah</u> to battle, but kept them down by the seashore, leaving men in every city to maintain and defend it." "And thus, <u>he</u> [Amalickiah] went on, **<u>taking possession of many cities, the city</u> <u>of Nephihah,</u>** and the city of **Lehi,** and the city of **Morianton,** and the city of **Omner,** and the city of **Gid,** and the city of **Mulek,** all of which <u>were on the</u> **east borders by the seashore.**" "And thus had the **Lamanites obtained <u>by the cunning of Amalickiah, so many</u> <u>cities,</u>** <u>by their numberless hosts,</u> **<u>all of which were strongly fortified</u> <u>after the manner of the fortifications of Moroni; all of which</u> <u>afforded strongholds for the Lamanites.</u>**" "And it came to pass that **<u>they</u>** [Amalickiah and his Lamanite armies, Aztecs]**<u>marched to the</u> <u>borders of the land Bountiful</u>**[where Christ later came and visited], **<u>driving the Nephites</u>**[Mayans] **<u>before them and slaying many.</u>**" (Alma 51:23-28, Book of Mormon)*

Amalickiah went conquering down along the seashore, going from city to city, until he came to Bountiful, where he and his men were headed off by Teancum and his army. Bountiful, was situated in the area at the mouth of the narrow neck of land, leading west, across to the land northward. Teancum is angry at Amalickiah for his ambitions to put the Nephites/Mayans into subjection and make them slaves. Teancum knows that it is an unnecessary and an evil thing that Amalickiah is doing, causing so much murder, and suffering of the Nephites, not to mention the murderous way he pulled off his selfish plans for personal gain, power, and profit. Teancum resolved to end this war right now.

In other words, *"The buck stops here"*. The Lamanite/Aztec armies had to use their vast numbers to get any courage to even attempt confronting the Nephites/Mayans. The Nephites/Mayans were very courageous, and had a duty first, to **God, then Country, then fellow man,** and these are the things that motivated them at this time. They had taken covenants to defend their country, their religion and their families to the death, and they were obeying the commandments of God, and God gave them great strength and courage[power of the priesthood], that enabled the Nephites/Mayans to go up against great odds, fearing nothing.

The Lamanites/Aztecs were extremely terrified of the Nephites/Mayans, because of their great faith in God. Whenever they fought the Nephites/Mayans in battle, they were terrified of them because, Nephites/Mayans fought with an insurmountable passion, continually calling on God to bless them, and bless them he did. For the Lamanite/Aztec at this time, to come face to face in battle was like that of coming face to face with "William Wallace" in battle during the wars of Scotland and England. William Wallace was said to have been seven feet tall, and he had a massive brute strength. Picture yourself having to stand face to face with him, in battle. If you were an Englishman on Scotland's land, where you shouldn't be. That Englishman knows for a surety that he is going to die today.

Picture the terror when you know you are wrong, and you are going to die in an instant, like every one of the enemy did, facing William Wallace. This is the same feelings the Lamanite/Aztecs felt facing off against the armies of Moroni, especially if it was found that either Moroni, Lehi, or in this case, Teancum, were leading that particular battalion of men coming at you, preparing to chop your heads off. God gave them the explicit commands to not be guilty of the first offense(invading them in their country), but he gave them deliberate blessings to defend their families even at the shedding of blood if necessary. Is all they wanted is peace, and for all men to have the same, and come to know Christ and be saved.

It showed in the way, that after they soundly, whipped the enemy; the Lamanites/Aztecs, the Nephites/Mayans would then spare the rest. Time and time again, if the Lamanites/Aztecs would enter into covenant to never take up arms again, they would then allow them to go back to their homes. Then the next evil communist-bastard looking for power, would promise the Lamanites/Aztecs riches, power, or compel them to break their covenants, and be back to war. A liberal's/communist's word means nothing. However, the Lamanites/Aztecs met their match in **Captain Teancum.**

> *"**And it came to pass that Teancum stole privily into the tent of the king, and he put a javelin to his heart; and he did cause the death of the king immediately that he did not awake his servants.**" "And he returned again privily to his own camp, and behold, his men were asleep, **and he awoke them and told them all the things that he had done.**" "And he caused **that his armies should stand in readiness, lest the Lamanites**[Aztecs] had awakened and should come upon them." "**And thus endeth the twenty and fifth year** of the reign of the judges over the people of Nephi[Mayans]; **And thus endeth the days of Amalickiah.**" (Alma 51:34-37, Book of Mormon)*

> *"And now, it came to pass in the **twenty and sixth year[65 B.C.]** of the reign of the judges over the people of **Nephi[Mayans]**, behold, when the **Lamanites[Aztecs]** awoke on the first morning of the first month, behold, **they found Amalickiah was dead in his own tent; and they also saw that** Teancum[Mayan Captain] was ready to give them battle on that day." "And now, when the **Lamanites**[Aztecs] saw this they were affrighted; and they abandoned their design in marching into the land northward, and retreated with all their army into the **city of Mulek,** and sought protection in their fortifications."(Alma 52:1-2, Book of Mormon)*

> *Teancum did secure the "Narrow Pass", which led into the land northward, and Moroni caused Bountiful to receive much fortification.*

*"And Moroni[Mayan General] <u>sent orders unto him[Teancum] that</u> <u>he should retain</u> **all the [Aztec] prisoners who** <u>fell into his</u> hands; for as the Lamanites[Aztecs] had <u>taken many prisoners, that he should</u> <u>retain all prisoners of the Lamanites[Aztecs]</u> **as a ransom** <u>for those</u> <u>whom the</u> Lamanites[Aztecs] had taken." "And he also sent orders unto him that he should* **fortify the land Bountiful, and secure** **the narrow pass which led into the land northward, lest the** **Lamanites[Aztecs] should obtain that point** <u>and should have</u> <u>power to harass them on every side."</u> *"And Moroni sent unto him that he would be faithful in <u>maintaining that quarter of the land, and that</u> <u>he would seek every opportunityt to</u> **scourge the Lamanites[Aztecs]** <u>in that</u> quarter, as much as was in his power, that perhaps he might take again by* **strategem or some other way those cities which had been** **taken** *out of their hands;and that he also would fortify and strengthen the cities round about, which had not fallen into the hands of the Lamanites[Aztecs]." "And he also said unto him, I would come unto you, <u>but behold, the Lamanites[Aztecs]</u>* **are upon us in the borders** **of the land by the west sea;** *and behold, <u>I go against them, therefore</u> <u>I cannot come unto you."</u> (Alma 52:8-11, Book of Mormon)*

There was no more war until **64 B.C.**, and Bountiful, bordering Panama, became a very important stronghold of the Nephites/Mayans, as it guarded the Nephite/Mayan lands to the north, we know as North America. The Nephites could not afford to let the Lamanites/ Aztecs get around them.

"And it came to pass that **Moroni** **did arrive with his** **army at the land Bountiful,** <u>at the latter end of the</u> **twenty and** **seventh year** *of the reign of the judges[***64 B.C.***] over the people of Nephi[Mayans]." "And in the commencement of the <u>twenty and</u> eighth year[***63 B.C.***] , Moroni and Teancum and many of the chief** **captains held a council of war---<u>what they should do to cause the</u> **Lamanites[Aztecs]** <u>to come out against them[the Nephite/Mayan</u> <u>armies] to battle; or that</u> they might by some means flatter them[the Lamanites/ Aztecs] out of* **their strongholds,** <u>that they[the Nephites/</u> <u>Mayans]might</u> gain advantage over them[Lamanites/Aztecs] and take **again the city of** <u>Mulek.</u>*" "And it came to pass they[the Nephites/*

Mayans] sent **embassies to the army of the Lamanites[Aztecs]***, which protected the ciy of* **Mulek***, to their leader, whose name was* **Jacob***, desiring him that he should* <u>come out with his armies</u> *to meet them[the Nephite/Mayan armies] upon the plains between the two cities. But behold,* **Jacob** <u>who was a</u> **Zoramite,** <u>would</u> *not come out with his army to meet them upon the plains."(Alma 52:18-20, Book of Mormon)*

"And it came to pass that **Moroni***[Mayan general], having no hopes of meeting them[Lamanites/Aztecs] upon fair grounds, therefore, he resolved upon a plan that he might* **decoy** <u>the Lamanites[Aztecs]</u> <u>out of their strongholds.</u>*" "Therefore he caused that* **Teancum** *should take a* <u>small number of men and march down near the seashore;</u> *and* **Moroni** <u>and his army, by night, marched in the wilderness,</u> *on the west of the city* **Mulek***; and thus, on the morrow, when the* <u>guards of</u> <u>the Lamanites[Aztecs] had discovered</u> **Teancum,** <u>they ran and told it</u> <u>unto</u> **Jacob,** <u>their leader.</u>*" "And it came to pass that the armies of the* <u>Lamanites[Aztecs] did march forth against</u> **Teancum,** <u>supposing by</u> <u>their numbers to overpower</u> **Teancum** <u>because of the smallness of his</u> <u>numbers.</u>*" "And as* **Teancum** *saw the armies of the Lamanites[Aztecs] coming out against him* <u>he began to retreat down by the seashore,</u> <u>northward.</u>*" (Alma 52:21-23, Book of Mormon)*

"And it came to pass that when the Lamanites[Aztecs] saw that he began to flee, they took **courage** *and pursued them* <u>with vigor. And</u> <u>while</u> **Teancum** <u>was thus leading away the Lamanites[Aztecs] who</u> <u>were pursuing them in</u> **vain,** *behold,* **Moroni** <u>commanded that a part</u> <u>of his army who were with him should march forth into the city, and</u> <u>take possession of it.</u>*" "And thus they[the Mayans] did,* **and slew all those who had been left to protect the city,** *yea, all those who would not yield up their weapons of war." "And thus* **Moroni** <u>had</u> <u>obtained possession of the city of Mulek</u> *with a part of his army, while he marched with the remainder to meet the Lamanites[Aztecs]*<u>when</u> <u>they should return from the pursuit of</u> **Teancum.***" "And it came to pass that the Lamanites[Aztecs] did pursue Teancum until they came near the* **city Bountiful,** <u>and then they[Aztecs] were met by</u> **Lehi** <u>and a small army, which had been left to protect the city</u> **Bountiful.***"*

"And now behold, when the chief captains of the Lamanites[Aztecs] had beheld **Lehi** *<u>with his army coming against them, they</u>* **<u>fled</u>** <u>*in much*</u> <u>*confusion,*</u> *lest perhaps they should not obtain the city* **Mulek** *before <u>Lehi should overtake them; for they[Aztecs] were wearied because</u> <u>of their march, and the men of</u>* **<u>Lehi</u>** <u>*were fresh.*</u>" *"And it came to pass that before the* **Lamanites[Aztecs]** *had retreated far they <u>were</u> <u>surrounded by the</u>* **<u>Nephites[Mayans]</u>***<u>,</u>, by the* **men of Moroni** *on one hand, and the men of* **Lehi** *on the other, <u>all of whom were fresh</u> <u>and</u>* **<u>full of strength</u>**<u>;</u> *but the Lamanites[Aztecs] were wearied because of their long march."* **(Alma 52: 24-31, Book of Mormon)**

"And **Moroni** <u>*commanded his men[Nephites/Mayans] that*</u> <u>*they should fall[attack] upon them[the Aztecs] until they[Aztecs] had*</u> <u>*given up their weapons of*</u> *war."* *"And it came to pass that* **Jacob,** <u>*being also a*</u> **<u>Zoramite</u>***<u>[dissenter/traitor]</u>, and having an unconquerable spirit[stubborn], he led the Lamanites[Aztecs]<u>forth to battle with</u> <u>exceeding fury against</u>* **<u>Moroni.</u>**" "**<u>Moroni</u>** <u>*being in their course of*</u> <u>*march[in their way],*</u> *therefore Jacob was determined to slay them and cut his way through to the city of Mulek. But behold,* **Moroni** <u>*and*</u> <u>*his men were more powerful; therefore they did not give way before the*</u> **<u>Lamanites[Aztecs]</u>**<u>.</u>" *"And it came to pass that they fought on both hands <u>with exceeding fury;</u> and there were many slain on both sides; yea, and* **Moroni[Mayan general] was wounded** *and* **Jacob[Aztec general] was killed.**" *"And Lehi[Mayan captain] <u>pressed upon</u> <u>their[Aztecs] rear with such</u>* **<u>fury with his strong men,</u>** *that the Lamanites[Aztec warriors] <u>in the rear delivered up their</u>* **<u>weapons</u>** **<u>of war;</u>** *and the remainder of them, <u>being much confused, knew not</u> <u>whither to go or strike."</u>* **(Alma 52:32-36, Book of Mormon)**

"Now **Moroni** *seeing their confusion, he said unto them: <u>If ye will</u> <u>bring forth your weapons of war and deliver them up, behold we will</u> <u>forbear[cease] shedding your</u> blood."* *"And it came to pass that when the* **Lamanites[Aztecs]** <u>*had heard these words,*</u> **<u>their chief captains,</u>** **<u>all those who were not slain, came forth and threw down their</u>** **<u>weapons of war at the feet of Moroni[chief Mayan general], and</u>** **<u>also commanded their men that they should do the same.</u>**" *"But behold, there were many that would not; and those who would not*

deliver up their swords were <u>taken and bound, and their weapons of</u> *<u>war were taken from them, and they were compelled to march with their</u>* *<u>brethren[fellow Aztec prisoners] forth into the</u>* **land Bountiful.***" "And now the <u>number of prisoners who were taken[of the Lamanites/Aztecs]</u>* **<u>exceeded more than the number of those who had been slain, yea,</u>** **<u>more than those who had been slain on both sides</u>**[combined].*"* (Alma 52:37-40, Book of Mormon)

More fortifications were added to Bountiful by digging a trench around it, and building a breastwork upon the heaped up earth, and they did all of this by using Lamanite/Aztec prisoners to accomplish this task. The Nephites/Mayans figured, that if they had to feed such an enormous host of prisoners, then the prisoners might as well **earn** their keep, and when the prisoners are busy working , they will always be easier to guard and control. Reminds us of the days of the chain gangs, we often read about in the early days of this country. If you decide to let them live, them make them work.

"And it came to pass that they[Moroni's Mayan soldiers] did set guards over <u>the prisoners of the Lamanites[Aztecs], and did</u> **<u>compel</u>** *<u>them to go forth and bury their dead, yea, also the dead of</u>* *<u>the Nephites[Mayans] who were slain; and</u>* **Moroni** *<u>placed men over</u>* *<u>them to guard them while they should perform their labors.</u>" "And* **Moroni** *went to the city of* **Mulek** *with* **Lehi**, *<u>and took command of</u>* *<u>the city</u> and gave it unto* **Lehi**. *Now behold, <u>This</u>* **<u>Lehi</u>** *<u>was a man</u>* *<u>who had been with Moroni in the more part of all his battles;</u>* **<u>and</u>** **<u>he was a man like unto Moroni,</u>** *and they rejoiced in each other's safety; yea, they were beloved by each other, and also beloved by all the people of Nephi[Mayan people]." "And it came to pass that after the Lamanites[Aztecs] had finished burying their dead and also the dead of the Nephites[Mayans], they were marched back into* **the land Bountiful;** *and* **Teancum, by the orders of Moroni** *<u>caused that they</u>* *<u>should commence laboring in digging</u>* **a ditch round about the land,** **or the city, Bountiful.***" "And he caused that they should build a* **breastwork of timbers upon the inner bank of the ditch;** *and <u>they</u>* *<u>cast up dirt out of the ditch against the breastwork of timbers; and</u>* *<u>thus they[Mayan soldiers] did cause the Lamanites[Aztec prisoners]</u>*

to labor until they had encircled the **city of Bountiful** round about with a strong wall of timbers and earth to an exceeding height." "And this city became an exceeding **stronghold ever after;** and in this city they did guard the prisoners of the Lamanites[Aztecs]; yea, **even within a wall which they[Moroni's Mayan soldiers]had caused them[Lamanite/Aztec prisoners] to build with their own hands.** Now Moroni was compelled to cause the Lamanites to labor, because it was easy to guard them while at their labors; and he desired all his forces when he should make an attack upon the Lamanites[Aztecs]."
"And it came to pass that **Moroni** had thus **gained a victory over one of the greatest of the armies of the Lamanites[Aztecs],** and had obtained possession of the city of **Mulek, which was one of the strongest holds of the Lamanites[Aztecs]** in the land of Nephi; and thus he had also built a stronghold to retain his prisoners."(Alma 53:1-6, Book of Mormon)

Chapter 13

Destruction of the Nephit/Mayan Government up to Death of Christ

Helaman leads 2,000 sons of Ammon into battle, to the aid of Moroni in the west!

More dissensions among the Nephites/Mayans, because of selfish, liberal/communist thinking reprobates. This insurrection erupted in the southwest of the Nephite/Mayan lands along the west sea, which caused a loss of ground, and cities were lost that once were held by the Nephites/Mayans, but now were occupied by the Lamanites/Aztecs and traitors. This put the Nephites/Mayans at a huge security risk. This ended **63 B.C.**

> *"And now it came to pass that the armies of the Lamanites[Aztecs], on the **west sea, south,** while in the absence of **Moroni** <u>on account of of some **dissensions amongst them**</u>[the Nephites/Mayans], had gained ground over the Nephites[Mayans], yea, insomuch that they[Lamanites/Aztecs] <u>had obtained possession of a number of their cities</u> in that part of the land." "And thus because <u>of iniquity amongst themselves</u>, yea, because of dissensions and <u>intrigue</u> among <u>themselves they were placed in the **most dangerous circumstances**</u>." "And now behold, I have somewhat to say concerning the **people of Ammon, who in the beginning, were <u>Lamanites[Aztecs]</u>;** but by Ammon and his brethren, or rather by the <u>power and word of God, they had</u>*

*been converted unto the Lord; and they had been brought down into the **land of Zarahemla**, and had ever since been protected by the Nephites[Mayans].*" "*And because of their **oath**[covenant/promise] they had been kept from taking up arms against their brethren; **for they had taken an oath that they never would shed blood more;** and according to their oath they would have perished; yea, they would have suffered themselves to have fallen into the hands of their brethren, had it not been for the pity and exceeding love which **Ammon and his brethren had had for them.***"(Alma 53:8-11, Book of Mormon)*

"*Andforthiscausetheywerebroughtdownintothelandof Zarahemla; and they ever had been **protected by the Nephites[Mayans].***" "*But it came to pass that when they saw the danger, and the many afflictions and tribulations which the Nephites[Mayans] bore for them, they were moved **with compassion and were desirous to take up arms in the defence of their country.***" "*But behold, as they were about to take their weapons of war, they were overpowered by the persuasions of Helaman and his brethren, for they were about to break the oath which they had made.*" "*And **Helaman** feared lest by so doing they should lose their souls; therefore all those who had entered into this covenant were compelled to behold their brethren wade through their afflictions, in their dangerous circumstances at this time.*" "*But behold, it came to pass they had many sons, who had not entered into a covenant that they would not take their weapons of war to defend themselves against their enemies; therefore they did assemble themselves together at this time, as many as were able to take up arms, **and they called themselves Nephites[Mayans].***" *(Alma 53:12-16, Book of Mormon)*

"*And they entered into a **covenant to fight for the liberty of the Nephites[Mayans], yea, to protect the land unto the laying down of their lives; yea, even they covenanted that they never would give up their liberty, but they would fight in all cases to protect the Nephites and themselves from bondage.***" "*Now behold, there were **two thousand of those young men, who entered into this covenant** and took their weapons of war to defend their country.*"(Alma 53: 17-19, Book of Mormon)*

Helaman, the Chief Judge, stepped down from the judgment seat for a time, to lead this brave band of converted, God loving, God fearing, Lamanites/Aztecs, now calling themselves Nephites/Mayans, or the sons of Ammon, who were domiciled in the Land of Jershon. They came together in the defense of the newly lost cities in the south. It was now **62 B.C.**, and the mindset of the Lamanites/Aztecs, was to destroy the Nephites/Mayans.

> *"And now behold, as they never had hitherto been a disadvantage to the Nephites[Mayans], they became now <u>at this period of time also a</u> <u>great</u> support; for they took their weapons of war,* **and they would that Helaman should be their leader."** *"And they were* **all young men, and they were exceedingly <u>valiant for courage</u>,** *and also for strength and activity; but behold, this was not all---**<u>they were men who were</u> <u>true at all times in whatsoever thing they were entrusted.</u>"** "Yea, **<u>they were men of truth and soberness, for they had been taught</u> <u>to keep the commandments of God and to walk uprightly before</u> <u>him.</u>"** "And now it came to pass that* **Helaman** *did march at the head of his* **<u>two thousand stripling soldiers,</u>** *to the support of the people in the borders of the land on the south by the west sea." "And thus ended the twenty and eighth year[63 B.C.] of the reign of the judges over the people of Nephi[Mayans]." (Alma 53:19-23, Book of Mormon)*

Moroni sends wine to his enemies in order to conquer the city of Gid!

Moroni, the chief general of the Nephites/Mayans, wrote a letter to the new king of the Lamanites/Aztecs, telling him to withdraw his designs, and give back the lands that he is occupying in order to spare so many more lives. He warned that if Ammoron failed to do this, that he, Moroni, would come after him and his armies, and destroy them. Of course, Ammoron, after all he was the king now, had to spout his lies and threaten Moroni. Moroni doesn't let Ammoron, intimidate him, but sees a necessity to use trickery to begin getting his cities back, otherwise, to attack the cities while inhabited by the enemy would cause the lives of so many needed soldiers. So he devised a plan to send wine to the guards on duty to get them drunk. The saying goes"anything is fair in love and war". It was now **61 B.C.**

The armies of Moroni on the north initiated plans to go against the Lamanites/Aztecs.

"And now it came to pass that When **Moroni had said these words,** *he caused that a search should be made among his men, that perhaps he might find a man who was a* <u>descendant of Laman</u>*[an Aztec]* <u>among them.</u>*" "And it came to pass that they* **found one,** <u>whose name was Laman;</u> **and he was one of the servants of the king** <u>who was murdered by Amalickiah</u>*[Nephite traitor]." "Now Moroni caused that Laman and a small number of his men should go forth* <u>unto the guards who were over the Nephites</u>*[Mayan prisoners]." "Now the Nephites[Mayan prisoners] were* <u>guarded in the city of Gid;</u> *therefore Moroni appointed Laman and caused that a small number of men should go with him." "And when it was evening Laman went to the guards who were over the Nephites[Mayans], and behold, they saw him coming and they hailed him; but he saith unto them:* **Fear not; behold, I am a Lamanite[Aztec]. Behold, we have escaped from the Nephites[Mayans] and they sleep; and behold we have taken of their wine and brought with us.***"(Alma 55:4-8, Book of Mormon)*

"Now when the Lamanites[Aztecs] heard these words they received him with joy; and they said unto him: <u>Give us of your wine, that we may drink ; we are glad that ye have thus taken wine with you for we are weary.</u>*" "But Laman said unto them:* <u>Let us keep of our wine till we go against the Nephites[Mayans] to battle. But this saying only made them more desirous to drink of the wine;" "For, said they:</u><u>We are weary, therefore let us take of the wine, and by and by we shall receive wine for our rations, which will strengthen us to go against the Nephites[Mayans].</u>*" "And Laman said unto them:* <u>You may do according to your desires."</u>*(Alma 55:9-12, Book of Mormon)*

And it came to pass that they did take of the <u>wine freely;</u> *and it was pleasant to their taste, therefore they took of it* <u>more freely;</u> *and it* <u>was strong, having been prepared in its strength.</u>*" "And it came to pass they* <u>did drink and they were merry, and by and by</u> **they were all drunken.***" "And now when Laman and his men saw that they* were all drunken, and _were in a deep sleep,_ they returned to **Moroni** and told him all the things that had happened." "And now this was _according to the design[plan] of Moroni._ And Moroni had prepared his men with weapons of war; and he went to the **city of Gid,** while the Lamanites[Aztecs] were in a deep sleep and drunken, _and cast in weapons of war unto the prisoners, insomuch that they were all_ armed;" "Yea, even to _their women and children,_ as many as were able to use a weapon of war, when Moroni had armed all those prisoners; and all those things were done _in profound silence."_ (Alma 55:13-17, Book of Mormon)

"But had they awakened the Lamanites[Aztecs], behold they were drunken and the Nephites[Mayans] could have slain[killed] them." "But behold, this was not the desire of Moroni; _he did not delight in murder or bloodshed,_ but he delighted in the saving of his people from destruction; and for this cause **he might not bring upon him injustice, he would not fall upon the Lamanites[Aztecs] and destroy them in their drunkenness.**" "But he had obtained his desires; for he had armed those prisoners of the Nephites[Mayans] who were within the wall of the city, and had given them power to gain possession of those parts which were within the walls." "And then he caused the men who were with him to _withdraw a pace from them, and surround the armies of the Lamanites[Aztecs]."_ "Now behold this was done in the night-time, so that when the Lamanites[Aztecs] awoke in the morning they beheld that they were surrounded by the Nephites[Mayans] without, and that their prisoners were armed within."(Alma 55:18-22, Book of Mormon)

"And thus they saw that the _Nephites[Mayans] had power over them;_ and in these circumstances they found that it was not _expedient that they should fight with the Nephites[Mayans];_ therefore their chief captains demanded their weapons of war, and they[the Lamanites/Aztecs] brought them forth and cast them _at the feet of the Nephites[Mayans],_ **pleading for mercy.**" "Now behold, this was the desire of Moroni. He took them prisoners of war, and took _possession of the city,_ and caused that all the prisoners should be liberated, who were Nephites[Mayans]; and they did join the army of Moroni, and were a *great strength to his army." "And it came to pass that he did cause the* **Lamanites[Aztecs]** *, whom he had taken prisoner, that they should commence a labor in strengthening the fortifications round about the city **Gid**."(Alma 55:23-25, Book of Mormon)*

This war that Moroni is fighting is a prime example of how God outsmarted his enemies to their own defeat. He uses their ignorance, their vices, their own lusts of the flesh, and lusts for power, and even uses their fear, and their own labor to beat themselves. In fact, it is quite ironic to picture how many of those Lamanite[Aztec] soldiers and leaders felt, when they came to the realization that they beat themselves time and again. They even worked for the Nephites/Mayans, free of charge, to fortify the cities they once held. They worked to keep themselves in as prisoners, and the others out , who want to get in, to liberate them.

*"Many times did the Lamanites[Aztecs] attempt to encircle them[the Nephites/Mayans] about by night, but in these attempts they [the Aztecs] did lose many prisoners." "And many times did they attempt to administer of their wine to the Nephites[Mayans], that they might **poison** or with drunkenness." "But behold, the Nephites[Mayans] were not slow to remember the Lord their God in this their time of affliction. They could not be taken in their snares; yea, they would not partake of their wine, save they had first given to some of the Lamanite prisoners." "And they were thus cautious that no poison should be administered among them; **for if their wine would poison a Lamanite[Aztec] it would also poison a Nephite[Mayan]**; and thus they did try all their liquors."(Alma 55: 29-32, Book of Mormon)*

Former Chief Judge Helaman, updates how his sons of Ammon are faring in the South!

General Helaman now sends a letter to Moroni in the North telling him about the exploits of the 2,000-Lamanite warriors, who came to the Nephites/Mayans aid when they needed them most. These young warriors were the sons of the Lamanites/Aztecs now

Nephites/Mayans, who had joined with the Nephites/Mayans, when they accepted Christ, and refused to take up their weapons of war against their fellow Nephites/Mayans or Lamanites/Aztecs. Because of this act of faith, the Nephites/Mayans took them in, protected them, and gave them lands of their own. Because these 2,000 young men did not enter in to the same covenants as their fathers, they were free to enlist.*(Alma 56:3-5, 9-13, Book of Mormon)*

Prophet, Chief Judge, and General, Helaman tells Moroni of his war with the Lamanites/Aztecs in the south. The war in the south was going on at the same time as Moroni and his army was fighting in the north, therefore the years may overlap with each area, north and south, of the conflict. It is now **61 B.C.** With Helaman, remembering he entered the conflict with his 2,000 stripling, Lamanite warriors in **65 B.C.,** so he is recounting to Moroni in the north, 4–years later to let him know the state of the union in the south.

*"And these are the words which he wrote, saying: My dearly beloved brother, **Moroni**, as well in the Lord as in the tribulations of our warfare; behold, my beloved brother, I have somewhat to tell you concerning our warfare in this part of the land." "Behold, **two thousand** of the sons of those men whom Ammon brought down out of the land of Nephi[Ecuador/Peru/Bolivia/southern Colombia]--- now ye have known that these descendants of **Laman,** who was the eldest son of our father **Lehi;**" "Therefore it sufficeth me that I tell you that two thousand of these young men have taken their weapons of war, and would that I should be their leader;and we have come forth to defend our country." "And now we also know concerning the covenant which their fathers made, that they would not take up their weapons of war against their brethren to shed blood." "But in the twenty and sixth year[65 B.C.], when they saw our afflictions and our tribulations for them, they were about to break the covenant which they had made and take up their weapons of war in our defense." "But I would not suffer them that they should break this covenant which they had made, **supposing that God would strengthen us,** insomuch that we should not suffer more because of the fulfilling **the oath** which they had taken."(Alma 56:2-3, 5-8, Book of Mormon)*

*"But behold, here is one thing in which we may have **great joy**. For behold, <u>in the twenty and sixth year[65 B.C.],</u> I, **Helaman**, did march at the head of these two thousand young men to the city of **Judea**, to assist **Antipus**, whom ye had appointed a leader over the people of that part of the land." "And <u>I did join my two thousand sons, (for they are worthy to be called sons) to the army of Antipus, in which strength Antipus did rejoice exceedingly; for behold, his army had been reduced by the Lamanites[Aztecs] because their forces had slain a vast number of our men, for which cause we have to mourn."</u> "(Alma 56:9-10, Book of Mormon)*

*"And the Lamanites[Aztecs] had also <u>retained many prisoners, all of whom are **chief captains, for none other have they spared alive.**</u> And we suppose that they are now at the time in the land of Nephi[Ecuador, Peru, southern Colombia]; it is so if they are not slain." "And now these are the cities of which the **<u>Lamanites[Aztecs] have obtained possession by the shedding of the blood of so many of our valiant men;</u>**" "The land of **Manti, or the city of Manti,** and the city **of Zeezrom, and the city of Cumeni, and the city of Antiparah.**" "And these are the cities which they possessed when I arrived at the city of Judea; and **found Antipus** and his men toiling with their might to fortify the city." "Yea, and they <u>were depressed in body as well as in spirit, for they had fought valiantly by day and toiled by night to maintain their cities; and thus they had suffered great afflictions of every kind."</u>**(Alma 56:12-16, Book of Mormon)***

The 2,000-stripling, Lamanite[Aztec] warriors, were converted to the truth, gathered with the Nephites[Mayans] for the good of their freedom, and faith. Because they had the courage to come forward, they were seen as very refreshing and encouraging to the Veteran Nephite/Mayan army, and because they were never tried in battle, and were so young, they at first were used as decoys to get the Lamanites out of their strongholds.

*Now when we saw that the Lamanites[Aztecs] began to grow uneasy on this wise, we were desirous to bring **a stratagem into effect upon them;** therefore **Antipus** ordered that I should march* *forth with my **little sons** to a neighboring city, as if we were carrying provisions to a neighboring city." "And we were <u>to march near the city</u> <u>of **Antiparah**</u>, as if we were going to the city beyond, in the borders by the seashore." "And it came to pass that we did march forth, as if with our <u>provisions, to go to that city.</u>" "And it came to pass that **Antipus** <u>did march forth with a part of his army,</u> leaving the remainder to maintain the city. But <u>he did not march forth until I had gone forth</u> <u>with my little army, and came near the city</u> **Antiparah**." "And now, <u>in the city of</u> **Antiparah were stationed the strongest army of the Lamanites[Aztecs]; yea, the most numerous**." "And it came to pass that when they had been informed by their **spies**, they came forth with their army and <u>marched against us.</u>" "And it came to pass that we did **flee** before them, <u>northward. And thus we</u> <u>did lead away the most</u> <u>powerful army of the Lamanites[Aztecs];</u>" "Yea, even to a considerable distance, insomuch that when they saw the <u>army of Antipus pursuing</u> <u>them, with their might, they did not turn to the right nor to the left,</u> <u>but pursued their march in a straight course after us; and as we suppose,</u> **it was their intent to slay us before Antipus should overtake** **them, and this that they might not be surrounded by our people.**" "**(Alma** 56:30-36, Book of Mormon)*

The young sons of Ammon, being led by their general Helaman, were given orders to go past the city, towards the land of Zarahemla. If the Lamanites/Aztecs sensed they were being led into a trap by going towards Zarahemla, deep into Nephite/Mayan country, they might get them to change their course. However, the Lamanites/Aztecs, so to speak, knew they were between a rock and a hard spot, and chose to go after Helaman and his smaller army first.

*"And now **Antipus**, beholding our danger, did speed the march of his army. But behold, it was night; therefore they[the Aztecs] did not overtake us, neither did Antipus overtake them; therefore we did camp for the night." "And it came to pass that before dawn of the morning, behold, the Lamanites[Aztecs] were pursuing us. Now we were not sufficiently strong to contend with them; yea, I would not suffer that my **little sons should fall** into their hands; therefore we did continue our march, and we took our march into the <u>wilderness.</u>"*

*"Now they[Aztecs] durst not turn to the right nor to the left lest they should be surrounded; neither would I turn to the right nor to the left lest they should overtake me, and we could not stand against them, but be slain, and they would make their escape; and thus <u>we did flee all that day into the wilderness, even until it was dark.</u>" "And it came to pass that again when the light of the morning came <u>we saw the Lamanites[Aztecs] upon us, and we did flee before them.</u>" "But it came to pass that <u>they did not pursue us far before they halted; and it was in the morning of the **third day** of the seventh month.</u>" (Alma 56:38-42, Book of Mormon)*

Antipus and his veteran soldiers caught up to the Lamanites/Aztecs from the city of Antiparah, whom, were attempting to catch Helaman and his young warriors to destroy them. You know full well, because of the concern of Antipus and his soldiers, for the welfare of the young stripling warriors, they went harder after the Lamanite/Aztec armies, to catch them before the Lamanites/Aztecs could destroy the 2,000-stripling, Lamanite warriors. That was a gracious act on the part of Antipus and his army, and doing so, made them very tired, when the Lamanites/Aztecs turned, and a huge battle began. The Lamanites/Aztec army then turned and began to fight Antipus and his army of Nephites/Mayans. Helaman and his band of 2,000 born-again stripling warriors, whose parents were once Lamanites/Aztecs, now converted Christians, and taught in the faith of God, now turned and came up on the Lamanites/Aztecs in their rear, and began to do very much damage to the Lamanite/Aztec army.

★★★*"And now, whether they were overtaken by Antipus we knew not, but I said unto <u>my men: Behold, we know not but they have halted for the purpose that we should come against them, that they might catch us in their snare;</u>" "Therefore what say <u>ye, my sons, will ye go against them to battle?</u>" "And now I say unto you, **<u>my beloved brother Moroni, that never had I seen so great courage, nay not amongst all the Nephites[Mayans].</u>**" "For as I had <u>**ever called them my sons(for they were all of them very young) even so they said unto me: Father, behold our God is with us, and he will not suffer that we should fall; then let us go forth; we would not slay**</u>*

our brethren if they would let us alone; therefore let us go, lest they should overpower the army of Antipus." "Now they* never had fought, yet they did not fear death; and they did think more upon the liberty of their fathers than they did upon their lives; yea, they had been taught by their mothers, that if they did not doubt, God would deliver them."* "And they* rehearsed unto me the words of their mothers, saying: We do not doubt our mothers knew it."* "(Alma 56:43-48, Book of Mormon)*

"And it came to pass **that I did return with my two thousand** against these Lamanites[Aztecs] who had pursued us. And now behold, **the armies of Antipus had overtaken them, and a terrible battle had commenced."** "The army of Antipus being weary, because of their long march in so short a space of time, **were about to fall into the hands of the Lamanites[Aztecs]; and had I not returned with my two thousand they would have obtained their purpose."** "For Antipus had fallen by the sword, and many of his leaders, because of their weariness, which was occasioned by the speed of their march-- -therefore the men of Antipus, being confused because of the fall of their leaders, began to give way before the Lamanites[Aztecs]."* "And it came to pass that the Lamanites[Aztecs] took* courage, and began to pursue them; and thus were the Lamanites[Aztecs]* pursuing them with great vigor when Helaman came upon their rear with his two thousand, and began to slay them exceedingly, insomuch that the whole army of the Lamanites[Aztecs] halted and turned upon Helaman."* "Now when the people of* **Antipus saw that the Lamanites[Aztecs] had turned them about, they gathered together their men and came again upon the rear of the Lamanites[Aztecs]."(Alma** 56:51-53, Book of Mormon)*

*** "And now it came to pass that we, **the people of Nephi[Mayan people], the people of Antipus, and I with my two thousand, did surround the Lamanites[Aztecs], and did slay them; yea insomuch that they were compelled to deliver up their weapons of war and also themselves as prisoners of war."** "And now it came to pass that when they had surrendered themselves up unto us, **behold, I numbered those young men who**

had fought with me, fearing lest there were many of them slain." *"But behold, to my great joy, there had not one of them fallen to the earth; yea, and they had fought as if with the strength of God; yea, never were men known to have fought with such miraculous strength; and with such mighty power did they fall upon the Lamanites[Aztecs], that they did frighten them; and for this cause did the Lamanites[Aztecs] deliver themselves up as prisoners of war."* *"And as we had no place for our prisoners, that we could guard them to keep them from the armies of the Lamanites, therefore we sent them to the land of Zarahemla, and a part of those men who were not slain of Antipus, with them; and the remainder I took and joined them to my stripling Ammonites, and took our march back to the city of Judea."* *(Alma 56:54-57, Book of Mormon)*

The battle between the Nephites/Mayans and the Lamanites/ Aztecs raged on fiercely, but as you will soon see, the Nephites began to prevail, despite the wickedness of the dissenting Nephites/Mayans traitors/liberals, and those invading Lamanites/Aztecs. As long as the Nephites/Mayans remembered to call upon God, they were blessed and able to win, and reclaim the city of Antiparah.

"And now it came to pass that I received an epistle from Ammoron, the king, stating that if I would deliver up those prisoners of war whom we had taken that he would deliver up the city of Antiparah unto us." *"But I sent an epistle[letter of reply] unto the king, that we were sure our forces were sufficient to take the city of Antiparah by our force; and by delivering up the prisoners for that city we should suppose ourselves unwise, and that we would only deliver our prisoners on exchange."* *"And Ammoron refused mine epistle, for he would not exchange prisoners; therefore we began making preparations to go against Antiparah."* *"But the people of Antiparah did leave the city, and fled to their other cities, which they had possession of, to fortify them; and thus the city of Antiparah fell into our hands."* *"And thus ended the twenty and eighth year of the reign of the judges."* *"And it came to pass that in the commencement of the twenty and ninth year, we received a supply of provisions, and also an addition to our army, from the land of Zarahemla, and from the land round about, to*

the number of six thousand men, besides sixty of the sons of the Ammonites who had come to join their brethren, my little band of two thousand. And now behold, we were strong, yea, and we had also plenty of provisions brought unto us." "(Alma 57:1-6, Book of Mormon)

Because of the fierceness of the report of the battle, and the talk of how few Nephites destroyed the hosts of the Lamanites/Aztec armies, the remainder, got scared and left the city of Antiparah without a fight. The next city the Nephites planned to take was Cumeni. This ended the year of **63-62 B.C..** Not one of the converted stripling Ammonite/Lamanite/Aztec warriors were killed, because of their great faith in their God.

"And it came to pass that it was our desire to wage a battle with the army which was placed to protect the **city Cumeni.** *" "And now behold, I will show unto you that we soon accomplished our desire; yea, with our strong force, or with a part of our strong force, we did surround, by night, the city Cumeni, a little before they were to receive a supply of provisions." "And it came to pass that we did camp[lay siege] round about the city for many nights; but we did sleep upon our swords, and keep guards, that the Lamanites[Aztecs] could not come upon us by night and slay us, which they attempted many times; but as many times as they[Aztecs] attempted this their blood was spilt." "At length their[Aztecs] provisions did arrive, and they were about to enter the city by night. And we[Mayan soldiers] instead of being Lamanites[Aztecs], were Nephites[Mayans]; therefore, we did take them[Aztecs] and their provisions." "And notwithstanding the Lamanites[Aztecs] being cut off from their support after this manner, they were still determined to maintain the city; therefore it became expedient that we should take those provisions and send them to Judea, and our prisoners to the land of Zarahemla."(Alma 57:7-11, Book of Mormon)*

"And it came to pass that **our [Aztec] prisoners were so numerous that notwithstanding the enormity of our numbers, we were obliged to employ all our force to keep them, or put them to death.** *" " behold, they would break out in great numbers,*

and would fight with stones, and with clubs, or whatsoever thing they could get into their hands, insomuch that we did slay upwards of two thousand of them after they had surrendered themselves prisoners of war." "Therefore it became expedient for us, that we should put an end to their lives, or guard them, sword in hand, down to the land of Zarahemla; and also our provisions were not any more sufficient for our own people[Mayan soldiers], notwithstanding that which we had taken from the Lamanites[Aztec soldiers]." "(Alma 57:13-15, Book of Mormon)

"...we did resolve to send them[Aztec prisoners] down to the land of Zarahemla; therefore we selected a part of our men, and gave them charge over our prisoners to go down to the land of Zarahemla." "But it came to pass that on the morrow they did return. And now behold, we did not inquire of them concerning the prisoners; for behold, the Lamanites[Aztecs] were upon us, and they returned in season to save us from falling into their hands. For behold, Ammoron had sent to their support a new supply of provisions and also a numerous army of men." "And it came to pass that those men whom we had sent with the prisoners did arrive in season to check them, as they were about to overpower us." (Alma 57:16-18, Book of Mormon)

Helaman informed Moroni of the miracles surrounding the preservation of his 2,000 stripling warriors, and gives an account of how valiantly they fought. He also explains to Moroni, that once more, that not one was killed in battle, but all were accounted for, while many veterans from the regular army were killed. Now however, they had an added sixty more Lamanite/Aztec, warriors, from the land of Jershon. They too, were preserved because of their faith and courage.

It makes you wonder if God had sent a protecting or guardian angel to accompany each of these 2,060-stripling Lamanite/Aztec warriors, because of their faith in him. Those angels were just out of sight of mortal men behind the veil, just as it was during the days of Elisha, when God told Elisha that he was being protected by legions of angels. Elisha heard the rustling in the air and the trees, and was told to look up, and sure enough, he saw armies of angels, in full military regalia to do as God directed them to do. *(2 kings 6:17-23, KJV)*

It was also the same in the days of Hezekiah, king of Judah, because he was a good king, he needed not fear the Assyrian armies approaching, because God promised him, through the prophet Isaiah, that he would fight the kings battles. Then that night angels of God slew 185,000 of the Assyrians, because they mocked the God of Israel, through Sennecharib, the Assyrian ambassador, and they even turned upon each other because of the fear of the Lord, for they knew not who was their enemy and who was doing this. The remainder fled back into their own country. God wanted to show the world that he means what he says, that if his people will obey his commandments, they need not fear. *(2 Kings 19:35 , KJV)*

"**But behold, my little band of two thousand and sixty fought most desperately; yea, they were firm before the Lamanites[Aztecs], and did administer death unto all those who opposed** *them.*" "*And as the remainder of our army were about to give way before the Laqmanites[Aztecs]. Behold, those **two thousand and sixty were firm and undaunted.**" "*Yea, **and they did obey and observe to perform every word of command with exactness; yea, and even according to their faith it was done unto them; and I did remember the words which they said unto me that their mothers had taught them.**" "**And now behold, it was these my sons, and those men who had been selected to convey the prisoners, to whom we owe this great victory; for it was they who did beat the Lamanites[Aztecs]; therefore they were driven back to the city of Manti.**" "*And we retained our city Cumeni, and were not all destroyed by the sword; nevertheless, we had suffered **great loss.**" (Alma 57:19-23, Book of Mormon)*

"*And it came to pass that there were two hundred, out of my two thousand and sixty, who had fainted because of the loss of blood; nevertheless, according to **the goodness of God, and to our great astonishment, and also the joy of our whole army, there was not one soul of them who did perish; yea, and neither was there one soul among them who had not received many wounds.**" "And now, **their preservation was astonishing to our whole army, yea, that they should be spared while there was a thousand of our brethren** *who were slain. And we do justly ascribe it to the miraculous power of God, because of their exceeding faith in that which they had been taught to believe---that there was a just God, and whosoever did not doubt, that they should be preserved by his miraculous power." "Now this was the faith of these of whom I have spoken; they are young, and their minds are firm, and they do put their trust in God continually."(Alma 57:25-27, Book of Mormon)*

"And now it came to pass that after we had thus taken care of our wounded men, and had buried our dead and also the dead of the Lamanites[Aztecs], which were many, behold,we did inquire of Gid concerning the prisoners whom they had started to go down to the land of Zarahemla with." "Now Gid was the chief captain over the band[Mayan soldiers] who was appointed to guard them down to the land." "And now these are the words which Gid said unto me: Behold, we did start to go down to the land of Zarahemla with our prisoners. And it came to pass that we did meet the spies of our armies[Mayans], who had been sent out to watch the camp of the Lamanites[Aztecs]." "And they cried unto us, saying---Behold, the armies of the Lamanites[Aztecs] are marching towards the city of Cumeni; and behold, they will fall upon them, yea, and will destroy our people[Nephites/Mayans]." "And it came to pass that our prisoners did hear their cries[shouts], which caused them to take courage; and they did rise up in rebellion against us." "And it came to pass because of their rebellion we did cause that our swords should come upon them. And it came to pass that they did in a body run upon our swords, in the which, the greater number of them were slain; and the remainder of them broke through and fled from us." "And behold, when they had fled and we could not overtake them, we took our march with speed towards the city Cumeni; and behold, we did arrive in time that we might assist our brethren in preserving the city."
(Alma 57:28-33, Book of Mormon)

Chapter 14

The Death of Christ and His Visit to Central America ; Bountiful

General Moroni censors the central governments Chief
Judge Pahoran, for neglect!

At this point, in the Nephite/Mayan and Lamanite/Aztec war, the Nephite/Mayan government appeared to be showing neglect towards their military, by failing to send reinforcements and provisions to keep their military going and strong. The Nephite/Mayan general, Helaman, and the main army's next objective was to take back the city of Manti, and Helaman voiced his concern about not having enough supplies and reinforcements to hold the cities that they have taken, without added help.

> "And it came to pass that I thus did send an embassy to the government of our land, to acquaint him concerning the affairs of our people. And it came to pass that we did wait to receive provisions and strength from the land of Zarahemla." "But behold, this did profit us but little; for the Lamanites[Aztecs] were also receiving great strength from day to day, and also many provisions; and thus were our circumstances at this period of time." And it came to pass that we <u>did wait in these difficult circumstances for the space of many months, even until we were about to perish for the want of food.</u>" "But it came to pass that we did <u>receive food, which was guarded to us by an army of</u>

two thousand men to our assistance; and this is all the assistance which we did receive, to defend ourselves and our country from falling into the hands of our enemies, yea, to contend with an enemy which was innumerable." "(Alma 58:4-5,7-8, Book of Mormon)

"And now the cause of these our embarrassments, or the cause why they did not send more strength unto us, we knew not; therefore we were grieved and also filled with fear, lest by any means the judgments of God should come upon our land, to our overthrow and utter destruction." "Therefore we did **pour out our souls in prayer to God, that he would strengthen us and deliver us out of the hands of our enemies, yea, and also give us strength that we might retain our cities, and our lands, and our possessions, for the support of our people.** *"Yea, and it came to pass that the* **Lord our God did visit us with assurances that he would deliver us;** *yea, insomuch that he did speak peace to our souls, and did grant unto us great faith, and did cause us that we should hope for our deliverance in him." "And we did take courage with our small force which we had received, and were fixed with a determination to conquer our enemies, and to maintain our lands, and our possessions, and our wives, and our children,* **and the cause of liberty.** *"(Alma 58:9-12, Book of Mormon)*

However, because of the Nephite/Mayan government's apparent lack of concern for the welfare of their military, was quite disconcerting, and an embarrassment, therefore, it required a lot of prayer, faith, and stratagem to get the largest host of Lamanites/Aztecs out of the city of Manti. This ends the year of **62 B.C..**

"And thus we did go forth with all our might against the Lamanites[Aztecs], who were in the city of **Manti***; and we did pitch our tents by the wilderness side, which was near to the city." "And it came to pass that on the morrow, that when the Lamanites[Aztecs] saw that we were in the borders by the wilderness which was near the city, that they sent out spies round about us that they might discover the number and the strength of our army." "And it came to pass that when they[the Aztecs] saw that we were not strong, according to our [Mayan army] numbers, and fearing that we should cut them off from*

*their support except they should come out to battle against us and kill us, and also supposing that they could easily destroy us <u>with their numerous hosts</u>, therefore they began making preparations to come out against us to battle." "And when we saw that they were making preparations to come out against us, behold, I [Helaman] caused that [captain]***Gid***, <u>with a small number of men, should secrete himself in the wilderness, and also [captain]**Teomner** and a small number of men should secrete themselves also in the wilderness.</u>"(Alma 58:13-16, Book of Mormon)*

"Now <u>Gid and his men were on the right and the others on the left; and when they had thus secreted themselves,</u> behold, <u>I [Helaman] remained with the remainder of my army, in that same place where we had first pitched our tents</u> against the time[expecting] that the Lamanites should come out to battle." "And it came to pass that the <u>Lamanites[Aztecs] did come out with their numerous army against us.</u> **And when they had come and were about to fall upon us with the sword, I caused that my men, those who were with me, should retreat into the wilderness."** *"And it came to pass that the* **Lamanites[Aztecs] did follow after us with great speed,** <u>*for they were exceedingly desirous to overtake us that they might slay us; therefore they did follow us into the wilderness;*</u>**and we did pass by in the midst of Gid and Teomner, insomuch that they were not discovered by the Lamanites[Aztecs]."** *"And it came to pass that when the* **Lamanites[Aztecs] had passed by, or when the army had passed by, <u>Gid and Teomner did rise up from their secret places, and did cut off the spies of the Lamanites[Aztecs] that they should not return to the city.</u>"** *"And it came to pass that* <u>**when they had cut them off, they ran to the city and fell upon the guards who were left to guard the city, insomuch that they did destroy them and take possession of the city.**</u>*"* *"Now this was done because*<u>the Lamanites[Aztecs] did suffer their whole army, save a few guards only, to be led away into the wilderness.</u>*"(Alma 58: 17-22, Book of Mormon)*

"And when the Lamanites[Aztecs] saw that we were marching towards the land of **Zarahemla***[heartland of the Mayan people], they*

were exceedingly **afraid**, *lest there was a plan laid to lead them on to destruction; therefore they began to retreat into the wilderness again, yea, even back by the same way which they had come." "Now it came to pass that when it was night, I caused that my men should not sleep, but that they should march forward by another way towards the land of Manti." "And because of this our march in the night-time, behold, on the morrow we were beyond the Lamanites[Aztecs], insomuch that we did arrive before them at the city of* **Manti.** *" "And thus it came to pass, that* **by this stratagem we did take possession of the city of Manti without the shedding of blood.** *" "(Alma 58:24,26-28, Book of Mormon)*

"And it came to pass that when the armies of the Lamanites[Aztecs] did arrive near the city, and saw that we were prepared to meet them, **they were astonished exceedinly and struck with great fear, insomuch that they did flee into the wilderness.** *" "Yea, and it came to pass that the armies of* **the Lamanites[Aztecs] did flee out of all this quarter of the land. But behold, they have carried with them many women and children out of the land.** *" "And those cities which had been taken by the* **Lamanites[Aztecs], all of them are at this period of time in our possession;** *and our fathers and our women and our children are returning to their homes, all save it be those who have been taken prisoners and carried off by the Lamanites[Aztecs]." (Alma 58:29-31, Book of Mormon)*

General Moroni gives the federal government an ultimatum to support their country, or else!

The Mayan General, Moroni sees the need to censor the government, and give the Judges an ultimatum to either support liberty or the military was going to revolt against them, and march against Zarahemla, and clean them out. A nation is only as free, and the rule of law only as strong and binding as those who the people elect and entrust to act in positions of public-trust, who take an oath of office to defend that system of law which governs we the people, from all enemies, foreign and domestic. When Presidents, governors, judges, representatives, sheriffs, law enforcement officers, clerks, attorneys, military officers, even down to a simple notary-public, violate their oaths for power and gain, that system of law is hanging by a thread. Our Constitution is hanging by a thread, because of the dishonesty, of communist thinking traitors all throughout government at all levels. They oppress the people instead of respecting their rights under the Constitution. Moroni had this concern at this time.

*"And it came to pass that while **Moroni** was thus making preparations to go against the Lamanites[Aztecs] to battle, behold, the people of **Nephihah,** who were gathered together from the city of **Moroni and the city of Lehi and the city of Morianton,** were attacked by the Lamanites[Aztecs]." "Yea, even those who <u>had been compelled to flee from the land of **Manti,** and from the land round about, had come over and joined the Lamanites[Aztecs] in this part of the land</u>." "And thus being exceedingly numerous, yea, and receiving strength from day to day, by the command of Ammoron they came forth against the people of Nephihah[Mayans], and they did begin <u>to slay[kill] them with and exceedingly great slaughter.</u>" "And their armies were <u>so numerous that the remainder of the people of Nephihah were obliged to flee before them; and they came even and joined the army of Moroni.</u>" "(Alma 59:5-8, Book of Mormon)*

*"And now, when Moroni saw that the city of **Nephihah** was lost[again] he was exceedingly sorrowful, and **began to doubt, <u>because of the wickedness[evilness] of the people, whether they should not fall into the hands of their brethren."</u> "<u>Now this was the case with all the chief captains. They doubted and marveled also because of the wickedness[evilness] of the people,</u>** and this because of the <u>success of the Lamanites[Aztecs] over them.</u>" "And it came to pass that **<u>Moroni was angry with the government[Bidens, Pelosis, Romneys, Pences, etc], because of their indifference concerning the freedom of their country."</u>**(Alma 59:11-13, Book of Mormon)*

Moroni sends a scorching rebuke to the Chief Judge: Pahoran, at the end of the 29th year of the judges, or **62 B.C.,** and also receives a reply in the beginning of the 30th year, or **61 B.C.** *"And it came to pass that he[Moroni] wrote again to the governor of the land, who was*

Pahoran, *and these are the words which he wrote, saying:* **Behold, I direct mine epistle to Pahoran, in the city of Zarahemla, who is the chief governor over the land, and also to all those who have been chosen by this people[Nephite/Mayan people] to govern and manage the affairs of this war.**" *"For behold,* **I have somewhat to say unto them by the way of condemnation; for behold, ye yourselves know that ye have been appointed to gather together men and arm them with swords, and with cimeters, and all manner of weapons of war of every kind, and send forth against the Lamanites[Aztecs], in whatsoever parts they should come into our land.**" *(Alma 60:1-2, Book of Mormon)*

"But behold, **great has been the slaughter among our people;** *yea, thousands have fallen by the sword, while it might have otherwise been if ye had rendered unto our armies sufficient strength and succor for them. Yea, great* **has been your neglect towards us.**" **"And now behold, we desire to know the cause of this exceedingly great neglect; yea, we desire to know the cause of your thoughtless state." "Can you think to sit upon your thrones in a state of thoughtless stupor, while your enemies are spreading the work of death around you? Yea, while they are murdering thousands of your brethren---" "Yea, even they who have looked up to you for protection, yea, have placed you in a situation that you might have succored them, yea, ye might have sent armies unto them to have strengthened them, and have saved thousands of them from falling by the sword."** *"But behold,* **this is not all---ye have withheld your provisions from them, insomuch that many have fought and bled out their lives because of their great desires which they had for the welfare of this people; yea, and this they have done when they were about to perish with hunger, because of your exceedingly great neglect towards them"** *"(Alma 60:5-9, Book of Mormon)*

"Behold, **could ye suppose that ye could sit upon your thrones, and because of the exceeding goodness of God ye could do nothing and he would deliver you? Behold, if ye have supposed this ye have supposed in vain."** *"And now behold,* **I say unto you, I fear exceedingly that the judgments of God will come upon this people,**

because of their exceeding slothfulness, yea, even the slothfulness of our government, and their exceedingly great neglect towards their brethren[fellow man], yea, towards those who have been slain." "For were it not for the wickedness[evilness] which first commenced at our head, we could have withstood our enemies that they could have gained no power over us." "Yea, had it not been for the war which broke out among ourselves; yea, were it not for these king-men[Democrats/liberals/socialists], who caused so much bloodshed among ourselves; yea, at the time we were contending among ourselves, if we had united our strength as we hitherto have done; yea, had it not been for the desire of power and authority which those king-men had over us; had they been true to the cause of freedom, and united with us, and gone forth against our enemies, instead of taking up their swords against us, which was the cause of so much bloodshed among ourselves; yea, if we had gone forth against them in the strength of the Lord, we should have dispersed our enemies, for it would have been done, according to the fulfilling of his word." _(Alma 60:11,14-16, Book of Mormon)

★★★ *"But why should I say much concerning this matter? For we know not but what ye yourselves are seeking for authority. We know not but what ye are also "traitors" to your country." "Or is it that ye have neglected us because ye are in the heart of our country and ye are surrounded by security, that ye do not cause food to be sent unto us, and also men to strengthen our armies?" "And now, except ye do repent of that which ye have done, and begin to be up and doing, and send forth food and men unto us, and also unto Helaman, that he may support those parts of our country which he has regained, and that we may also recover the remainder of our possessions in these parts, behold it will be expedient that we contend no more with the Lamanites[Aztecs] until we have first cleansed our inward vessel, yea, even the great "head of our government"." "And except ye grant mine epistle, and come out and show unto me a true spirit of freedom, and strive to strengthen and fortify our armies, and grant unto them food for their support, behold I will leave a part of my freemen to maintain this part of our land, and I will leave the strength and the blessings of God upon them, that none other power can operate against them---"_(Alma 60:18-19,24-25,Book of Mormon)*

***"And I will come unto you, and if there be any among you that has a desire for freedom, yea, if there be even a spark of freedom remaining, behold I will stir up insurrections among you, even until those who have desires to usurp power and authority shall become extinct." "Yea, behold I do not fear your power nor your authority, but it is my God whom I fear; and it is according to his commandments that I do take my sword to defend the cause of my country, and it is because of your iniquity that we have suffered so much loss." "Behold it is time, yea, the time is now at hand, that except ye do bestir yourselves in the defense of your country and your little ones, the sword of justice doth hang over you; yea, and it shall fall upon you and visit you even to your utter destruction." "Behold, I wait for assistance from you; and, except ye do administer unto our relief, behold, I come unto you, even in the land of Zarahemla, and smite you with the sword, insomuch that ye can have no more power to impede the progress of this people in the cause of our freedom." "Behold, I am Moroni, your chief captain. I seek not for power, but to pull it down. I seek not for honor of the world, but for the glory of my God, and the freedom and welfare of my country. And thus I close mine epistle."(Alma 60:27-30, 36, Book of Mormon)*

This chapter about the wars during the time of Moroni, Chief General of the Nephites/Mayans and the Lamanites/Aztecs is to illustrate what selfishness of dissenters, and Democrats liberals/communists/king-men, and the unwillingness to call upon God, looks like, and how rebellion against God, causes a constant chaos. Also being without God , does irreparable harm. These are exactly the same things that the Communists/liberals are doing today. What the secret orders, violation of the innocent, the homosexuality, the illegal immigration, the corruption of the Christian churches, the evolution theories, the public schools, the Satan worship, witchcraft, the murders/

abortions, and the pedophilia, etc., is enough to send judgment upon our civilization. We need not think we are better than the Nephites/Mayans, or the Lamanites/Aztecs, because, at one time long ago, the Nephites/Mayans, from the land of Nephi/Peru/Ecuador etc., were greatly blessed of the Lord, until they went whoring after strange gods.

The Chief Judge, Pahoran, of whom, reminds me of Donald Trump, and informs Moroni of the cause of the neglect by his government. He admits that there are too many liberals/communists, filling the seats of government, that nothing can get done. He also talks about the interference by those who would seek to alter the laws in their plan to have a king, and give him all power, and authority. The evil communists, Democrats and liberals seized upon the opportunity to get their way during this war with the Lamanites/Aztecs, having failed early on, now are using it to their advantage. They want control and authority over the people, and are willing to sacrifice their own freedom, just to get their way. The corporate beast never gets satisfied.

Chief Judge Pahoran's Reply to General Moroni!

★★★ *"I Pahoran[Donald J. Trump], who am the chief governor of this land, do send these words unto Moroni, the chief captain over the army. Behold, I say unto you, Moroni, that I do not joy in your great afflictions, yea, it grieves my soul."* ***"But behold, there are those****[liberals/socialists/Democrats/Rat-Bastards]* ***who do joy in your afflictions, yea, insomuch that they have risen up in rebellion against me, and also those of my people who are freemen, yea, and those who have risen up are exceedingly numerous."*** *"And it is those* <u>*who have sought to take away the judgment-seat from me that have been the cause of this great iniquity; for they have used great flattery[disinformation/fake news/lies], and they have led away the hearts of many people, which will be the cause of*</u> ***sore affliction*** *among us; they have withheld our provisions, and have daunted[threatened, and lied to] our freemen that they have not come unto you."(Alma 61:2-4, Book of Mormon)*

"And behold, they[the liberals/Democrats/communists] have driven me out before them, and I have fled to the land of ***Gideon***,

with as many men as it were possible that I could get." "And behold, I have sent a proclamation **throughout this part of the land; and behold, they are flocking to us daily, to their arms, in the defense of their country and their freedom, and to avenge our wrongs."**

"And they have come unto us, insomuch that those[Democrats/liberals/ communists/liars/Rat bastards] who have risen up in rebellion against us are set at defiance, yea, **insomuch that they do fear us** and durst not come out against us to battle." **"They have got possession of the land of Zarahemla[Mayan heartland]; they have appointed a king over them, and he hath written unto the king of the Lamanites[Aztecs/ Nephite traitor-Ammoron], in the which he hath joined an alliance[collaboration] with him; in the which alliance[agreement] he hath agreed to maintain the city of Zarahemla [seat of Nephite/ Mayan government], which maintenance he supposeth will enable the Lamanites[Aztecs] to conquer the remainder of the land, and he shall be placed king over this [Nephite/Mayan] people when they shall be conquered under the Lamanites[Aztecs system of force].***"(Alma 61:5-8, Book of Mormon)*

"Gather together whatsoever force ye can upon your march hither[here], and we will go, speedily against those dissenters[communists, Democrats/liberals/kingmen], in the strength of our God according to the faith which is in us."
"And we **will take possession of the city of Zarahemla[center of government], that we may obtain more food to send forth unto Lehi and Teancum; yea, we will go forth against them in the strength of the Lord, and we will put an end to this great iniquity[evil]."** *"And now,* **Moroni, I do joy in receiving your epistle, for I was somewhat worried concerning what we should do, whether it should be just in us to go against our brethren."**
"But ye have said, except they repent[change] **the Lord hath commanded you that ye should go against them." "See** *that ye* **strengthen Lehi and Teancum in the Lord; tell them to fear not, for God will deliver them, yea, and also all those who stand fast in that liberty wherewith God hath made them free. And now I close mine epistle to my beloved brother, Moroni."***(Alma 61:17-21, Book of Mormon)*

As we the people observe the much police brutality, the disrespect by the ones put into power by the voice of the people, and who are paid by the people as their servants. The same who are entrusted with taking an oath to uphold and protect the Constitution from all enemies, foreign and domestic, they neglect their obligations, by doing just the opposite. The Constitution hangs by a thread **because those put into power to protect the Supreme Law of the Land make it only as strong as those who respect the rights of the people under the Constitution.** If they do what they are entrusted to do, then our country is strong, and the thread is like an unbreakable chain. President Trump was right, when he called on Mike Pence to do what was right, to protect his country, but Mike Pence was a coward, and violated his oath of office to support his country and our Constitution. He played into the hands of the kingmen, and their Democracy/ socialist form, of democratic government. He wanted to be liked by the rich, for he surely wasn't trying to help his country. He showed a great weakness of indifference, when he could have upheld his oath to protect the Constitution, against all enemies foreign and domestic.

In order to make that thread a strong chain, the people need to step up and know the Constitution. We must know of ourselves the truth, and be the ones to step up when the laws are violated by the ones who are entrusted to these fiduciary positions. The huge overreaches of power and jurisdiction is ridiculous and despicable. Give a communist a hand, they take an arm, and when they get your arm, they take your freedom.

> *"And now it came to pass that when* **Moroni had received this epistle his heart did take courage, and was filled with exceedingly great joy because of the faithfulness of Pahoran [Donald J. Trump],* *that he was not also a traitor [communist] to the freedom and cause of his country."* *"And it came to pass that* <u>*Moroni took a small number of men, according to the desire of Pahoran, and gave Lehi and Teancum command over the remainder of his army, and took his march towards the land of*</u> **Gideon."** **"And he did raise the standard of liberty [national flag] in whatsoever place he did enter, and gained whatsoever force he could in all his march towards the land of Gideon"** *"And* <u>**it came to pass that thousands did flock unto his**</u>

standard, and did take up their swords in the defence of their freedom, that they might not come into bondage[communism/ socialism, etc.]."(Alma 62:1,3-5,Book of Mormon)

***"*And behold, Pachus[appointed liberal/communist king, Joe Biden] was slain and his men were taken prisoners, and Pahoran[Donald J. Trump] was restored to his judgment-seat.*" "*And the men of Pachus[Joe Biden] received their trial, according to the law, and also those king-men who had been taken and cast into prison; and they were executed according to the law; yea, those[liberals/Democrats/communists, etc.] men of Pachus and those king-men, whosoever would not take up arms in the defence of their country, but would fight against it, were put to death.*" "And thus *it became expedient that this law should be strictly observed for the safety of their country; yea, and whosoever was found denying their freedom was speedily executed according to the law.*" "And thus ended *the thirtieth year of the reign of the judges over the people of Nephi[Mayans]; Moroni and Pahoran having restored peace to the land of Zarahemla, among their own people, and having inflicted death upon all those who were not* true to the cause of freedom.*"(Alma 62: 8-11, Book of Mormon)

The Nephites/Mayans were very intelligent and merciful to the Lamanites/Aztecs and always released them after a war or battle, if they promised to lay down their arms, and promise and covenant that they would not return again. If they did this they were allowed to live, and given their freedom to return to their lands and families. Whereas, the Lamanites/Aztecs were very opposite when they were in control, and they showed virtually no mercy when the tables were turned. The Lamanites/Aztecs were a people who wouldn't create jobs or industry, but were always around to steal or kill the Nephites/Mayans because they wanted what they had and didn't want to work for it. They would finally cause the Nephites/Mayans to move in order for them to have any peace. At this time the Lamanites/Aztecs still had many Nephite/Mayan women and children as prisoners, that they needed to account for.

"*And it came to pass that Moroni and Pahoran, leaving a large body of men in the land of Zarahemla, took their march with a large body of men towards the land of* **Nephihah,** *being determined to overthrow the Lamanites[Aztecs] in that city.*" "*And as it came to pass as they were marching towards the land , <u>they took a large body of men of the Lamanites[Aztecs], and slew many of them, and took their provisions and their weapons of war.</u>*" "*And it came to pass after they had taken them, <u>they caused them to enter into a covenant that they would no more take up their weapons of war against the Nephites[Mayans].</u>*" "*And when <u>they had entered into this covenant they[the Mayans/Nephites] sent them to dwell with the people of Ammon, and they were in number about four thousand who had not been slain.</u>*" *(Alma 62:14-17, Book of Mormon)*

The Lamanites/Aztecs were now very afraid of the Nephites/Mayans because of the many battles won by them, with so few, and because their exceedingly great courage, and faith in their God. In fact, the Lamanites/Aztecs were terrified, especially of the army of Moroni, knowing he was leading it. Even the many instances the Lamanites recalled, that even a small Nephite/Mayan army devastated numerous hosts of the Lamanites/Aztecs. There was not any war started by the Nephites/Mayans, unless it was dissenters from the Nephites/Mayans, who were the cause, most often, started by the selfish, liberal thinking Lamanites/Aztecs.

And it came to pass that when they had sent them away they[the Nephite/Mayan army] pursued their course towards the land of **Nephihah.** *And it came to pass that when they had come to the city of* **Nephihah,** *they did pitch their tents in the plains of Nephihah, which is near the city of Nephihah,*" "<u>**Now Moroni was desirous that the Lamanites[Aztecs] should come out to battle against them, upon the plains; but the Lamanites[Aztecs], knowing of their exceedingly great courage, and beholding the greatness of their numbers, therefore they durst not come out against them;**</u> *therefore they did not come to battle that day.*" *(Alma 62:18-19, Book of Mormon)*

Moroni and his army, in the retaking of the city of Nephihah, did so without losing a single man, as the Lamanites/Aztecs surrendered and became the Nephite's/Mayan's prisoners.

> *"And when the night came, Moroni went forth in the darkness of the night, and came upon the top of the wall to spy out in what part of the city the Lamanites[Aztecs] did camp with their army."* *"And it came to pass that they were on* **the east, by the entrance and they were all asleep. And now Moroni returned to his army, and caused that they should prepare in haste** **strong cords and ladders, to be let down from the top of the wall into the inner part of the wall.** *" "And it came to pass that Moroni caused that his men should march forth and come upon the top of the wall , and let themselves down into that part of the city, yea, even on the west, where the Lamanites[Aztecs] did not camp with their armies." "And it came to pass* **that they were all let down into the city by night,** by the means of their strong cords and their ladders; **thus when the morning came they[the Mayan soldiers] were all within the walls of the city.** *"(Alma 62:20-23, Book of Mormon)*

> *"And now, when the Lamanites[Aztecs] awoke and saw that the armies of Moroni[Nephites/Mayans] were within the walls, they were affrighted[terrified/shocked] exceedingly, insomuch that they did* **flee** out by the pass." *"And now when Moroni saw that they* were **fleeing before him, he did march forth against them, and slew many, and surrounded many others, and took them prisoners;** *and the remainder of them fled into the land of* **Moroni, which was in the borders by the seashore.** *" "Thus had Moroni and Pahoran obtained the possession of the city of* **Nephihah** *without the loss of one [Nephite/Mayan] soul; and there were many of the Lamanaite[Aztecs] who were slain." (Alma 62:20-26, Book of Mormon)*

When the Lamanite[Aztec] prisoners saw how good the "Children of Ammon" were treated, and how happy and free they were, they wanted to join them, and as they desired, it was granted unto them.

*"Now it came to pass that many of the **Lamanites[Aztecs], that were prisoners were desirous to join the people of Ammon and become a free people.**" "And it came to pass that <u>as many as were desirous, unto them it was granted according to their desires.</u>" "Therefore, **all the prisoners of the Lamanites[Aztecs] did join the people of Ammon, and did begin to labor exceedingly, tilling the ground, raising all manner of grain, and flocks and herds of every kind; and thus were the Nephites[Mayans] relieved from a great burden; yea, insomuch that they were relieved from all the prisoners of the Lamanites[Aztecs].**"(Alma 62:27-29, Book of Mormon)*

All of the Lamanites/Aztecs soldiers fled north now, from the armies of Helaman, out of the land of Manti, to the city of Nephihah in the north to strengthen the armies of their king, Ammoron, the brother of Amaleckiah, who at the start of the war, Teancum, slipped into his camp and thrust a spear into his heart. This reminds me of the British during the Revolutionary war, and how all of the British fled to the eastern coast to unite with their General Cornwallis[Ammoron], for the last great battle, before the war ended. He just dreaded the moment when George Washington[Moroni] came with his armies to finish the conflict. This is the same scenario playing out before Cornwallis's time, with Ammoron, the Lamanite/Aztec king. All of the Lamanite/Aztec armies are now fleeing before Moroni's armies, from city to city, until the final meeting on the seashore, although in different areas. This was the end of the 30th year, **61 B.C.,** of the Judges and the beginning of **60 B.C.**

The same Teancum, the captain of Bountiful, that headed Amalickiah, king of the Lamanites/Aztecs at the beginning of the war, then slipped into his camp at night and put a spear threw his heart. He did the same to his brother, Ammoron, also king of the Lamanites/Aztecs, at the end of the war. Both of these wicked kings were the cause of so much murder, and stress, and conflict. Now Teancum, being very angry with what traitors to his country can do, he slipped into the camp of Ammoron at night, and threw a javelin into his heart. However, Ammoron stirred enough to awaken his body guards, and they chased Teancum to the wall, and before he could get over and away, he was killed.

> "*And thus they did encamp for the* **night. For behold, the Nephites[Mayans] and the Lamanites[Aztecs] were weary because of the greatness of the march; therefore they did not resolve upon any stratagem in the night-time, save it were Teancum; for he was exceedingly angry with Ammoron, insomuch that he considered that Ammoron, and Amalickiah his brother, had been the cause of this great and lasting war between them and the Lamanites[Aztecs], which had been the cause of so much war and bloodshed, yea, and so much** *famine.*" "*And it came to pass that* **Teancum** *in his anger did go forth into the camp of the Lamanites[Aztecs], and did let himself down over the walls of the city. And he went forth with a cord, from place to place, insomuch that he did find the king; and he did cast a javelin at him, which did pierce him near the heart. But behold, the king did awaken his servants before he died, insomuch that they did pursue Teancum, and slew him.*"(Alma 62:35-36, Book of Mormon)

The next day, Moroni and his armies attacked the Lamanites[Aztecs], capitalizing on Teancum's sacrifice of his own life to end the war. Teancum had virtually ended the war by killing Ammoron, king of the Lamanites/Aztecs because now, without a leader to feed their frenzy, chaos ensued, and terror commenced. The Lamanites/Aztecs then fled back south to their own lands, if they could escape. This ended the 32nd year of the reign of the Judges. Now **59 B.C.**

> "*Now it came to pass that* **Moroni marched forth on the morrow, and came upon the Lamanites[Aztecs], insomuch that they did slay them with a great slaughter; and they did drive them out of the land; and they did flee, even that they did not return at that time against the Nephites[Mayans].*" "*And thus ended* the thirty and first year of the reign of the judges over the people of Nephi[Mayans]; and thus they had had wars, and bloodsheds, and famine, and affliction, for the space of many years.*" "*And there

*had been murders, and contentions, and dissensions, and all manner of iniquity among the people of Nephi[Mayans]; nevertheless for **the righteous sake, yea, because of the <u>prayers of the righteous, they were spared</u>**.*"(Alma 62:38-40, Book of Mormon)

The last thing Moroni did before he hung up his sword at the end of the war, was to oversee the fortification of many of the cities surrounding Zarahemla, we know today as northern Colombia, before returning to his home. Helaman also returned south to the land of Nephi, in Peru, to teach the gospel of Jesus Christ and reestablish the Church, because the length of the war, had caused many to become hardened in their faith.

*"And it came to pass that after <u>Moroni had fortified those parts of the land which were most exposed to the Lamanites[Aztecs], until they were sufficiently strong</u>, **he returned to the city of Zarahemla; and also Helaman returned to the place of his inheritance; and there was once more peace established among the people of Nephi.**"*
*"**And Moroni yielded up the command of his armies into the hands of his son, whose name was Moronihah; and he retired to his own house that he might spend the remainder of his days in peace.**"(Alma 62:42-43, Book of Mormon)*

General Moroni died at about the age of 31-years old, more or less. He was 25-years old when he assumed the responsibility of the safety and well being of his people. He endured much physical, as well as mental stress that goes along with this monumental responsibility. Moroni was a fine man, and we can all be proud of Moroni's unwavering courage, his integrity, his sense of what right is, and his unshakable faith in his God. To bad there is not more men just like him. This now ended the year, **55 B.C.**

*"**<u>And it came to pass that Moroni died also. And thus ended the thirty and sixth year of the reign of the judges.</u>**"(Alma 63:3, Book of Mormon)*

Chapter 15

Final Battle and Destruction of the Nephites/Mayans: Hill Cumorah, NY

The North American Migration of the Nephites[Mayans]
The building of ships, and the corruption by secret orders

In the beginning of the 37ᵗʰ year of the Judges, there was a large migration of Nephites/Mayans from the land of Zarahemla, or northern Colombia. Their first company consisted of 5,400 men, not including all of their women, and children, but added to the 5,400-men, that left Zarahemla, or Northern Colombia, South America. They went west across the narrow neck of land that separated the sea on the west and the sea on the east, going through Panama, Desolation, Nicaragua, Costa Rica Guatemala, Mexico, and on northward, including the land that had many great rivers and lakes. to inhabit many parts of what today we know as America-Republic. This first group was only the beginning, as there were many more to follow. This mass migration by land took place beginning in **54 B.C.**

> *"And it came to pass that in the <u>thirty and seventh year of the reign of the judges</u>, **there was a large company of men, even to the amount of five thousand and four hundred men, with their wives amd their children, departed out of the land of Zarahemla into the land which was northward.**"* *"(Alma 63:4,9, Book of Mormon)*

In this same year, was a Nephite/Mayan, who built ships. He built a very large ship at a place known as the land of Desolation, east of Bountiful, on the narrow neck of land, where he was able to launch it. It was launched in the west sea/Pacific Ocean, and many did enter therein and sailed Northward.

> *"And it came to pass that **Hagoth, he being an exceedingly curious man, therefore he went forth and built him an exceedingly large ship, on the borders of the land Bountiful, by the land Desolation, and launched it forth into the west sea, by the narrow neck which led into the land northward[North America].*" "*And behold, there were many of the Nephites[Mayans] who did enter therein and did sail forth with much provisions[supplies],and also many women and children; and they took their course northward. And thus ended the thirty and seventh year.*"(Alma 63:5-6, Book of Mormon)*

Hagoth built one other ship and it did sail forth northward, and the first ship did return, and carried many more men, women, and children northward, and neither ship was heard from again. This year began **54 B.C. ended 53** B.C., and there continued to be much migration to the land northward, by land and by water.

> *"And in the <u>thirty and eighth year[53 B.C.], this **man[Hagoth] built other ships. And the first ship did also return, and many more people[Nephites/Mayans] did enter into it; and they also took much provisions, and set out again to the land northward.*" "*And it came to pass that t**hey were never heard of more. And we suppose that they were drowned in the depths of the sea. And it came to pass that one other ship also did sail forth; and whither she did go we know not.*" "*And it came to pass that in this year there were many people[Nephites/Mayans] who went forth into the land northward. And thus ended the thirty and eighth year.*"(Alma 63:7-9, Book of Mormon)*

More ships were built and more people continued to migrate, looking for more opportunity. This is why the Polynesians,

Hawaiians,and the Tongans, etc. exist. They inhabited the isles of the sea. They also are remnants from the tribes of Israel, predominantly from the tribe of Joseph, who was sold into Egypt. *"And it came to pass in the thirty and ninth year of the reign of the judges, [52 B.C.] Shiblon died also, and Corianton had gone forth to the land northward[North America] in a ship, to carry forth provisions unto the people who had gone forth into that land."* *"Therefore it became expedient for Shiblon to confer sacred things, before his death, upon the son of Helaman, who was called Helaman, being called after the name of his father."* *"Now behold, all those engravings which were in the possession of Helaman were written and sent forth among the children of men throughout all the land, save it were those parts which had been commanded by Alma should not go forth."(Alma 63:10-12, Book of Mormon)*

Meanwhile, the center point for the continuous onslaught from the Lamanites/Aztecs was that narrow neck of land that they couldn't access. It was the Lamanites/Aztecs desire to overrun the north, being as they were hemmed off by the military of the Nephites/Mayans, beginning at the land Bountiful, also part of the land of Zarahemla. It was for this reason the Nephites/Mayans were guarding against the Lamanites/Aztecs getting access to the land north, and why the narrow neck of land was so advantageous to them.

"And it came to pass also in this year[52 B.C.] there were some dissenters[Democrats/liberals] who had gone forth unto the Lamanites[Aztecs]; and they were stirred up again to anger against the Nephites[Mayans]." *"And also in this same year they[Aztecs] came down[from the land of Nephi/Ecuador/ Peru etc.] to war against the people of Moronihah, or against the army of Moronihah[Nephites/Mayans], in the which they[Lamanites/Aztecs] were beaten and driven back again to their own lands, suffering great loss".(Alma 63:14-16, Book of Mormon)*

The Nephites/Mayans had the same system of law as we have under the Constitution today, whereas, the leaders are appointed by the voice of the people. They had those who constantly stood for Freedom/Almighty God, and many that stood for control/Slavery/

Satan. These were the kingmen/Democrats/Liberals. The Nephites/ Mayans were constantly having to guard against the lies these evil, selfish people spread, causing the Lamanites/Aztecs to even consider the source that these lies came from, and take them seriously, in light of the fact, that many Lamanites/Aztecs always ended up dead. They lost many more as always, compared to the Nephites/Mayans.

> *"Now these are their names <u>who did contend[ran for office] for the Judgment-seat[run for President], who did also cause the people to contend[get behind, campaign for]:Pahoran, Paanchi, and Pacumeni."</u>* *"Now these are not all the sons of Pahoran<u>(for he had many), but these are they who did contend[run for office] for the judgment-</u>* **<u>seat; therefore, they did cause three divisions [Conservatives, Libertarians,and Democrats] among the</u>** <u>people.</u>*"* *"Nevertheless, it came to pass that* **Pahoran**[i.e. Donald J. Trump] **was appointed by the voice of the people** *of Nephi[Mayans]."* *"And it came to pass that* **Pacumeni**<u>, when he saw that he could not obtain the judgment-seat, he</u> **did unite with the voice of the people.**"*(Helaman 1:3-6, Book of Mormon)*

Those who desired power over the people used many fraudulent methods to alter the laws, i.e. voter fraud, and manipulation, that threatened the liberty of the people, as was the case of Paanchi[Biden,Pelosi/Schiff], and they began to swear false accusations, and secretly met to conspire to assassinate, impeach, and falsely accuse, to cause them trouble, and difficulty, by immorally attacking in an attempt to defame [D.Trump etc] those who were appointed by the voice of the people, to push their Democracy/socialist agendas.

> *"But behold,* **<u>Paanchi, [Biden],and those part of the people that were desirous that he should be their governor[president] was exceedingly wroth[angry]; therefore, he was about to flatter away those people to rise up in rebellion against their</u>** <u>brethren.</u>*"* *"And it came to pass as* **he was about to do this, behold, <u>he was taken[arrested], and was tried according to the voice of the people[trial by jury/ Constitution], and condemned[convicted&sentenced] unto death; for he had raised up in rebellion[sedition] and sought</u>**

to destroy the liberty of the people[committed treason]." "*Now when those people who were desirous that he should be their governor saw that he was condemned[sentenced] unto death, therefore they were angry, and behold, they sent forth one Kishkumen[a Jesuit assassin, i.e.John Wilkes Booth] even to the judgment-seat of Pahoran, and murdered Pahoran[Lincoln, Garfield, Kennedy, etc.] as he sat upon the judgment-seat.*" "*And he was pursued by the servants of Pahoran[secret service] but behold, so speedy was the flight of Kishkumen, that no man could overtake him.*" "*And he went unto those[Vatican/Jesuits i.e. John Paul] that had sent him, and they all entered into a covenant[secret oath], yea, swearing by their everlasting Maker, that they would tell no man that Kishkumen[jesuit assassin] had murdered Pahoran.*" "*Therefore, Kishkumen[Jesuit assassin] was not known among the people of Nephi[Mayans], for he was in disguise at the time that he murdered Pahoran, and Kishkumen and his band[Jesuits/liberals/Democrats], who had covenanted with him, did mingle themselves among the people, [business owners, governors, congress men and women, church leaders, military leaders, county workers, judges, law enforcement, attorneys, etc.] in a manner that they all could not be found; but as many as were found were condemned[convicted & sentenced] to death.*" "*(Helaman 1:7-12, Book of Mormon)*

Chapter 16

Coriantumr Leads an Army of Lamanites Into The Land of Zarahemla!

Because of the slothfulness of the Nephites/Mayans, The Lamanites/Aztecs invaded them again, this time better prepared than ever before, and even sent a *Goliath* of a man as their general to lead them. This giant was a descendant of Zarahemla[Toltecs], who they found still alive in the land, the last remaining giant from the people who preceded him and his people, the Mulekites/Toltecs. This Last giant, was the last king of the Jaredites/Olmecs, and lived 9-moons/9-months with the king of the Mulekites/Toltecs. His name was Coriantumr, and he was a large and mighty man. The story of his reign, is talked about in the first chapter of this book and in the Book of Ether, in the Book of Mormon.

In 9-months a lot of things can happen. Do you not think that Coriantumr didn't marry one of the daughters of the people of Zarahemla within 9-months to keep his seed alive? How convenient for Zarahemla's descendant to also be named Coriantumr, after his grandfather, or great grandfather, who at one time was called King Coriantumr, of the whole kingdom of the Jaredites/Olmecs.

★*"And it came to pass in the <u>forty and first year</u>[**50 B.C.**] of the reign of the judges, that the Lamanites[**Aztecs**] had gathered together an <u>innumerable army of men, and armed them with swords, and with</u>*

cimeters and with bows, and with arrows, and with head-plates, and with breastplates, and with all manner of shields of every kind." "And they came **down**[from the AndesMountains of Ecuador, Peru, Bolivia, southern Colombia] *that they might pitch battle against the Nephites[Mayans]. And they were led by a man whose name was "Coriantumr"; and he was a descendant of Zarahemla; and he was a "dissenter from among the Nephites[Mayans]"; and he was a "large and a mighty man".* " "Therefore, the king of the Lamanites[Aztecs], whose name was **Tubaloth, and who was the son of Ammoron, supposing that Coriantumr, being a mighty man,** could stand against[whip] the **Nephites[Mayans], with his strength and also with his "great wisdom", insomuch that by sending him forth he should gain power over the Nephites[Mayans]---** (Helaman 1:14-16, Book of Mormon)

"Therefore, he did stir them up to anger, and he did gather together his armies, **and he [Tubaloth] did appoint Coriantumr to be their leader, and did cause that they should go down to the land of Zarahemla to battle against the Nephites[Mayans]."** "And it came to pass that because of so much contention[conspiracy, treason, criminals in high places/liberals] and so much **difficulty in the government, that they had not kept sufficient guards in the land of Zarahemla**[heartland of the government of the **Nephites/ Mayans**];**for they had supposed that the Lamanites[Aztecs] durst not come into the heart of their lands to attack that great city Zarahemla[N. Colombia]**" "But it came to pass that **Coriantumr** *did march forth at the head of his numerous host, and came upon the inhabitants of the city, and their march was with* **such exceedingly great speed that there was no time for the Nephites[Mayans] to gather together their armies,"** "Therefore **Coriantumr did cut down the watch by the entrance of the city, and did march forth with his whole army into the city, and did slay[kill] everyone who did oppose them, insomuch that they did take posession of the whole city[Capital City, Zarahemla]."** "(Helaman 1:17-20, Book of Mormon)

"And it came to pass that __Pacumeni[newly elected judge] who__ __was the chief judge, did flee before[chased by] Coriantumr, even__ __to he walls of the city. And it came to pass that Coriantumr__ __did smite[fling/beat/throw] him against the wall, insomuch__ __that he died, And thus ended the days of Pacumeni.__" *"And now when __Coriantumr__ saw[realized] __that he was in possession of the__ __city Zarahemla, and realized that the Nephites[Mayans] had__ __fled before them, and were slain, and were taken[captured], and__ __thrown into prison, and that he had obtained the "strongest hold__ __in all the land", his heart took courage[confident] insomuch__ __that he was about to go forth against all the land[realm of the__ __Nephites[Mayans].__"* *"And now he did not tarry[let opportunity go to waste]__in the land of Zarahemla, but he did march forth with__ __a large army, even towards the city of "Bountiful";__ for it was __his__ determination to go forth and cut his way through with the __sword, that__ __he might obtain the "north parts of the land"[North America].__"* (Helaman 1:21-23, Book of Mormon)

Now Coriantumr and the Lamanites/Aztecs had invaded the Land of Zarahemla without a struggle, and now were headed for Bountiful to overthrow the fortified city, that guarded the mouth of the narrow neck of land that led into the north country/North America. He now realized that if he succeeded in his ambition to conquer such a people as the Nephites/Mayans and take all of their lands for himself, he would become a great man in the eyes of his Lamanite/Aztec king. He saw great fame and fortune and power, and he was not about to let the "grass grow under his feet".

We will soon see that Coriantumr's "great wisdom" was not so great. There is a true saying that goes like this: *"If something seems too good to be true, it usually is!"* His god, Satan was inspiring him with false confidence. Surely, he had heard about the prowess of the people of God, the Nephites/Mayans, their unconquerable spirit and their courage. A truly wise man would have been concerned, and have been looking for answers, and fast. He had placed himself, and his Lamanite /Aztec armies into a terrible situation, and one that was to be very costly, and knowing the Nephites/Mayans, and knowing what they were capable of, made him a very foolish general.

"And, supposing that their[Nephites/Mayans] greatest strength was in the center of the land, therefore he did march forth, giving them no time to assemble[organize] themselves together save it were in small bodies; and in this manner they did fall upon them[Nephites/ Mayans] and cut them down to the earth." **"But behold, this march of Coriantumr through the center of the land gave Moronihah[high- general of the Nephite /Mayan armies] great advantage over them[Lamanites/Aztec armies], notwithstanding the greatness of the number of the Nephites who were** *slain[killed]."* **"For behold, Moronihah had supposed that the Lamanites[Aztecs] durst not come into the center of the land, but that they would attack the cities** *round about in the borders as they had hitherto done; therefore* Moronihah **had caused that their[Nephite/Mayan] strong armies should maintain those parts round about by the borders."** *"But behold, the Lamanites were not frightened according to his[Coriantumr's] desire,* **but they had come into the center of the land, and had taken the capital city which was the city of Zarahemla, and were marching through the most capital parts[most populated] of the land, slaying the people with a great slaughter, both men, women, and children, taking possession of many cities and of many strongholds." "But when Moronihah had discovered this, he immediately sent forth [mighty captain] Lehi with an army round about to head them[Lamanites/Aztecs] before they should come to the land "Bountiful"" "And thus he did; and he did head them before they came to the land Bountiful, and gave unto them battle, insomuch that they[the Lamanites/ Aztecs] began to retreat back towards the land of Zarahemla."** *"(Helaman 1:24- 29, Book of Mormon)*

So much for all of Coriantumr's supposed glory and fame and fortune. He allowed himself to be deceived by lies, and pictures of becoming king himself of all the land. He greatly and foolishly underestimated the fighting courage and strength of true "Sons of God". Moronihah, the son of the great general Moroni, headed them in their rear, by catching up to Coriantumr, and his army from behind, and began to kill them, in the which Coriantumr was also killed.

The Nephites/Mayans then surrounded the Lamanites/Aztecs, and commenced to destroy them until they surrendered. It is now **49 B.C.**

> *"And it came to pass that* **Moronihah did head them in the retreat, and did give unto them battle, insomuch that it became an exceedingly bloody battle; yea, many were slain, and among the number who were slain Coriantumr was also found.** *" "And now, behold,* **the Lamanites[Aztecs] could not retreat either way, neither on the north, nor on the south, nor on the east, nor on the west, for they were surrounded on every hand by the Nephites[Mayans].** *" "And thus had* **Coriantumr plunged the Lamanites[Aztecs] into the midst of the Nephites[Mayans], insomuch that they were in the power of the Nephites[Mayans], and he himself was slain and the Lamanites[Aztecs] did yield themselves into the hands of the Nephites[Mayans].** *" "And it came to pass that* **Moronihah took possession of the city of Zarahemla again, and caused that the Lamanites[Aztecs] who had been taken prisoners should depart out of the land in peace.** *"*
> *"And thus ended the* forty and first year of the reign of the judges. *"*
> *(Helaman 1:30-33, Book of Mormon)*

Chapter 17

Signs and wonders up to Christ's Birth
Secret-order-network, Bands of Gadianton Robbers/Liberals

To think that this exciting story is so real and true. As it is in every civilization, selfish people uphold Communism/liberalism in their governments. It is because the natural man seeks for power and riches, and the praise of the world. They conspire with the evil one, through secret orders, i.e. illuminati, Jesuits, Masons, etc.. They murder, lie, steal, and war, etc., and their judgment seats were filled with traitors, and they followed a chain of leadership, and today I am sure who the "Whore of All the Earth" is. Just follow the lies and the Money. Meanwhile we continue forward with the voice of the people, to put things back in order.

"And it came to pass *in the forty and second year of the reign of the judges[49B.C.], after Moronihah had established again peace between the Nephites[Mayans] and the Lamanites[Aztecs], behold there was no one to fill the judgment-seat; therefore there began to be a contention again among the people concerning who should fill the judgment-seat[a new election].*" "And it came to pass that **Helaman,** who was the son of Helaman[the general], was appointed[elected] to fill the judgment-seat, by the *voice of the people.*" "But behold, **Kishkumen[***the same mob-family hitman], who had murdered Pahoran, did lay wait to destroy Helaman also; and he was upheld by his band[of i.e. jesuits/illuminatti/***

Liberals], who had entered into a covenant that no one should know his wickedness." "For there was one "Gadianton" who was exceedingly expert in many words, and also in his craft, to carry on the "secret work of murder" and of robbery; therefore he became the leader of the band of Kishkumen[crime families/ Democrats/liberals/communists]." (Helaman 2:1-4,Book of Mormon)

"Therefore he [Gadianton] did flatter them, and also Kishkumen, that if they would place him in the judgment-seat[as president] he would grant unto those who belonged to his band[democrat club] that they should be placed in power and authority among the people; therefore Kishkumen [Joe Biden, etc.,]sought to destroy Helaman[i.e. Donald J. Trump]." "And it came to pass as he went forth towards the judgment-seat to destroy Helaman, behold one of the servants of Helaman[undercover detective/secret service/ etc.], having been out by night, and having obtained, through disguise, a knowledge of those plans which had been laid by this band[Jesuit/communists] to destroy Helaman[Donald Tump]---" "And it came to pass that he[undercover detective] met Kishkumen[crime family hitman/ liberal/Jesuit/communist], and gave unto him a sign[sign of the secret orders/illuminatti handshake]; therefore Kishkumen made known unto him the object of his desire, desiring that he would conduct him to the judgment-seat that he might murder Helaman." "(Helaman 2:5-7, Book of Mormon)

"And when the servant of Helaman had known all the heart of Kishkumen, and how that it was his object to murder, and also that it was the object of all those [jesuits/democrats/communists] who belonged to his band to murder, and to rob, and to gain power, "(and this was their secret plan, and their combination[contract/ covenant/oath]) the servant of Helaman said unto Kishkumen; Let us go forth unto the judgment -seat." "Now this did please Kishkumen exceedingly, for he did suppose that he should accomplish his design; but behold, the servant of Helaman, as they were going forth unto the judgment-seat, did stab Kishkumen even to the

*heart, that he fell dead without a groan. And he ran and told Helaman all the things which he had seen, and heard, and done." "And it came to pass that **Helaman[Donald J. Trump] did send forth to take this band of [deep state] robbers[Democrats/ liberals/communists] and "secret murderers", that they might be executed according to the law[Constitution].** "(Helaman 2:8-10, Book of Mormon)*

*"And more of this **Gadianton[Barack Obama]** shall be spoken hereafter. And thus ended the forty and second **year[49 B.C.]** of the reign of the judges over the people of Nephi[the Mayan people]."* ***"And behold, in the "end of this book" ye shall see that this "Gadianton[Democrat/liberal/communist party/Democracy/ secret orders]" did prove the overthrow, yea, almost the "entire destruction of the people of Nephi[Mayans]."***(Helaman 2:12-13, Book of Mormon)

It was not any secret that liberal thinking arose in every civilization, and Democrats/Liberals/Communists were the reason for every civilization to dwindle in unbelief in Almighty God. They are also the reason for so many wars, and so much control and bloodshed. This ended the 43rd -year of the reign of the Judges, over the Nephites/ Mayan people. It is now **48 B.C.**

*"And it came to pass in the forty and third year of the reign of the judges, there was no contention among the people of Nephi[Mayan people] save **it were a little pride which was in the church, which did cause** some little **dissensions[controversy] among the people, which affairs were settled in the ending of the forty and third year[48 B.C.].**"(Helaman 3:1, Book of Mormon)*

Chapter 18

Land differentiation of Land Lehi and Land of Mulek

More Migrations to the North American Continent
And their building and their shipping

In the 46th-year of the reign of the Judges, or **44 B.C.,** more contentions and dissensions arose, and many more Nephites/Mayans migrated into the North country/North America, this time as far as the northeast coast[New England, NY, PA, Canada, etc.], and any place in between, and began populating all regions. America and Canada, and the New Territories, including Alaska, where vast amounts of land, was open for the taking.

> *"And it came to pass in the forty and sixth year[44 B.C.], yea, <u>there was much contention[controversy] and many dissensions[disagreements]; in the which **there were an exceedingly great many who departed out of the land of Zarahemla**[Northern Colombia, Cental America], **and went forth unto the land northward to inherit the land.**"</u> "And <u>**they did travel to an "exceedingly great distance", insomuch that they came to [great lakes: Michigan, Wisconsin, Illinois, Indiana, Ohio, etc.]"large bodies of water and many rivers"[Mississippi, Ohio, Missouri, Hudson, etc.] .**</u>" "Yea, <u>**and even they[Nephites/Mayan people] did spread forth into all parts of the land, into whatever parts it had not been rendered**</u>*

desolate, and without timber, because of the "many inhabitants who before inherited the land[Olmecs/Jaredites/Giants/people of Coriantumr]." "And now _no part of the land was desolate, save it were for timber; but_ **because of the "greatness" of the destruction of the people[Jaredites/Olmecs] who had before inhabited the land it was called desolate."** " (Helaman 3:3-6, Book of Mormon)

★★★ "And _there being but little timber upon the face of the land, nevertheless the people[Nephites/Mayans] who went forth became "exceedingly expert in the working of cement"; therefore they did build houses of cement, in the which they did dwell."_ "And it came to pass that _**they[Nephites/Mayans] did multiply and spread, and did go forth from the land southward[Central America/Colombia/Land of Zarahemla] to the land northward[even as far as Greenland/on the east /extremities of Canada on the North to Arctic Ocean, and Alaska, Dutch Harbor on the west], and did "spread insomuch that they began to cover the face of the whole earth, from the sea south[Gulf of Mexico/ Carribean] to the sea north[Arctic Ocean/North Pole], from the sea west[Pacific Ocean] to the sea east[Atlantic Ocean]."**_ "And the **people who were in the land northward did dwell in tents, and in houses of cement,** _and they did suffer whatsoever_ **tree should spring up upon the face of the land that it should grow up, that in time they might have timber to build their houses, yea,** _their cities, and their_ **temples, and their synagogues,** _and their sanctuaries,, and all manner of their buildings._" (Helaman 3:7-9, Book of Mormon)

★★ "And it came to pass as _**timber was exceedingly scarce in the land northward, "they did send forth MUCH by the way of "shipping"." "And thus they did enable the people in the land northward [North America] that they might build many cities, both of wood and of cement."**_ "And it came to pass _**that there were "many of the people of Ammon who were Lamanites[Aztecs] by birth, did "also go forth into this land.[North America]."**_ (Helaman 3:10-12, Book of Mormon)

There were many of the Lamanite/Aztecs who had joined to the Church of God among the Nephites/Mayans, had also been able to migrate into the country in the north, and records that are innumerable, have been kept, chiefly by the Nephites. Anytime some alleged expert uses the term: "Prehistoric" people, you know immediately they are ignorant and many times on purpose. There is nothing prehistoric about any child of God from Adam to this time. There were many records kept, especially among Godly people. The Nephites/Mayans were commanded of God to keep records. They passed the responsibility of keeping a history of the people down from generation to generation, for the purpose of future generations to learn from.

They kept baptismal records, ordination records, temple records, marriage records, they had rooms and rooms full of records. They had mostly records testifying of God and his commandments to his sons and daughters. If this was not the case, then why did the Cardinal from Spain come with the Catholic Jesuit military, when conquering the Lamanites/Aztecs, in South America, after 1492 and discover the Island of all white natives, and their huge rooms of records. The history states that not only did they murder them, but they burned rooms full of records, and there were thousands upon thousands of the Nephite/Mayan records that were destroyed. It seems to me that having an opportunity to know more about these people, that just for the history alone, a civilized country would want to preserve the records for resource material out of curiosity, if not for any other reason. However, the Roman Empire/Catholic Church serves a different master, and there is always a spiritual war going on, Worlds without end.

The war was fought before we, as mortals came to earth, and it is being fought in the physical world here now and it will continue to be fought after this world, infinitely. The Catholic Church was organized in approximately 210 A.D. to battle and contradict the Church of Jesus Christ. The Catholic Church was trying to extinguish any knowledge of Christ it could, and it ruled with blood and horror upon the face of the earth. It attempted to stamp out any opposition to Satan it could, everywhere the worship of Christ burst into light. This was the reason that the Cardinal burnt those Mayan /Nephite records, and went on to kill thousands of natives, even after conquering the people into submission. This is the same thing that Hitler did to the Jewish people in Germany. It was to wipe out, and extinguish possibly the knowledge of Jesus Christ. The Catholic Church wanted to control their minds, not just their country, or their labor. Satan wants all of us to forget in fear, who you are serving, other than submission to his lies, and servitude. This is why institutions like the Smithsonian Institute is withholding evidence of these ancient Americans, This is why the Democrats are trying to destroy our government under the Constitution, and this is why the liberals push evolution and "Prehistoric". They don't want you to know your true history.

*"And now there are **many records kept of the proceedings of this people[Nephites/Mayans], by many of this people, which are particular and 'very large concerning them.'** " "But behold, **a hundredth part of the proceedings of this people[Nephites/ Mayans], yea, the account of the Lamanites[Aztecs] and of the Nephites[Mayans], and their wars, and contentions[disagreements], and dissensions[insurrections], and their preaching, and their prophecies, and their shipping and their building of ships, and their building of temples, and of synagogues, and their sanctuaries, and their righteousness, and their wickedness, and their murders, and their robbings, and their plundering, and all manner of abominations and whoredoms, cannot be contained in this work.** " "But behold, there are many books and many records of every kind, and they have been kept chiefly by the Nephites[Mayans].*" (Helaman 3:13-15, Book of Mormon)*

*"And they have been handed down from generation to generation by the **Nephites[Mayans], even until they have fallen into transgression and have been muredered, plundered, and driven forth, and slain, and scattered upon the face of the earth, "and mixed with the Lamanites[Aztecs] until they are no more called the Nephites[Mayans], becoming wicked, and wild, and ferocious, yea, even becoming Lamanites[Aztecs][ignorant of God].*"(Helaman 3:16, Book of Mormon)*

These records talk about anything and everything, including the murders, and plunders, and the Nephites/Mayans dissenting and joining with the Lamanites/Aztecs, willingly in rebellion against God and their country, and also those at the end of the Nephite/Mayan period, who mixed with the Lamanites/Aztecs rather than be killed, and their families be offered up as sacrifices. They all turned their backs on God, just like a true liberal/Democrat/communist, and eventually find themselves of their own doing, in outer darkness. An ignorant people, become a wild and ferocious people, believing in tradition and superstition, and not refraining from anything that satisfies their own selfish ambitions. As Helaman stated: "*...yea, even becoming Lamanites[Aztecs]."* What more could he say? It is now the year of **42 B.C.**

> "*And it came to pass in the forty and ninth year[42 B.C.] of the reign of the judges, there was continual peace established in the land, all save it were[secret deals, contracts]* **secret combinations which Gadianton the robber[and Democrats] had established in the more settled parts of the land, which at that time were not known unto those who were at the head of government; therefore they were not destroyed out of the** land." "*And it came to pass that in this same year there was exceedingly great prosperity in the church, insomuch that there were* **thousands who did join themselves unto the church and were baptized unto repentance.**" "*And so* **great was the prosperity of the church and so many blessings which were poured out upon the people[Nephites/Mayans], that even the high priests and teachers were themselves astonished beyond measure.**" "*And it came to pass that the* **work of the Lord did prosper unto the baptizing and uniting to the Church of God, many souls, yea, even tens of thousands.**" "*Thus we may see that* **the Lord is merciful unto all who will, in the sincerity of their hearts, call upon his holy name.**"*(Helaman 3:23-27, Book of Mormon)*

Continual peace was once again established, except for the *"secret orders"*, being used by the liberals/Democrats/communists, still working to destroy the government in the bigger settled cities(i.e. Washington

D.C., New York, Milwaukee, Chicago,San Francisco, Las Angeles, Minneapolis, etc.), many came to God at this time also. It is now **40 B.C.**

> And in the *fifty and first year* of the reign of the judges there was peace also, *save it were the* **pride** *which began to enter the church---not into the church of God, but into the hearts of the people who professed to belong to the church of God---*" "*And it came to pass that the fifty and second year [39 B.C.]ended in* **peace** *also save it were the* **exceedingly great pride which had gotten into the hearts of the people[Nephites/Mayans];** *and it was because of their exceedingly great riches and their prosperity in the land; and it did* **grow upon them from day to day.**" (Helaman 3:33, 36, Book of Mormon]

Pride began again to enter into the Church because of the much learning, and riches they obtained from their educations, therefore they were beginning to believe they were superior to the regular citizen who toiled with his hands to support his family, and it got even worse before Helaman died. Then his son, Nephi, was appointed/elected, Chief Judge by the voice of the people of Nephi/Mayans. It is now **38** B.C. Helaman dies and his son: Nephi takes over as chief Judge of the Nephites/Mayans. Meanwhile the pride and hypocritical thinking, which comes by way of Democrat/liberal, selfish thinking, and wanting to justify their own selfish acts.

> "And it came to pass in the *fifty and third year of the reign of the judges, Helaman died, and his son Nephi began to reign in his* stead. And it came to pass that he *did fill the judgment-seat with* **justice and equity**; *yea, he did keep* **the commandments of God, and did walk in the ways of his father.**" (Helaman 3:37, Book of Mormon)

Chapter 19

The Both South, & North American Inhabitants Belonged To Church Of Christ

Wars leading up to the Birth of Christ

In **37 B.C.** There were more dissenters, wishing to be in the world, of the anti-Godly, therefore, they went up to the Lamanites/Aztecs and joined with them. Many people would rather live in their ignorance of the laws of God, therefore they pull any card/excuse to throw their tantrums, blame someone else for their own weaknesses, instead of wanting to listen to reason, especially, they don't want to listen to someone who believes in God. In order to not have to listen to the truth, they have to get out of the same room or from among the people who are telling it. Many people don't want to hear it, so in order to avoid the truth or the voice of God, they hate God, and in order to do this, they have to hate those who keep reminding them of God. Therefore they have to find a cause, or excuse, right or wrong, to get angry and go join those who are ignorant, in order to justify their own lies, and short comings. The love of money, or riches, has proven over and over to be the "root of all evil."

"And it came to pass in the _fifty and fourth year[37 B.C.] there were many_ **dissensions [controversy] in the church, and there** **was also a contention[disagreement, and fighting] among the** **people[Nephites/Mayans], insomuch that there was much**

244

*bloodshed." "And the rebellious part were slain and driven out of the
land, and they did go <u>unto the king of the Lamanites[Aztecs].</u>" "And
it came to pass that they did endeavor <u>to stir up the Lamanites[Aztecs]</u>
<u>to war against the Nephites[Mayans]; but behold, **the**</u>
<u>Lamanites[Aztecs] were exceedingly afraid , insomuch that they</u>
**<u>would not hearken[listen] to the words of those dissenters.</u>" "But
it came to pass in the <u>fifty and sixth year[35 B.C.] of the reign of the</u>
<u>judges, there were dissenters who went **up** from the Nephites[Mayans]</u>
<u>unto the Lamanites[Aztecs]; and they **succeeded** with those others</u>
<u>in stirring them up to anger against the Nephites[Mayans]; and they</u>
<u>were all that **year preparing for war.**" (**Helaman** 4:1-4, Book of*
Mormon)*

*"And in the <u>fifty and seventh year[34 B.C.] they did come **down**</u>
<u>against the Nephites[Mayans] to battle</u>, and they did <u>commence</u>
<u>the work of death; yea, insomuch that in the fifty and eighth year[33</u>
<u>B.C.] of the reign of the judges they succeeded in obtaining **possession**</u>
<u>of the land of Zarahemla; yea, and also all the lands, even</u>
**<u>unto the land which was near the land "Bountiful".</u>" "and the
<u>Nephites[Mayans] and the armies of Moronihah were driven</u>
<u>even into the land of Bountiful[just before the narrow neck of</u>
**<u>land];</u>" "And there they did fortify against the <u>Lamanites[Aztecs],</u>
<u>from the **west sea[Pacific Ocean], even unto the east[Atlantic**</u>
<u>Ocean]; it being a day's journey for a Nephite[Mayan], on</u>
<u>the line which they had fortified and stationed their armies to</u>
<u>defend their north</u> <u>country.</u>" " And thus those dissenters[traitors]
of the **Nephites[Mayans], with the** help of <u>a numerous army of</u>
<u>the Lamanites[Aztecs], **had obtained all the possession of the**</u>
<u>Nephites[Mayans]which was in the land southward[Colombia].</u>
<u>And all this was done</u> in the fifty and eighth year[33 B.C.], and
ninth year[32 B.C.] of the reign of the judges." (Helaman 4:5-8,
Book of Mormon)*

The battles that followed between the Nephites/Mayans and the
Lamanites/Aztecs, because of these traitors of the Nephites/Mayans,
cost the Nephites/Mayans, even the Land of Zarahemla, clear to the
borders of the Land Bountiful, at the beginning of the Narrow Neck

of land. The Nephites/Mayans lost all of their lands in South America. It is now **31 B.C.**

> *"And it came to pass in the <u>sixtieth year[31 B.C.] year of the reign</u>* <u>*of the judges, Moronihah did succeed with his armies in obtaining many*</u> <u>*parts of the land;Yea, they regained many cities which had fallen into*</u> <u>*the hands of the Lamanites[Aztecs].*</u> *" "And it came to pass in the sixty and first year of the reign of the judges <u>they[Nephite/Mayan armies]</u>* <u>*succeeded in regaining even* **half of all their possessions.**</u> *" "Now this* <u>*great loss of the* **Nephites[Mayans], and the great slaughter which**</u> **<u>was among them, would not have happened had it not been for</u>** **<u>their wickedness and their abomination which was among them;</u>** **<u>yea, and it was among those also who professed to belong to the</u>** **<u>church of God.</u>** *" (Helaman 4:9-11, Book of Mormon)*

General Moronihah, Nephite/Mayan General of the armies of the Nephites/Mayans succeeded in reclaiming only half of their lands back. Most of the harm done to their own people was done **by those who professed to be in the Church of God.** To violate any commandment of God knowingly and deliberately, leads to abomination. Treason, insurrection, pedophilia, homosexuality, fraud, murder, joining secret societies/secret orders, conspiracies, lies, fraud etc., all of which are abominations in the sight of God. It is now **30 B.C.**

> *"And thus ended the <u>sixty and first year[30 B.C.] of the reign</u>* <u>*of the judges." "And it came to pass in the sixty and second year[29*</u> <u>*B.C.] of the reign of the judges, that* **Moronihah could obtain no**</u> **<u>more possessions over the Lamanites[Aztecs].</u>** *" "Therefore they did <u>abandon their design[plans] to obtain the remainder of their lands,</u>* <u>*for* **so numerous were the Lamanites[Aztecs] that it became**</u> **<u>impossible for the Nephites[Mayans] to obtain more power</u>** **<u>over them; therefore Moronihah did employ all his armies in</u>** **<u>maintaining those parts which he had taken.</u>** *" "And it came to pass, <u>because of the greatness of the number of the Lamanites[Aztecs] the</u>* <u>*Nephites[Mayans] were in great fear, lest they should be overpowered*</u> <u>*and trodden down, and slain, and destroyed."*</u>*(Helaman 4:17-20, Book of Mormon)*

"Yea, and they began to remember the prophecies of Alma, and also the words of Mosiah; and they saw that they had been a stiffnecked[stubborn] people, and that they had set at naught[ignored/ violated;] the commandments of God[The Constitution]:" *"And that they had altered[abrogated] and trampled[broke their oaths of public trust]under their feet the laws[Constitution/ Common Law] of Mosiah, or that which the Lord commanded him to give unto the [we the]people; and they[the Nephites/ Mayans] saw that their law[Constitution/Common law] had become corrupted, and that they the Nephites[Mayans] had become a wicked people, insomuch that they were wicked even like unto the Lamanites[Aztecs]."* *"And because of their iniquity the church had begun to dwindle[go backwards in progress/numbers]; and they began to disbelieve in the spirit of prophecy and in the spirit of revelation; and the judgments of God did stare them in the face."*(Helaman 4:21-23, Book of Mormon)

★★★ *"And they [Nephites/Mayans] had become weak, like unto their brethren, the Lamanites[Aztecs], and that the Spirit of the Lord[truth&light] did no more preserve them; yea, it[truth&light] had withdrawn from them because the Spirit of the Lord [light & truth] doth not dwell in unholy temples[ruled by lies/Satan]---"* *"Therefore the Lord did cease to preserve them by his miraculous and matchless power, for they the [Nephites/Mayans] had fallen into a state of unbelief and awful wickedness[evil doings]; and they saw that the Lamanites[Aztecs] were exceedingly more numerous than they, and except they should cleave unto the Lord their God they must unavoidably perish."* *"For behold, they saw that the strength of the Lamanites[Aztecs] was as great as their strength, even "man for man". And thus had they fallen into this "great transgression"; yea, thus had they become "weak", because of their transgression, in the space of not many days."* (Helaman 4:24-26, Book of Mormon)

It was now only 30-years before the coming of the Messiah/ the Holy One of Israel, as had been prophesied to come for thousands of years in advance. The judgments of God were staring the people of the land, those who professed to belong to the Church of God, in the face. This same year, Helaman felt moved to give up the Judgment Seat as Chief Judge, and go through the land preaching and warning the people to repentance.

"For as their[Nephites/Mayans] laws and their governments were established "by the voice of the people", and they who chose evil were more numerous than they who chose good, therefore they were ripening for destruction, for the laws had become corrupted. [through state codes abrogating the Constitution]." "Yea, and this was not all; they [the Nephites/Mayans] were a stiffnecked[stubborn/ selfish/treasonous, evil] people, insomuch that they could not be governed by the law nor justice, save it were to their destruction [putting them to death for their crimes]." (Helaman 5:2-4, Book of Mormon)

Helaman remembered the words of his father, that they needed to preach the truth of the gospel of Jesus Christ. Helaman, and those that maybe went with him began converting the Lamanites/Aztecs, who at this time were inhabiting the Nephite/Mayan city of Zarahemla, that they had just recently lost. They then went into the land of Nephi, that the Nephites/Mayans once held, and showed many wonders.

"Therefore they[Nephi & Lehi-Nephite/Mayan prophets] did speak unto the great astonishment of the Lamanites[Aztecs], to the convincing them, insomuch that there were eight thousand of the Lamanites[Aztecs] who were in the land of Zarahemla and round about "baptized" unto repentance, and were convinced of the wickedness of their traditions of their fathers." "And it came to pass that Nephi and Lehi[Mayan prophets] did proceed from thence to go[up] to the land of Nephi." "And it came to pass that they were taken by an army of the Lamanites[Aztecs] and cast into prison; yea, even that same prison in which Ammon and his brethren were cast[land of Shilom where 1st temple was built] by the servants of Limhi." "And after they had been cast[jailed] into prison many days without food, behold, they[the Lamanites[Aztecs] went forth into the prison to take them[Lehi & Nephi, sons of Helaman] that they

might _slay them_." "And it came to pass that _Nephi and Lehi were_
encircled about as if by fire, even insomuch that they durst[dared] not
lay their hands upon them for fear they [the Lamanites/Aztecs] should
be burned. Nevertheless _Nephi and Lehi were not burned;_ **and they**
were standing in the midst of fire and were not burned." "And
when they saw that they[Nephi and Lehi] were encircled about
with a pillar of fire, and that it burned them not, their hearts did
take courage."   (Helaman 5:19-24, Book of Mormon)

"And also **again the third time the voice came, _and did speak_**
unto them _marvelous words which **cannot be uttered by man;** and_
the walls did tremble again, and the earth shook as if it were about
to divide asunder." "And it came to pass that the _Lamanites[Aztecs]_
could not **flee** because of the **darkness which did overshadow them**;
yea, and also **they were immovable because of the fear which did**
come upon them." "Now there was _one among them who was a_
Nephite by birth _who had **once** belonged to the **church of God**_
but had **dissented**[left the church/had become a **jack Mormon**]from
them." "And it came to pass that _he turned him about, and behold,_
he saw through the cloud of darkness the faces of Nephi and Lehi;
and behold, **they did shine exceedingly, even as the face of angels.**
And he beheld that they[Nephi and Lehi] did lift their eyes to
heaven; and they were In the attitude as if talking or lifting their
voices to some being whom they beheld." "And it came to pass
that this man did cry[shout] unto the multitude, _that they might turn_
and look. And behold, **they did turn and look.** And behold, **there**
was power given unto them that they[Lamanites/Aztecs] did turn
and look; and they did behold the faces of Nephi and Lehi[the
Nephite/Mayan_ missionaries/prophets]." "And they said unto the
man[Nephite dissenter/jack Mormon] Behold, what do all these things
mean, and **who is it with whom these men do converse?**" "Now
the mans name was _Aminadab. And Aminadab said unto them: **They**_
do converse with the angels of God."   (Helaman 5:33-39, Book
of Mormon)

"And Aminadab said unto them: **You must repent[change], and**
cry[pray] unto the voice, even until ye shall have faith in Christ,

who was taught unto you by Alma, and Amulek, and Zeezrom[former prophets]; And when ye shall do this, **the cloud of darkness**[cloud of misunderstanding] **shall be removed from overshadowing you.**" "And it came to pass that they **all** did begin to cry[**pray**] unto the voice of him[**God**]who had shaken the earth; yea, they did cry[**pray**] even until the cloud of darkness[lies/ disinformation] was dispersed." "And it came to pass that when they cast their eyes about, and saw[their eyes were opened] that the cloud of darkness was dispersed[they now understood]from overshadowing them, behold, **they saw that they were encircled about, yea every soul, by a pillar of fire**[God's arms of redeeming love]." "And **Nephi and Lehi were in the midst of them; yea, they were as if in the midst of a flaming fire, yet it did harm them not, neither did it take hold upon the walls of the prison; and they were filled with that "joy which is unspeakable and full of glory."** (Helaman 5:41-44, Book of Mormon)

"And it came to pass that there came a voice, as if it were a whisper saying: **Peace, peace, be unto you, because of your "faith" in my Well Beloved, who was from the foundation[with him in the creation] of the world.**" "And now, when they heard this they cast their eyes as if to behold from whence the voice came; **and behold, they saw the heavens open; and angels came down out of heaven and ministered unto them.** And there were about **three hundred souls who saw and heard these things; and they were bidden to go forth and marvel not**[accept as fact], **neither should they doubt**[but have a resolve of what they just witnessed is true]." "And it came to pass that they[the Lamanites/Aztecs who witnessed these things] did go forth, and did minister[teaching and testifying] unto the people, **declaring throughout all regions round about all the things which they had heard and seen, insomuch that the more part of the Lamanites[Aztecs] were convinced of them, because of the greatness of the evidences which they had received**." "And as many as were **convinced did lay down their weapons of war and also their hatred and the traditions of their fathers.**" "And it came to pass that **they**[the Lamanites/Aztecs] **did yield**[give back] **up unto the Nephites**[Mayans]**the lands of their possession.**" **(Helaman** 5:46-52,Book of Mormon)

Helaman's sons, Nephi's and Lehi's missionary efforts were very successful and God truly blessed them and the lives of those they touched, even though from the depths of a prison. God is so gracious and kind, that everyone is so precious to him, that if they will exercise faith in him, and call upon him continually, that there is almost nothing that we can't receive forgiveness for. It doesn't matter how rich or poor, or the color of your skin, or how educated you or others think you are, he just wants a sincere heart, and a teachable spirit. He doesn't care if you once were in trouble with the law, no matter what you did, or are doing now, or if you are a Jack Mormon/dissenter, or a Catholic or Muslim, he wants your heart.

God wants you to change/repent from what you are doing now, and call upon him before he withdraws from you, because of continual rejection of the truth, because this is what causes the shadows of darkness to overshadow the ungodly. If you will exercise your faith, and pray always to God the Father in the name of Jesus Christ, in everything you do, until the eyes of your understanding are opened, you can have God's redeeming love encircle you also. We don't listen to what man or the world thinks of you, or how the world judges you, but it is what God thinks of you, is what is important. Nephi and Lehi were so successful, even though they were in prison, waiting to be executed unjustly, but remaining faithful to what they knew without a doubt was true, great things happened to the Nephites/Mayans and the Lamanites/Aztecs, reuniting their family for a time. At one time, most all of the Lamanites/Aztecs were converted, and they did become more righteous than the Nephites/Mayans. It is now **28 B.C.**

*"And it came to pass that when the <u>sixty and second year</u> of the reign of the judges had ended, all these things **had happened_ and the Lamanites[Aztecs] had become, the more part of them, a righteous people**[right with God], **insomuch that their righteousness did exceed that of the Nephites[Mayans], because of their firmness and their steadiness in the faith.**" "For behold, <u>there were many of the Nephites[Mayans] who had become</u> **hardened and impenitent and grossly wicked,** <u>insomuch that they did</u> **reject** <u>the word of God</u> and all the preaching and prophesying which did come upon them." "Nevertheless, the <u>people of the church did have</u>*

*great joy because of the conversion of the **Lamanites[Aztecs]**, yea, because of the **church of God, which had been established among them. And they did fellowship one with another, and did rejoice one with another, and did have great joy.**" (Helaman 6:1-3, Book of Mormon)*

★*"And it came to pass that many of **the Lamanites[Aztecs] did come "down" into the land of Zarahemla**[from Peru, Ecuador/ land of Nephi], **and did declare**[witness, testify] **unto the people of the Nephites[Mayans] the manner of their conversion, and did exhort**[encourage] **them to faith and repentance**[change]."* *"Yea, and **many**[Lamanites/Aztecs] **did preach with exceedingly great power**[conviction] **and authority**[priesthood of God], **unto the bringing down many**[Nephites/Mayans/jack-Mormons/those professing Christians] many of them **into the depths of humility, to be the humble followers of God and the Lamb**[Jesus Christ/ last blood sacrifice for us]."* *"And it came to pass that **many of the Lamanites[Aztecs] did go into the land northward**[North America]; **and also Nephi and Lehi went into the land northward, to preach unto the people. And thus ended the sixty and third year."* (Helaman 6:4-6, Book of Mormon)*

As you can clearly see, that the closer we are getting to the **year-0**, the closer it is to when Christ comes into the world. These were now the years when the Nephites/Mayans and the Lamanites/Aztecs from South America had open borders, to come and go freely. They had open commerce because they had all things in Common, because they believed and worshiped the same God, and belonged to the same Church of God. **26 B.C.**

★★*"And behold, **There was peace in all the land, insomuch that the Nephites[Mayans] did go into whatsoever part of the land they would, whether among the Nephites[Mayans] or the Lamanites[Aztecs]."* *"And it came to pass that **the Lamanites[Aztecs] did also go whithersoever they would, whether it were among the Lamanites[Aztecs] or among the Nephites[Mayans]; and thus they did have free intercourse**[trade/*

movement/travel] one with another, to buy and sell, and to get gain, according to their desire.""And it came to pass that they *became exceedingly rich, both the Lamanites[Aztecs] and the Nephites[Mayans]; and they did have an exceeding plenty of gold, and of silver, and of all manner of precious metals, both in the land south and in the land north."* (Helaman 6:6-9, Book of Mormon)

Chapter 20

Birth of Christ, and change of reckoning of Time

The Land of Lehi and the Land of Mulek because of where they landed

★★★ *"Now the land* **south** *[South America]* <u>**was called Lehi, and the land north**</u> *[North America]* <u>**was called Mulek, which was after the son of Zedekiah; for the Lord did bring Mulek into the land north, and Lehi into the land south.**</u> *" "And behold, there was all manner of* **gold in both these lands, and of silver, and of precious ore** <u>**of every kind; and there were also curious workmen, who did work all kinds of ore and did refine it; and thus they did become rich.**</u> *" "They did raise* <u>grain in abundance,</u> **both in the north and in the south; and they did flourish exceedingly, both in the north and in the south. And they did multiply and wax exceedingly strong in the land. And they did raise many flocks and herds, yea, many fatlings.** *" "Behold* <u>their women did toil and spin, and did make all manner of cloth, of fine twine linen and cloth of every kind, to clothe their nakedness. And thus the sixty and fourth year did pass away in peace</u>.*" **(Helaman** *6:10-13, Book of Mormon)*

Because of their much prosperity and everyone was getting rich, that the people set their hearts upon their riches, and they quickly forgot what was right with God. Satan and selfish, liberal/communist ideas began creeping into their hearts again. The "secret societies" began to grow due to the selfish desires of those who didn't want to work honestly for their keep, and who sought to control and rob others who did. Socialist/communist/liberal ideas once more were raging in the thinking of the Lamanites/Aztec, mostly at this point, but give the wicked an idea, and they were joined rapidly by the Nephites/Mayans, who had the same liberal viewpoints, and wanting to compete.

> *"And it came to pass in the <u>sixty and sixth</u> **year[25 B.C.]** of the* **reign of the judges, behold,** *Cezoram <u>was murdered by an unknown</u>* <u>hand as he sat upon the judgment-seat.</u> *And it came to pass that <u>in</u>* <u>the same year, that his son, who had been</u> **appointed[elected] by** **the people in his stead, was also murdered.** *And thus ended the* <u>sixty and sixth year."</u> *"And in the commencement of the sixty and seventh* **year[24 B.C.]** *the people began to grow <u>exceedingly wicked</u>* <u>again."</u> *"For behold, the Lord had blessed them so long <u>with riches</u>* <u>of the</u> **world** <u>that they had not been stirred up to anger, to wars, nor</u> <u>to bloodshed;</u> **therefore they began to set their hearts upon their** **riches;** *yea, they began to seek <u>to get gain that they might be lifted</u>* <u>up one above another[titles of nobility/kings];</u> **therefore they began** **to commit secret murders, and to rob and to plunder, that they** **might get gain."** *(Helaman 6:15-17, Book of Mormon)*

The people began seeking out those secret combinations/secret orders to get gain and power. They began again, doing their secret murders through the secret bands; Jesuits, illuminati, Masons, skull & Bones, crime families, etc. that existed to hide their works handed down through Kishkumen and Gadianton, that one time seethed with Communism, and force and control. Now they are the liberals and Democrats, and evil GOP who have joined with them. They are the kingmen/communists today, and Satan is where they get their power for a time only.

> ★ *"And now behold,* **those murderers and plunderers** *were a band who had been formed by Kishkumen and Gadianton[Bilderburgers/International Bankers].* *And*

now it had come to pass *that there were many, even among the Nephites[Mayans], of Gadianton's band*[evil empathizing GOP]*. But behold, they were more numerous among the more wicked part of the Lamanites[Aztecs]. And they were called Gadianton's[International Bankers/Jesuit's/Democrat's, etc.] robbers and murderers." "And it was they who did murder the chief judge Cezoram[Lincoln, Garfield, Kennedy, etc. etc.], and his son, while in the judgment-seat; and behold, they were not found."* "And now it came to pass that *when the Lamanites[Aztecs] found that there were robbers among them they were exceedingly sorrowful; and they did use every means in their power to destroy them off the face of the earth."*(Helaman 6:18-20, Book of Mormon)

"But behold, *Satan did stir up the hearts of the more part of the Nephites[Mayans], insomuch that they did unite with those bands of robbers[Liberals/Democrats/Bankers/secret orders, etc.] and did enter into their covenants and their oaths, that they would protect and preserve one another in whatsoever difficult circumstances they should be placed, that they should not suffer for their murders, and their plunderings, and their stealings."* "And it came to pass that *they did have their signs that, yea, their secret signs, and their secret words; and this that they might distinguish a brother who had entered into the covenant, that whatsoever wickedness his brother should do he should not be injured by his brother, nor by those who did belong to his band, who had taken this covenant."* "And thus *they might murder and plunder, and steal, and commit whoredoms and all manner of wickedness[evil] contrary to the laws of their country[Constitution] and also the laws of their God."* "And whosoever *of those who belonged to their band should reveal unto the world of their wickedness[evil] and their abominations[evil acts], should be tried, not according to the laws of their country, but according to the laws of their wickedness[oaths], which had been given by Gadianton and Kishkumen."*(Helaman 6:21-24, Book of Mormon)

"Now behold, it is *those secret oaths and covenants which Alma commanded his son should not go forth unto the world,* *lest they should be a means of bringing down the people unto destruction.*" "*Now behold, those* secret oaths and covenants did not come forth unto Gadianton from the records which were delivered unto Helaman; *but behold, they were put into the heart of Gadianton by that same being who did entice our first parents to partake of the forbidden fruit---*" "*Yea, that that same being who did plot with Cain, that if he would murder his brother Abel it should not be known unto the world. And he did plot with Cain and his followers from that time forth.*" "*And also it is that same being[Satan] who did put it into the hearts of the people to build a tower* sufficiently high that they might get to heaven. And it is that same being[Satan] *who led on the* people who came from that tower into this land[Jaredites/Olmecs/giants]; who spread the works of darkness and abominations over all the face of the land, until he dragged the people[Jaredites/Olmecs] down to an entire destruction, and to an everlasting hell.*" (Helaman 6:25-28, Book of Mormon)

" *Yea, it is that same being who put it into the heart* of Gadianton[liberals, Democrats, Bilderbergers, Jesuits, etc.] to still carry on the work of darkness, and of secret murder; and he has brought it forth from the beginning of man even down to this time[2023+].*" "*And behold,* it is he who is the author of all sin. And behold, he doth carry on his works of darkness and secret murder, and doth hand down their plots, and their oaths, and their covenants, and their plans of awful wickedness[evil] from generation to generation according as he can get hold upon the hearts of the children of men.*" "*And now behold, he[Satan]had got great hold upon the hearts of the* Nephites[Mayans]; yea, insomuch that they had become exceedingly wicked[evil]; yea, the more part of them had turned out of the way of righteousness, and did trample under their feet the commandments of God, and did turn unto their own ways, and did build up unto themselves idols of their gold and their silver.*"(Helaman 6:29-31, Book of Mormon)

All scripture and records are preserved to be passed on from generation to generation, and civilization to civilization for the benefit and learning of those who come after. The bridge has already been established for the offspring of God to cross over the deep chasm, and return to him. The good and evil examples both, have been put before us, therefore hindsight is easy if we compare what happens when people obey God's commandments, and when they don't. We must choose who we want to serve, and understand why. We must liken the scriptures to ourselves if we seek to return to our Heavenly Father. If not, do what the Jaredites/Olmecs and the Nephites/Mayans did as well. By now, Satan had gotten quite a hold on the hearts of the Nephites/Mayans, and the signs of the coming of Christ was not far distant, but the majority of the Nephites/Mayans had chosen to idolize Satan and the temptations of power, riches, murder, control, homosexuality, witchcraft, etc. etc.. Obviously they refused to believe the prophets of old, and even their prophets in their midst at that time. Now **23 B.C.**

> *"And it came to pass that all these iniquities did come unto them in the space of not many years, insomuch that a more part of it had come unto them in the sixty and seventh year of the reign of the judges over the people of Nephi[Mayans]." "And they did grow in their iniquities in the **sixty and eighth year** also, to the great sorrow and lamentation of the righteous[right with God]." "And thus we see that the* **Nephites[Mayans] did begin to dwindle in unbelief, and grow in wickedness[i.e. Voter fraud, murders, etc] and abominations[i.e. pedophilia, sex traficking, homosexuality, etc], while the Lamanites[Aztecs] began to grow exceedingly in the knowledge of their God; yea, they did begin to keep his[God's] statutes and commandments, and to walk in "truth" and uprightness before him." *"And thus* **we see that the Spirit of the Lord began to withdraw from the Nephites[Mayans], because of the wickedness and the hardness of their hearts."** *"And thus we see that the* **Lord began to pour out his Spirit upon the Lamanites[Aztecs], because of their easiness and willingness to believe in his words.** *" (Helaman 6:32-36, Book of Mormon)*

This is why the Nephites/Mayans, disappeared from history, or are extinct as civilizations. After having been blessed with such great knowledge, and are prospered and after having been blessed with all of these things, yet they began to deny that God, who has continually preserved them. The Lamanites/Aztecs continued to serve the Lord by being deliberate and obedient by hunting those evil Gadianton robbers out of their midst. Once they believed, there was very little that could change their minds. They remained faithful to the Lord no matter what, or who tried to tempt them. This is also why the hispanics today, who are a remnant, of the tribe of Joseph who was sold into Egypt, and as promised by the Lord, were preserved to inhabit the dwellings left to them by the Jaredites/Olmecs, Mulekites/Toltecs, and the Nephites/Mayans, and even us, the gentiles.

> *"And it came to pass that the Lamanites[Aztecs] did hunt the band of robbers[communists] of Gadianton; and they did preach the word of God among the more wicked part of them, insomuch that this band of of robbers was utterly destroyed from among the Lamanites[Aztecs].*" "*And it came to pass on the other hand, that the Nephites[Mayans] did build them up and support them, beginning at the more wicked part of them, until they overspread all the land[infested government, businesses, colleges, churches, law enforcement, military, etc.] of the Nephites[Mayans], and had seduced[deceived] the more part of the righteous until they had come down to believe in their works and partake of their spoils, and to join with them[aid and abet] in their secret murders and combinations.* (Helaman 6:37-39, Book of Mormon)

The Lamanites/Aztecs were more righteous than the Nephites/Mayans, because they hunted out the Communists/Liberals/Democrats/rat-bastards, and destroyed the *"secret orders"* from among themselves. Whereas, the Nephites/Mayans joined to the communists/Democrats, until the sole management of their government was controlled by the liberals/Democrats/Communists, who were seeking to overthrow the government. They trampled upon the rights of the people, for whom they were put into positions of public-trust to insure that their God-given rights were not violated. Even all the churches, have caused the people to err. Just look around you today, who is it that is trying to sell us out. Christ calls them the whore of all the earth.

Even the churches deceive the people into believing that whatever the government does must be right, or follow your church leaders without question, or they are threatened with excommunication, until the ignorant people give in and reap the benefits thinking that if they are required to do it they might as well get paid, thus, they begin to aid and abet the criminals in government who are still on television, and walking the streets. Wake up people, this is the way it was with the Nephites/Mayans, and it is happening to our civilization right in front of our eyes, and most are party to it, there are very few who are not. It is now **22 B.C..**

Nephi returns from preaching the gospel in the land Northward. (MN, WI, New England, NY, IA, GA? etc. etc.,)finding that all of those Nephites/Mayans that migrated north, including converted Lamanites/Aztecs, rejected the truth, and refused to hear about God. After all, what the people knew before they migrated, ended up being in just a few years, ignorant of the truth, and rejecting it.

> *"Behold, now it came to pass in the sixty and ninth year[22 B.C.] of the reign of the judges over the people of the Nephites[Mayans] that Nephi, the son of Helaman, returned to the land of Zarahemla from the land northward." "For he had been forth <u>among the people who were in the land northward[North America], and did preach the word of God unto them, and did prophesy many things unto them;"</u> <u>"And they did reject all his words, insomuch that he could not stay among them, but returned again unto the land of his nativity." "And* ***seeing the people in a state of such awful wickedness, and those Gadianton robbers[Democrats/Jesuits, Pelosi, Biden, Obama, Clintons, etc.] filling the judgment-seats---having usurped the power and authority of the land; laying aside the commandments[Constitution] of God, and not in the least aright before him; doing no justice unto the children of men;"*** <u>*"Condemning the righteous[Donald Trump, Gatz, etc.] because of their righteousness;*</u> ***letting the guilty[Bidens, Obamas, Pelosis, Clintons, etc.] and the wicked go unpunished because of their money; and moreover to be held in office at the head of government, to rule and do according to their wills, that they might get gain and glory of the world, and moreover, that they might the more***</u>

easily commit adultery, and steal, and kill, and do according to their wills---" (Helaman 7:1-5, Book of Mormon)

When he returned, Nephi found the criminals walking the streets unpunished[i.e. Pelosi, Obama, Schiff, Clintons, Romney, Biden, etc.]. It is exactly like our situation today in our American-Republic. Nephi told them of their sins and why the Nephites/Mayans would be destroyed. Many cities and their populations were destroyed, because of the evilness and abominations going on in them. Nephi got back to his house in the land of Zarahemla, and went upon his tower/pyramid, to get as close to God as possible, and was praying for the people to repent. While he was pouring out his heart to God, men came by, and observed what he was doing, and raced to tell the news to the whole city of Zarahemla. Considering the wicked state they were in, it must have been a rare sight to see anyone praying to Almighty God. Obviously they were treating it as very uncommon. When he saw them galking at him because he was praying, and the spectacle, and the focus of the gathering, he asked them some frank questions to break the silence. He asks them what they have gathered there for, so that he could tell them about their sins and wickedness? He tells them what will happen to them if they don't get right with God.

"And now, when Nephi arose he beheld the multitudes of people who had gathered together." "And it came to pass that Nephi opened his mouth and said unto them: Behold, why have ye gathered yourselves together? That I may tell you of your iniquities?" "Yea, how could you have given way to the enticing of him who is seeking to hurl away your souls down to everlasting misery and wo?" "And behold, instead of gathering you, except you repent[change], behold, he shall scatter[drive you] you forth that ye shall become [destroyed by the sword, and left on the ground to rot] meat for dogs and wild beasts." "O how could you have forgotten your God in the very day that he has delivered you?" "But behold, it is to get gain, to be praised of men, yea, and that ye might get gold and silver. And ye have set your hearts upon the riches and the vain things of this world, for the which ye do murder, and plunder, and steal, and bear false witness[lie] against your neighbor, and do

all manner of iniquity[evil]."*(Helaman 7:12-13, 16, 21, Book of Mormon)*

** "For behold, thus saith the Lord: **I will not show unto the wicked of my strength[have strength of common man], to one more than the other, save it be unto those who repent of their sins, and hearken unto my words**[God rewards those who diligently seek him]. Now therefore, I would that ye should behold, my brethren, **that it shall be better for the Lamanites[Aztecs] than for you except ye shall repent[speedily change your** ways]." "For behold, **they are more righteous than you, for they have not sinned against great knowledge which ye have received; therefore the Lord will be merciful unto them; yea, he will lengthen out their days and increase their seed[population], even when thou shalt be utterly destroyed except thou shalt repent[change your ways].**" "*(Helaman 7:23-25, Book of Mormon)*

"Yea, **wo be unto you because of that "great abomination" which has come among you; and ye have united yourselves unto it, yea to that "secret band" [Bilderbergers/Jesuits/Democrats/liberals, etc] which was established by Gadianton[Master Mahan]!**" "Yea, **wo shall come unto you because of that pride which ye have suffered to enter your hearts, which has lifted you up beyond that which is good because of your exceedingly great** riches!" "*Yea, wo be unto you because of* **your wickedness[evil] and** abominations[depravity]!" "And **except ye repent ye shall perish; yea, even your lands shall be taken from you, and ye shall be destroyed from off the face of the earth.**"*(Helaman 7:26-28, Book of Mormon)*

Nephi gained favor of some of the people, because he was proven to be right when telling them about their murders, and secret orders. He told the crowd that even now their judge was murdered upon the judgment-seat, and immediately five men ran to see if it was true, and it was. This revelation by God, to Nephi, converted a few to believe in his words. However, because the wicked still put him through a deposition, trying to get him to contradict himself, trying to find a word that might give them reason to arrest Nephi.

"*Yea, behold it is now even at your doors; yea, go ye in unto the judgment-seat, and search; and behold, your judge is murdered, and he lieth in his blood; and he hath been murdered by his brother, who seeketh to sit on the judgment-seat.*" "**And behold, they both belong to your secret band, whose author is Gadianton[Master Mahan] and the evil one[Satan] who seeketh to destroy the souls of men[God's work and glory].**" "*(Helaman 8:27-28, Book of Mormon)*

"*And it came to pass that they ran with all of their might, and came in unto the judgment-seat; and behold, the chief judge had fallen to the earth, and did lie in his blood.*" "*And now behold, when they saw this they were astonished exceedingly, insomuch that they fell to the earth; for they had not believed the words which Nephi had spoken concerning the chief judge.*" "*But now, when they saw they believed, and fear came upon them lest all the judgments which Nephi had spoken should come upon the people[Mayans]; therefore they did quake, and had fallen to the earth.*" "*Now, immediately when the judge had been murdered---he being stabbed by his brother by a garb of secrecy, and he fled, and the servants ran and told the people, raising the cry of murder among them;*" "*And behold the people did gather themselves together unto the place of the judgment-seat---and behold, to their astonishment they saw those five men who had fallen to the earth.*" *(Helaman 9:3-7, Book of Mormon)*

"*And thus also those judges who were at the garden of Nephi, and heard his words, were also gathered together at the burial.*" "*And it came to pass that they inquired among the people, saying: Where are the five who were sent to inquire concerning the chief judge whether he was dead? And they answered and said: Concerning this five whom ye say ye have sent, we know not; but there are five who are the murderers, whom we have cast into prison.*" "*And it came to pass that the judges desired that they should be brought; and they were brought, and behold they were the five who were sent; and behold the judges inquired of them to know concerning the matter, and they told them all that they had done, saying:*" "*We ran and came to the place of the judgment-seat, and when we saw all things even as Nephi had testified, we were astonished insomuch that we fell to the earth[fainted]; and when we were recovered from our astonishment, behold they cast us into prison"(Helaman 9:11-14, Book of Mormon)*

"Nevertheless, they caused that Nephi should be taken[falsely arrested] and bound[handcuffed] and brought before the multitude[court], and they began to question him in <u>divers ways</u>[deposition]that they might cross him[trick him], that they might accuse him to death---." *"Saying unto him: <u>Thou art confederate[collaborated]; who is this man that hath done this murder? Now tell us, and acknowledge thy fault; saying, behold here is money[bribe]; and also we will grant unto thee thy life if thou wilt tell us, and acknowledge the agreement which thou has made with him[plea bargain].</u>"(Helaman 9:19-20, Book of Mormon)*

"And because I have done this[told them their chief judge was dead] <u>ye say that I have agreed with a man that he should do this thing;</u> yea, because I showed unto you this sign <u>ye are angry with me, and seek to destroy my life.</u>" *"And now behold, I will show unto you <u>another sign, and see if ye will in this thing seek to destroy me.</u> "* *"<u>Behold I say unto you:</u>* **Go to the house of Seantum, who is the brother of Seezoram, and say unto him---"** *"**Has Nephi, the pretended prophet, who doth prophesy so much evil concerning this people agreed with thee, in the which ye have murdered Seezoram, who is your brother?**"* *"<u>And behold, he shall say unto you,</u>* **Nay.**" *"And ye shall say unto him:* **Have ye murdered your brother?**" *"And he shall stand with* **fear and wist not[won't know] what to say.** *And behold, <u>he shall deny unto you; and he shall make as if he were astonished; nevertheless, he shall declare unto you that he is innocent.</u>" (Helaman 9:24-30, Book of Mormon)*

"But behold, **<u>ye shall examine him, and ye shall find blood upon the skirts of his cloak.</u>** *"* *"And when ye have seen this, <u>ye shall say:</u>* **From whence cometh this blood? Do ye not know that it is the blood of your brother?**" *"And* **then shall he tremble, and shall look pale, even as if death had come upon him.** *"* *"And then shall ye say:* **Because of this fear and this paleness which has come upon your face, behold, we know that thou art guilty.**" *"**And then shall greater fear come upon him; and then shall he confess unto**"*

*you, and deny no more that he has done this murder." "And **then**
shall he say unto you, that I, Nephi, know nothing concerning
this matter save it were given unto me by the power of God. And*
*then shall ye know that I am an honest man, and that I am sent **unto***
***you from God.**" "And it came to pass that they went and did, even*
*according as Nephi had said unto them. **And behold, the words which***
he had said were true; for according to the words he did deny;
***and also according to the words he did confess.**"(Helaman 9:25-37,*
Book of Mormon)

The wicked set about to silence any that spoke up for Nephi. Nephi still continued to prophecy of the coming of the birth of Jesus Christ. However, I, the author, was told by a wise old man, and it has proven to be true: "That you can't beat an honest man". Nephi wasn't afraid of any man, nor could they shut him up. He was identical to Daniel in the Bible, in that, if you asked him a question, then expect to hear the truth, or don't ask him anything, because he won't lie to you. The truth really scares and maddens the wicked/evil, but that is what is meant by the saying: "putting the fear of God into him". It is now **20 B.C.**

*" But behold, the **power of God was with him[the Mayan***
***prophet/man of God],** and they could not take him to cast him into*
*prison, for he **was taken by the Spirit and conveyed away out of the***
midst of them.**" "And it came to pass that thus he did go **forth in the
Spirit, from multitude to multitude, declaring the word of God,
even until he had declared it unto them all, or sent it forth among
***all the people**[of the Nephites and Lamanites]." "And it came to pass*
*that they would not hearken[listen] unto his words; insomuch that **they***
were divided against themselves and began to slay one another
***with the sword**" "And thus ended the seventy and first year of the*
reign of the judges over the people of Nephi[Mayan people]."(Helaman
10:16-19, Book of Mormon)

There began to be a war/revolution among the people, because of the evil Communists/liberals/ Democrats, who infested the government. There was no justice, but only selfish ambition by those who have sworn to uphold freedom. It is now **19 B.C.** The Communists are only in government for themselves and not for the people. They want money, power, control, and a secret–order–network. They cause the problems, then they turn and offer a solution, their solution, that they can control for profit.

> *"And now it came to pass in the <u>seventy and second year</u>[19 B.C.] of the reign of the judges that the <u>contentions[fighting] did increase, insomuch that there were **wars** throughout all the land **among all the people of Nephi[Mayans].**" "And it was[without a doubt] this secret band of robbers[communists/socialists/Democrats/Jesuits] who did carry on this work of destruction and wickedness. And this war[civil war] did last all that year; and in the seventy and third year[18 B.C.] it did also last."</u>(Helaman 11:1-2, Book of Mormon)*

It was Nephi: the Nephite/Mayan prophet who saved the Mayan people from destroying themselves by war, because civil war hurts everyone, as we in America are still healing from the effects of our early civil war. Nephi the Nephite/Mayan prophet, asked God, on behalf of the Nephites/Mayans, if he would send instead, a famine in all the land to teach the people a lesson. The famine ended in **15 B.C.**

> *"And it came to pass in this year[18 B.C.] <u>Nephi did cry[pray] unto the Lord, saying:" "Oh Lord, **do not suffer that this people shall be destroyed by the sword; but oh Lord, rather let there be a famine in the land, to stir them up in rememberance of the Lord their God, and perhaps they will repent and turn unto thee**." "And so it was done</u> according to the words of Nephi. **And there was <u>a great famine upon the land, among all the people of Nephi[Mayan people]. And thus in the seventy and fourth year[17 B.C.] the famine did continue, and the work of destruction did cease by the sword but became sore by famine." "And this work of destruction did also continue in the seventy and fifth year[16 B.C.].</u>** <u>For the earth was smitten that it was dry, and did not yield forth grain in the season of grain; **and the whole earth was smitten, even among the Lamanites[Aztecs] as well as among the Nephites[Mayans], that they did perish by the thousands in the more wicked parts of the land."**</u>" (Helaman 11:3-6, Book of Mormon)*

*"And it came to pass that the people[Aztecs & Mayans alike] saw that they were about to <u>perish by famine, and they began to remember</u> the **Lord their God;** <u>and they began to remember the words of Nephi.</u>"* *"And the people <u>began to plead with their chief judges and their leaders, that they would say unto Nephi: Behold, we know that thou art a man of God, and therefore cry[pray] unto the Lord our God that he turn away from us this famine, lest all the words which thou hast spoken concerning our destruction be fulfilled.</u>" "And it came to pass that the judges did say unto Nephi, according to the words which had been desired. And it came to pass that when <u>Nephi[Mayan prophet] saw that the people had repented[changed their ways] and did humble themselves in sackcloth, he cried[prayed] again unto the Lord, saying.</u>" "<u>O Lord, behold this people repenteth[have changed and are sorry];</u> and they have swept away the band of Gadianton[communists/socialists/Democrats/ Jesuits/rat bastards] from amongst them insomuch that they have become extinct, and they have concealed their secret plans in the earth."*(Helaman 11:7-10, Book of Mormon)

★★ *"And it came to pass that in the <u>seventy and sixth year[15B.C.]</u> the Lord did turn away his anger from the people[both Nephite[Mayan] and Lamanite[Aztec], and caused that rain should fall upon the earth, <u>insomuch that it did bring forth her fruit in the season of her fruit. And it came to pass that it did bring forth her grain in the season of her grain.</u>" "And behold, the people did <u>rejoice and glorify God, and the whole face of the land was filled with rejoicing; and they did no more seek to destroy Nephi, but they did esteem him as a great prophet,</u> and a man of God, having great power and authority[Priesthood] given unto him from God."* "And it came to pass that the <u>seventy and sixth year[15B.C.] did end in peace. And the seventy and seventh[14B.C.] year began in peace;</u> and the ★church did spread throughout the face of ALL the land; and the more part of the people, BOTH the Nephites[Mayans] and the Lamanites[Aztecs], "did belong to the church;" and they did have exceedingly great peace in the land; and thus ended the seventy and seventh year[14B.C.]."*(Helaman 11:17-18, Book of Mormon)

Chapter 21

Government Destroyed, Secret Orders Were Reinstated

War against the Gadianton robbers, and secret Societies Houses dotted the earth, both North and South Americas. And most belonged to the Church of Jesus Christ

It was now only 14-years before Christ was to be born, as the Holy men of God had prophesied for thousands of years in advance, of the birth of a Messiah. The people had begun to prosper and there was a <u>great peace</u>, as the majority of the wicked were destroyed during the <u>great famine</u>.

★★"*And thus it did come to pass that the people of Nephi[Mayans] began to prosper again in the land, <u>and began again to build up their</u> <u>**waste places, and began to multiply and spread, even until they did**</u> <u>**cover the whole face of the land, both on the northward[North**</u> <u>**America] and on the southward[South America], from the sea**</u> <u>**west[Pacific Ocean] to the sea east[Atlantic Ocean].**</u>" "*And it came to pass that the <u>seventy and sixth year[15 B.C.] did end in</u> <u>peace. And the seventy and seventh[14B.C.] year began in peace; **and**</u> <u>**the church did spread throughout the face of ALL the land; and**</u> <u>**the more part of the people, BOTH the Nephites[Mayans] and**</u> <u>**the Lamanites[Aztecs], "did belong to the church;" and they**</u> <u>**did have exceedingly great peace in the land; and thus ended the**</u>

seventy and seventh year[14B.C.]. *"(Helaman 11:20-21, Book of Mormon)*

The people dotted the whole land, both North and South, until 2-years later, when the secret societies began to spring up again. It is amazing just how quickly people turn back to their vomit, because of letting Satan enter their hearts, and giving way to temptations. They want to be the first to take advantage, and position themselves in a position of power and control. They see dollar signs circling in their small pea brains. They yearn for titles of nobility, because of their money and great riches. They know that they have been blessed by God, but then begin to tell themselves and others that they did it their way, leaving God out of having anything to do with their prosperity and not giving Him any credit at all. It now being: **11 B.C.**

"And in the seventy and ninth year[12 B.C.] there began to be **much strife**. *But it came to pass that Nephi and Lehi, and many of their brethren who knew concerning the true points of doctrine, having many revelations daily, therefore they did preach unto the people, insomuch that they did put an end to their strife." " And it came to pass that in the eightieth year[11 B.C.] of the reign of the judges over the people of Nephi[Mayans], there were a certain number of the dissenters[seditionists/traitors] from the people of Nephi[Mayans], who had some years before gone over unto the Lamanites[Aztecs], and taken upon themselves the name of* **Lamanites[Aztecs]** *, and also* **a certain number who were real descendants of the Lamanites[Aztecs], being stirred up to anger by them, or by those dissenters[traitors/unbelievers], therefore they commenced a war with their brethren[the Nephites/Mayans].** *" (Helaman 11:23-24,Book of Mormon)*

"And thus in time, yea,even in the space of not many years, they became an exceedingly great band of robbers; and they did search out all the secret plans of Gadianton and his secret orders [communism/socialism/Jesuits/Democrats/liberals/illuminati etc.]; and thus they became robbers of Gadianton[i.e. Illuminatti, Jesuit secret societies of Satan]." "Now behold, these robbers[i.e.

Democrats, and Jesuits/secret societies] did make great havoc, *yea, even great destruction among the people of Nephi[Mayans],* *and also among the people of the Lamanites[Aztecs]." "And it* *came to pass that it was expedient[essential] that there should be a stop* *put to this work of destruction; therefore they[Mayans,Aztecs] sent an* *army of strong men into the wilderness and upon the mountains[central* *Colombia] to search out this [lowlife-communist] band of robbers,* *and to destroy them." "But behold, it came to pass that in that same* *year[11B.C.] they were* **driven back even into their own** *lands.* *Thus ended the eightieth year[11B.C.] of the reign of the judges over* *the people of Nephi."(Helaman 11:26-29, Book of Mormon)*

"And it came to pass in the commencement of the eighty and *first year[**10 B.C.**] they did go forth again against this band of* *robbers, and did* **destroy many; and they were also visited with** **much destruction**. " "And they were again obliged to return out of the* *wilderness and out of the mountains unto their own lands, because of* *the exceeding greatness of the numbers of* **those robbers who infested** **the mountains and the wilderness**. " "And it came to pass that* *thus ended this year[10 B.C.]. And the robbers did still increase and* *wax strong, insomuch that they did* **defy the whole armies of the** **Nephites[Mayans], and also of the Lamanites[Aztecs]; and** **they did cause great fear to come unto the people upon all the** **face of the land.**" "Yea, for they did visit many parts of the land,* *and did do great destruction unto them; yea, did kill many, and did* *carry away others captive into the wilderness, yea, and more* **especially** **their women and their children.**" "Now this great evil, which came* *unto the people because of their iniquity, did stir them up again in* *remembrance of the Lord their God." "And thus ended the eighty and* *first year[10 B.C.] of the reign of the judges."(Helaman 11:30-35,* *Book of Mormon)*

As this Satanic band grew stronger and more numerous, they began infiltrating businesses, churches, county and city governments, schools and colleges, private practices, state governments, and even national governments, every departmental agency, and even the military. Anyone with eyes to see knows what I am talking about. The term used today in America is: "**Woke**". In a speech our great President Donald J. Trump gave, after watching stupid Biden and General Milly give away our billions of dollars worth of the most advanced military weaponry money could buy. Also watching the 2020 Olympics, where every liberal team or single competitor lost miserably, i.e. the American soccer team, all of which are embarrassments to a proud American citizen. President Trump observed and stated that: "everything woke turns to shit", and he is right.

The blessings of God are not with those people, but God's curse is. So if you are violating the commandments of God by joining with this band, then change. The Communists/Democrats are a scourge, a cancer to a free society. In just a few years the people again forgot about God, and were joining to Communist ideas and practices. They wanted ease and comfort , and not having to work for it. They want riches and control, they want the people as slaves, they want your children's minds, they want all to be subservient, or like Hitler, they find a way to destroy their freedom and their lives. Now **6 B.C.**

*"And it came to pass in the <u>eighty and fifth year they did wax stronger and stronger in their pride, and in their wickedness[evilness]; and thus they were ripening</u> **again for destruction.**" "And thus ended the <u>eighty and fifth year[6 B.C.]</u>." (Helaman 11:37-38, Book of Mormon)*

Because of the ease and money they were making, and the power and control they appear to have, still, they didn't have time for their only true friend, except they be brought down to extreme sorrow. People like that don't want God to rule over them, because they would have to stop. They were forgetting who created them and all of the power he has. Successful people, so to speak, because of their great possessions, think that nothing can stop them. What happens when they die, what have they really gained ? They managed to get to rub shoulders with Satan and like minded, knuckle-headed intelligence for the rest of eternity. I especially don't envy those people. Actually, I think how could they be so stupid, and so selfish, so insane. The answer to that is, they are listening to the wrong source.

"O how foolish, and how vain, and **how evil, and devilish,** *and how quick to do evil, and how slow to do good, are the children of men; yea,* **how quick to hearken unto the words of the evil one, and to set their hearts upon the vain things of the world!"** *"Yea, how quick to be lifted up in pride; yea, how quick to boast, and do all manner of that which is iniquity; and how slow are they to remember* **the Lord their God, and to give ear unto his counsels, yea, how slow to walk in wisdom's paths!"** *"Behold,* **they do not desire that the Lord their God, who hath created them, should rule and reign over them; notwithstanding his great goodness and his mercy towards them, they do set at naught his counsels, and they will not that he should be their guide.** *" "O how great is the* **nothingness of the children of men; yea,** *even they are less than the dust of the earth."* *(Helaman 12:4-7, Book of Mormon)*

"And may God grant, in his great fulness, that men might be brought unto *repentance* **and good works, that they might be restored unto grace for grace, according to their works.** *" "And* **I would that all men might be saved. But we read that in the great and last day there are some who shall be cast off from the presence of the Lord;"** *"Yea, who shall be* *consigned to a state of endless misery, fulfilling the words which say:* **They that have done good shall have everlasting life; and they that have done evil shall have everlasting damnation. And thus it is** *. Amen." (Helaman 12:24-26, Book of Mormon)*

Chapter 22

Communist Revolution, War With The Gadianton Robbers

The Birth of Christ and Change in the Reckoning of Time

The Nephite/Mayan people were so unthoughtful, forgetful, and rebellious, that it was necessary to send a Lamanite/Aztec prophet to remind them of the covenants they have made, and tell them what was to happen to them if the people of Nephi didn't change. It happened in just a few years, even as Samuel the Lamanite/Aztec prophet said it would. It is now **5 B.C.**

    ** *"And now it came to pass in the eighty and sixth year[5 B.C.] the <u>Nephites[Mayans] did still remain in wickedness[without change],</u> while* **<u>the Lamanites[Aztecs] did observe strictly to keep the commandments of God, according to the law of Moses.</u>**" "*And it came to pass that in this year[5B.C.] there was* **<u>one Samuel, a Lamanite[Aztec], came into the land of Zarahemla, and began to preach unto the people[Nephites/Mayans].</u>** *And it came to pass that he did preach, <u>many days, repentance unto the people,</u>* **<u>and they did cast him out, and he was about to return to his own</u>** *land."* "*But behold, the* **<u>voice of the Lord came unto him, that he should return again, and prophesy unto the people whatsoever things should come into his heart.</u>**" "*And it came to pass that they would* not suffer[allow] that he should enter into the city; <u>therefore he went and got upon the wall thereof, and</u> **stretched forth his hand and cried with a loud voice, and prophesied unto the people[Mayans] whatsoever things the Lord put in his heart.** "(Helaman 13:1-4, Book of Mormon)

     ***"And he said unto **them:** <u>**Behold, I, Samuel, a Lamanite[Aztec], do speak the words of the Lord which he doth put into my heart; and behold he hath put it into my heart to say unto this people[Nephites/Mayans] that the sword of justice hangeth over this people; and four hundred years pass not away save the sword of justice falleth upon this people[the** *Nephites/ Mayans].*</u>" "Yea, **<u>heavy destruction awaiteth this people, and it surely cometh unto this people, and nothing can save this people save it be faith on the Lord Jesus Christ, who surely shall come into the world, and shall suffer many things and shall be slain for his people</u>**[those who believe and receive His gospel]." "And behold, an **angel of the Lord hath declared it unto me, and he did bring glad tidings to my soul.** <u>And behold, I was sent unto you also, that ye might have glad tidings; but behold ye would not receive me.</u>"(Helaman 13:5-7, Book of Mormon)

     ***"Therefore, <u>**thus saith the Lord: Because of the hardness of the hearts of the people of the Nephites[Mayans], except they repent I will take away my word from them, and I will withdraw my Spirit from them, and I will suffer them no longer, and I will turn the hearts of their brethren[Lamanites/Aztecs] against them.**</u>" "**<u>And four hundred years shall not pass away before I will cause that they shall be smitten; yea, I will visit them with the sword and with famine and with pestilence.</u>**" "Yea, I will **<u>visit them in my fierce anger, and there shall be those of the fourth generation who shall live, of your enemies, to behold your utter destruction; and this shall surely come except ye repent[change], saith the Lord; and those of the fourth generation shall visit your destruction.</u>**" "(Helaman 13:8-10, Book of Mormon)

Samuel, the Lamanite/Aztec prophet, tells the Nephites/Mayans, that they will be destroyed if they don't change their ways. He goes on to point out certain cities to be destroyed and how it will be done. Zarahemla, was to be burned by fire now, if it wasn't for those who were right with God. When Christ was crucified 34-years later, Zarahemla was burned by fire, because all were wicked by that time. Samuel also mentions the city Gideon, and all of the cities of the Nephites/Mayans, for their many depravities, and abominations, within them.

"But blessed are they who will repent[change and do what's right], for them will I spare. But behold, if it were not for the righteous who are in this great city, behold, I would cause that fire should come down out of heaven and destroy it." *"But behold, **it is for the righteous sake that it is spared**. **But behold** the time cometh, saith the Lord, that when ye shall cast out the righteous from among you, then shall ye be ripe for destruction; yea, wo be unto this great city[Zarahemla], because of the wickedness and abominations which are in her."* *"Yea, wo be unto the city of Gideon,[just south of Zarahemla] for the wickedness and abominations which are in her."* *"Yea, **wo be unto all the cities which are in the land round about, which are possessed by the Nephites[Mayans], because of the wickedness and abominations which are in them.**"(Helaman 13:13-16, Book of Mormon)*

*"Ye do not remember the Lord your God in the things with which he hath blessed you, but ye do always remember your riches, not to thank the Lord your God for them; yea, your hearts are drawn out unto **great pride,** unto boasting, and unto great swelling, envyings, strifes, malice, persecutions, murders, and all manner of iniquities."* *"For this cause hath the Lord God caused that a curse should come upon the land, and also **upon your riches, and this because of your iniquities.**"* *"Yea, wo unto this people[Nephites/Mayans], because of this time which has arrived, that ye do cast out the prophets, and do mock them, **and cast stones at them, and do slay them, and do all manner of iniquity unto them, even as they did of old time.**"* *(Helaman 13:22-24, Book of Mormon)*

"And now when ye talk, ye say: <u>if our days had been in the days</u> <u>of our fathers of old, we would not have slain the prophets; we would</u> <u>not have stoned them, and cast them out.</u>" "Behold, ye are **worse** **than they; for as the Lord liveth, if a prophet** <u>come among you and</u> <u>declareth unto you the</u> **word of the Lord, which testifieth of your** **sins and iniquities, ye are angry with him, and cast him out and** **seek to destroy him; yea, you will say that he is a false prophet,** **and that he is a sinner, and of the devil, because he testifieth that** **your deeds are evil.**" *(Helaman 13:25-26, Book of Mormon)*

⋆*"But behold, <u>your days of probation are past; ye have</u> <u>procrastinated the day of your salvation until it is everlastingly</u> <u>too late, and your destruction is made sure; yea, for ye have</u> <u>sought for happiness in doing iniquity, which thing is contrary</u> <u>to the nature of that righteousness which is in our "great and</u> <u>Eternal Head[God Almighty]</u>." "O ye people of the land[of the Nephites/Mayans], that ye would hear my words! And I pray that the anger of the Lord be turned away from you, and that ye would repent[change and turn to God] and be saved."* (Helaman 13:38-39, Book of Mormon). **Now 5 B.C.**

Samuel the Lamanite/Aztec, prophesies next, of the birth of the Messiah to come in just 5-more years. The birth of Jesus Christ is pinpointed right to the exact day, so if anyone thinks God is not in charge and controls the times and seasons, think again. He is more intelligent and organized than we could ever think to be, and he knows all of his offspring by name, worlds without end. When I think about how great my God is, and how kind and merciful he is, it just makes my heart swell with pride. I am not ashamed to talk about my God in any crowd. "Joshua's long day" when he was fighting wars against the people across the river Jordan, that the children of Israel were involved in, as they fought to conquer the Phillistines, required the same sign at the birth of Jesus Christ, as it was truly a long day.

*"Yea, **by the power of his voice, do the foundations rock, even to the very center.**" "Yea, and if <u>he say unto the earth---Move---</u> <u>it is moved.</u>" "Yea, and if <u>he say unto the earth---Thou shalt go</u>*

back, that it lengthen out the day for many hours---it is done;" "And thus, *according to his "word" the earth goeth back, and it appeareth that the sun standeth still; Yea, and behold, this is so; for surely it is the earth that moveth and not the sun."* (Helaman 12:12-15, Book of Mormon)

 # *"And now it came to pass that* **Samuel, the Lamanite[Aztec] did prophesy a great many more things which cannot be written." "And behold, he said unto them[the Nephites/Mayans in Zarahemla/Colombia]: **Behold, I give unto you a sign; for five more years cometh, and behold, then cometh the Son of God to redeem all those who shall believe on his name."** "And behold, this will I give unto you for a **sign** at the time of his coming; for behold, there shall be **great lights in heaven, insomuch that in the night before he cometh, there shall be no darkness[the earth stands still], insomuch that it will appear unto man as if it was a day."** "Therefore, **there shall be one day and a night and a day, as if it were one day and there were no night; and this shall be unto you for a sign; for ye shall know of the rising of the sun and also of its setting; therefore they shall know of a surety that there shall be two days and a night; nevertheless the night shall not be darkened; and it shall be the night before he is born."** "And behold, **there shall a new star arise, such an one as ye have never beheld; and this also shall be a sign unto you."**(Helaman 14:1-3, Book of Mormon)

"And if ye believe on his name ye will repent of all your sins, that thereby ye may have a remission of them through his merits." "And behold, another sign I give unto you, yea, a **sign of his death."** "Yea, **at the time that he shall yield up the ghost** there shall be thunderings and lightnings for the space of many hours, and the earth shall shake and tremble; and the rocks which are upon the face of this earth, which are both above the earth and beneath, which ye know at this time **are solid, or the more part of it is one solid mass, shall be broken up;"** "Yea, they shall be rent in twain, and shall ever after **be found in seams and in cracks, and in broken fragments upon the face of the whole earth, yea, both**

above the earth and beneath," "And behold, **there shall be tempests, and there shall be many** <u>mountains laid low, like unto a valley, and there shall be many places which are now called valleys which shall become mountains, and whose height is great."</u> *"And* <u>many highways shall be broken up, and many cities shall become desolate."</u> "And <u>many graves shall be opened, and shall yield up many of their dead; and many saints shall appear unto many."</u> *(Helaman 14:13,21-25, Book of Mormon)*

"And now remember, remember, my brethren[Nephites/Mayans/ believers], <u>that whosoever **perisheth, perisheth unto himself[is responsible for his own sins]; and whosoever doeth iniquity, doeth it unto himself [knowingly of his own free will]; for behold, ye are FREE[**under the law of your Constitution, and the laws of God]; and ye are permitted to act for yourselves; for God hath given unto you a knowledge[of the truth] and he hath made you free[under the law]."</u> "He hath <u>given unto you that ye might **know good from evil, and he hath given unto you that ye might choose life [freedom] or death[slavery]; and ye can do good[uphold the laws of God], and be restored unto that which is good[freedom], or ye can do evil[violate the laws of God] and have that which is evil[slavery] restored unto you."</u>*(Helaman 14:30-31, Book of Mormon)*

Samuel continues to tell them that the Nephites/Mayans, unless they repent now, their houses shall be left desolate, and their families will have no refuge. Was it not so in the end? As we all, world wide, can see, that all of the cities of North America once inhabited by the Nephites/Mayans, are left empty, and without inhabitants. Lots of evidence exist that witness they were here, having such great knowledge, some to surpass our technology today. No expert can seem to understand where these people have gone, leaving their houses and cities intact and still standing, but there are no people. They also cannot understand where they came from or where they went.

"And now, behold my brethren, behold, I declare unto you that <u>except ye shall repent[change from your evil ways],</u> "your houses *shall be left unto you desolate." "Yea, except ye repent, your women shall have great cause to mourn in the day that they shall give suck; for ye shall attempt to flee and there shall be no place for refuge; yea, and wo unto them which are with child, for they shall be heavy and cannot flee; therefore they shall be trodden down and shall be left to perish." "Yea, wo unto this people who are called the people of Nephi[Mayans] except they shall repent[change], when they shall see all these signs and wonders which shall be showed unto them; for behold, they have been a chosen people of the Lord; yea, the people of Nephi[Mayan people] hath he loved, and also hath he chastened them; yea, in the days of their iniquities hath he chastened them because he loveth them." (Helaman 15:1-3,* Book of Mormon)

Then Samuel the Lamanite/Aztec prophet talks about his people, the Lamanites/Aztecs, and why they will remain on the land long after the Nephites/Mayans are gone.

"But behold, my brethren, the Lamanites[Aztecs] hath he hated because their deeds have been evil continually, and this because of the iniquity of the tradition of their fathers, But behold, salvation hath come unto them through the preaching of the Nephites[Mayans]; and for this intent hath the Lord prolonged their days." "And I would that ye should behold that the more part of them are in a path of their "duty", and they do observe to keep the "commandments and "his statutes" and "his judgments according to the law of Moses." "Yea, I say unto you that the more part of them[Lamanites/Aztecs] are doing this, and they are striving with unwearied "diligence" that they may bring the remainder of their brethren to the "knowledge of the truth"; therefore there are many who do add to their numbers daily." "And behold, ye know of yourselves, for ye have witnessed it, that as many of them as are brought to the knowledge of the truth, and to know of the wicked and abominable traditions of their fathers, and are led to believe in the holy scriptures, yea, the prophecies of the holy prophets, which are written, which leadeth them to faith and

repentance"bringeth a change of heart unto them---" *(Helaman 15:4-7, Book of Mormon)*

"Therefore, as many as have come to this, ye know of yourselves are firm and steadfast in the faith, and in the thing wherewith they have been made free" "And ye know also that they[Lamanites/ Aztecs] have buried their weapons of war, and they fear to take them up lest by any means they should sin; yea, ye can see that they fear to sin---for behold they will suffer themselves to be trodden down and slain by their enemies, and will not lift their swords against them, and this because of their faith in Christ." "And now, because of their[the Lamanites/Aztecs] "steadfastness when they do believe in that thing which they do believe, for because of their firmness when they are once enlightened, behold, the Lord shall bless them and "prolong their [Lamanites/Aztecs] days, notwithstanding[inspite] of their previous many sins, because if they repent he will remember [their sins] no more their iniquity---" "Yea, even if they should dwindle in unbelief the Lord shall prolong their days, until the time shall come which hath been spoken of by our fathers, and also by the prophet Zenos, and many other prophets, concerning the restoration of our brethren, the Lamanites[Aztecs], again to the knowledge of the truth---[Jesus Christ]" *(Helaman 15:8-11, Book of Mormon)*

⋆*"Yea, I say unto you, that "in the latter times[today-2023, etc.] the promises of the Lord have been extended to our brethren, the Lamanites[Aztecs, people of South America]; and notwithtanding[despite] the many afflictions which they shall have, and notwithstanding[in spite of] they shall be driven to and fro upon the face of the earth, and be hunted, and shall be smitten and scattered abroad, having no place of refuge, the Lord shall be merciful unto them." "And this is according to the prophecy, that they shall again be brought to the true knowledge, which is the knowledge of their redeemer, and their great and true shepherd, and be numbered among his sheep." "Therefore I[Samuel, the Lamanite/Aztec prophet] say unto you[Nephites/ Mayans] that it shall be better for them[Lamanites/Aztecs]*

than for you[Nephites/Mayans] except you repent[change]."
"For behold, had the __mighty works been shown unto them which__
__have been shown unto you, yea, unto them[the Lamanites/__
*__Aztecs] who have dwindled in unbelief__ because of the **traditions**__*
*__of their fathers,__ ye can see for yourselves that they **never would**__*
*__again have dwindled in unbelief.__ " "Therefore, **saith the Lord: "I**__*
__will not utterly destroy them, but I will cause that in the day__
__of my wisdom they SHALL RETURN AGAIN UNTO ME,__
__saith the Lord.__" "And now behold,, saith the Lord, __concerning the__
*__people of the__ **Nephites[Mayans]: "If they will not repent[change**__*
__and   seek God in all things, and observe to do MY WILL, I__
__will UTTERLY DESTROY THEM, saith the Lord, because of__
__their UNBELIEF notwithstanding[despite] the many "mighty__
__works" which I have done among them[Nephites/Mayans];__
__and as SURELY AS THE LORD LIVETH SHALL THESE__
__THINGS BE, saith the Lord__."(Helaman 15:12-17, Book of
Mormon)

Samuel continues to emphasize the destruction of the Nephites/
Mayans,, if they don't change. If they don't change, Samuel promises
their utter destruction. Is/was it not so? No one knows, except me,
and those who have the Spirit of Revelation and Prophesy, having
searched the scriptures, and believing in God, where the Jaredites/
Olmecs, or the Nephites/Mayans,Toltecs, Incas, came from, they
don't know where they went, or why their cities are empty and still
in good shape and standing. They also do not understand that the
Lamanites/Aztecs are right in front of them, in South and Central
America as the Lamanites/Aztecs. The promise to them is that they
will all be brought to a knowledge of the truth, of who their great
Shepherd is, and that being Catholic doesn't fit the description of what
the Lord has in mind. Satan, move out!, Because the Lord Jesus Christ
is moving in!

Samuel, the Lamanite's /Aztec's people are inhabiting the towns
and cities of the Ancient Jaredites/Olmecs, and of the Nephite's/
Mayan's, Toltec's, Inca's. The experts can't figure out who they were,
where they came from, or where they went. The houses and cities
are still standing, the architecture is superb, but they can't figure out

where they went and why. Samuel is telling everyone when, why, and how, their destruction is to come. Samuel told the Nephites/Mayans that in exactly **400 years** after the Birth of Christ that the Nephites/ Mayans, Incas, total destruction would take place.

The Nephites/Mayans who believed Samuel, repented and sought out Nephi and were baptized and went forward confessing their sins, but the majority sought to shoot him with arrows, or hit him with stones from their slingshots, but seeing this failed tried to chase him down to lay their hands upon him/Samuel, with the desire to kill him some other way.

> "And now, it came to pass that there _were many[Nephites/ Mayans]_ **who heard the words of Samuel, the Lamanite[Aztec],** which he spake upon the walls of the city[Zarahemla]. And as many as believed on his word went _forth and sought for Nephi[the Nephite/ Mayan prophet]; and when they had come forth and found him they_ **confessed unto him their sins and denied not[owned up to their faults and wrong doing], desiring that they might be baptized unto the Lord.[Born again]**" "But as many as there were who did not believe in the words of Samuel were angry with him; _and they cast stones at him upon the wall, and also many shot arrows at him as he stood upon the wall; but the_ **Spirit of the Lord was with him, that they could not hit him with their stones or their arrows**." "Now when they saw that they could not hit him, **there were many more who did believe in his words, insomuch that they went away unto Nephi[the Nephite/Mayan prophet] to be** baptized." "For behold, Nephi was baptizing, and prophesying, and preaching, crying repentance unto the people[Nephites/Mayans], showing **signs and wonders, working miracles among the people, _that they might know that the Christ must shortly come---_**" "(_Helaman_ 16:1-4, Book of Mormon)

> "And as they[the Nephites/Mayans] went forth to lay their hands upon him, behold, _he did cast[jump] himself down from the wall, and did flee out of their[the Nephite/Mayan] lands, , yea, even unto his own country[South America, Land of Nephi, etc.], and began_ to preach and to prophesy among his own people[the Lamanites/

*Aztecs]." "And behold, **He was never heard of more among the Nephites[Mayans];** and thus were the affairs of the [Nephite/ Mayan] people." "And thus ended the <u>eighty and sixth year[5 B.C.]</u> <u>of the reign of the judges over the people of Nephi[Mayans]</u>(Helaman 16:7-9, Book of Mormon)*

4-years more had gone by, and the majority of the people of Nephi[Mayans], were more hardened in iniquity. **Signs and wonders** were beginning to take place, just as was prophesied by holy men thousands of years earlier, beginning at the year before Christ was born. It is now **1 B.C.**

> *But it came to pass <u>in the **ninetieth year[1 B.C.]** of the reign</u> <u>of the judges,</u> **there were great signs given unto the people, and wonders;** <u>and the words of the prophets began to be fulfilled.</u>" "And **angels did appear unto men, wise men, <u>and did declare unto</u> <u>them glad tidings of great joy;</u>** thus in this year the scriptures began to be fulfilled." "Nevertheless, the people began to <u>harden</u> <u>their hearts, all save it were the most believing part of them,</u> **both** <u>**of the Nephites[Mayans] and also of the Lamanites[Aztecs],**</u> <u>**and began to depend**</u> upon their own strength and wisdom, saying:" "**Some things they may have <u>guessed</u> right among so many; but behold, we know that all these <u>great and marvelous works cannot</u> <u>come to pass, of which has been spoken.</u>" (Helaman 16:13-16, Book of Mormon)*

The Nephites/Mayans began to badmouth the Jews and were doubting the ones who foretold these things about Christ coming so many years in advance. Oh, but the experts, those who are learned, but now think they are wise, influence the people who are easily led, because they want to see them as experts, and all wise, in order to justify their own sins. Instead of the alleged experts humbling themselves, and searching, reading, understanding, and believing what good and holy men before them said, who actually talked with God, and lived what they taught. A liberal minded sinner, will normally **imagine and hope** that the people of God are wrong, to make themselves feel better about themselves. They, like a common Democrat/Liberal, imagine myriads of ways to "**spin the truth**", to take the spotlight off of themselves, and their dastardly, and despicable deeds.

"And they began to reason among themselves, saying: That it is not reasonable that such a being as a **Christ shall come;** if so, and he be the **Son of God, the Father of heaven and earth,** as it has been spoken, why will he not show himself unto us as well as unto them who shall be at **Jerusalem?"** *"But behold,* we know that this is a wicked tradition[Lie], handed down unto us by our fathers, to cause us that we should believe in some great and marvelous thing which shall come to pass, **but not among us, but in a land which is far distant,** a land which we know not; therefore they can keep us **in ignorance,** for we cannot witness with our own eyes that they are **true.**" *"And they will,* by the cunning and the mysterious arts of the evil one, work some great miracle which we cannot understand, which will keep us down to be servants to their words, and also servants unto them, for we depend upon them to teach us the word; **and thus they keep us in ignorance if we will yield ourselves** unto them, all the days of our lives."**(Helaman** *16:16-21,Book of Mormon)*

"And many more things did the people[Nephites/Mayans] **imagine** up in their hearts which were **foolish and vain;** and they were much disturbed[feeling guilty and bothered], **for Satan did stir them up to do iniquity continually;** yea, he did go about **spreading rumors[disinformation and propaganda] and contentions[riots and vandalizing] upon all the face of the land, that he might harden the hearts of the people against that which was good[truth and light] and against that which should** come[fighting to keep Christ from coming to judge against their evil]." *"**And notwithstanding[despite] the signs and wonders which were wrought[done,seen, witnessed and performed] among the people of the Lord, and the many mighty miracles** which they **did, Satan did get great hold upon the hearts of the people upon all the face of the land**[mostly among the Nephites/Mayans]." "Thus ended* the ninetieth year[**1 B.C.**] of the reign of the judges **over the people of Nephi[Mayans].**"*(Helaman 16:22-24, Book of Mormon)*

The **final year-1 B.C.,** before Christ was to be born passed away, and in this same year, Lachoneous was appointed Chief Judge over the Nephites/Mayans. People had begun, even more so, to doubt Christ's coming, believing that the prophets were lying to them, at least they were hoping this was the case in order to justify their own wickedness. They didn't just doubt, but they were actively resisting the idea that Christ would come, because there were many, many wicked people who would just as soon have the mountains fall upon them, than have to look into the piercing eyes of some indignant God. Many mountains did bury them up, among other things that happened, so they must have known that **Justice** was coming for them. If they were doing what was right, and changing their ways, and born again, they would have no need to fear. The sad truth, is those who fought against God, breaking all of his commandments and reveled in doing so, chose to fight against the people of God, even as is going on today in America, and around the world.

So far, **600 years** had gone by since the first Nephi; first leader of theMayan people, left Jerusalem with his father, Lehi, to come to the Americas. This same year, Nephi the Prophet, having inherited his good name, from generation to generation, from the first Nephi, who had been taken up to be with God, many believing he was translated because of his faithfulness, and rightly so. Before Nephi left, he turned charge of the records of the people of Nephi to his son, also named Nephi.

*"Now it came to pass that the **ninety and first year had passed away**[now in the year 0, or meridian of time] and it was <u>six hundred years from the time that Lehi</u>[and Nephi, etc.] had <u>left Jerusalem;</u> and it was in the year that Lachoneus was the <u>chief judge and governor</u> over the land[of the Nephites/Mayan people]." "And **Nephi** the son of **Helaman**, <u>had departed out of the land of Zarahemla</u>[Northern Colombia, South America], giving **charge** unto his son **Nephi**, who was his eldest son, **concerning the "brass plates"** [Old Testament writings/five books of Moses etc.], and <u>all records w</u>hich had been kept, and all those things[sword of Laban, Liahona/compass,etc.] which had been kept sacred from the departure of Lehi out of Jerusalem" "Then he departed out of the land, <u>and whither he went, **no man knoweth;**</u> and his son **Nephi** did keep the*

*records in his stead, yea the records of this people[Nephites/Mayans
people]."(3 Nephi 1:1-3, Book of Mormon)*

The Nephites/Mayans who wanted God to be wrong were
beginning to mock God, and the people of God, because things were
not happening as they had imagined it should. Basically, they didn't
understand the words of the prophets. They figured everything should
have started within the final year leading up to the birth of Christ,
but Samuel the prophet had plainly said that 5 more years cometh,
then cometh the Son of God *(Helaman 14:2, Book of Mormon)*. 4-years
definitely passed, and then commenced in the fifth year, before Christ
was born. Like many people today, they don't listen to the wording,
because of what they are desperately wanting. In fact, because they
love what they are doing, and not wanting to change, they pull the
ignorant card, they won't read, listen, and won't take a stand, and they
won't vote. They figure that if they bury their heads in the sand, or
deny the facts long enough, it won't really happen to them.

First the 5th year had to go by before the time was up, and like any
normal pregnancy, 9-months, it all depends on the day of conception.
In this case, Christ was born in the spring, on April 6th, in the year
"0", meaning the Meridian of Time. If Christ was born before
the year had expired down to 0, it would have made a liar of his
prophet, Samuel, like it was prophesied. It is all in the wording, but
the natural man of the world wants to jump to conclusions, without
understanding. So, after the 91st year of the Reign of the Judges,
finalized the waiting period then, which ended early within the next
year, which was the year Christ was to be born. Christ knows how to
confound the wise, and destroy the plans of the wicked.

Obviously, he could see and hear the plans of the Satanic, conspiring
communists, and of the dastardly liberals, who conspired to destroy the
people who reverence him. He knew what they were planning against
his righteous people, those who believed in him, had faith in him,
received his gospel, and kept his commandments. Christ baited them
by not coming, until just the day before they had arranged to destroy/
kill the people of Christ, if he didn't come, as was foretold. Now you
try to convince me, that Jesus Christ is not more powerful than Satan,
and all of his followers combined. Because that very night, Christ

made fools out of Satan, and all of the ungodly minions, worldwide, because he did come, and still lives today. He is still continuing to make fools out of anyone and any institution who thinks that they will destroy the freedom and the belief/faith, his people have in him. He has always said: **My people need not fear.** Many times we find ourselves in situations, that begins to look like there is no way out, but then the door opens right at the last minute, and instead of a storm, we see the sunshine.

> *"And it came to pass in the <u>commencement of the ninety and second year</u>[0-- year Christ was to be born], behold, the prophecies of the prophets began to be **fulfilled more fully**; for there began to be greater signs and greater miracles wrought among the people."* **"But there were some who began to say that the time was past for the words to be fulfilled,** *which were spoken by Samuel, the Lamanite[Aztec]."* *"<u>And they began to rejoice</u>[ridicule and celebrate] <u>over their brethren, saying</u>:* **Behold the <u>time is past</u>, and the words of Samuel are not fulfilled; therefore, your <u>joy and your faith</u> concerning this thing hath been in vain.** *"And it came to pass that they[unbelievers/communists/libtards] did make a great uproar throughout the land; and the people who <u>believed began to be very</u>* **<u>sorrowful[in case the ungodly communists were right], lest by any means those things which had been spoken might not come to pass.</u>** *(3 Nephi 1:4-7, Book of Mormon)*

> *"But behold, <u>they did watch</u>* **<u>steadfastly for that day and that night and that day which should be as "one day" as if there were no night,</u>** *that they might know that their faith had not been in vain."* *"Now it came to pass that <u>there was a day set apart by the unbelievers</u>[communists/liberals], that* **<u>all those who believed[Christians] in those traditions should be put to death except the sign should come to pass, which had been given by Samuel the prophet.</u>** *"Now it came to pass that when Nephi, the son of Nephi, saw this wickedness of his people, his heart was exceedingly sorrowful."* *"And it came to pass that he went out and bowed himself down upon the earth, and <u>cried</u>[prayed] <u>mightily to his God in behalf of his people, yea, those</u>* **<u>who were about to be destroyed because</u>**

of their faith in the tradition of their fathers."(3 Nephi 1:8-11, Book of Mormon)

"And it came to pass that he cried[prayed] mightily unto the Lord all that day; and behold, the voice of the Lord came unto him, saying:" "Lift up your head and be of good cheer; for behold, the time is at hand, and on this night shall the sign be given, and on the morrow "come I into the world", to show unto the world[Satan's kingdom/hell] that I will fulfill all that which I have caused to be spoken by the mouth of "my holy" prophets." "Behold, I come unto my own, to fulfill all things which I have made known unto the children of men from the foundation of the world[for thousands of years], and to do the will, both of the Father and of the Son---of the Father because of me, and of the Father and of the Son because of my flesh. And behold, the time is at hand, and "this night shall the sign be given."(3 Nephi 1:12-14, Book of Mormon)

Once again, God spoiled the plans of the wicked and made fools out of them. Christ was born in the spring and not the winter, because too many facts testify to this. Shepherds were watching their flocks by night as they grazed on the new grass of spring. Many people were guilty concerning their plans against the people of God. The same is in the process of happening even now as we speak, what the unbelievers, communists/liberals/Democrats etc., have planned for the people of God, something is going to go terribly wrong with their plans, you can have full faith in that.

★★ *"And there were many, who had not believed the words of the prophets, who fell to the earth and became as if they were dead, for they knew that the great plan of destruction which they had laid for those who believed in the words of the prophets had been frustrated; for the sign which had been given was already at hand." "And they began to know that the Son of God must shortly appear; yea, in fine, all the people upon the face of the whole earth from the west to the east, both in the land north and in the land south, were so exceedingly astonished that they fell to the earth." "For they knew that the prophets had testified of these things for many years, and that the sign which had been given was already at hand; and they began to fear because of their iniquity and their unbelief."(3 Nephi 1:16-18, Book of Mormon)*

*"And it came to pass that there was **no darkness in all that night, but it was as light as though it was mid-day.** And it came to pass that the sun did rise in the morning again, according to its proper order; and they knew that "it was the day that the Lord should be born", because of the sign which had been given."* *"And it had come to pass, yea, all things, every whit, according to the words of the prophets."* *"And it came to pass also that "a new star did appear, according to the words of the prophets." (3 Nephi 1:19-21, Book of Mormon)*

Even then did disinformation, and lies go out trying to deceive the people, both **Nephite/Mayan** and Lamanite/Aztec, but there were many who came to Christ at this time forward. Just like a hardened communist, or a self-seeking liberal, to lie and spread disinformation, when the truth would do them the most good. I'll tell you this, that I would believe the words of someone, in this case, the Lord, seeing as he can bring the earth to a complete stop for two whole days, and then start it on time without missing a beat. What power and majesty! Can Satan do that? No, Satan can't even muster up his own body. Satan can't even create a speck of dirt! Satan was thrown out of Heaven by God, along with a third of all the hosts of Heaven, at the same time! Where is Satans power? I can show you God's/Christ's power!

*"And it came to pass that from this time forth there began to be lyings [disinformation/propaganda] sent forth among the people, by Satan, to harden their hearts, to the intent that they might not believe in those signs and wonders which they had seen[witnessed themselves]; but notwithstanding[in spite of /despite] these lyings and deceivings the more part of the people did **believe and were converted unto the Lord.**" "And it came to pass that Nephi went forth among the people[Nephites/Mayan and Lamanites/Aztecs], and also many others, baptizing unto repentance, in the which there was a great*

remission of sins[complete change /turn about]. And thus the people began again to have **peace in the land**.*"(3 Nephi 1:22-23, Book of Mormon)*

You see, the Nephites/Mayans, and Lamanites/Aztecs, as almost all of them were now members of the Lord's Church, and were Christian people, the Lamanites/Aztecs, even more so. They all had been observing the *"Law of Moses"* as was still required by God, for 33-34 years more, before Christ was hung on the cross. Some of the Nephites/Mayans, in their wisdom, were now trying to prove that there was no need to continue the Law of Moses, now that Christ had been born, but they didn't understand that Christ was the last sacrifice by the shedding of blood, and He was to resemble the sacrificial Lamb without blemish, and He was the only one that could finish it.

*"And there were no contentions, save it were a few that began to preach, endeavoring to prove by the scriptures that it was no more expedient to observe the"***law of Moses"***. Now in this thing they did err, having not understood the scriptures."(3 Nephi 1:24, Book of Mormon)*

The Nephites/Mayans now began to reckon their time/calendar at the birth of Christ, when the sign was first given of his birth. As time passed year by year, down to the day **when** the sign of Jesus Christ's birth was fulfilled, the time from then on was reckoned as **"0"** A.D. meaning "In the Year of Our Lord".

"And nine years had passed away **from the time when the sign was given, which was** *spoken of by the prophets,* **that Christ should come into the world.**" **"Now the Nephites[Mayans] began to reckon their time from this period when the sign was given, or "from the coming of Christ"***; nine years had passed away[***now 9 A.D.].*"(3 Nephi 2:7-8, Book of Mormon)*

Chapter 23

Mormon Observes The Destruction Of The Nephites/Mayans Corrupt Government

Secret-Societies Infesting the Mayans and Aztecs
Leading up to the Death of Christ

14 A.D.

Even the people having the knowledge that the King of All The Earth, the Messiah, was born 14-years earlier went back to their vomit, by reinstating the *secret orders* of Satan, and thereby filling the seats of government with Democrats/Gadianton Robbers, same as Communists. They were once again altering the laws of the people, and instituting a Democracy, where the rich few ruled over the people without justice, only <u>Just Us.</u> Many people were forsaking the Lord, wanting to be numbered with the Elite Class, and having power and riches.

They were joining to the Democrats/Liberals because they were promised *Free Benefits. This is w*hat happens to a people when the majority of the people, especially the young, strong , able, and educated youth, won't work and produce anything, but would rather be dependent on the Liberal government. This mentality grieved the people who were trying to contribute to the upkeep of the people, by working on the farms,etc.. It especially grieved the Lamanites/Aztecs, because at this time there were more faithful Lamanite/Aztecs in the Church of Jesus Christ, than there were Nephites/Mayans.

It was the Nephites/Mayans mostly responsible for reviving the evil orders at this time in history, and encouraging the growth of this Democrat/communist infestation, without doing anything at all to get the communists out of their government, or repent. However, on the other hand, The Lamanites/Aztecs, once they were converted to the truth, they would not compromise or go backwards, for the rest of their lives, until the later generations came along. It was them, that were more numerous, and more diligent in searching out the Criminals in their land, and they hunted and searched them out, and brought speedy justice to them. It was their children in the next generation who were joining steadily to them, because they were deceived into believing the lies and disinformation and propaganda, hoping to have a life of ease without working and producing something, or some service. Everyone was trying to become rich on their investments, much of it at the expense of their fellowman.

At this time among the Lamanites/Aztecs, you wouldn't have found the voter fraud going unpunished, or the abortions, or the many other abominations happening as they are happening in America. They would have hunted out the Obamas, Clintons, Bidens, Pelosis, Romneys, Gates, Soros, Pences, etc. etc.. If a liberal can't get something for free out of you by deceitfulness, then they are going to take it by force, either by changing the rules, or bringing the woke military down on you. Therefore, there began to be continual wars in the land.

*"And it came to pass in the _thirteenth year_**[13 A.D.] there began to be wars and contentions throughout all the land;** _for the Gadianton robbers[Democrats/communists]had become so numerous, and did slay many of the people, and did lay waste so many cities[i.e. Portland, St. Louis, Chicago], and did spread so much death and carnage throughout the land, that it became expedient that all the people,_ **both the Nephites[Mayans] and the Lamanites[Aztecs], should take up arms against them.** _" "Therefore,_ **all the Lamanites[Aztecs] who had become converted unto the Lord did unite with their brethren, the Nephites[Mayans], and were compelled, for the safety of their lives and their women and their children, to take**

up arms against those Gadianton [Democrat/communist] robbers, yea, and also to maintain their rights, and the privileges of their church[religion] and of their worship, and their freedom and their liberty." "And it came to pass that before this thirteenth year had passed away the Nephites[Mayans] were threatened with utter destruction because of this war, which had become exceedingly sore." "And it came to pass that those Lamanites[Aztecs] who had united with the Nephites[Mayans] were numbered among the Nephites[Mayans];" (3 Nephi 2:11-14, Book of Mormon)

***"And *their curse was taken from them, and their skin became white like unto the Nephites[Mayans];" "And their young men and their daughters became exceedingly fair, and they were numbered among the Nephites[Mayans], and were called Nephites[Mayans].* Thus ended *the thirteenth year[13 A.D.]* (3 Nephi 2:15-17, Book of Mormon)

Obviously, the Communist/liberal/Democrat/Gadianton Robbers, were carrying on *"business as usual"*, forgetting about the fact, that in just about 15-18 years or more, that Christ would die, and what repercussions that would bring upon the wicked. Selfish, greedy people, don't look that far ahead, or even care, so long as they get what they want for the moment. *Riches, Power?* What good is all of that if you can't take it with you when you die? It doesn't belong to any of us anyway. It belongs to the creator of all, and is all we have is control for only a short time, and then we have to answer to Him that gave us life.

To make a long story short, about these Communists/Gadianton Robbers, they couldn't get away with just robbing the people at will, because the people of God gathered together, to protect what was their's, both, Nephite/Mayan, and Lamanite/Aztec alike, seeing the necessity of needing to join forces against these robbers for self preservation. These wars sound more like the communist revolutions stirred up by the communists in Russia, Germany, and many other places throughout our more recent history, of this world. The same thing the communists/liberals/democrats are trying to start even today in America. They start the uprising, and then offer the solution for compromise that they would control, called slavery.

After all of the loss of life, because of the wars and destruction, the people of God, called upon God in their time of need, and He did answer their prayers/cries. The Communists/liberals were forced to hide in the Wilderness, which would be approximately, in the northeast region beyond Zarahemla across the River Sidon/Rio Magdalena, close to the seashore in the narrow strip of wilderness, dividing the Nephites/Mayans from the Lamanites/Aztecs country. We know today, this area, as north central Colombia.

The Nephites/Mayans and Lamanites/Aztecs, were continuously on the lookout, and watched diligently to make sure these bands of robbers didn't come upon them when they weren't prepared to meet them in battle. The Robbers were continually threatening to come down out of the mountains of the Wilderness and lay waste to their land and homes, and kill their families, but the people of God were prepared to meet them, because they had all of their food/crops already harvested, and then took it with them, so there was nothing that the invading army could find to feed themselves.

> *"And now it came to pass that <u>in the sixteenth year</u>[**16 A.D.**] <u>year from the coming of Christ, Lachoneus, the governor[president]</u> <u>of the land,</u> **received an epistle[letter] from the leader and the** **governor of this band of robbers[communists/Democrats];** and these were the words which were written, saying:"* *"Lachoneus, most noble and chief governor of the land, behold, <u>I write this epistle unto</u> <u>you, and do give unto you exceedingly great praise because of your</u> <u>firmness, and also the firmness of your people, in maintaining that</u> which **ye suppose to be your right and liberty;** <u>yea, ye do stand well,</u> <u>as if ye were</u> **supported by the hand of a god**, <u>in the defense of your</u> **liberty, and your property, and your country,** <u>or that which ye so</u> <u>call so.</u>"* *"And it seemeth a pity unto me, most noble Lachoneus, that ye should be so foolish and vain as to suppose that ye can stand against so many <u>brave[twisted,lying, thieving, murdering] men[communist/</u> <u>liberals] who are at my command, who do now at this time stand in</u> <u>their arms, and do await with great anxiety for the word</u>---**Go down** **upon the Nephites[Mayans] and destroy them.**"* *"And I know of*

their unconquerable spirit, having proved them in the field of battle, and knowing of their everlasting hatred towards you because of the many wrongs which ye have done unto them, therefore if they should come **down** *against you they would visit you with* **utter destruction.** *" (3 Nephi 3:1-4, Book of Mormon)*

Therefore I have written this epistle[letter], sealing it with mine own hand, feeling for your welfare[sure he does], because of your firmness in that which ye believe to be right, and your noble spirit in the field of battle." "Therefore I write unto you, desiring that ye would yield up unto this [communist/liberal/band of thieves] my people, your cities, your lands, and your possessions, rather than that they should [have to work for their keep] visit you with the sword and that destruction should come upon you[us, meaning themselves]." "Or in other words[become our slaves], yield yourselves up unto us, and unite with us[become just as worthless as we are] and become **acquainted with our "secret works",** *and become* **our brethren that ye may be like unto us---not our slaves, but our brethren[accomplices] and partners of all our** substance[they don't have any substance]." "And behold, I swear unto you, if ye will do this, with an oath, ye shall not be destroyed; but if ye will not do this, I swear unto you with an oath, that on the morrow month[month after next] I will command that my armies shall come down against you, and they shall not stay their hand[no quarter] and shall spare not, but shall slay you, and shall let fall the sword upon you even until ye shall become extinct[famous last words]."(3 Nephi 3:5-8, Book of Mormon)*

And behold, I am Giddianhi; and I am the governor[chief communist/liberal/Democrat robber] of this the **secret society of Gadianton[Catholic Church]; which society and the works thereof I know to be good; and they are of ancient date and they have been handed down unto us [by** *Satan &* **his minions].**" *"And I write this epistle[letter] unto you, Lachoneus, and I hope that ye will deliver up your lands and your possessions[betray your own people], without the shedding of blood, that this my people[won't be killed instead] may recover[something they never had] their rights[by forfeit to your very lives] and government, and except ye do this, I will* *avenge their wrongs. I am Giddianhi." (3 Nephi 3:9-10, Book of Mormon)*

"And now it came to pass <u>when Lachoneus received this epistle[letter] he was exceedingly astonished, because of the boldness of Giddianhi demanding the possession of the land of the Nephites[Mayans], and also of threatening the people and avenging the wrongs of those that had received no wrong, save it were they had wronged themselves by dissenting away unto those wicked[evil] and abominable robbers[communists/democrats].</u>"(3 Nephi 3:11, Book of Mormon)

All that these Communists did in those days, are the same as the communists are doing today in our own America. There is nothing different in their dishonest, self-serving practices, except the year. . As King Solomon writes in Proverbs, "there is nothing new under the sun". The people were constantly needing to make decisions, like us today also. The decisions they were constantly having to make were, to call upon God for their blessings, protection, health, safety and defense. If they failed to respect God, then God was slow to answer the people's cries/needs/prayers.

If you want a look/idea at who the Communists are in our own government today, observe the Democrats in Congress, along with many GOP. Those who are wanting to bring our country to believing we have a Democracy, when actually, it is a Republic. Those who fill positions of public-trust, yet trample all over your rights and laws, and commandments from God. These are the **"<u>whore of all the earth</u>"**.

*And it came to pass that in the <u>eighteenth year[**18 A.D.**] those armies of the robbers[communists] had prepared for battle, and began to come down and to sally forth from the hills, and out of the mountains, and the wilderness, and their strongholds, and their secret places, and began to take possession of the lands, both which were in the land south and which were in the land north, and began to take possession of all the lands deserted by the Nephites[Mayans], and the cities which had been left</u> desolate." "But behold, there **<u>were no wild beasts nor game in those lands which had been deserted by the</u>***

Nephites[Mayans], and there was no game for the robbers save it were in the wilderness." "And the <u>robbers could not exist save it were in the wilderness, for the want of food;</u> **for the Nephites had left their lands desolate, and had gathered their flocks and their herds and all their substance, and they were in one body**."*(3 Nephi 4:1-3, Book of Mormon)*

"*Therefore, there was no chance for the robbers[communists/ liberals] to plunder and to obtain food, save it were to come <u>up in open battle against the Nephites[Mayans]; and the Nephites[Mayans] being in one body, and having so great a number, and having reserved for themselves provisions,</u>and* **horses and cattle, and flocks of every kind, that they might subsist for the space of seven years,** *in the <u>which time they did hope to destroy the robbers[communists] from off the face of the land;</u>" "And it came to pass that in the <u>nineteenth year[19 A.D.]</u> Giddianhi found that it was expedient[necessary] that he should,go up to* **battle against the Nephites[Mayans], for there was no way they could subsist** <u>save it were to plunder and rob and murder."</u> *(3 Nephi 4:4-5, Book of Mormon)*

Chapter 24

High Priests And Judges Collaborated To Get Gain, And Cover Up Secret Murders

The **Mayans witnessed their own Bolshevic Revolution** *, They refused to feed the good for nothing robbers, and instead destroyed them in battle!*

The Nephites/Mayans gathered together around Zarahemla and Bountiful, but by taking their food sources with them into the walled city, leaving their farms for a while. Even though the fertile land was now open for the Robbers to grow food, they didn't dare let their guard down, when they needed every man to stay vigilant, in case of attack from the Nephites/Mayans. Nevertheless, There was not anytime to grow food without being attacked by the Nephites/Mayans. Therefore, as usual, the liberals not being willing to work, they needed to steal from Paul, to pay John, but if there is nothing to steal, then there will always be war, as was in this case.

"And they durst[dared] not spread themselves upon the face of the land insomuch that they could raise grain, lest the Nephites[Mayans] should come upon them and slay them; therefore Giddianhi gave commandment[orders] unto his armies that in this year[19 A.D.] they should go up to battle against the Nephites[Mayans]." "And it came to pass that they did come up to battle; and it was in the sixth month[June]; and behold, great and terrible was the day that

they did come up to battle; and they were girded about after the manner of robbers; and they had a lamb-skin about their loins, and they were dyed in blood, and their heads were shorn, and they had headplates upon them; and great and terrible was the appearance of the armies of Giddianhi[the communists], because of their armor, and because of their being dyed in blood[red army]. (3 Nephi 4:6-7, Book of Mormon)

The day the Gadianton Robbers/[Bolshiveks]/Communists, came out to battle, the Nephites/Mayans and Lamanites/Aztecs, bowed themselves to the ground before God in prayer, when they saw the appearance of the Gadianton Robbers/Red Army/Communists, as the Robbers/ Communists had their garments dyed in blood, and marked with red on their foreheads. The people of God were asking for the blessings of God, but the Communists judged this to be a weakness of fear, and rushed in for the kill. However, they did err, because the people of God were strengthened, and they withstood the Robbers/ Communists, and slaughtered them all day. The Communist/Robbers then retreated, but were killed by the thousands, clear back into the wilderness of Colombia. This was the greatest slaughter since Lehi had left Jerusalem, with his families.

*"And it came to pass that the armies of the Nephites[Mayans], when they **saw the appearance of the army of Giddianhi[red army/communists], had fallen to the earth, and did lift their cries[prayers] to the Lord their God, that he would spare them and deliver them out of the hands of their enemies.*" *"And it came to pass that when the armies of Giddianhi[communists] saw this they began to shout with a loud voice, because of their joy, for they had supposed that the Nephites[Mayans] had fallen with fear because of the terror of their armies."* "But in this thing **they were disappointed, for the Nephites did not fear them; but they did fear their God and did supplicate him[asked for strength and his blessings] for protection; therefore, when the [communists] armies of Giddianhi did rush upon them they were prepared to meet them; yea, in the strength of the Lord they did receive them.**"* (3 Nephi 4:8-10, Book of Mormon)

*"And the **battle commenced in this the sixth month[June, 19 A.D.]; and great and terrible was the battle thereof, yea, great and terrible was the slaughter thereof, insomuch that there never was known so great a slaughter among all the people of Lehi since he left Jerusalem.** "And notwithstanding[in spite of] **the threatenings and the oaths which Giddianhi had made[and the master he served], behold, the Nephites[Mayans] did beat them, insomuch that they[the communists] did fall back from before them.** "And it came to pass that **Gidgiddoni[general of the Nephites/Mayans] commanded that his armies should pursue them as far as the borders of the wilderness, and that they should not spare any that should fall into their hands by the way; and thus they did pursue them and did slay them, to the borders of the wilderness, even until they had fulfilled the commandment of Gidgiddoni.** "And it came to pass that **Giddianhi, who had stood and fought with boldness, was pursued as he fled; and he was weary because of his much fighting he was overtaken and slain.** And thus was the end of Giddianhi the robber."(3 Nephi 4:11-14, Book of Mormon)*

to the grief and sadness of the older generation of the Lamanites, who had united with the Nephites/Mayans, as they had joined themselves to the Church of God, and were numbered among them, many of the younger generation/ their children, were joining to the liberals/ Democrats/Gadianton Robbers/Communists. The Democrats/ Robbers, were led primarily by dissenters and traitors, from the ranks of the Nephites/Mayans. The Communists now, because they had been beaten in battle, attempted to lay siege to the land of Zarahemla, which proved a futile effort. Therefore, because of the preparedness of the people of God, they thought to march around Zarahemla, northwest, past Bountiful, to the narrow neck of land separating the sea on the east and on the west, and go into the land northward[North America]. Their plans were to go into the land northward and infiltrate and rob the people on the north, however, the people of God knew their plans and put a stop to the robbers.

*"And in the twentieth and first **year[21 A.D.]** they[the robbers/ communists of Giddianhi] did not come up to battle, but they came*

up on all sides to lay siege round about the people of Nephi[Mayans]; for they did suppose that if they should cut off the people of Nephi[Mayans] from their lands, and should hem them in on every side, and they should cut them off from all their outward privileges, then they could cause them to yield themselves up according to their wishes." "Now they had appointed unto themselves another leader, whose name was Zemnarihah; therefore it was Zemnarihah that did cause that this siege did take place." "But behold, this was an advantage to the Nephites[Mayans]; for it was **impossible**[a futile effort] *for the robbers[communists] to lay siege sufficiently long to have any effect upon the Nephites[Mayans], because of* **their much[preparedness] provision which they had laid up in store,"** *"And because of the scantiness of provisions among the [communist/liberal] robbers; for behold, they had nothing[because they expected to take the hard working people's supplies] save it were meat for their subsistance, which meat they did obtain in the wilderness;" "And it came to pass that the wild game became scarce in the wilderness insomuch that the robbers[communists]* **were about to perish[starve to death] with hunger."** *(3 Nephi 4:16-20, Book of Mormon)*

"And the Nephites[Mayans] were continually marching out by day and by night, and falling upon their armies, and cutting them off **by the thousands and by tens of thousands**. *"And thus it became the desire of the people of Zemnarihah to withdraw from their design, because of the great destruction which came upon them by night and by day." "And it came to pass that Zemnarihah did give command unto his people[the communist/liberal/robbing rat-bastards] that they should withdraw themselves from the siege, and march into the furthermost parts of the land northward." "And now, Gidgiddoni being aware of their design, and knowing of their weakness because of the want of food, and the great slaughter which had been made among them,* **therefore he did send out his armies in the night-time, and did cut off the way of their retreat, and did place his armies in the way of their retreat.** *"And this did they do in the night-time, and got on their march beyond the robbers[communists], so that on the morrow, when the robbers began their march, they were met by the armies of the Nephites[Mayans] both in their front and in their rear."*

"And the robbers[communists] who were on the south were also cut off in their places of retreat. And all these things were done by command of Gidgiddoni[General of the Nephites/Mayans]." (3 Nephi 4:21-26, Book of Mormon)

★★ "And there were many thousands who did yield themselves up prisoners unto the Nephites[Mayans], and the remainder of them were slain[killed]." "And their leader, Zemnarihah, was taken and hanged upon a tree, yea, even upon the top thereof until he was dead. And when they had hanged him until he was dead they did fell the tree to the earth, and did cry[shout] with a loud voice, saying:" "May the Lord preserve his people in righteousness and in holiness of heart, that they may cause to be felled to the earth all who shall seek to slay them[the people] because of power[wanting power] and secret combinations[secret orders, i.e. Jesuits/illuminati], even as this man hath been felled to the earth." *(3 Nephi 4:27-29, Book of Mormon)*

There is very much history to do with the ancient inhabitants of the Americas that these alleged experts don't understand, or more likely, don't want to understand, or even better yet, hide the **truth**, so no one can understand. They only guess how old these civilizations are, because of artifacts, and the remains they find, and judge the age through *Carbon Dating*. The Smithsonian Institution, a liberal/Communist society placed there to cover-up and spread disinformation about the history of the Americas, just as it was when the Spaniards invaded and destroyed evidence/records/books, that these ancient people had left behind. These Spaniards were Jesuits, under the orders of the Pope of the Catholic Church, as the facts will show.(see: Mystery History: https://youtu.be/Uho8VRLaOsA)

The Nephites/Mayans, and Lamanites/Aztecs, worked together often for their own, self preservation, and many times, warred against one another, and often warred among themselves, as all nationalities have in the past, and still do. In most all cases, when the people of God prevail, they give glory and honor to God Almighty, for their blessings.

"And they did rejoice and cry again with one voice, saying: <u>May</u> <u>*the God of **Abraham, and the God of Isaac, and the God of***</u> <u>***Jacob, protect this people in righteousness, so long as they shall***</u> <u>***call on the name of their God for protection***</u>*." "And it came to pass that they did break forth, all as one, in singing, and praising their God for the great thing which he had done for them, in preserving them from falling into the hands of their enemies." "Yea, they did cry:* <u>**Hosanna to the Most High God. And they did cry: Blessed**</u> <u>**be the name of the Lord God Almighty, the Most High God.**</u>*" "And their hearts were swollen with joy, unto the <u>gushing out of many</u>* <u>*tears, because of the great goodness of God in delivering them   out*</u> <u>*of the hands of their enemies; and* **they knew it was because of**</u> <u>**their repentance[change] and their humility that they had been**</u> <u>**delivered from an everlasting destruction.**</u>*"(3 Nephi 4:30-33, Book of Mormon)*

After the Robbers/Communists were defeated, and silenced, the remaining sympathizers, still persisting in their *secret orders* and secret murders, when detected, were judged and sentenced to death, as is the justice for someone committing treason against their own country. Through this method, the Nephites/Mayans and Lamanites/Aztecs put an end to **Communism/Socialism,** among their people then. Jesus Christ was now 25-years of age, and teaching, and doing many miracles in Jerusalem; healing the sick, walking on water, making the blind see, healing the lepers, and the maimed, raising the dead, turning water into wine, confounding the pharisees and sadducees, etc.. 10-years more before he would be crucified, and visit the Nephites/Mayans, and Lamanites/Aztecs as well, in the Americas.

*"And now it came to pass that when they had taken all the robbers prisoners, insomuch that **none did escape who were not slain,** they did cast their prisoners into prison, <u>and did cause the word of God to be</u>* <u>*preached unto them; and as many as would repent[change] of their sins*</u> <u>*and enter into a covenant that they murder no more, were set at liberty.*</u>*" "But as many as there were who did enter into a covenant, and who did still continue to have those* **secret murders in their hearts**<u>*, yea, as*</u> <u>*many as were found breathing out threatenings against their brethren*</u>

were condemned and punished according to the law." "And thus they did put an end to **all those wicked, and secret, and abominable combinations[secret societies], in the which there was so much wickedness, and so many murders committed**_." "And thus had the twenty and second year[22 A.D.] passed away, and the twenty and third year also, and the twenty and fourth, and the twenty and fifth; and thus had twenty and five years passed away[25 A.D.]" (3 Nephi 5:4-7, Book of Mormon)_

Chapter 25

Death Of Christ, Destruction Of Wicked

The Destruction of the Mayan Government Leading up to the death of Jesus Christ

25 A.D.

Mormon, the last and final general of the Nephites/Mayans, at the last, is abridging many of the records of the Nephites/Mayans, and he is making this abridgement while he is awaiting the final battle with the Lamanites/Aztecs, as the final chapter of this book shall soon show. First however, this chapter will show what happened among the Nephites/Mayans and the Lamanites/Aztecs, at the death of Christ, which is shortly to come in the next 5-8 years.

Mormon is a pure descendant of Lehi, of whom, is the first father of the people of Nephi/Mayan, and the people of Laman//Aztec, who came from Jerusalem in 600 B.C.. Mormon is a true disciple of Jesus Christ, with the *"Spirit of Revelation"*, and by him abridging the records of his people, through the wisdom of God, once again, outsmarted Satan/the Roman Catholic Empire/the Pope, who thought to destroy all of the records of this ancient people, but instead, God has preserved the records of the people of Nephi/the Mayan people, through General Mormon.

> *"And behold, I am called **Mormon**, being called after the land of Mormon, the land in which Alma did establish the church among*

the people , yea, the first church which was established among them
after their transgression." "Behold, I am a disciple of Jesus Christ,
the Son of God. I have been called of him to declare his word among
this people [Nephites/Mayans], that they might have everlasting life. "
"And it hath become expedient[necessary] that I, according to the will
of God, that the prayers of those who have gone hence, who were the
holy ones, should be fulfilled according to their faith, **should make a
record of these things which have been done---**" "Yea, **a small
record of that which hath taken place from the time that Lehi left
Jerusalem, even down until the present time.**"(3 Nephi 5:12-15,
Book of Mormon)

**Therefore I do make my record from the **accounts which have
been given by those who were before me, until the commencement
of my day;**" "And I do make a record of the things which I have
seen with my own eyes." "**And I know the record which I make
to be a just and true record; nevertheless there are many things
which, according to our language, we are not able to write.**"
"And now I make an end of my saying, which is of myself[my personal
introduction], and proceed to give an account of the things which have
been before me[have seen]." "**I am Mormon, and a pure descendant
of Lehi.** I have reason to bless my **God and my Saviour Jesus
Christ,** that he brought our fathers **out of the land of Jerusalem,**
(and no one knew it save it were himself and those whom he brought
out of that land[Jerusalem]) and that he hath given me and my people
so much knowledge unto the salvation of our souls." (3 Nephi 5:16-
20, Book of Mormon)

"And insomuch as the children of Lehi have kept his commandments
he hath blessed them and prospered them according to his word." "Yea,
and surely shall **he again bring a remnant of the seed of Joseph to
the knowledge of the Lord their God**." "And as surely as the Lord
liveth, **will he gather in from the four quarters of the earth all the
remnant of the seed of Jacob, who are scattered abroad upon all
the face of the earth**."(3 Nephi 5:22-24, Book of Mormon)

The Nephites/Mayans and the Lamanites/Aztecs once again returned to their lands and their homes after the war with the Communists, the Gadianton robbers. They were thankful to God, having prevailed against the Communist/liberal army, and against tyranny. To bad the churches are not Holy enough to have faith like earlier Christians, and use their God given rights to tell the liberals/communists/socialists to go pound sand, and try them for treason. Instead they have joined with the communists, so as not to offend, or they have their hearts set on their possessions. They are ashamed of being right, and knowing and exercising the truth. They are ashamed of God, and they will not act, and they hunker down in fear and become like sheep.

"And now it came to pass that the people of the Nephites[Mayans] did all return to their own lands in the twenty and sixth year[26 A.D.], every man, with his family, his flocks and his herds, his horses and his cattle, and all things whatsoever did belong unto them." "And it came to pass that they had not eaten up all their provisions; therefore they did take with them all that they had not devoured, of all their grain of every kind, and their gold, and their silver, and all their precious things, and they. did return to their own lands and their possessions, both on the north and on the south, both on the land northward[North America] and on the land southward[South America]." "And they granted unto those robbers who had entered into a covenant to keep the peace of the land, who were desirous to remain Lamanites[Aztecs], lands, according to their numbers, that they might have, with their labors, wherewith to subsist upon; and thus they did establish peace in all the land." (3 Nephi 6:1-3, Book of Mormon)

★*"And they began again to prosper and to wax great; and the twenty and sixth and seventh years passed away, and there was great order in the land; and they had formed their laws according to equity and justice." "And now there was nothing in all the land to hinder the people from prospering continually, except they should fall into transgression." "And it came to pass that there were many cities built anew, and there were many old cities repaired." "And there were many highways cast up, and many roads made, which led*

from city to city, and from land to land, and from place to place."
"*And thus passed away the twenty and eighth year[28 A.D.], and the people had continual peace.*" *(3 Nephi 6:4-5, 7-9, Book of Mormon)* *https://youtu.be/i-N3NYOL0c0 : 25-thousand miles of road.*

29 A.D.

Then again pride, and elitism, entered into their hearts, whereas, they began again to compete against each other according to how much they were able to accumulate through commerce, and they began comparing their riches, and their education, and high degrees of learning. They began again to form their secret orders, and monopolies, corporations, and began to differentiate in classes, the rich and the poor. They once again sought to alter the laws of the land, and to have many lawyers and policemen who abused the people, and violated their oaths of office, to bring in revenue for a wicked government. They were beginning to forget *the laws of God* again in just such a short period of time. This shows just how selfish the ***natural man*** really is. They ignored the Commandments of God, and instead, focused on their riches, at the expense of the poor and needy.

The Church of Jesus Christ among the Nephites/Mayans was corrupted. The Lamanites/Aztecs however, were firm in their covenants to Christ, and never deviated from what they knew to be just and true, and there was many more righteous among them, at this point in time, than there were among the Nephites/Mayans.

"*And there were many merchants in the land, and also many lawyers, and many officers.*" "***And the [Nephites/Mayans] people began again to be distinguished by ranks, according to their riches and their chances for learning; yea, some were ignorant because of their poverty, and others did receive great learning because of their riches.***" "*Some were lifted up in pride, and others were exceedingly humble; some did return **railing for railing,** while others would receive railing and persecution and all manner of afflictions, and would not turn and revile again, but were humble and penitent before God.*" "*And thus there became a great inequality in all the land, insomuch* *that **the church began to be broken up; yea, insomuch that in the thirtieth year[30 A.D.] the church was broken up in all the land save it were among a few of the Lamanites[Aztecs] who were converted unto the true faith; and they would not depart from it, for they were firm, and steadfast, and immovable, willing with all diligence to keep the commandments of the Lord.***"(3 Nephi 6:11-14, Book of Mormon)*

*"**Now the cause of this iniquity of the people was this--- Satan had great power, unto the stirring up of the people to do all manner of iniquity, and to the puffing them up with pride, tempting them to seek for power, and authority, and riches, and the vain things of the world.**" "And thus Satan did lead away the hearts of the people to do all manner of iniquity[evil]; **therefore they had enjoyed peace but a few years.**" "And thus, in the commencement of the thirtieth year[30 A.D.]---the people[Nephites/Mayans] having been delivered up for the space of a long time to be carried about by the temptations of the **devil whithersoever he desired to lead them,** and to do whatsoever iniquity he desired they should---and thus in the commencement of this, the thirtieth year, they **were in a state of awful wickedness.**" "Now **they did not sin ignorantly, for they knew the will of God concerning them, for it had been taught unto them; therefore they did "willfully rebel against God."** (3 Nephi 6:15- 18, Book of Mormon)*

30 A. D.

In this year, the laws were really corrupted by the lawyers and judges, and the high Priests of the Church of Jesus Christ were holding hands with the World, in the support of the world, and were attempting to convict and put to death those who believed contrary to them. They were violating the *Right to Religion and freedom of speech*(1st Amendment)among others.

★★★#*"And there began to be **men inspired from heaven and sent forth, standing among the people in all the land,**

Steven Sego

preaching and testifying boldly of the sins and iniquities of the people, and testiying unto them concerning the redemption which the Lord would make for his people, or in other words, the resurrection of Christ; and they did testify boldly of his death and sufferings." "_Now there were many of the people[Mayans] who were exceedingly angry because of those who testified of these things; and those who were angry were chiefly the chief judges, and they who had been high priests and lawyers; yea, all those who were lawyers were angry with those who testified of these things[told them of their sins, and a greater king was coming soon to a city near you]._" (3 Nephi 6:20-21, Book of Mormon)

★"_Now there was no lawyer nor judge nor high priest that could have power to condemn[pass sentence/ruling from the bench, without due process of law/6th and 7th Amendments/ process of jury and appeals etc.] any one to death save their condemnation[sentencing] was signed by the governor of the land[Supreme Court]._" "_Now there were many of those who testified of the things pertaining to Christ who testified boldly, who were taken and put to death secretly by the judges, that the knowledge of their death came not unto the governor of the land until after their death[now expecting qualified immunity because of their feduciary-position]._" "_Now behold, this was contrary to the laws of the land, that any man should be put to death except they had power from the governor of the land[without due process, and is not honoring their oaths of office, sacred]---_" (3 Nephi 6:22-24, Book of Mormon)

"_Therefore a complaint came up to the land of Zarahemla, to the governor of the land[Supreme Court], against these who had [ruled from the bench unjustly]condemned[sentenced] the prophets of the Lord unto death, not according to the law[without due process through the courts]._" "_Now it came to pass that they[those evil liberal judges/high priests/and lawyers involved, and party to this organized crime/collaboration] were taken[indicted, and arrested] to be judged of the crime[deprivation of rights, and murder] which they had done, according to the law[Constitution] which had been given by [we] the people._" (3 Nephi 6:25-26, Book of Mormon)

★*"Now it came to pass that those <u>judges had many friends and</u> <u>kindreds; and the remainder, yea,</u> **even almost all the lawyers and** **the high priests, did gather themselves together, and unite with** **the kindreds of those judges who were to be tried according to** **the law**[their Constitution]." "And they did **enter into a covenant** **one with another, yea, even into that covenant which was given** **by them of old, which covenant was given and administered by** **the devil, to combine**[collaborate] **against all** <u>righteousness</u>[against Christ coming soon]." "Therefore **they did combine against the** **people of the Lord, and enter into a covenant to destroy them,** **and deliver those who were guilty of murder from the grasp of** **justice, which was about to be administered "according to the** **law.""** "**And they did set at defiance**[hold in contempt] **the law** **and the rights of their country; and they did covenant one with** **another to destroy the governor, and to establish a king over** **the land, that the land should no more be at liberty but should** **be subject unto kings."**[liberal, whitewashed sepulchres/ evil selfish libtards, like they are in Wash. D.C. etc. Many who are self acclaimed Christians with their secret orders and signs of the brotherhoods of Demon-crats, Jesuits, Illuminati, Skull and Bones, Masons, you name it, they all wreak of evil depravity and murders](3 Nephi 6:27-30, Book of Mormon)

They violated their *oaths of office*, thus destroying their *Law of the Land created and put into effect by the voice of the people*[Constitution]. A country is only as free as the ones placed into the positions of public trust, who after taking an oath to protect the law of the land, against all enemies , foreign and domestic, fail to do so. Instead, abuse the people they are paid and sworn to protect. (see Audit America You Tube channel; Lackluster channel) Communists continually rear their ugly, evil heads. The secret societies once again were established by the want-to-be elite-class, the liberals/Democrats[i.e. Pelosis, Clintons, Bidens, etc.], with their *Democracy,* and those wanting a *dictator or king,* and they want that king to be the Pope, under the **Roman** Empire. *The "Democrats"* are called Democrats because they support the *Socialist System,* called a **Democracy.** *Republicans* are called Republicans, because they support the American-Republic which is free and brings equality and justice to all: rich and poor, regardless of color, male or female, educated or simple, and all are kings and queens under the law of the land: **Constitution,** just as were the **Nephites/Mayans,** under their Common-law, comparable to the Constitution of today. **Now 30 A.D.**

★★ *"Now behold, I will show unto you that <u>they did not establish a king over the land; but in this same year, yea, the</u> **thirtieth year, [30A.D.] they did destroy upon the judgment-seat, yea , they did murder the chief judge of the land.**" "And the <u>people[Mayans] were divided one against another[like the native Indian tribes of today]; and they did separate one from another</u> **into tribes,** <u>every man according to his family and his kindred and friends;</u> **and thus they did destroy the government of the land.**" "And **every tribe did appoint a chief or a leader over them; and** <u>thus they became tribes and leaders of tribes</u>." (3 Nephi 7:1-3, Book of Mormon)*

★*"<u>**And the Regulations of the government were destroyed, because of the "secret combinations"**[Jesuits/Democrats/ illuminati,etc.] **of the friends and kindreds of those who murdered the prophets.**</u>" "And they did cause a <u>great contention in the land, [uproar], insomuch that the more</u> **righteous part of the people had nearly all become wicked; yea, there were but few righteous[good]men among them.**" "And thus <u>six years</u> had not passed away <u>since the</u> **more part** of **the people**[Mayans] **had turned from their righteousnes**[doing that which was right], **like the dog to his vomit,** or **like the sow to her wallowing** mire." "Now this <u>secret combination[secret order] which had brought so great iniquity upon the [Nephite/Mayan] people, did gather themselves together, and did place at their head a man whom they did call</u> **Jacob;**" " <u>And they did call him</u> **their king; therefore he became a king over this wicked band; and he was one of the chiefest who had given his voice against the prophets who testified of Jesus.**" (3 Nephi 7:6-10, Book of Mormon)*

After the Democrats/liberals destroyed their government in this case, for the time being, the people divided into tribes/groups/

clans, which included their families, relatives, close friends and their families, etc.. Some tribes were more numerous than others, therefore, Jacob[liberal Mayan President] knowing his days were in jeopardy if he didn't act fast, influenced the other libtards to gather with him and flee out of the area to the north. He, with his followers, went across the *narrow neck of land,* we know as Panama, Nicaragua, Costa Rica, Guatemala, through Mexico, and into the land of the American-Republic, and out of contact, and out of reach of justice, with the intentions of waiting for more dissenters over time, to join them.

When these communist king-men gathered sufficient strength, they intended to build a kingdom, and usurp authority over the people through a civil war and force. I believe this group of Jacob's went as far as southern Wisconsin, to the area we know as Madison, which today is the state capitol for the State of Wisconsin. There is a lake there named Rock Lake, and just under the surface of the lake is a sunken city, possibly named **Mocum,** by the Nephites/Mayans, that was destroyed at the death of Christ.(see: https://youtu.be/3EXvsiKBLzA). Many other cities around were burned, Like Zarahemla was burned at the death of Christ. Jacob and his followers named their city **Jacobagath, also like Zarahemla, was burned by fire**. However, their plans backfired, as you will soon see.

*"And it came to pass that they[Jacob's/Biden's followers] were not so strong in number as the **tribes** of the people, who were united together **save it were the leaders did establish their laws, every one according to his tribe;** nevertheless they were enemies; notwithstanding[despite the fact] they were not a righteous people, **yet they were united in the hatred of those who had entered into a covenant to destroy the government.** "Therefore, **Jacob** seeing that their enemies were more numerous than they, he being the **king** of the band, therefore he commanded his people **that they should take their flight into the northernmost part of the land,** and there build up unto themselves a kingdom, until they were **joined by dissenters,** (for he flattered them that there would be many dissenters) and they become sufficiently strong to contend[war] with the tribes of the people; **and they did so**. "And so speedy was their march[flight] that it could not be impeded until they had gone forth out of the reach of the*

*people. And thus ended the thirtieth year[**30 A.D.**]; and thus were the affairs of the [Mayans] people of Nephi*." *(3 Nephi 7:11-13, Book of Mormon)*

The Mayan prophet at this time was named Nephi, after so many of his forefathers before him. Nephi went from tribe to tribe, preaching repentance, and condemning the wickedness of the people for letting this happen. The people were much more interested chasing wealth, than paying attention to things that really mattered, like *Freedom, and calling upon God, and seeing to the needs of the poor, and most importantly: getting involved in their government.* So quickly did the people give up their rights, and very few sought God, but rather found delight in their ignorance of God. In fact, it was going to take an act of God(pun intended), to get their attention.

"*And it came to pass that the thirty and first year[31 A.D.] did pass away, and there were very few who were converted unto the Lord; but as many as were converted[born again] did truly signify unto the people that they* **had been visited by the power and Spirit of God, which was in Jesus Christ, in whom they believed.** *(3 Nephi 7:21, Book of Mormon)*

Chapter 26

The Three Days Of Darkness After The Destruction

The death of Jesus Christ!
The destruction of the wicked cities, of the wicked

Now 33 A.D.

Nephi, the Mayan prophet was knowledgeable to the fact that Christ was to come very shortly, so he was up and doing all he could to set the Church of Christ back in order as fast and diligently as he could. He also knew the crucifixion/death of Christ was imminent. Jesus Christ was now 33-years old, known from the signs at His birth, and the reckoning of time according to these same signs, and wonders, and messengers telling of these things to come. Now you wicked, selfish, liberals, communists, who are trying to destroy your country, by first attempting to destroy the government, those who are busy celebrating Satan, saying that evil Spirit, that doesn't even have a body, is more powerful than God. Ask yourselves, just how can Satan tempt mankind into worshiping him unless it is through your own desires of depravity, promising money, and power, etc. etc.

Ask him: How many times has God ultimately came to destroy such Satanic people, because they can only enjoy such depravity and power for only a short time? How many times has Christ went and destroyed worlds, civilizations, cities, kingdoms, individuals when they turn away and sin against light and truth, and abuse their fellow man? So, this question should be a no brainer for any one to consider, but it takes a Democrat/liberal, who has no brain, to think Satan is more powerful than God. If you want to see **_Global warming_**, it won't be long until you are going to help fuel that fire, unless you change your ways quickly, and cease the destruction of your fellowman and our own government.

"*Now I would have you to remember also, <u>that there were none brought unto **repentance** who were not **baptized with water**</u>[immersion]." "Therefore, there was <u>ordained of Nephi[Mayan prophet], men unto this ministry, that all such as should come unto them should be baptized with water[immersion], and this as a **witness and a testimony before God[outward showing], and unto the people, that they had repented[changed] and received a remission of their sins</u>*." "<u>And there were many in the commencement of this year[33 A.D.] that were **baptized unto repentance**; and thus the more part of the year[33 A.D.] did pass away</u>.*"(3 Nephi 7:24-26, Book of Mormon)*

Now 34 A.D.

When He died, there was great earthquakes, thunders and lightnings, and many cities were destroyed in South, Central, and North America, in various ways. The Capitol city of the Nephites/ Mayans was Zarahemla. It was located just southwest of the narrow neck of land, bordering Panama, and Colombia, and then was just southwest of Bountiful, in northern Colombia, just west of the Rio Magdalena River. Zarahemla, as it was built out of lumber mostly, was burned by fire at Christs death, while other cities were destroyed using other means. After the great storm that had arisen, and the great tempests and the great thunder and lightnings that arose at the death of Jesus Christ, the earth was also shaken as if by a mighty hand.

"*And it came to pass in the <u>thirty and fourth year[**34 A.D.**], in the first month[January], on the fourth day of the month, **there arose a great storm, such an one as never had been known in all the**</u>*

land." "*And there was also a **great and terrible tempest; and there was terrible thunder, insomuch that it did shake the whole earth as if it was about to divide asunder**.*" "*And there were exceedingly sharp lightnings, such as never had been known in all the land*." "*And **the city of Zarahemla did take fire**.*" "*and the city of **Moroni** did sink into the depths of the sea, and the inhabitants thereof were drowned.*" "*And the earth was carried up upon the city of **Moronihah,** that in the place of the city there became a great mountain*." "*And there was a great and terrible destruction in the land southward[lands of the Nephites/Mayans].*" "*But behold, **there was a more great terrible destruction in the land northward**[North America among the Nephite/Mayan people]; **for behold, the whole face of the land was changed,** because of the tempest and the whirlwinds, and the thunderings and the lightnings, and the exceedingly great quaking of the whole earth;*" *(3 Nephi 8:5-12, Book of Mormon)*

★"*And the **highways were broken up, and the level roads were spoiled, and many smooth places became rough**." "**And many great and notable cities were sunk, and many were burned, and many were shaken till the buildings thereof had fallen to the earth, and the inhabitants thereof were slain, and the places were left desolate**." "And there were some cities which remained; but the damage thereof was exceedingly great, and there were many in them who were slain[killed]*." "*And there were some who were carried away in the whirlwind; and whither[where] they went no man knoweth, save they know that they were carried away.*" "*And thus the face of the whole earth **became deformed,** because of the tempests, and the thunderings, and the lightnings, and the quaking of the earth.*" "*And behold, **the rocks were rent in twain; they were broken up upon the face of the whole earth, insomuch that they were found in broken fragments, and in seams and in cracks, upon all the face of the land.**" (3 Nephi 8:13-18, Book of Mormon)*

Some cities were buried in the ground and became large mountains, while some fell down from earthquakes, others were blown down, while others were sunken in the earth and covered with water, and some were sunken in the depths of the ocean. Then there was pitch darkness, so dark that there was not any light, nor could a light be lit. Just imagine, darkness so thick that nothing will burn. Imagine what *"outer darkness"*, will be like for the ungodly, and wicked.

> *"And it came to pass that when the thunderings, and the lightnings, and the storm, and the tempest, and the quakings of the earth did cease---for behold, they did last for about the space **of three hours;** and it was said by some that the time was greater; nevertheless, all these great and terrible things were done in about the **space of three hours---**and then behold, **there was darkness upon the face of the land**."* *"And **there could be no light, because of the darkness, neither candles, neither torches; neither could there be fire kindled with their fine and exceedingly dry wood, so that there could not be any light at all;**"* *"And **there was not any light seen, neither fire, nor glimmer, neither the sun, nor the moon, nor the stars, for so great were the mists of darkness which were upon the face of the land**."* *"And it came to pass that **it did last for the space of three days that there was no light seen;** and there was **great mourning, and howling and weeping among all the [Mayan] people continually; yea, great were the groanings of the people, because of the darkness** and the great destruction which had come upon them."* *(3 Nephi 8:19-23, Book of Mormon)*

> *"And **in one place they were heard to cry, saying: O that we had repented before this great and terrible day, and then would our brethren have been spared, and they would not have been burned in that great city** Zarahemla."* *"**And** in another place they were heard to cry and mourn, saying: **O that we had repented before this great and terrible day, and had not killed and stoned the prophets, and cast them out; then would our mothers and our fair daughters, and children have been spared, and not have been buried up in that great city Moronihah.** And thus were the howlings of the [Mayan] people great and terrible."* *(3 Nephi 8:24-25, Book of Mormon)*

Then came a voice which was heard by all that were spared, of the most righteous of the people, declaring the destruction of Zarahemla, along with other cities that were destroyed using many different methods. In every instance, among every city that was destroyed with the inhabitants therein, there was crying and weeping, and mourning for their lost ones, who all admitted that, if they had listened to those who were trying to warn them of these things to come, the destruction would not have befell their loved ones. Instead of thinking, that they could just ignore the truth(*voice of God),* or just will it in their own minds to not happen, while they did nothing as liberal/democrats, and set about to imprison or kill those who were inspired by God to declare the truth, didn't make it not happen. Today America is on the verge of being destroyed itself, if we as a nation do not repent/change, especially in those liberal sanctuary cities. Picture in your own minds what it would be like if New York City, or Chicago, etc. was all of a sudden destroyed because of what goes on there. There are still a lot of good, Godly people who still remain in those places. Actually, that is why those cities are still standing, and haven't been destroyed yet, because it is for the righteous sake.

"*And it came to pass that there was **a voice heard among all the inhabitants of the earth, upon all the face of this land, crying:**" "**Wo, wo, wo unto this [Mayan] people; wo unto the inhabitants of the whole earth except they shall repent; for the devil laugheth, and his angels rejoice,** because of the slain of the fair sons and daughters of my people; and it is because of **their iniquity and abominations that they are fallen!**" "Behold, that great city **Zarahemla have I burned with fire, and the inhabitants** thereof.*" "*And behold, that great **city Moroni have I caused to be sunk in the depths of the sea, and the inhabitants** thereof to be drowned.*" "*And behold, that great city **Moronihah** have I covered with earth[a whole big mountain], and the inhabitants thereof, **to hide their iniquities and their abominations** from before my face, that the blood of the prophets and the saints shall not come any more unto me against them.*" (3 Nephi 9:1-5, Book of Mormon)*

"*And behold, the **city of Gilgal have I caused to be sunk,** and the inhabitants thereof to be buried up in the depths of the earth;*" "*Yea, and the **city of Onihah** and the inhabitants thereof, and the city*

of **Mocum[Rock Lake, WI]** and the inhabitants thereof, and the city of **Jerusalem** and the inhabitants thereof; **and waters have I caused to come up in the stead thereof, to hide their wickedness and abominations from before my face, that the blood of the prophets and the saints shall not come up any more unto me against** _them._"
"_And behold, the city of **Gadiandi,** and the city of **Gadiomnah,** and the city of **Jacob,** and the city of **Gimgimno,** all these have I caused to be sunk and made **hills and valleys in the places thereof;**and the inhabitants thereof have I buried up in the depths of the earth, to hide their wickedness and abominations from before my face, that the blood of the prophets and the saints should not come up any more unto me against them._" "_(3 Nephi 9:6-8, Book of Mormon)_

*** "_And behold, **that great city Jacobagath, which was inhabited by the people of king Jacob, have I caused to be burned with fire because of their wickedness, which was above all the wickedness of the whole earth because of their secret murders and combinations; for it was they**[liberals/democrats/communists] **that did destroy the peace of my people and the government of the land; therefore I did cause them to be burned, to destroy them from before my face, that the blood of the prophets and the saints should not come up unto me any more against them.**_"
"_And behold, the city of **Laman,** and the city of **Josh,** and the city of **Kishkumen,** have I caused to be burned with fire, and the inhabitants thereof, because of their wickedness **in casting out the prophets, and stoning those whom I did send** to declare unto them concerning their wickedness and their **abominations**._" "_And because they did cast them out,[all a mass of sheep, they gave the few a yes vote, by staying silent] that **there were none righteous among them,** I did send down fire and destroy them, that their wickedness and abominations might be hid from before my face, that the blood of the prophets and the saints whom I sent among them might not cry unto me from the ground against them._" _(3 Nephi 9:9-11, Book of Mormon)_

"_And many great destructions have I caused to come upon this land[the Americas], and upon this [Nephite/Mayan] people, **because of their wickedness and their abominations**._" "**O all ye that are** *spared because ye were more righteous than they, will ye not now return unto me, and repent of your sins, and be converted[to the truth and born again], that I may heal you?"* "*Yea, verily I say unto you, if ye will come unto me ye shall have "eternal life".* Behold, *mine arm of mercy is extended towards you, and whosoever will come, him will I receive; and blessed are those who come unto me."* "Behold, *I am Jesus Christ the Son of God. I created the heavens and the earth, and all things that in them are. I was with the Father from the beginning. I am in the Father, and the Father in me; and in me hath the Father glorified his name."* (3 Nephi 9:12-15, Book of Mormon)

Satan laughs at those people in South America and North America when they celebrate Halloween, and the Mardi Gras, etc., by parading his effigy up and down the streets of New Orleans, and Rio De Janeiro, saying he is more powerful than God. If that were so, you would at least think that low-life Satan, would at least be powerful enough to have his own body. He excercises his power through temptations, and intimidations, to destroy if they can, the creations of God, through disinformation. How pathetic, and ignorant can people be, because of their lusts, and their need to be worshiped? They ultimately will give up their freedom to Satan for eternity. The voice also declared that *blood sacrifice was now ended, and* **the law of Moses** was now all fulfilled.

"And as **many** *as have received me[his gospel],* **to them have I given to become the "sons of God"; even so will I to as many as shall believe on my name, for behold, by me redemption cometh, and in me is the "law of moses fulfilled."** "**I am the light and the life of the world. I am Alpha and Omega, the beginning and the end."** "And ye shall offer for a **sacrifice unto me a broken heart and a contrite spirit. And whoso cometh unto me with a broken heart and a contrite spirit, him will I baptize with fire and with the Holy Ghost,** *even as the* **Lamanites[Aztecs],** *because of their faith* **in me at the time of their conversion, and were baptized with fire and with the Holy Ghost, and they knew it not."** "Behold, I have come unto the **world[Satan's kingdom]** *to bring redemption unto* *the world[those enslaved by Satan], to save the world from sin[those who will follow Christ away from Satan's kingdom]." "Therefore, whoso repenteth[desire change] and cometh unto me[follows by receiving his gospel and living it] as a little child[having full faith as a child, trusting his all to Christ] him will I receive, for of such is the kingdom of God. Behold, for such I have laid down my life, and have taken it up again; therefore repent[change over to the one who gives life, not death], and come unto me ye ends of the earth, and be saved."(3 Nephi 9:17-18, 20-22, Book of Mormon)*

Chapter 27

Christ's 2nd Day, Mighty and Strong
*Christ came down and stood at the temple and taught
and blessed the people.*

Christ's crucifixion was towards the end of the year, 34 A.D., and it was the end of this year that Christ did show himself to the remaining Nephites/Mayans and Lamanites/Aztecs alike. This is why that Central America is the Bountiful that Christ visited when he came. There were more righteous Lamanites/Aztecs than Nephites/Mayans at this time, believe it or not, and they were just as important as anyone else, as they were obeying the commandments of God with more resolve, and more humility. It was Samuel, the Lamanite/Aztec prophet who, prophesied of Christ's birth and of His death, and that he would come, and also the destruction of the Nephite/Mayan people.

Christ did show himself to His remaining people, both Nephite/Mayan, and Lamanite/Aztec alike, to those who waited and believed in His return, just as He promised. He descended down to Central America, in the Land of Bountiful, to the temple there, and there is no mistake. The Lamanites/Aztecs are also from the *Tribe of Joseph,* of him who was sold into Egypt by his brothers, and they, because of their firmness in keeping the commandments of God, once they were enlightened, were just as important as any one else. Christ, knowing his people were in captivity to Satan, in his kingdom of Hell, had the mercy, and the graciousness of a Great King of valor, to walk right up to Satan's kingdom, to the people imprisoned there, brazen as brass, telling the people to come on, now is your opportunity to escape. He is telling them, in front of Satan's face, in front of his witches, zombies, demons, secret orders, his military etc., if you follow me and do the things you both, see me do, and hear my words and do them, you can leave Satan in Hell, in his own misery. Now, that is courage, and integrity, and power, making Satan look awfully puny, and pitiful, wouldn't you say?

> *"Yea, the prophet Zenos did testify of these things, and also Zenock spake concerning these things, because they testified <u>particularly concerning us, who are the remnant of their seed.</u>" "Behold, <u>our father Jacob[father of Joseph, sold into Egypt] also testified concerning a</u>* **<u>remnant of the seed of Joseph.</u>** *And behold,* **<u>are not we a remnant of the seed of Joseph?</u>** *And these <u>things which testify of us, are they not written upon the</u>* **plates of brass**[Bible] **<u>which our father Lehi brought out of Jerusalem?</u>**" "*And it came to pass that in the <u>ending of the thirty and fourth year</u>[34 A.D.], <u>b</u>ehold, I will show unto you that the people of Nephi[Mayans] who were spared, and also those who had been called Lamanites[Aztecs] who had been spared, <u>did have great favors shown unto them, and great blessings poured out upon their heads, insomuch</u>* **that soon after the ascension of Christ into heaven he truly did manifest himself unto them---**" "**<u>Showing his body unto them; and an account of his ministry shall</u>** <u>be given hereafter. ...</u>"*(3 Nephi 10:16-19, Book of Mormon)*

Each one there had the privilege and opportunity to go forward and feel for themselves, and see his wounds, and see firsthand that it truly was he, Jesus Christ in real life. Can you honestly imagine the excitement they must have had, when realizing who this was, and seeing the kindness, and understanding of the *Son of God* while looking at you, with His *all piercing gaze*, into your very soul?

> *"And it came to pass that there were a great multitude gathered together, of the people of Nephi[Mayans], round about the* **temple which was in the land Bountiful;** *and they were marveling and wondering one with another, and were showing one to another the great and marvelous change <u>which had taken place</u>." "And they were*

also conversing about this **Jesus Christ,** *of whom the sign had been given concerning his death." "And it came to pass that while they were thus conversing one with another, they heard a voice as if it came out of heaven; and they cast their eyes round about, for they understood not the voice which they heard; and it was not a harsh voice neither was it a loud voice; nevertheless, and notwithstanding it* **being a small voice it did pierce them that did hear to the center, insomuch that there was no part of their frame that it did not cause to quake; yea, it did pierce them to the very soul, and did cause their hearts to burn.** *" "And it came to pass that again they heard the voice, and they understood it not." "And again the third time they did hear the voice, and did open their ears to hear it; and their eyes were towards the sound thereof;* **and they did look steadfastly towards heaven, from whence the sound came.** *" (3 Nephi 11:1-6, Book of Mormon).*

★*"And behold,* **the third time they did understand the voice which they heard;** *and it said unto them:" "Behold my* **Beloved Son, in whom I am well pleased, in whom I have glorified my name---hear ye him.** *" "And it came to pass, as they understood they cast[looked up] their eyes towards heaven; and behold,* **they saw a Man descending out of heaven[Quetzalcoatl]; and he was clothed in a white robe; and he came down and stood in the midst of them;** *and the eyes of the whole multitude were turned upon him, and they durst[dared] not open their mouths, even one to another, and wist[knew] not what it meant, for they thought it was an angel that* **had appeared unto them**. *" (3 Nephi 11:7-8, Book of Mormon).*

"And it came to pass that **he stretched forth his hand and spake unto the people**[*Mayan and Aztec present*], **saying: Behold, I am Jesus Christ, whom the prophets testified shall come into the world**[*Hell*]. *" "And behold,* **I am the light and life of the world; and I have drunk of the bitter cup which the Father hath given me, and have glorified the Father in taking upon me the sins of the world**[*Christ voluntarily championed the cause of the kingdom of Hell, to save those out of it*], **in the which I have suffered the will of the Father in all things from the beginning**[*worlds without end*]. *" "And it came to pass that when* **Jesus had spoken these words the**

*whole multitude fell to the earth for they remembered that it had
been prophesied among them that Christ should show himself
unto them after his ascension into heaven. [they realized they were
in the presence of God] (3 Nephi 11:9-12, Book of Mormon).*

Jesus Christ explains to the people there that they, both the
Nephites/Mayans and the Lamanites/Aztecs, are all remnants of
the tribe of Joseph, and that they all are the *other sheep,* as explained
by Christ himself, as being the only other ones to whom he would
personally appear in person, and he is here with them now. It just blew
their minds, that it was now a reality, not just words.

*"Behold, **I have given unto you the commandments; therefore
keep my commandments. And this is the law and the prophets** [love
God and love your neighbor]**, for they truly testified of me.** " "And
now it came to pass that when **Jesus had spoken these words, he said
unto twelve whom he had** chosen [among the Nephites [Mayans]:"
"**Ye are my disciples; and ye are a light unto this people, who are
a remnant of the house** [tribe] **of Joseph.** " "And behold, **this is the
land of your inheritance; and the Father hath given it unto you.** "
"And **not at any time hath the Father given me commandment
that I should tell it unto your brethren at Jerusalem.** " "(3 Nephi
15:10-24, Book of Mormon) compare (John 10:16, KJV)*

Jesus Christ just told the Nephites/Mayans and the Lamanites/
Aztecs present, that this land of the Americas, as they were a remnant
of the tribe of Joseph, and that the Father/Almighty God, had given
the land forever as an inheritance to the tribe of Joseph. Are the people
today listening? God's hand is in what is happening now, using his
enemies, the Democrats/liberals/ secret orders. To give the land back
to the remnants of the tribe of Joseph, by overrunning the country
northward. Jesus Christ also mentioned other sheep, meaning the
gentiles in the Latter-Days, [this is us] who also will hear his voice, but
only through the Holy Ghost. He will not appear to us, the Gentiles,
as he had done to them, so when the Gentiles hear the truth, and
know it is the truth, then that is the voice of his Spirit speaking unto
us. When we hear it and know it is truth, and then reject it, we have

just denied the Holy Ghost. If we continue to do this, then he begins to withdraw from those who reject his voice, until they are in outer darkness, and find themselves in an awful state, touching elbows with Satan's very own, and he/Satan is laughing at you, because you have been deceived.

"And _blessed are the_ **Gentiles because of their belief in me, in and of the Holy Ghost, which witnesses unto them of me and of the Father.**" "Behold, **because of their belief in me, saith the Father, and because of the unbelief of you**[Nephites/Mayans & Lamanites/Aztecs], **O house of Israel, in the latter days**[today in America, since the pilgrims] **shall the truth come unto the Gentiles**[us, Europeans, etc.,], **that the fulness of these things shall be made known unto them**[through Joseph Smith and the Book of Mormon, etc.,]." "**But wo, saith the Father, unto the unbelieving of the Gentiles---for notwithstanding**[in spite of the fact] **they have come forth upon the face of this land, and have scattered my people who are of the house**[tribes] **of Israel ;...**"(3 Nephi 16:6-8, Book of Mormon)

★"And thus commandeth _the Father that I should say unto you:_ **At that day when the Gentiles shall sin against my gospel, and shall reject the "fulness of my gospel", and shall be lifted up in the pride of their hearts above all nations, and above all people of the whole earth, and shall be filled with all manner of lyings, and of deceits, and of mischiefs, and all manner of hypocrisy, and murders, and priestcrafts, and whoredoms, and of secret abominations; and if they shall do all those things, and shall reject the "fulness of my gospel", behold, saith the Father, I will bring the fulness of my gospel from among them.**" "And **then will I remember my covenant** people[through Abraham, Isaac, and Jacob], **O house of Israel, and I will bring my gospel unto them.**" "And **I will show unto thee, O house of Israel, that the Gentiles shall not have power over you; but I will remember my covenant unto you, O house of Israel, and ye shall come unto the knowledge of the "fulness of my gospel."** (3 Nephi 16:10-12, Book of Mormon)

"But if [big word] the Gentiles will repent[change]and return unto me, saith the Father, behold, they shall be numbered among my people[the tribes of Israel], O house of Israel." "And I will not suffer my people, who are of the house of Israel, to go through among them[the Gentiles/us], and tread them down[destroy them], saith the Father." "But if they[the Gentiles] will not turn unto me, and hearken[listen] unto my voice[truth], I will suffer them[the Lamanites/Aztecs], yea, I will suffer my people[remnants of Lamanites/Aztecs], O house of Israel, that they shall go through among them[the Gentiles], and shall tread them [Gentiles/us] down, and they [the Gentiles] shall be as the salt that hath lost its savor, which is thenceforth good for nothing but to be cast out, and trodden under foot of my people[South/Central Americans/remnants of the tribe of Joseph], O house of Israel." (3 Nephi 16:13-15, Book of Mormon)

"Verily, Verily, I say unto you, thus hath the Father commanded me---that I should give unto this people this land for their inheritance." "And then the words of Isaiah shall be fulfilled, which say: Thy watchmen shall lift up the voice; with the voice together shall they sing, for they shall see eye to eye when the Lord shall bring again Zion." "Break forth into joy, sing together, ye waste places of Jerusalem; for the Lord hath comforted his people, he hath redeemed Jerusalem." "The Lord hath made bare his holy arm in the eyes of all the nations; and all the ends of the earth shall see the salvation of God."(3 Nephi 16:16-20, Book of Mormon)

Christ affirms to the Nephites/Mayans, and Lamanites/Aztecs, that this Land of the Americas, will still be the land of their inheritance as He had promised, to those who obey His commandments. We still are waiting for Christ to come again, this time in judgment, so beware you Gentiles, you Communists who pervert the ways of God. Also you covenant breakers, who sin against the fulness of Christ's gospel, you GOP who form alliances with the enemy, your corporations, your secret orders. Do you actually think your fake money, and your puny military is going to keep Jesus Christ from coming to replace you out of your cozy jobs or country, because you think it is impossible to defeat such an ominous force or obstacle because of advanced technology? You will not inherit this land in the end unless you change your wicked ways, and there will be no king here in America, with the exception of Jesus Christ, and only him. So, what people are going to replace the Gentiles, you may ask?

As it was during the days of the son of Nebuchadnezzar, the king of Assyria, who had already been on the move against him, and it was because of the audacity of him, the son of Nebuchadezzar to defy the God of heaven and earth. It was that very night, that Babylon was turned over to the Assyrians and Meads/Turkey, just by such a simple means of diverting the Euphrates river away from the city and going under the wall on dry ground in the night-time when the son of Nebuchadnezzar was in the very act of defying God and his covenant people. So what is America's Achilles heel/weakness, so to speak? Where is God on the move, and beginning to fulfill his promises to the remnants of Israel, the Lamanites/Aztecs who are a mixture of those dissenters from the Nephites/Mayans?

The people were very saddened when it came time for him to depart from them that first day, and he could read their thoughts and knew their feelings, and he knew that they already were missing him before he left. Because he was moved with love and compassion, and empathy, Christ asked them to bring their little ones/children, and he blessed them, and left his blessings on all of them who were there before he ascended back to his Father, who was in Heaven.

*"And he said unto them: **Behold, my bowels**[inward organs/ heart] **are filled with compassion towards you.**" "**Have ye any that are sick among you? Bring them hither. Have ye any that are lame, or blind, or halt**[diseased], **or maimed, or leprous, or that are withered, or deaf, or that are afflicted in any manner? Bring them hither and I will heal them, for I have compassion upon you; my bowels are filled with mercy.**" "For **I perceive that ye desire that I should show unto you what I have done unto your brethren at Jerusalem, for I see that your faith is sufficient that I should heal you.**" "And it came to pass that when he had thus spoken, all the multitude with one accord, did go forth with their sick and their afflicted, and their lame, and with their blind, and with their*

dumb[halt], and with all them that were afflicted **in any manner;** **and he did heal them every one as they were brought forth unto** **him.** *"(3 Nephi 17:6-9, Book of Mormon)*

"And **they did all, both they who had been healed and they** **who were whole, bow down at his feet, and did worship him; and** **as many as could come for the multitude** *[congested, and everyone pressing forward]* **did kiss his feet, insomuch that they did bathe** **his feet with their** *tears[they were so grateful]*. *" "And it came to pass* **that he commanded that their little children should be brought.** *"* *"So they[Mayans&Aztecs]* **brought their little children and set** **them down upon the ground round about him, and Jesus stood** **in the midst; and the multitude gave way till they had all been** **brought unto him.** *" "And it came to pass that when they* **had all** **been brought, and Jesus stood in the midst , he commanded the** **multitude that they should kneel down upon the ground.** *" "And it came to pass that* **when they had knelt upon the ground,** **Jesus** **groaned within himself, and said: Father, I am troubled because** **of the wickedness of the people[Mayans&Aztecs] of the house of** **Israel.** *" "And when* **he had said these words, he himself also knelt** **upon the earth; and behold he prayed unto the Father, and the** **things which he prayed cannot be written, and the multitude did** **bear record who heard him.** *"(3 Nephi 17:10-15, Book of Mormon)*

"And after this manner do they bear record: **The eye hath never** **seen, neither hath the ear heard, before, so great and marvelous** **things as we saw and heard Jesus speak unto the Father;** *" "***And** **no tongue can speak, neither can there be written by any man,** **neither can the hearts of men conceive so great and marvelous** **things as we both saw and heard Jesus speak; and no one can** **conceive of the joy which filled our souls at the time we heard** **him pray for us unto the Father.** *" "And it came to pass that when* **Jesus had made an end of praying unto the Father, he arose; but** **so great was the joy of the multitude that they were overcome.** *"* *"And it came to pass that* **Jesus spake unto them, and bade them** **arise.** *"* **"And they arose from the earth, and** **he said unto them:**

Blessed are ye because of your faith. And now behold, my joy is full."(3 Nephi 17:16-20, Book of Mormon)

*"And when he had said these words, **he wept, and the multitude bare record of it, and he took their little children, one by one, and blessed them, and prayed unto the Father for them.**" "And when he had done this he wept again;" "And he spake unto the multitude, and said unto them: Behold your little ones." "And as they looked to behold they cast their eyes towards heaven, and they saw the heavens open, and they saw angels descending out of heaven as it were in the midst of a fire; and they came down and encircled those little ones about, and they were encircled about with fire; and the angels did minister unto them." "And the multitude did see and hear and bear record; and they know that their record is true for they all of them did see and hear, every man for himself; and they were in number about two thousand and five hundred souls; and they did consist of men, women, and children."* (3 Nephi 17:21-25, Book of Mormon)

Since the *Law of Moses* was ended, Christ now called twelve apostles, while he was there, and one by one conferred upon them the Holy Melchizedek Priesthood, by himself laying his hands upon them, so now they could confer this higher and lower priesthoods upon others in like manner. Through the giving twelve disciples the priesthood authority to act in his/Jesus's name, they then once again established the Church of Jesus Christ, and the government back into it's original order, under the rule of the Judges.

"And it came to pass that when Jesus had made an end of these sayings, he touched with his hand the disciples whom he had chosen[among the Nephites/Mayans], one by one, even until he had touched them all, and spake unto them as he touched them[called them by name and conferred his priesthood authority upon them by the laying on of hands]." "And the multitude heard not the words which he spake, therefore they did not bear record; but the disciples bare record that he gave them power[authority to act in his name] to give the Holy Ghost." "And I will show unto you

*hereafter that this record is true." "And it came to pass that when **Jesus** **had touched them all, there came a cloud and overshadowed the** **multitude that they could not see Jesus." "And while they were** **overshadowed he departed from them, and ascended into heaven.** **And the disciples saw and did bear record that he ascended again** **into heaven."** (3 Nephi 18:36-39, Book of Mormon)*

Jesus Christ then ascended back into Heaven, and the people immediately busied themselves all night long, sending messengers,and spreading the word that that they had seen Jesus Christ, and that he had administered unto them. You can just imagine the other sayings and things passed along , about the miracles they saw and trying to explain things that they were unable to explain in the language of any civilization. That night must have been some what of a pony express night, get it on night, but there was no Paul Revere there. Jesus Christ continued to teach the Nephites/Mayans and Lamanites/Aztecs, by visiting them every day, three days in a row.

The three days of darkness talked about after the tempests took place while the body of the crucified Lord/Jesus Christ, was hanging on the cross in Jerusalem, for two of those days, and the third, was while he was lying in the tomb, also in Jerusalem. Christ was true to his word with the thief that was on the cross next to him, who asked to be remembered by Jesus when he ascended into his kingdom. He believed in Christ, and wanted to follow Him, even at the last moment, Christ forgave him of his sins and told the thief saying: "This day shall thou be with me in paradise." Paradise is where Christ went in the spirit, during those three days, to teach those who were in the Spirit Prison, the place where every believer can rest from his labors. Christ also used these three days to organize the redemption of those who were once rebellious, during the days when Noah was still building the ark, and when the waters came and took them all away, etc..

*"And now it came to pass that **when Jesus had ascended into** **heaven,** the multitude did disperse, and every man did take his wife and his children and did return to his own home." "And it was noised abroad among the people[both in the land northward and the land southward] **immediately, before it was yet dark,** that the multitude*

had seen Jesus, and that he had ministered unto them, and that he would show himself on the morrow unto the multitude." "Yea, and even all the night it was noised abroad concerning Jesus; and insomuch did they send forth unto the people[both Mayan and Aztec]*that there were many, yea, an exceedingly great number, did labor exceedingly all that night, that they might be on the morrow in the place when Jesus should show himself unto the multitude." (3* Nephi 19:1-3, Book of Mormon)

" *And it came to pass that on the morrow, when the multitude was gathered together, behold, Nephi[Mayan prophet] and his brother whom he had raised from the dead, whose name was* **Timothy**, *and also his son, whose name was* **Jonas, and also Mathoni, and Mathonihah, his brother, and Kumen, and Kumenonhi, and Jeremiah, and Shemnon, and Jonas, and Zedekiah, and Isaiah---Now these were the names of the disciples whom Jesus had chosen---***and it came to pass that they went forth and stood in the midst of the multitude." "And behold the multitude was so great that they did cause that they should be separated into twelve bodies." "And the twelve did teach the multitude; and behold, they did cause that the multitude should kneel down upon the face of the earth, and should pray unto the* **Father in the name of Jesus.**" *(3 Nephi 19:4-6, Book of Mormon)*

"And the disciples did pray unto the Father also in the name of Jesus. And it came to pass that they arose and ministered unto the people." "And when they had ministered those same words which Jesus had spoken---nothing varying *from the words which Jesus had spoken--behold, they knelt again and prayed to the Father in the name of Jesus.*" "And they did pray for that which *they most desired that the* **Holy Ghost should be given unto them.**" "And when they had thus prayed they went down unto the **waters edge, and the multitude followed them.**" "And it came to pass that **Nephi**[The Mayan prophet] **went down into the water and was baptized**[immersed under the water]." "**And he came up out of the water and began to baptize. And he baptized all those whom Jesus had chosen.**" "And it came to pass **when they were all baptized and had come** *up out of the water, the Holy Ghost did fall upon them, and they were filled with the Holy Ghost and with fire."(3 Nephi 19:7-13. Book of Mormon)*

"And behold, they were encircled about as if it were by fire; and it came down from heaven, and the multitude did witness it, and did bear record; and angels did come down out of heaven and did minister unto them." "And it came to pass that while the angels were ministering unto the disciples, behold, Jesus came and stood in the midst and ministered unto them." (3 Nephi 19:14-15, Book of Mormon)

Chapter 28

Blesses 12-Disciples, They See Unspeakable Things

Christ returned the second day!

Christ appeared again the second day, in the which he did say, and did teach them specifically, that they, the Nephites/Mayans and the Lamanites/Aztecs were from the twelve tribes of Israel, and that the Americas were to be *their inheritance* as promised through the covenants with Abraham, Isaac, and Jacob.

> ⋆⋆ *"And the* ___Father hath commanded me that I should give unto you this land, for your inheritance.___ *" "And* ___I say unto you, that if the Gentiles do not repent after the blessing which they shall receive, after they have scattered my people___---*[Mayans/ Aztecs]" "Then* ___shall ye, who are a remnant of the house of Jacob, go forth among them; and ye shall be in the midst of them who shall be many; and ye shall be among them as a lion among the beasts of the forest, and as a young lion among the flocks of sheep, who, if he goeth through both treadeth down and teareth in pieces, and none can deliver.___ *" "Thy hand shall be lifted up upon thy* ___adversaries, and all thine___ ___enemies shall be cut off.___ *" "(3 Nephi 20:14-17, Book of Mormon)*

"And it shall come to pass, **saith the Father, that the sword of my justice shall hang over them at that day; and except they repent it shall fall upon them, saith the Father, yea, even upon all the nations of the** Gentiles." "And it shall come to pass that I will establish my people, O house of Israel." "And behold, **this people**[remnants of Israel/Mayans /Aztecs] **will I establish in this land, unto the fulfilling of the covenant which I made with your father Jacob; and it shall be a New Jerusalem. And the powers of heaven shall be in the midst of this people; yea, even I will be in the midst of you.**" (3 Nephi 20:20-22, Book of Mormon)

"The Father having raised me up unto you first, and sent me to bless you in turning away every one of you from his iniquities; and **this because ye are the children of the covenant---**" "And after that ye were blessed then fulfilleth the Father the covenant which **he made with Abraham, saying: In thy seed shall all the kindreds of the earth be blessed---unto the pouring out the Holy Ghost through me upon the Gentiles, which blessing upon the Gentiles**[Europeans, etc./us] **shall make them mighty above all, unto the scattering of my people**[Nephites/Mayans&Lamanites/Aztecs]**, O house of Israel.**" "And they[Gentiles] **shall be a scourge unto the** [natives/ American Indians] **people of this land. Nevertheless**[in spite of]**, when they shall receive the fulness of my gospel, then if they shall harden their hearts against me I will return their iniquities upon their own heads, saith the Father.**" (3 Nephi 20:26-28, Book of Mormon)

Christ also explains some of the sayings and writings of Isaiah from the Old Testament, concerning us, the Gentiles, sinning against the *"Fullness of His Gospel"*. Christ also promises, that when this happens, **that the remnants of the tribes of Israel shall tread upon the Gentiles**, and implies, that the one chosen to lead them, His servant, will come from the South[America], and he will be *Mighty and Strong*. The scripture also implies that he will be a Lamanite/Aztec, who has seen many battles, and his countenance will be scarred. The way things are going, it could be happening very subtley, even now. He has been referenced as being one who is "mighty and strong", and will have the

Spirit of God about him, and will be led by him and protected by him, and he will come from the south.

★★★ *"Behold my servant shall deal prudently; he shall be exalted and extolled and be very high." "As many were atonished at thee---his visage was so marred, more than any man, and his form more than the sons of men---"* "So shall he <u>sprinkle many nations;</u> <u>the kings shall shut their mouths at him, for that which had not been</u> <u>told them shall they see; and that which they had not heard shall they</u> <u>consider."</u> *(3 Nephi 20:43-45, Book of Mormon)*

★★ *"For in that day, for my sake shall the Father <u>work a work</u>* *, which shall be a great and marvelous work among them: and there shall be among them those who will not believe it, although a man shall declare it unto them." "But behold, the <u>life of my servant shall</u> <u>be in my hand; therefore they shall not hurt him, although</u>* **he shall** **be marred because of them. Yet I will heal him, for I will show** <u>unto them that my wisdom is greater than the cunning of the devil.</u>**"** *"Therefore it shall come to pass that whosoever will not believe in my words,* **<u>who am Jesus Christ, which the Father shall cause him</u>** **<u>to bring forth unto the Gentiles,</u>** <u>and shall give unto him power</u> <u>that, (it shall be done even as Moses said)</u> **<u>they shall be cut off from</u>** **<u>among my people who are of the covenant."</u>** *"And* **my people** **who are a remnant of Jacob shall be among the Gentiles, yea, in** **the midst of them as a lion among the beasts of the forest, as a** **young lion among the flocks of sheep, who if he go through both** **treadeth down and teareth in pieces, and none can deliver."** *(3 Nephi 21:9-12, Book of Mormon)*

★★ *"Their hand shall be lifted up upon their adversaries, and all their enemies shall be cut off."* **"Yea, wo be unto the Gentiles[us]** **except they repent; for it shall come to pass in that day, saith** **the Father, that I will cut off thy horses out of the midst of** **thee, and I will destroy thy chariots;"** *"And I will cut off thy cities of thy land, and throw down all thy strongholds;"* **"<u>And I will</u>** **<u>cut off witchcrafts out of thy land, and thou shalt have no more</u>** **<u>soothsayers;"</u>** **"<u>Thy graven images I will also cut off, and thy</u>** **<u>standing images</u>[**S*tatue of Liberty, etc.]out of the<u> midst of thee, and</u>*

*thou shalt **no more worship the works of thy hands;**" "And I will pluck up thy **groves out** of the midst of thee; **so will I destroy thy cities.**" "And it shall come to pass that **all lyings, and deceivings, and envyings, and strifes, and priestcrafts, and whoredoms, shall be done away.**" (3 Nephi 21:13-19, Book of Mormon)*

★"*But if they[the Gentiles] will repent and hearken unto my words, and harden not their hearts, I will establish my church among them, and they shall come in unto the **covenant and be numbered among this the remnant of Jacob, unto whom I have given this land for their inheritance;**" "And **they**[the Gentiles] shall assist my people, the remnant of Jacob, and also as many of the house of Israel as shall come, that they may build a city, **which shall be called the New Jerusalem.**" "And then shall they[the Gentiles] assist my people[Mayans/Aztecs] that they **may be gathered in, who are scattered upon all the face of the land, in unto the New Jerusalem.**" "And then shall the power of heaven come down among them; and I[Jesus Christ] also will be in the midst.**" (3 Nephi 21: 22-25, Book of Mormon)*

Christ expounds on many prophecies and scriptures taught by Isaiah concerning the *remnants of the tribes of Israel*, and about them, the Nephites/Mayans and Lamanites/Aztecs, and about the Gentiles[**us**] in the Latter-days/these days. Christ also asked Nephi, the Mayan prophet, to come forward with the record he was responsible for keeping, and reminded him to write things in the record that he had neglected to do. The things that he failed to write was about Samuel the Lamanite/Aztec prophet, who prophesied of things that happened, but were not recorded.

*"And it came to pass that when **Jesus** had said these words he said unto them again, after he had expounded all the scriptures unto them which they had received, he said unto them: **Behold, other scriptures I would that ye should write, that ye have not.**" "And it came to pass that he said unto Nephi: **Bring forth the record which ye have kept.**" "And when Nephi had brought forth the records, **and laid them before him, he cast his eyes upon them and said:**"*

"Verily I say unto you, I commanded my servant Samuel, the Lamanite[Aztec], that he should testify unto this people[the Nephites/Mayans], that at the day that the Father should glorify his name in me that there were many saints who should arise from the dead, and should appear unto many, and should minister unto them: Was it not so?" *"And his disciples answered him and said: Yea, Lord, Samuel did prophesy according to thy words, and they were all fulfilled."* *"And Jesus said unto them: How be it that ye have not written this thing, that many saints did appear unto many and did minister unto them?"* *"And it came to pass that Nephi[Mayan/Nephite prophet] remembered that this thing had not been written."* *"And it came to pass that Jesus commanded that it should be written; therefore it was written according as he had commanded."(3 Nephi 23:6-13, Book of Mormon)*

This 2nd day also, Jesus expounds all things from beginning to end, and he explains to them how their voice shall cry from the dust, and references the Gentiles to bring forth the record.

"And now it came to pass that when Jesus had told these things he expounded[explained] them unto the multitude and he did expound all things unto them, both great and small." *"And he saith: These scriptures, which ye had not with you, the Father commanded that I should give unto you; for it was wisdom in him that they should be given unto future generations."* *"And he did expound all things, even from the beginning until the time that he should come in his glory---yea, even all things which should come upon the face of the earth, even until the elements should melt with fervent heat, and the earth should be wrapt together as a scroll, and the heavens and the earth should pass away;"* *"And even unto the great and last day, when all people, and all kindreds, and all nations and tongues shall stand before God, to be judged of their works, whether they be good or whether they be evil---"(3 Nephi 26:1-4, Book of Mormon)*

"And now there cannot be written in this book even a hundredth part of the things which Jesus did truly teach unto

the people;" *"But behold **the plates of Nephi***[the gold plates] **do contain the more part of the things which he taught the people.***"*

*"And these things have I written, <u>which are a lesser part of the things which he [Jesus]taught the people;and I have written them to the intent that they may be brought again unto this people</u>[the remnants of both Nephite/Mayan and Lamanite/Aztec], from the **Gentiles**[us], **according to the words which Jesus hath spoken.***"* *"And when they <u>shall have received this, which is expedient that they should have first</u>[What Joseph Smith brought forth], **to try their faith, and if it shall so be that they shall believe these things then shall the greater things be made manifest unto them**[both for Gentile and Nephite/Lamanite].*" **"And if it so be that they will not believe these things, then shall the greater things be withheld from them, unto their condemnation."***(3 Nephi 26: 6-10, Book of Mormon)*

Chapter 29

Secret Societies Got Above The People

Christ returned a third day, and by the third day, the crowd of people had tripled!

On the third day, Christ explains his gospel to the multitude, because now the number of people had pretty much tripled, as some of them had been traveling all through the first two nights, nonstop, in order to get to see Christ in the flesh, as was prophesied thousands of years in advance, that he would come, and was now within walking distance, or even within sailing distance. Wouldn't you want to go and be in his presence and be a witness, if you were in their positions?

Before Christ ascends up to his Father for the last time, he calls his twelve-disciples to come forward, and he asks them what they desired of him before he goes. Ten of them tell him that they simply want to come and be with him when their time comes to die, and leave this earth. The other three were quiet, and wouldn't openly say, but Christ read their thoughts, and knew they desired to be as it was with John the Beloved, that they would never taste of death, but would live to see Christ come again in His glory. Those three disciples/Apostles to Jesus Christ, of the Nephites/Mayans, had their wishes granted, and they are here ministering and observing and keeping record until Christ comes again in His Glory, as is John the Beloved.

That means that, there are four disciples who are still alive today walking the earth and waiting for Christ to return again. As Mormon and Moroni both testify, that the disciples have ministered unto them at the last, even before their people, the Nephites/Mayans, are destroyed, or else have joined with the Lamanites/Aztecs, rather than be destroyed.

*"And it came to pass when Jesus had said these words, **he spake unto his disciples** [Nephite/Mayan disciples], **one by one, saying unto them: What is it that ye desire of me, after that I am gone to the Father?**" "And they all spake, save it were three, saying: We desire that after we have lived unto the age of man, that our ministry, wherein thou hast called us, may have an end, that we may speedily come unto thee in thy kingdom." "**And he said unto them: Blessed are ye because ye have desired this thing of me; therefore, after that ye are seventy and two years old ye shall come unto me in my kingdom; and with me ye shall find rest.**" 3 Nephi 28:1-3, Book of Mormon)*

*✱✱ "And when he had spoken unto them, **he turned himself unto the three, and said unto them: What will ye that I should do unto you, when I am gone unto the Father?**" "And they sorrowed in their hearts, for they durst [dared] not speak unto him the things which they desired." "And he said unto them: **Behold, I know your thoughts, and ye have desired the thing which John, my beloved, who was with me in my ministry, before that I was lifted up by the Jews, desired of me.**" "Therefore, **more blessed are ye, for ye shall never taste of death; but ye shall live to behold all the doings of the Father unto the children of men, even until all things shall be fulfilled according to the will of the Father, when I shall come in my glory with the powers of heaven.**" "**And ye shall never endure the pains of death; but when I shall come in my glory ye shall be changed in the twinkling of an eye from mortality to immortality; and then shall ye be blessed in the kingdom of my Father.**" (3 Nephi 28:4-8, Book of Mormon)*

*And again, ye shall **not have pain while ye shall dwell in the flesh, neither sorrow save it be for the sins of the world; and all this will I do because of the thing which ye have desired of me, for ye have desired that ye might bring the souls of men unto me, while the***

world[Hell] _shall stand." "And for this cause ye shall have fulness_
of joy; and ye shall sit down in the kingdom of my Father[the
Celestial kingdom];_yea, your joy shall be full, even as the Father_
hath given me fulness of joy; and ye shall be even as I am, and I
am even as the Father; and the Father and I are one[in purpose];
" "And the _Holy Ghost beareth record of the Father and me; and the_
Father giveth **the Holy Ghost unto the children of men, because**
of me." "And it came to pass when **Jesus had spoken these words,**
he touched every one of them with his finger save it were the
three who were to tarry, and then he departed." "And behold, **the**
heavens were opened, and they were caught up into heaven, and
saw and heard unspeakable things[the planet where God dwells/
Mount Olympus]."_(3 Nephi 28:9-13, Book of Mormon)_

★★" _And now I, Mormon, make an end of speaking concerning_
these things for a time." "Behold, I was about to write the names of those
who were never to taste of death, but the Lord forbade; therefore I write
them not, for they are hid from the world[Hell/Telestial Kingdom]."
"But behold, **I have seen them, and they have ministered unto**
me." "And behold **they will be among the Gentiles**[us]_, **and the**_
Gentiles shall know them not." "**And they will also be among**
the Jews, and the Jews shall know them not." "And it shall come
to pass, _when the Lord seeth fit in his wisdom that they shall minister_
unto all the scattered tribes of Israel, and unto all nations, kindreds,
tongues and people, and shall bring many souls, that their desire may be
fulfilled, and also because of the convincing power of **God which is in**
them." "And **they are as the angels of God, and if they shall pray**
unto the Father in the name of Jesus they can show themselves
unto whatsoever man it seemeth them good." " _(3 Nephi 28:24-_
30, Book of Mormon)

"And now behold, _as I spake concerning those whom the Lord_
hath chosen, yea, even three who were caught up into the heavens, that I
knew not whether they were cleansed from mortality to immortality---"
"But behold, **since I wrote, I have inquired of the Lord, and he**
hath made it manifest unto me that there must needs be a change
wrought upon their bodies, or else it needs be that they must taste

of death;" "Therefore, *that they might not taste of death there was a change wrought upon their bodies, that they might not suffer pain nor sorrow save it were for the sins of the world.*"*(3 Nephi 28:36-38, Book of Mormon)*

Chapter 30

Ammarron Buries Records In Hill Shim, And Notifies Mormon

The Destruction of the Nephites/Mayan Civilization
By the Lamanites/Aztecs

35 A.D. thru 59 A.D.

From the time Christ ascended back to His Father in Heaven, the people, both Nephites/Mayans, and Lamanites/Aztecs, all belonged to the true Church of Jesus Christ, and they all prospered in the land. There were no contentions for at least 24-years, nor were there any disputes among them, and they had all things in common-law. They were not divided into class or ranks, but everyone dealt justly with one another. The Lamanites/Aztecs were free to go anywhere they chose, as could the Nephites/Mayans. There were many Lamanites/Aztecs that migrated to North America at this time. Also all of the lands of the Nephites/Mayans were returned to them. i.e. The land of Nephi in Peru and Ecuador, Bolivia, Colombia, etc..

   ★★★*"And it came to pass that the* _thirty and fourth year[34A.D.]_ _passed away. And also the thirty and fifth year[35A.D.], and behold_ _the disciples of Jesus had formed a_ **church of Christ in all the lands** **round about. And as many as did come unto them, and did truly** **repent of their sins, were baptized in the name of Jesus; and** *they did also receive the Holy Ghost.* " *"And it came to pass in the thirty and sixth year[36A.D.], the people were all converted unto the Lord, upon all the face of the land, both Nephites[Mayans] and Lamanites[Aztecs], and there were no contentions and disputations among them, and every man did deal justly one with another."* "And they had all things common among them; therefore there were not rich and poor, bond and free, but they were all made free, and partakers of the heavenly gift."(4 Nephi 1:1-3, Book of Mormon)*

★ *And the* **the Lord did prosper them exceedingly in the land; yea, insomuch that they did build cities again where there had been cities burned.*** " *"Yea, even that great city Zarahemla did they cause to be built again." "But there were many cities which had been sunk , and waters came up in the stead thereof; therefore these cities could not be renewed." "And now, behold, it came to pass that the* **people of Nephi***[Mayan people]* **did wax strong, and did multiply exceedingly fast, and became an exceedingly fair and delightsome people.*** " *"And they were married and given in marriage, and were blessed according to the multitude of the promises which the Lord had made unto them." "And they did not walk any more after the performances and ordinances of the "law of Moses"; but they did walk after the commandments which they had received from their Lord and their God, continuing in fasting and prayer, and in meeting together oft both to pray and to hear the word of the Lord." "and it came to pass that there was no contention among all the people[Mayan and Aztec], in all the land;* **but there were mighty miracles wrought among the disciples of Jesus.*** " (4 Nephi1:7-13, Book of Mormon)*

"And it came to pass that the seventy and first year[71 A.D.] passed away, and also the seventy and second year[72A.D.], yea, and in fine, till the seventy and ninth year[79A.D.] had passed away; yea, **even an hundred years had passed away[100 A.D.], and the disciples of Jesus had all gone to the paradise of God, save it were the three who should tarry;*** *and there were other disciples ordained in their stead; and also many of that generation had passed away." "And it came to pass that there was no contention in the land,*

because of the love of God which did dwell in the hearts of the people[Mayan and Aztec people]." "And there were no envyings, nor strifes, nor tumults, nor whoredoms, nor lyings, nor murders, nor any manner of lasciviousness; **and surely there could not be a happier people among all the people who had been created by the hand of God."** "T*here were no robbers, nor murderers, neither were there Lamanites, nor any manner of -ites; but they were in one, the children of Christ, and heirs to the kingdom of God."*(4 Nephi 1:14-17, Book of Mormon)

Zarahemla, the Capitol City of the Nephites/Mayans, was rebuilt after being burned by fire at the coming of Christ. The Law of Moses was not observed anymore, so the sacrificial alters were not used anymore at all. The Lord's Day was now observed on the 1st day of the week, not the 7th day.

79 A.D. thru 100 A.D.

The 9-Apostles of the Nephites/Mayans, were now gone to the Lord as they had desired, and only the three tarried, as John tarries to await to the end of time, when Jesus Christ comes again in his Glory.

110 A.D.

There was still peace in all the land, and the first generation from the days Christ visited Bountiful, at the temple in Northern Colombia, had all passed away. These plates/records of Nephi were now passed down to Nephi's son, Amos. Amos kept the plates of Nephi 84-years, and there was still continual peace in the land, save for a small rebellious group who had revolted from the Church of Christ, and began again to call themselves **Lamanites/Aztecs.** Amos the Nephite/Mayan prophet died in **194 A.D.**, and his son, also named Amos after his father, continued to keep the record, on the plates of Nephi/gold plates, as gold is easy to write on, and will last forever.

"And how blessed were they! For the Lord did bless them in all their doings; yea, even they were blessed and prospered until

an hundred and ten years[110A.D.] had passed away; and the first generation from <u>Christ had passed away,</u> and there was no contention in all the land." "And it came to pass that <u>200 years had passed away[200 A.D.]; and the second generation had all passed away save it were for a few.</u>" *(4 Nephi 1:18, 22, Book of Mormon)*

Chapter 31

Spirit Of God Was Withdrawn From The Nephites/Mayans

Pride entered into the hearts of men/women, divisions, and classes were reinstated!

200 A.D. thru 201A.D.

Pride began to surface in the land, and Satan was beginning to get a hold on the hearts of the people, both Nephites/Mayans and Lamanites/Aztecs. *"And now, in this two hundred and first year[201A.D.] there began to be among them those who were lifted up in pride, such as wearing of costly apparel, and all manner of fine pearls, and of fine things of the world."* *"And from that time forth they did have their goods and their substance no more common among them."* *"And they began to be divided into classes; and they began to build up* **churches unto themselves to get gain, and began to deny the true church of Christ.**"(4 Nephi 1:24-26, Book of Mormon)

210 A.D.

In this year, churches were formed and built up to get gain and power over the people. It was about this period that the Catholic Church was formed, and began to destroy the 12-apostles of Christ, in Jerusalem, and around the Mediterranean countries. It took about 210-years to destroy the Church of Christ, but that only happened because of the wickedness of the people, of the Church of Jesus Christ in Jerusalem, and in other areas the disciples had built up the Church. The Church of Jesus Christ predated the Catholic Church by at least 200-years.

The Common-Laws of the land[Constitution] were corrupted, and the Freedom of Religion and the Freedom of Speech was discouraged by harassment, and by unlawfully arresting the teachers and disciples of Christ, and putting them into prisons. Even the three disciples who tarried were thrown into prisons unjustly, but those prisons were destroyed because the three disciples could not be held.

***"And it came to pass that *when two hundred and ten years[210A.D.] had passed away there were many* **churches in the land; yea, there were many churches which professed to know the Christ, and yet they did deny the more parts of his gospel**[like is done today, 2023]**, insomuch that they did receive all manner of wickedness, and did administer that which was sacred unto him to whom it had been forbidden because of unworthiness.**" "And **this church did multiply exceedingly because of iniquity, and because of the power of Satan who did get hold upon their hearts.**" "And again, there was another church which denied the Christ; and they did persecute the true church of Christ, because of their humility and their belief in Christ; and they did despise *them because of the many miracles which were wrought among them.*" "Therefore they did exercise power and authority over the disciples *of Jesus who did tarry with them, and they did cast them into prison; but by the* **power of God, which was in them, the prisons were rent in twain, and they went forth doing mighty miracles among them.**" "(4 Nephi 1:27-30, Book of Mormon)

"Nevertheless, and notwithstanding[in spite of]all these *miracles, the people did harden their hearts, and did seek to kill them, even as the Jews at Jerusalem sought to kill Jesus, according to his word.*" "And they did *cast them into furnaces of fire, and they came forth receiving no harm.*" "And they did also **cast them into dens of wild beasts, and they did play with the wild beasts even as a child with a lamb; and they did come forth from among them, receiving no harm.**"(4 Nephi 1:31-33, Book of Mormon)

The people were led by many *false priests and false prophets*, who practiced priest-craft to make religion a big business. It just got worse continually. Where are the General Moroni's of today? *"Nevertheless, the people did harden their hearts, for they were led by many priests and false prophets to build up many churches, and to do all manner of iniquity. And they did smite upon the people of Jesus; but the people of Jesus did not smite again. And thus they did dwindle in unbelief and wickedness, from year to year, even until two hundred and thirty years[230A.D.] had passed away."* (4 Nephi 1:34, Book of Mormon)

230 A.D.

There began to be a **great division** again, among the people, Mayans and Aztecs, it was like a dog going back to it's vomit. There were those who rejected the *gospel of Jesus Christ,* and they again began to call themselves Lamanites, Lemuelites, and Ishmaelites/Aztecs, and they **wilfully rebelled against God and the Truth.** They were taught to hate those people who believed in the Church of God, because they made them feel guilty. They were true liberals/Democrats, because they think completely opposite to those who love God.

Watch what is happening today in America, since the year 1776, when our forefathers declared the independence of the American-Republic, to now 2024, it has been **248 years**. The people came here in the beginning, as Christians, seeking *freedom,* and now in 2024, only 248-years later, the Democrats/Communists, have divided our country, trying to alter the Constitution, and establish a king/ or dictator, where only the rich rule. You can see the pride, secret murders going on among high ranking liberal "Elite rich", with their secret plans to enslave the people. You can see they are divided into class, divided by titles of Nobility, representing a Democracy, in other words a Socialist/communist kingdom. Whereas those who love God and believe in Christ are loyal to a Republic-America, and uphold their Constitutional Law of the land, Where everyone is equal under the law and free from tyranny.

*"And now it came to pass in this year, yea, in the two hundred and thirty and first year[231A.D], there was a **great division***

among the people[Nephites/Mayans and Lamanites/Aztecs]."
"And it came to pass that in this year there arose a people who were called the Nephites[Mayans], and they were true believers in Christ; and among them there were those who were called by the Lamanites[Aztecs]---Jacobites, and Josephites, and Zoramites;" *"Therefore the true believers in Christ, and the true worshipers of Christ , (among whom were the three disciples of Jesus who should tarry)were called Nephites, and Jacobites, and Josephites, and Zoramites."* *"And it came to pass that they who rejected the gospel were called Lamanites, and Lemuelites, and Ishmaelites; and they did dwindle in unbelief, but they did wilfully rebel against the gospel of Christ; and they did teach their children that they should not believe, even as their fathers, from the beginning, did dwindle."* *"And it was because of the wickedness and abominations of their fathers, even as it was in the beginning. And they were taught to hate the children of God, even as the Lamanites[Aztecs] were taught to hate the children of Nephi[Mayans]."(4 Nephi 1:35-39, Book of Mormon)*

Liberals/Communists want to justify their despicable actions of whoring around, lying, stealing, homosexual activities, Evolution theories, getting rich, having control, etc.. To do this and feel justified in their own hearts and actions, they must think completely opposite to the commandments of God, and because the people of God remind them of their sins, they have to hate the people of God. Thus, the Democrats/ liberals/Communists are forcing themselves into outer darkness because they reject any light that illuminates them and their actions.

"And it came to pass that two hundred and forty and four years[244A.D] had passed away, and thus were the affairs of the people. And the more wicked part of the people did wax strong, and became exceedingly more numerous than were the people of God." *"And they did still continue to build up churches unto themselves, and adorn them with all manner of precious things. And thus did two hundred and fifty years[250 A.D.] pass away, and also two hundred and sixty years[260 A.D.]"(4 Nephi 1:40-43, Book of Mormon)*

Chapter 33

Treaty Between Lamanites And Nephites To Divide North And South Continents

The Churches became polluted again, and they joined themselves to the world!
They were beginning to sin against such great Light.

260 A.D.

Do you see where this is going America? The Nephites/ Mayan people, continued falling away from the **Truth/Christ** because of the ease and temptations of <u>money</u>. Everyone was trying to get rich, and it became their God and main focus. Money is the *"Mark of the Beast", The Beast being the Corporate System,* and money and riches bring all manner of temptations, and peer pressures, competitions, Elitism, Jealousy, and **Pride**. America in 2024 has been around as a country through the mercy of God for **248** years, equally as long, and in comparison, the people are heading downhill at breakneck speed, and on the road to destroying our own civilization. It got so bad, so quickly, that the wicked outnumbered the people of God. It is the same thing going on today, and if the Gentiles, "we the people", don't come to our senses, we will destroy our own civilization, because God will not allow the secret orders to continue after they get above us, and we rebel willingly against God. It was already to the point that the unbelievers out numbered the the true believers of Christ, and it didn't help at all, seeing the true believers beginning to be proud in their hearts, and to be vain like the others, seeking for power and riches.

> *"And it came to pass that **the wicked part of the people**[Nephites / Mayans or Lamanites/Aztec] **began again to build up the secret oaths and combinations of Gadianton.**" "And* also ***the people who were called the people of Nephi**[Mayans] **began to be proud in their hearts, because of their exceeding riches, and become vain like unto their brethren, the Lamanites**[Aztecs]." "And from this time **the disciples began to sorrow for the sins of the world**[Hell]." (4 Nephi 1:42-44, Book of Mormon)*

300 A.D.

The Nephites/Mayans and Lamanites/Aztecs had become equally evil. They gave into wanting to seek out and be rich. They all adopted the secret orders[i.e. Illuminati, Jesuits] into their midst and reveled in them. The secret orders and secret societies began to flourish and spread all over the South and the North American continents. All were party to the evil, except the three disciples who would never taste of death until Christ comes again in his glory and to judge the world/Satan's kingdom. Meanwhile they were left to sorrow for the speedy plunge from being such a righteous and blessed people to a people who were now becoming so evil, and there was nothing that they could say was going to make any difference.

Once a stubborn horse takes a bit into it's mouth, it is determined to run until something stops it cold, like a two by four between the ears, or getting back to the barn, because it envisions that can of tasty grain it is accustomed to getting, once back at the barn. It is the nature of mankind to want to fit in, and so everyone it seems, is trying to outdo the other, and therefore forge ahead with reckless abandonment to what they imagine will do them the most good. They don't want anything to get in their way, especially God.

If they would just stop one moment, while they are trying to build up all of their possessions, and think about what they are really trying to accomplish, who they are injuring, who and what are they going to sacrifice to meet their goals, and just who does all their great possessions really belong? Ask themselves, can they take their riches with them when they leave this earth. If they will just stop for one moment and think about this thing, they will come to the conclusion that they are injuring themselves,and all of the ones they really care about. Everything they have, even the air that they breathe, belongs to our creator. Even the air that we breathe belongs to someone greater than us, and we are only here on earth, for only a second, compared to forever, .

Ask yourselves, what is the point of all of this earth life? What can I take with me when I die? The answer to that is, our memories, our knowledge, a knowledge of what good we have accomplished while here. Did we do any good while here? Who did we help along the way? Will our loved ones be there, where we hope to end up, because of our faith and knowledge, or can we expect to end up rubbing shoulders with evil money grubbing, lowlife liberals, selfishly trying to kill and rob each other. My hope and prayer is, that I can be a beacon of knowledge to help my family understand the truth, and stay close to God. God is the only one who is ultimately the one I depend on for anything I have, or hope to achieve. I believe in God with all my heart. I can't think of anyone who can do for me what he can do. I don't care for people who are mean, and filthy, or try to tear me down, or lie to me, or take advantage of me, or mine. I can't tolerate a liberal attitude around me, because it wears on my goals and my confidence in myself and morals that I am trying to better.

I want to go up to God, not down to Hell, therefore, we must be focused on what is our priorities and of greatest importance, like family, and knowledge, and knowing by using your knowledge you have helped others to grip onto the **Iron Rod.** I wane to see the understanding fill, and enlighten their minds and hearts with Truth. This is what really matters, and brings the most glorious satisfaction. Once you see a really priceless jewel that is worth having, and it is just within your grasp, you will sell everything you have, and do without many worldly things, in order to put your hands on that precious jewel. I see those precious jewels, first and foremost, the kingdom of God, being back in my Father's presence again. Secondly, it is my family, thirdly, it is my fellowman. I refuse to give up my knowledge of God and my integrity for some fake money, no matter how much it is, because if God didn't give it to me, I don't want it. If it comes from Satan's schemes, originating through his minions, I refuse it. No temptation, no promise of power and riches is worth the loss of God, and family in that order.

To stay close to God means eternal freedom! To see your family close to God because of your efforts means eternal happiness and real Joy. To see your fellowman attain to the kingdom of God because you spoke boldly, brings eternal joy and satisfaction. God asks us to trust him, because reaching the Kingdom of God is **glorious,** like it was when the three apostles that were swept into Heaven, and they saw unspeakable things. **We cannot even start to imagine what unspeakable things are.** It takes much faith to believe what glorious is, but as you receive knowledge by exercising your faith, as this author has, you begin to understand, and begin to see hints of eternity, and the closer you get to our Father in Heaven, through the Truth, it begins to reveal just how glorious it can be.

***"And it came to pass that when three hundred years[300A.D.] had passed away, **both the people of Nephi[Mayans] and the Lamanites[Aztecs] had become exceedingly wicked one like unto another.**" "And it came to pass that the **robbers of Gadianton**[liberals/Demoncrats/secret-orders, Jesuits/illuminati/ mafia] **did spread over all the face of the land; and there were none that were righteous save it were the disciples of Jesus. And gold and silver did they lay up in store in abundance, and did traffic in all manner of traffic.**" "And it came to pass that after three hundred and five years[305A.D.] had passed away, (and the people did still remain in wickedness) Amos died; and his brother, Ammaron, did keep the record in his stead." "And it came to pass that when three hundred and twenty years[320A.D.] had passed away, **Ammaron, being constrained by the Holy Ghost, did hide up the records which were sacred---yea, even all the sacred records which had been handed down from generation to generation, which were sacred---even until the three hundred and twentieth year from the coming of Christ."*(4 Nephi 1:45-48, Book of Mormon)

Chapter 33

Mormon Refuses To Lead The Nephite Armies, As They Invade The Lamanites

General Mormon abridges the Plates of Nephi, and others, after he is of age, and General of the Nephites/Mayans. He hides up many sacred records unto the Lord!

305 A.D.

The Nephite/Mayan prophet, Amos the younger, now dies, and Amos's brother, Ammaron, then commences to keep the record on the plates of gold, until he was told to hide them up for their own preservation, to come forth in a later period. *"And he did hide them up unto the Lord, that they might come again unto the remnant of the house of Jacob, according to the prophecies and the promises of the Lord. And thus is the end of the record of Ammaron."(4 Nephi 1:49, Book of Mormon)*

320 A.D.

Ammaron was obedient to the voice of God, and he hid them up in the same hill that the Jaredites/Olmecs/giants, held their last battle. This was just north of Guatemala, into southern Mexico. After hiding up the plates of Nephi, Ammaron,and went north to New York and told Mormon, who was only 10-years old at the time, that when he was about 24-years old, to remember the things he observes about his people, the Nephites/Mayans, and then go to the Hill Shim, in the land of Antum. There he was to find, and retrieve the plates of Nephi, and record what he had seen and observed, and write them upon the plates, but leave all other records where they are in the Hill Shim. One year later, Mormon is carried south to the land of Zarahemla, by his father.

***"*And Now I, Mormon, make a record of the things which I have both seen and heard, and call it the "Book of Mormon""* "*And about the time that Ammaron hid up the records unto the Lord, he came unto me, (I being about ten years of age, and I began to be learned somewhat after the manner of learning of my people[Nephites/Mayans]) and Ammaron said unto me:I perceive that thou art a sober child, and art quick to observe;*" "*Therefore, when ye are about twenty and four years old I would that ye should remember the things that ye have observed concerning this [Nephite/Mayan] people; and when ye are of that age go to the land Antum, unto a hill which shall be called "Shim"; and there have I deposited unto the Lord all the sacred engravings concerning this people.*" "*And behold, ye shall take the "plates of Nephi" unto yourself, and the remainder shall ye leave in the place where they are; and ye shall engrave on the plates of Nephi all the things that ye observed concerning this people[the Nephites/Mayans].*" "*And I, Mormon, being a descendant of Nephi, (and my father's name was Mormon) I remembered the things which Ammaron commanded me.*" "*And it came to pass that I being eleven years old, was carried by my father into the land southward, even to the land of Zarahemla.*"*(Mormon 1:1-6, Book of Mormon)*

Mormon, at the time he was 10-years old, must have been living with his family in the land northward, in North America in and around the area of Palmyra, New York, and was very familiar with the Hill called Cumorah. Mormon relates that he was carried by his father into the land southward, just one year later, even to Zarahemla. Many years later, as general of the Nephite/Mayan armies, seeing that the destruction of his people are imminent., and on the verge of being swept off the face of the earth, writes to the king of the Lamanites/ Aztecs, an epistle or a letter, asking for time to gather his people together for the last battle to be fought back in New York around the Hill called Cumorah. He was thinking it would give his people much advantage over the Lamanites/Aztecs, and his epistle/request was granted. Mormon, the Nephite/Mayan, man of God, describes the beginning of a war between the Nephites/Mayans and the Lamanites/Aztecs, this very same year. The Nephites/Mayans consisted of Jacobites, Josephites,and Zoramites. The Lamanites/Aztecs included the Lamanites, Lemuelites, and ishmaelites. Thus, both parties were either Lamanites/Aztecs or Nephites/Mayans.

*"And it came to pass in this year there began to be a war between the Nephites, who consisted of the Nephites, and the Jacobites, and the Josephites, and the Zoramites; and this war was between the **Nephites and the Lamanites**, and the Lemuelites, amd the Ishmaelites."* *"Now the Lamanites,and the Lemuelites and the Ishmaelites were called Lamanites, **and the two parties were Nephites**[Mayans] **and Lamanites**[Aztecs]."(Mormon 1:8-9, Book of Mormon)*

The war began on the southern borders of Zarahemla, by the "Waters of Sidon"[Rio Magdalena] in Central Colombia. *"And it came to pass that the **war** began to be among them in the borders of Zarahemla, **by the waters of Sidon.**"* *"And it came to pass that the Nephites[Mayans] had gathered together a great number of men, even to exceed the number of thirty thousand. And it came to pass that they did have in this same year a number of battles, In which the Nephites[Mayans] did beat the Lamanites[Aztecs] and did slay[kill] many of them."* *"And it came to pass that the Lamanites[Aztecs] withdrew their design, **and there was peace settled in the land;** and peace did remain for the space of about four years, that there was no bloodshed."(Mormon 1:10-12, Book of Mormon)*

The Nephites/Mayans beat the Lamanites/Aztecs, and then there was peace for another 4-years, but because the Nephites/Mayans would not acknowledge God in all things, because from them, more was expected, especially after all of their many blessings, and how God had always preserved them, they now were only equal to the Lamanite/Aztecs as to the strength of regular men. It is so true, that God rewards those who diligently seek him. Remember that the Nephites were knowledgeable in the ways of God. They had the temples, the priesthood, and were commanded to not be guilty of any first offense, or even the second offense, if possible. If they remembered to do what the Lord had commanded them to do, and were honoring God at all times, then God blessed them with super strength to defend themselves, because they were right/righteous in the eyes of the Lord, and were obeying, his commandments.

Chapter 34

Mormon Leads Again As Nephites/ Mayans Begin To Be Swept Away

Mormon was visited by Christ! And the war began in earnest.

324 A.D.

Wickedness did prevail, and as you will soon see how God began withdrawing His Spirit from among the Nephites/Mayans, and began leaving them in their own strength. He took his disciples from among them, there were no gifts of the Spirit, the Holy Ghost was absent, because there was no priesthood during wickedness and disobedience to the commandments of God. The priesthood can only be exercised in long suffering, and gentle persuasion, and the Nephites/Mayans could only understand corruption, and force. They had all joined themselves to the corporate/communist system, Satan's system.

> *But wickedness did prevail upon the face of the <u>whole land, insomuch that the Lord did</u> **take away his beloved disciples, and the work of miracles and of healing did cease because of the iniquity of the people.**" "**And there were no gifts from the Lord, and the Holy Ghost did not come upon any, because of their wickedness[evilness] and unbelief.**" (Mormon 1:13-14, Book of Mormon)*

Mormon, the last Nephite/Mayan general and a prophet of God, gives an account of being visited by Jesus Christ when he was still only 15-years old, and he knew of the goodness of Jesus. He did endeavor/attempt to preach unto his people, but his mouth was shut, and he was forbidden to preach to them, because they had willfully rebelled against their God. Even though Mormon lived among them, they didn't want to hear the truth, so he was forced to keep his mouth shut because of the hardness of their hearts. Therefore the land became cursed, and their destruction became imminent. Wake up America, because, if this is home to the brave, then everyone needs to hold those who are trying to destroy our peace, and our liberty, accountable. There is no need to think that America is special in this current age, letting so many liberals force their Democracy/socialism down our throats. America is on the road to having God withdraw his Spirit and blessings from our land. When that happens, this civilization will be destroyed also.

The only one happy about that, is Satan himself, in fact he is laughing at you America, for being so foolish and cowardly to speak up. We need to change, or God is going to give this land to someone else. If it did any good, I can tell you, he is already on the verge of giving it back to the true remnants of the house of Israel, promised to them from the Lord. Those people are already coming in by the millions, and the day is coming, when you will either have to join with them or be destroyed. Thanks to your Democrats/Liberals/socialists/communists, who think they are beating God, but are only digging their own pit, for them and their families. If you think we are having Global Warming now, well no one has seen anything yet. When God comes again, those who are evil will be the source of the fuel that melts the whole earth with a fervent heat. Now, that is Global Warming!

The Gadianton Robbers[Liberals/Democrats/Communists] were also among the Lamanites/Aztecs, and they did infest the land as a scourge/plague and a detriment to the freedom of a once free people. Private corporations got control of the coinage of the money system, (i.e. Federal Reserve Bank, Internal Revenue Service, lawyers, judges, law enforcement agencies who make a man an offender for a word, senators, House Representatives, etc.etc.)

The people began hiding up their treasures in the earth, and they became slippery, that they were not able to hang onto them, from the cursings of the land. Magic, sorcery, and witchcraft were practiced upon the land. Instead of turning to God, the people were turning to Satan for their power, even as earlier prophets of God foretold. Samuel, the Lamanite/Aztec prophet had warned the Nephites/ Mayans, hundreds of years ago, about this happening.

> "And now I, being _fifteen years of age and being somewhat of a sober[serious/studious/calculating] mind. Therefore I was visited of the Lord, and tasted_ **and knew of the goodness of of Jesus.**" "_And I did endeavor to preach unto this [the Nephite/Mayan] people, but my mouth was shut,_ **and I was forbidden that I should preach unto them; for behold they had wilfully rebelled against their God; and the beloved disciples were taken away out of the land, because of their iniquity.**" "_But I did remain among them, but I was forbidden to preach unto them, bec_**ause of the hardness of their hearts; and because of the hardness of their hearts the land was cursed for their sake.**" "_And these Gadianton robbers[socialists], who were among the Lamanites[Aztecs],_ **did infest the land, insomuch that the inhabitants thereof began to hide up their treasures in the earth; and they became slippery, because the Lord had cursed the land, that they could not hold them, nor retain them again.**" "_And it came to pass that there_ **were sorceries, and witchcrafts, and magics; and the power of the evil one was wrought upon all the face of the land,** _even unto fulfilling of all the words of Abinadi, and also Samuel the Lamanite[Aztec prophet]._"(Mormon 1:15-19, Book of Mormon)

326 A.D.

Now the Nephite/Mayan civilization was at war because of the same scourge/plague that the civilization of the Jaredites/Olmecs had let get above them, and had destroyed them. The people of Nephi/ Mayan people, instead of humbling themselves and changing, they prepared for war. They were seeking out good men that would lead them into battle. This war was going to prove the undoing of the people who once championed the cause of Jesus Christ. Mormon, the man of God, was chosen because of his size, deliberateness, and his knowledge he possessed, at the age of only 16-years old, to lead the armies of the Nephites/Mayans, into battle.

> *"And it came to pass in that same year[326 A.D.] there began to be a war again between the* **Nephites[[Mayans] and the Lamanites[Aztecs]. And notwithstanding[despite] I being young, was large in stature: therefore the people of Nephi[Mayan people] appointed me that I should be their leader, or the leader of their armies.** *"Therefore it came to pass that* **in my sixteenth year I did go forth at the head of an army of the Nephites[Mayans], against the Lamanites[Aztecs]; therefore three hundred and twenty and six years[326 A.D.] had passed away.** *"And it came to pass that in the three hundred and twenty and seventh[327A.D.] the Lamanites[Aztecs]* **did come upon us with exceedingly great power, insomuch that they did frighten my armies; therefore they would not fight, and they began to retreat towards the north** countries*[narrow neck of Panama, Desolation, Nicaragua etc].* *"*
> *"(Mormon 2:1-3, Book of Mormon)*

At this point, it was easy to frighten the armies of the Nephites/ Mayans because they were as to the strength of their enemies, the Lamanites/Aztecs, and when the next year arrived, they were invaded by such a force, that they were afraid, and therefore, Mormon could not get them to fight. So, they gave up their land of Zarahemla, in northern Colombia, and fled as far across the narrow neck of land that separated the Pacific Ocean from the Atlantic Ocean, passing through Desolation/Panama, Teancum/Eastern Costa Rica, to Angola/Costa Rica. They were then driven further to David/Nicaragua, then again to Joshua/El Salvador.

As the armies of the Nephites/Mayans fled northwest across the *narrow neck of land* passing through all of these areas as mentioned, they attempted to gather in their people as fast as possible, but the land was full of Robbers and Lamanites/Aztecs, having let the Lamanites/ Aztecs early on, overrun their borders, and now they are going to pay the price for their bad decisions. The wisest thing for the people to do at this point is to teach the gospel to all people like their lives, and freedom depended on it.

*"And it came to pass that we did come to the city of **Angola**, and we did take possession of the city, and make preparations to defend ourselves against the Lamanites[Aztecs]."* *"And it came to pass that we did fortify the city with our might; but notwithstanding[in spite of] all our fortifications the Lamanites did come upon us and drive us out of the city."* *"And **they did also drive us forth out of the land of David**."* *"And we marched forth and came to the land of **Joshua**, which was in the borders west by the seashore."* *"And it came to pass that we **did gather our people as fast as it were possible, that we might get them together in one** body."* *"But behold, **the land was filled with robbers**[traitorous liberals/demoncrats/communists etc.] **and with Lamanites[Aztecs];** and notwithstanding[despite] **the great destruction which hung over my people**[Mayans], **they did not repent of their evil doings; therefore there was blood and carnage spread throughout all the face of the land, both on the part of the Nephites[Mayans] and also on the part of the Lamanites[Aztecs]; and it was one complete revolution throughout all the face of the land."**_(Mormon 2:4-8, Book of Mormon)*

330 A.D.

The Lamanites/Aztecs had a king named Aaron, and he attacked the Nephite/Mayan armies with a force of 44,000, and Mormon faced King Aaron's armies with a force of 42,000, and did beat the Lamanites/Aztecs, and did drive them back. It appeared to Mormon, the Nephite/Mayan general, that his people were being brought down into humility, and were beginning to repent and cry unto God, but is all they were sorry for, was the loss of their possessions that they couldn't hold onto, because of all the Robbers, and of the much witchcraft. They wanted to be saved in their wickedness. They neglected to offer up a truly broken heart and a contrite spirit, but rather cursed God, then hacked and killed with the sword, and were killed, and were heaped up, upon the face of the earth.

★*"Thus **there began to be a mourning and a lamentation in all the land because of these things, and more especially*** *among the people of Nephi.*" *"And it came to pass that when* **I, Mormon, saw their lamentation and their mourning and their sorrow before the Lord, my heart did begin to rejoice within me, knowing the mercies and the long-suffering of the Lord,** *therefore supposing that he would be merciful unto them that they would again become a righteous people.*" *"But behold this my* **joy was in vain, for their sorrowing was not unto repentance, because of the goodness of God; but** *it was rather the sorrowing of the damned, because the Lord will not always suffer them to* **take happiness in sin.** " *"And they did not come unto Jesus with broken hearts and contrite spirits, but* **they did curse God, and wish to die. Nevertheless they would struggle with the sword for their** *lives."(Mormon 2:11-14, Book of Mormon)*

344 A.D.

Remember the words of Samuel, the Lamanite/Aztec prophet, when he came to tell the Nephites/Mayans about the birth of Jesus Christ hundreds of years ago. The people wouldn't listen to him, and threw him out of their city, so he was leaving, and Christ told him to return to Zarahemla, which he obeyed. In order to get them to listen to him, he had to climb upon the high walls of the city, and foretold/ prophesied of the birth of Jesus Christ, and the signs to look for, and it was fulfilled even as he said. He then warned the Nephites/Mayans about the total destruction of the Nephites/Mayans, that would come in 400-years after the coming of Jesus Christ, and they were now in the 344th-year since Samuel had made that prediction. That prediction could only be changed if the people would repent.

Instead of listening, and understanding Samuel, it made the prideful Nephites/Mayan, tough guys angry, to think that a Lamanite/Aztec could foresee the destruction of so great a people as the Nephites/ Mayans who were tried and tested in battle, and could whip a Lamanite/ Aztec any day. Therefore, it injured their pride, and they tried to hit him with rocks and arrows, to kill him. You can clearly see, that now, the Nephites/Mayans are only as strong as to the strength of the Lamanites/Aztecs. God has withdrawn from them, because He will not strive with a stubborn and wicked man or woman. The Nephites/

Mayans are slowly losing all of their lands, even the land northward across the Narrow Neck of Land.

> *"And it came to pass that my sorrow did return unto me again, and I saw that* **the day of grace was passed with them, both temporally and spiritually; for I saw thousands of them hewn down in open rebellion against their God, and heaped up as dung upon the face of the land.** *And thus* three hundred and forty and four years[344A.D.] had passed away." *"And it came to pass that in the* three hundred and forty and fifth year[345A.D.] the Nephites[Mayans] **did begin to flee before the Lamanites[Aztecs]; and they were pursued until they came even to the land of Jashon, before it was possible to stop them in their retreat."** *"And now the city of* **Jashon was near the land where Ammaron had deposited the records unto the Lord, that they might not be destroyed. And behold I had gone according to the words of Ammaron, and taken the "plates of Nephi", and did make a record according to the words of Ammaron."** *(Mormon 2:15-17, Book of Mormon)*

Because the Nephites/Mayans, had no intentions of changing and humbling themselves before God, but only wanted revenge, they were driven again to the Land/City of Jashon/Guatemala. This is getting into the close proximity of where the Hill Shim is located, which is just north of Jashon in Antum/Southern Mexico, before the borders of Guatemala. This is where Ammaron hid up the records/Plates of Nephi on the plates of gold. Ammaron instructed Mormon, when he was ten years old on what to do, and where to find them. It was Mormon's responsibility to get them, and from then on, write down what he has observed of the people of the Nephites/Mayans.

> *"And upon* the plates of Nephi **I did make a full account of all the wickedness and abominations; but upon these plates**[abridgement] **I did forbear to make a full account of their**[the Nephites/Mayans] **wickedness and abominations,** for behold, a continual scene of wickedness and abominations has been before mine eyes ever since I have been sufficient to behold the ways of man." *"And it came to pass that in this* year[345A.D.] the people of Nephi[Mayans]

were again hunted and driven. And it came to pass that we were driven forth until we had come northward to the land which was called Shem."(Mormon 2:18, 20, Book of Mormon)

The Nephites were now driven further northward to the land of Shem, which is northwest of the the Hill Shim, where the civilization of the Jaredites/giants/Olmecs ended. The Nephites/Mayans had now lost all of their lands from Zarahemla, in northern Colombia, northwest past the Land of Bountiful, across the narrow neck of land, into now southern Mexico. Here the Nephite/Mayan armies fortified the land of Shem.

*"And it came to pass that we did fortify the city **of Shem, and we did gather in our people as much as it were possible, that perhaps we might save them from destruction.** " "And it came to pass in the three hundred and forty and sixth year[346A.D.] they began to come upon us again." "And it came to pass **that I did speak unto my people, and did urge them with great energy, that they would stand boldly before the Lamanites[Aztecs] and fight for their wives, and their children, and their homes.** " "And my words did arouse them somewhat to vigor, insomuch that they did not flee from before the Lamanites[Aztecs], but did stand with boldness against them." "And it came to pass that **we did contend with an army of thirty thousand against an army of fifty thousand. And it came to pass that we did stand before them with such firmness that they did flee from before us.** " "And it came to pass that when they had fled we did pursue them with our armies, and did meet them again, **and did beat them;** nevertheless the **strength of the Lord was not with us; yea, we were left to ourselves, that the Spirit of the Lord did not abide in us; therefore we had become weak like unto our brethren."(Mormon 2:21-26, Book of Mormon)*

349A.D.

In this year, Mormon, and his armies managed to get half of their lands back, including all parts even east, across the narrow neck of land to the borders of Bountiful, but not Bountiful itself, or Zarahemla.

Chapter 35

Battle At Cumorah, Ny, The Morning Of Terror When The Mayans Were Destroyed

Treaty that divided North and South America

350 A.D.

This year the Nephites/Mayans entered into a **Treaty** with the Lamanites/Aztecs, that officially divided the lands of the two continents. In this treaty, the Nephites/Mayans agreed to accept all of the land from Bountiful, across the Narrow neck of Land, and all of the land northward into what we know as North America. The Lamanites/Aztecs agreed to accept all of the land southward/South America, beginning at the narrow neck of land, including Bountiful, where the temple was/is. This very same Bountiful, where 350 years ago, **Jesus Christ, came down from heaven and blessed the people, not just the Nephites/Mayans, but also the Lamanites/Aztecs.**

> *"And my heart did sorrow because of this **great calamity of my people,** because of their wickedness and abominations. But behold, we did go forth against the Lamanites[Aztecs] and the robbers of Gadianton[communists/liberals/Democrats/socialists etc.], until we had again taken possession of the lands of our inheritance."*

*"And the <u>three</u> hundred and forty and ninth year[349A.D] had passed away, and in the thee hundred and fiftieth year[350 A.D.] we made a treaty[compromised] with the Lamanites[Aztecs] and the robbers[communists/liberals/Democrats] of Gadianton, in which <u>**we did get the lands of our inheritance divided.**</u>" "And the Lamanites[Aztecs]did give unto us the land northward, yea even to the narrow passage which led into the land southward. And we did give unto the Lamanites[Aztecs] the land southward." <u>(Mormon</u> 2:27-29, Book of Mormon)*

The Nephites/Mayans now had 10-years in which to fortify their holdings in Desolation/Panama, in which to keep the Lamanites/Aztecs from overrunning their lands northward. The Lamanites/Aztecs at this point had no honor, they were infested with liberalism/Robbers/and thieves, and they had a king who couldn't get enough power. The word of a Democrat is not to be trusted. What is a treaty mean to a liar? A treaty means nothing to a liberal, and to trust a liberal will put you into slavery before you know it. Their word is no good, as they break treaties when they see something they want. It is greed, and power, and riches that motivate the Devil's own. The corporation is the beast, and the beast can't get enough. And the mark of the beast is the money, if you can call it money.

While the Nephites/Mayans were fortifying the land of Desolation/Panama, The Lord came to Mormon and told him to preach the gospel to the Nephites/Mayans, giving them just one last chance, telling them to Repent and be baptized, and to build up the Church of Jesus Christ/Church of God, and if they repented/changed, they would be spared. However, Mormon's efforts to obey the Lord was all in vain. The NephitesMayans didn't want to hear it, they just wanted to get even.

*"And it came to pass that the Lamanites[Aztecs] did not come to battle again until <u>ten years more had passed away.</u> And behold, I had employed my people, the Nephites[Mayans], in preparing their lands and their arms against the time of <u>battle.</u>" "And it came to pass that **<u>the Lord did say unto me: Cry unto this people---Repent ye, and come unto me, and be ye baptized, and build up again my church, and ye shall be spared.</u>" "And I did cry unto this**

people, but it was in vain; and they did not realize that it was the Lord that had spared them, and granted unto them a chance for repentance. And behold they did harden their hearts against the Lord their God." (Mormon 3:1-3, Book of Mormon)

360 A.D.

The king of the Lamanites/Aztecs, after 10-years, informed Mormon, the top General of the Nephites/Mayans that he wanted to fight, and was coming to war against them for no apparent reason, except they wanted everything the Nephites/Mayans had, even their absolute destruction. Then again, on the other hand, if the Nephites/Mayans had listened to Mormon, and had changed from their wicked ways, and built up the Church of God, they would have been spared. Remember this, that God has written the play, and he is the narrator, and he directs it, knowing how it is going to play out ahead of time. He gave them just one last chance to have a change of heart, so in the end when standing before him, they will have no excuse for their judgment.

Robbers/liberals never get enough, unless they have it all, then they turn on each other. You have to ask yourself though, whose fault is this, the Lamanites/Aztecs, who at this time, were selfish, just like a democrat/liberal, or the Nephites/Mayans, who have been warned for hundreds of years what was going to happen if they didn't do certain things, and even at the end were given one more chance, but they turned it down, because they, themselves, were grieving over their lost possessions, and wanted justice and revenge, despite the great knowledge they had, knowing about and having experienced the priceless blessings they had witnessed in the past.

Nevertheless, Mormon prepared to meet the Lamanites/Aztecs in the land of Desolation/Panama. It was the most strategic spot at this point, as it was the narrowest point, that separated two oceans, one on each side, and being that narrow, would be more easily defended.

*"And it came to pass that after this tenth year[360A.D.] had passed away, making in the whole , three hundred and sixty years from the coming of **Christ**, the king of the Lamanites[Aztecs] sent an*

*epistle[letter] unto me, which gave unto me to know **that they were preparing to [break their treaty and]come again to battle against us.*** *"And it came to pass that I did cause my people that they should gather themselves together at the **land Desolation, to a city which was in the borders, by the narrow pass which led into the land southward.**" (Mormon 3:4-5, Book of Mormon)*

361 A.D.

This year, the Lamanites/Aztecs came down to Desolation/Panama to battle, just as King Aaron of the Lamanites/Aztecs said they would, and they were beaten by the Nephites/Mayans. The next year the Lamanites/Aztecs came again, and were beaten back again. This made the Nephites/Mayans think that they were better than the Lamanites/Aztecs, so they began to boast in their own strength, and it never occurred to them to give thanks to Almighty God, for preserving them and their families. If it did enter their minds, they didn't show it by their actions. Instead, they were feeling pretty confident in their own strength, that they swore to **avenge** those who had unjustly been slaughtered by the Lamanites/Aztecs, what hadn't occurred to them, was that they were more guilty, and that is why they were being swept off of the land.

*"And there **we did place our armies, that we might stop the armies of the Lamanites[Aztecs], that they might not get possession of any of our lands; therefore we did fortify against them with all our force.**" "And it came to pass that in the three hundred and sixty and first year[361A.D.] the Lamanites[Aztecs] **did come down to the city of Desolation to battle against us;** and it came to pass that in that year we did **beat them, insomuch that they did return to their own lands again.**" "And in the three hundred and sixty and second year[362A.D.] they did come down again to battle. And we did beat them again, and **did slay a great number of them, and their dead were cast into the sea.**" "And now because of this great thing which my people, the Nephites[Mayans], had done, they began to boast in their own strength, and **began to swear before the heavens that they would avenge themselves of the blood of***

their brethren who had been slain by their enemies." "*And they did swear by the heavens, and also by the throne of God, that they would go up to battle against their enemies, and would cut them off from the face of the land.*"*(Mormon 3:6-10, Book of Mormon)*

Chapter 36

The Conquering of the Lamanites/Aztecs by the Spaniards & Catholic Church

Mormon refused to be their general!

Nephites/Mayans committed the unpardonable sin, and denied the Holy Ghost, seeking revenge, They swore they would go south and wipe the Lamanites out! They invaded South America!

The Nephite/Mayan General, Mormon, at this point completely refused to any longer be their leader and commander of the Nephite/Mayan military, because of their wickedness, by the actions they did take to show their bravery and courage, in reality were worse than what the Lamanites/Aztecs were doing to this point. The Nephites up to this point had not been the first offender, but always the defender , and always prevailed. Now they did the unforgivable by swearing by everything to avenge their brethren, including the throne of God.

They knew better than this, but despite the knowledge they had, they ignored the Spirit of Truth, pretty much sealing their judgment, and their destruction was made sure, because they for one, were not blessed by God for their disobedience, and secondly, they were only man to man, as strong as one of the Lamanites/Aztecs, and in order to win they needed overwhelming numbers. The Lamanites/Aztecs were more numerous than they, so when they decided, despite Mormon's warning, to invade the Lamanites/Aztecs, they now were guilty of the first offense. The Nephites gave raised a national emergency, and a call to arms, because they were now being invaded by the Nephites/ Mayans. On top of all that, God had withdrawn from them, and now was moving upon the Lamanites/Aztecs to destroy the Nephites/ Mayans, because of their rebellion.

"*And it came to pass that I, __Mormon did utterly refuse from this time forth to be a commander and a leader of this [Nephite/ Mayan] people, because of their wickedness and__ abomination.*" "*Behold, I had led them notwithstanding their wickedness, I had led them many times to battle, and had loved them, according to the **love of God which was in me**, all my heart; __and my soul had been poured out in prayer unto my God all the day long for them;__* nevertheless, *it was without faith, because of the hardness of their hearts.*" "*And thrice have I delivered them out of the hands of their enemies, and they have repented not of their sins.*" "__And when they had sworn by all that had been forbidden them by our Lord and Savior Jesus Christ, that they would go up unto their enemies to battle, and avenge themselves of the blood of their brethren, behold the voice of the Lord came unto me, saying:__" "__Vengeance is mine, and I will repay; and because this people repented not after I had delivered them, behold, they shall be cut off from the face of the earth.__" "*And it came to pass that I __utterly refused to go up against mine enemies; and I did even as the Lord had commanded me; and I did stand as an idle witness to manifest unto the world the things which I saw and heard, according to the manifestations of the Spirit which had testified of things to__ come.*"(Mormon 3:11-16, Book of Mormon)

363 A.D.

This year the Nephites/Mayans went south into the land Bountiful, from their agreed to lands via the treaty they had made with the Lamanites/Aztecs 13-years ago. It is one thing for the Lamanites/Aztecs to break their end of the bargain, because God is always on the side of **Right**, and because the Lamanites/Aztecs were breaking the treaty, they were driven back. However, now that the Nephites/Mayans had broken it this time, opened another can of worms(so to speak).

The Nephites/Mayans went southeast out of the Land Desolation to attack the Lamanites/Aztecs in their own lands, looking for revenge, but the Nephites/Mayans were driven back to Desolation/Panama, and were now weary. While the Nephites/Mayans were yet weary, a fresh army of Lamanites/Aztecs came upon them in Desolation, and did slaughter many of the Nephites/Mayans, and did take many prisoners. The remainder fled to the next City of Teancum/Costa Rica, by the seashore.

> *"And now it came to pass that in the three hundred and sixty and third year[363 A.D.] the Nephites[Mayans] did go up with their armies to battle against the Lamanites[Aztecs], out of the land Desolation."* *"And it came to pass that the armies of the Nephites[Mayans] were driven back again to the land of Desolation. And while they were yet weary, a **fresh army of the Lamanites**[Aztecs] **did come upon them; and they had a sore battle, insomuch that the Lamanites[Aztecs] did take possession of the city Desolation, and did slay many of the Nephites[Mayans], and did take many** prisoners."* *"And the remainder did flee and join the inhabitants of the city **Teancum. Now the city Teancum lay in the borders by the seashore; and it was also near the city** Desolation."(Mormon 4:1-3, Book of Mormon)*

It was because the Nephites/Mayans, rather than listen to God, and use their forces only as a defense, went contrary to God's commandments. God would have blessed them in maintaining their *Narrow Neck* of land/Panama, and the Lamanites/Aztecs would have had no power over them. The Nephites/Mayans once again were disobedient to the commandments of God, and His judgments were beginning to be poured out.

> *"**And it was because the armies of the Nephites[Mayams] went up unto the Lamanites[Aztecs] that they began to be smitten; for were it not for that, the Lamanites[Aztecs] could have had no power over them.**"* *"But behold, **the judgments of God will overtake the wicked; and it is by the wicked that the wicked are punished; for it is the wicked that stir up the hearts of the children of men unto bloodshed.**"(Mormon 4:4-5, Book of Mormon)*

364 A.D.

The Lamanites/Aztecs attacked the City of Teancum, but were repulsed, and then the Nephites/Mayans went forward and took back Desolation, and began again to boast in their own strength. Teancum, is in Costa Rica, located just northwest of Desolation, and also borders the land of Panama, also on the narrow neck of land.(see ancient map of the Americas)

366 A.D.

This year passed, and the Lamanites/Aztecs came against the Nephites/Mayans in Desolation/Panama. Both the Lamanites/Aztecs, and the Nephites/Mayans hearts were so hardened, that they delighted in the shedding of blood continually, General Mormon, explained.

> *"And now all these things had been done, and there had been thousands slain[killed] on both sides, both the Nephites[Mayans] and the Lamanites[Aztecs]." "And it came to pass that the three hundred and sixty and sixth year[366] had passed away, and the Lamanites[Aztecs] came again upon the Nephites[Mayans] to battle; and yet the Nephites[Mayans] repented not of the evil they had done, but persisted in their wickedness continually." "And it is impossible for the tongue to describe, or for man to write a perfect description of the blood and carnage which was among the people, both of the Nephites[Mayans] and the Lamanites[Aztecs]; and every heart was hardened, so that they delighted in blood continually." "And there never had been so great wickedness among all the children of Lehi, nor even among all the house of Israel, according to the words of the Lord, as was among this people."(Mormon 4:9-12, Book of Mormon)*

This same year the Lamanites/Aztecs took the City of Desolation/Panama, because they were more numerous. The Lamanites/Aztecs then marched against Teancum/Costa Rica, and took that city. They also took many prisoners of women and children, and did offer them up as sacrifices to their idols, which were all Satanic. This is what the Demoncrats/Socialists are doing today, even after Roe v. Wade was repealed, attempting to destroy the children through abortions, to appease their idols, especially Satan, and make no mistake about it. Now they are going state by state, trying to pass abortion laws, under states rights, no matter the rights of everyone else, born or unborn, and denying them the right to life, liberty, and the pursuit of happiness.

> *"And it came to pass that the Lamanites[Aztecs] did take possession of the **city Desolation[Panama]**, and this because their **number did exceed the number of the Nephites[Mayans]**. And they did also march forward against the **city Teancum**, and did drive the inhabitants forth out of her, **and did take many prisoners both women and children, and did offer them up as sacrifices unto their idol gods.**" "(Mormon 4:13-14, Book of Mormon)

367 A.D.

The Nephites/Mayans were angry with the Lamanites/Aztecs for offering their wives and children to Idols, that they drove the Lamanites/Aztecs out of their lands, back to the City of Desolation. _"And it came to pass that in the three hundred and sixty and seventh year[367A.D.], the Nephites{Mayans]_ **being angry because the Lamanites[Aztecs] had sacrificed their women and children,** _that they did go against the Lamanites[Aztecs]_ **with exceedingly great anger,** _insomuch that they did beat again the Lamanites[Aztecs], and_ **drive them out of their lands.**_"(Mormon 4:15, Book of Mormon)_

375 A.D.

The Lamanites/Aztecs didn't come to war again against the Nephites/Mayans until this year, 375 A.D.. They used this time to gather such a large military, that they would overrun the Nephites/Mayans and destroy them once and for all. So when they came this year, they came with all of their powers; and they were not numbered because of the greatness of their numbers. From this time forth, the Nephites/Mayans could never again, gain any power, or advantage over the Lamanites/Aztecs, but the Nephites/Mayans began to be swept from the land, *as dew before the sun.* The Lamanites/Aztecs did come against the Nephites/Mayans in Desolation/Panama, and did drive them out of Desolation/Panama, through Teancum/Costa Rica, to Boaz/Nicaragua.

> *"And the Lamanitess[Aztecs] did <u>not come again against the Nephites[Mayans] until the three hundred and seventy and fifth year[375 A.D.]</u>." "And this year* **they did come down against the Nephites with all their powers; and they were not numbered because of the greatness of their** <u>number.</u>*" "And from this time forth did the Nephites <u>gain no power over the Lamanites[Aztecs], but began to be swept off by them, even as a dew by the sun"</u>."(Mormon 4:16-23, Book of Mormon)*

Chapter 37

General Mormon Empathizes With His People, And Once Again Leads Them In The Final Battle!

Mormon, changed had a change of heart, about leading his people into battle. He didn't have it in his heart to deny them of his leadership, because many looked upon him as if he could save them if he would just lead them. He knew the gospel, and that, only they could save themselves, but as long as the people turned their backs upon God, and ignored him, by not reverencing him, Mormon knew that he, himself could not do anything for them, except be an example and a ray of hope.. So Mormon, rather than watch as a neutral bystander, he saw it as his duty to lead his people knowing there was no hope that the judgments of God would be reversed. Mormon still loved his people and had pity upon them, and he was showing it by offering up his life to help them, and he did.

> And it came to pass _that the Lamanites[Aztecs] did come down against the_ **city Desolation;** _and there was an exceedingly sore battle fought in the land Desolation[Panama], in the which_ **they did beat the Nephites[Mayans].**" "_And they[Mayans] fled again from before them, and they came to the_ **city Boaz[Nicaragua]; and there they did stand against the Lamanites[Aztecs] with exceeding boldness,** _insomuch that the Lamanites did not beat them until they_

had come again the second time." "*And when they had come the second time, the Nephites[Mayans] were driven and slaughtered with an exceedingly great slaughter; their women and their children were again sacrificed unto idols[Satan].*" "*And it came to pass that the Nephites[Mayans] did again flee from before them, taking all the inhabitants with them, both in towns and villages.*" "*And now I, Mormon, seeing that the Lamanites[Aztecs] were about to "overthrow" the land, therefore I did go to the Hill Shim[Southern Mexican penninsula], and did take up the records which Ammaron had hid up to the Lord.*"*(Mormon 4:19-23, Book of Mormon)*

"*And it came to pass I[General Mormon] did go forth among the Nephites[Mayans], and did repent of the oath which I had made[changed his mind] that I would no longer assist them; and they gave me command again of their armies, for they looked upon me as though I could save them from their afflictions.*" "*But behold, I was without hope, for I knew of the judgments of the Lord which should come upon them; for they repented not of their iniquities, but did struggle for their lives without calling upon that Being who created them.*" "*And it came to pass that the Lamanites[Aztecs] did come against us as we had fled to the city of Jordan; But behold, they were driven back that they did not take the city at that time.*" "*And it came to pass that they came against us again, and we did maintain the city. And there were also cities which were maintained by the Nephites[Mayans], which strongholds did cut them off that they could not get into the country which lay before us, to destroy the inhabitants of our land[in the north].*" *(Mormon 5:1-4, Book of Mormon)*

379 A.D.

It became a matter of policy from this time forth, that wherever the army passed through in it's continual retreat ahead of the Lamanites/Aztecs army, the Nephites/Mayans needed to gather everyone including women, and children, otherwise when the Lamanite/Aztecs forces came through, and they surely would, as they were following the retreat of the Nephites/Mayans, they would take them prisoners and offer up the women and children to their Satanic Idols, and their cities would be burned if possible.

> "But it came to pass **that whatsoever lands we passed by, and the inhabitants thereof were not gathered in, were destroyed by the Lamanites[Aztecs], and their towns, and villages, and cities were burned with fire;** and thus three hundred and seventy and nine years[379A.D.] passed away." (Mormon 5:5, Book of Mormon)

380 A.D.

This year the Lamanites/Aztecs did come against the Nephites/Mayans with such great numbers, that they did tread the people of the Nephites/Mayans under their feet. Only those who were swifter than the Lamanites/Aztecs did escape. There was a continual scene of bloodshed and carnage, from city to city, that it is hard to comprehend.

> "And it came to pass that in the three hundred and eightieth year[380 A.D.] the **Lamanites[Aztecs] did come again against us**[the Mayans/Nephites] **to battle, and we did stand against them boldly; but it was all in vain, for so great were their numbers that they did "tread" the people of the Nephites[Mayans] under their feet**" "And it came to pass that we did again take to flight, **and those whose flight was swifter than the Lamanites[Aztecs] did escape, and those whose flight did not exceed the Lamanites[Aztecs] were swept down and destroyed.**" "And now behold, I, Mormon, do not desire to harrow up the souls of men in casting before them **such an awful scene of blood and carnage as was laid before mine eyes; but I, knowing that these things must surely be made known, and that all things which are hid must be revealed**[shouted from] **upon the roof-tops---**" "And also that a **knowledge of these things must come unto the remnant of these people, and also unto the Gentiles[us in America], who the Lord**[Jesus Christ] **hath said should scatter this people and this people should be counted as naught among them---therefore I [Mormon] write a small abridgment,** daring not to give a full account of the things which

*I have seen, **because of the commandment which I have received, and also that ye might not have too great sorrow because of the wickedness of this** [the Nephite/Mayan] **people.**" "**And now behold,** this I speak unto their **seed**[posterity],**and also to the Gentiles who have care for the house of Israel, that realize and know from whence their blessings come.**" (Mormon 5:6-10, Book of Mormon)*

Now anyone can see how the Lamanites/Aztecs have overrun the North American Continent and why the Nephites/Mayans are extinct, except for those who have joined the Lamanites/Aztecs or be destroyed, or somehow managed to hide, or escape by sea. Now Mormon was there as his people were driven from city to city, from land to land, and was watching the destruction of his people.

Chapter 38

The Gathering Of The Armies Of The Nephites/Mayans To The Land Of Cumorah/New York!

For the Morning of Terror when the Nephites/Mayans became extinct!

General Mormon, knowing the end of the Nephites/Mayans was inevitable, so instead of making his people, the Nephites/Mayans be torchered with always being hunted and driven, and knowing that the Lamanites/Aztecs were next, going to overrun the mainland of North America, wrote a letter to the king of the Lamanites/Aztecs asking him to grant the Nephites/Mayans the opportunity to gather together his people to the Land of Cumorah, by a Hill called Cumorah, and there meet him and his armies. This land of Cumorah is in the State of New York. The Hill Cumorah is near to where Joseph Smith lived at the time in Palmyra, New York. This is the same Hill where Joseph Smith received the Plates of Nephi recorded on gold plates, from General Mormon's son, Moroni. Don't you think that God told Mormon to do this thing, and ask for the epistle to be granted to his people, knowing his people were going to be destroyed?

It is my honest opinion, that the Lord told Mormon to ask for this epistle, in order to gather all of the Nephites/Mayans in for one major battle, so that he could position the records he was keeping, and bury them in the Hill Cumorah, knowing the purposes of God. The purposes of God in this thing was to give Joseph Smith the ability at such a young age to have access to these records, thus bringing them forth for the benefit of the Nephites/Mayans. Mormon knew these things before hand, and he deliberately asked for this area, knowing the will of the Lord, to give that young man a leg up, and thus fulfilling his own righteous purposes.

> "And **now** *I finish my record concerning the "destruction of my people, the Nephites[Mayans].* And it came to pass that *we did march forth before the Lamanites[Aztecs]."* "And **I, Mormon, wrote and epistle**[letter] **unto the king of the Lamanites[Aztecs], and desired of him that he would grant unto us[** the Nephites/ Mayans] **that we might gather together our people unto the land"of Cumorah," by a hill which was called"Cumorah,"** and there we could give battle." "And it came to pass that *the king of the Lamanites[Aztecs] did grant unto me[*Mormon]*the thing which I desired.*" "And it came to pass that we **did march forth to the land of Cumorah; and we did pitch our tents round about the hill Cumorah; and it was in a land of many** *waters[lakes], rivers, and fountains[springs/wetlands/etc.]; and here we had hoped to* **gain advantage over the Lamanites[Aztecs]."** (Mormon 6:1-4, Book of Mormon)

384 A.D.

All of the people of the Nephites/Mayans gathered in from coast to coast, from north to south within a 4-year period, as much as could be expected, as also were the Lamanites/Aztecs gathering their people for this last and final battle in the State of New York, at the Hill Cumorah. Now Mormon was beginning to be old, and so he saw fit to preserve all of the records that were entrusted to him, which were sacred. He could not allow the records of his people the Nephites/ Mayans, to fall into the hands of the Lamanites/Aztecs, because they would destroy them. Mormon, therefore, hid up all of the records in the Hill Cumorah, which had been entrusted to him by the Lord, save it were these few plates of Nephi, and his abridgment, which were passed to his son, Moroni, who later in the due time of the Lord, Moroni passed them on to the Prophet Joseph Smith.

"*And when three hundred and eighty and four years[384 A.D.] had passed away, **we had gathered in all the remainder of our people unto the land Cumorah.** [that would be gathered].*" "*And it came to pass that when we had gathered in **all our people in one** [one main body] unto **the land Cumorah, behold I, Mormon, began to be old; and knowing "it to be the last struggle of my people[the Nephites/Mayans], and having been commanded of the Lord that I should not suffer the records which have been handed down by our fathers, which were sacred, to fall into the hands of the Lamanites[Aztecs], (for the Lamanites[Aztecs] would destroy them) therefore I made this record** [on gold plates] **out of the "plates of Nephi", and hid up in the hill Cumorah all the records which were entrusted to me by the hand of the Lord, "save it were these few plates which I gave unto my son Moroni." (Mormon 6:5-6, Book of Mormon)*

In this same year, General Mormon of the Nephite/Mayan armies, gives a description of when the people of Nephi/Mayans watched as the masses of Lamanites/Aztecs were marching towards them ready to do battle. The hearts of the women and children were filled with terror, because of the greatness of their numbers.

"*And it came to pass **that my people[Nephites/Mayans], with their wives and their children, did now behold the armies of the Lamanites[Aztecs] marching towards them; and with that awful fear of death which fills the breasts of all the wicked, did they await to receive them.*" "*And it came to pass that **they came to battle against us, and every "soul was filled with terror because of the greatness of their numbers.***" "*And it came to pass **that they** [the Lamanites[Aztecs] **did fall upon my people** [the Nephites/Mayans] **with the sword, and with the bow, and with the arrow, and with the ax, and with all manner of weapons of war.***" "*And it came to pass **that my men were hewn down, yea, even my ten thousand who were with me, and I** [Mormon] **fell wounded in**

the midst; and they passed by me that they did not put an end to my life." "And when they had gone through and hewn down all my people save it were twenty and four of us, (among whom was my son Moroni) and we having survived the dead of our people, did behold on the morrow, when the Lamanites[Aztecs] had returned unto their camps, from the top of the hill Cumorah, ten thousand of my people who were hewn down, being led in the front by me[Mormon]." (Mormon 6:7-20, Book of Mormon)

Now the reader knows where they, who used to inhabit those cities in South and Central America, and North America, who they are, where they came from, where they went and how and why. Mormon in his last words , before he is killed, and his son, Moroni takes responsibility of these last plates of gold, known as an abridgment from the plates of Nephi. He now admonishes the Lamanites/Aztecs to lay down their weapons of war, with these last and parting words to them, and pleads with them to receive the **gospel of Jesus Christ and be saved**.

"And now, behold, I would speak somewhat unto the remnant of this people who are spared, if it so be that God may give unto them my words, that they may know of the things of their fathers; yea, I speak unto you, ye remnant of the house of Israel[Lamanites/ Aztecs]; and these are the words which I speak:" "Know ye that ye are from the house of Israel." "Know ye that ye must come unto repentance, or ye cannot be saved." "Know ye that ye must lay down your weapons of war, and delight no more in the shedding of blood, and take them not again, save it be that God shall command you." "Know ye that ye must come to the knowledge of your fathers, and repent of all your sins and iniquities, and believe in Jesus Christ, that he is the Son of God, and that he was slain by the Jews, and by the power of the Father he hath risen again, whereby he hath gained the "victory" over the grave; and also in him is the sting of death swallowed up." "And he bringeth to pass the resurrection of the dead, Whereby man must be raised to stand before his judgment-seat." "And he hath brought to pass the redemption of the world[those without knowledge and

_understanding], **whereby** he that is found **guiltless before him** at
the judgment day hath **it given unto him to dwell in the presence
of God in his kingdom,** to sing ceaseless praises with the choirs
above, unto the **Father, and unto the Son, and unto the Holy
Ghost, which are one God** [one in purpose, and united], **in a state
of happiness which hath no end**[throughout eternity/forever]"._
(Mormon 7:1-7, Book of Mormon)

"Therefore **repent, and be baptized in the name of Jesus, and
lay hold upon the gospel of Christ,** which shall be set before you,
not only in this record **but also in the record which shall come
unto the Gentiles from the Jews**[Bible] which record[**Bible**] shall
come from the Gentiles unto you." "For behold, this is written for the
intent that ye **may believe that;** and if ye believe that ye will believe
this also; and if ye believe this ye will know concerning your fathers,
and also the marvelous works which were wrought by the power of
God among them." "And ye also will know that ye are a remnant
of the seed of **Jacob;** Therefore, **ye are numbered among the people
of the first covenant;** and if it so be **that ye believe in Christ and
are baptized, first with water, then with fire and with the Holy
Ghost, following the example of our Savior,** according to that
which he hath commanded us, and it **shall be well with you in the
day of judgment. Amen.**"_(Mormon 7:8-10, Book of Mormon)_

Moroni, the last survivor out of 24-Nephites/Mayans was still
alive, being left for dead, as the Lamanites/Aztecs waded through
the Nephite/Mayan Armies in the last battle, now collects the Plates
of Nephi from his father Mormon, before Mormon is killed later,
when the Lamanites/Aztecs return to mop up, So to speak. After all,
Mormon was old and wounded and could not flee. Moroni, adds his
last words, and then buries these plates in the Hill Cumorah, later to
come forth, and be translated by Joseph Smith, also a direct descendant
of Joseph who was sold into Egypt. Joseph Smith was only 14-years
of age, when Moroni, an Angel of God, appeared to Joseph Smith
and told him about the abridged version by Mormon, from the Plates
of Nephi, onto plates of gold, for their preservation, for a very long,
period of time, and where they were hidden.

*"Behold I, **Moroni,** do finish the record of my father, **Mormon.** Behold, I have but a few things to write, which things I have been commanded by my father." "And now it came to pass <u>that after the great and tremendous battle **at Cumorah**</u>[in New York], <u>the Nephites[Mayans] who had escaped into the country southward were hunted by the Lamanites[Aztecs], **until they were all destroyed.**"* "And my father [Mormon] also was killed by them, and I even remain alone to **write the sad tale of the destruction of my people**[the Nephites/Mayans].But behold, they **are gone,** and I fulfill the commandment of my father. And whether they[the Lamanite/Aztecs] slay me, I know not." "Therefore I will **write and hide up the records in the earth;** and whither[where] I go it mattereth not." (Mormon 8:1-4, Book of Mormon)*

*"Behold, my father hath made this record, and he hath <u>written the intent thereof.</u> And behold, I would write it also if I had room upon the plates, but I have not; and **ore** I have none, for I am alone." <u>"My father hath been slain in battle, and all my kinsfolk, and I have not friends nor whither to go; and how long the Lord will suffer that I may live I know not.</u> **Behold four hundred years**[Now 400 A.D.] **have passed away since the coming of our Lord and Savior."** "And behold, <u>The **Lamanites[Aztecs] have hunted my people, the Nephites[Mayans], from city to city and from place to place, even until they are no more; and great and marvelous is the destruction of my people, the Nephites[Mayans].**</u>" "And behold, **it is the hand of the Lord which hath done it.** And behold also, the Lamanites[Aztecs] are at war one with another; <u>and the whole face of this land is one continual round of murder and bloodshed; and no one knoweth the end of the war.</u>"(Mormon 8:5-8, Book of Mormon)*

*"And now, behold, I say no more concerning them, for there <u>are none save it be the Lamanites[Aztecs] and robbers that do exist upon the face of the land</u>." "And there are none that do know the true God save it be the **disciples of Jesus, who did tarry in the land until the wickedness of the people was so great that the Lord would not suffer them to remain with the people;** and whether they be upon the face of the land no man knoweth." "But behold, **my***

father[Mormon] and I [Moroni] have seen them, and they have ministered unto us." "*And whoso receiveth[believes] this record, and shall not condemn it because of the imperfections which are in it, the same shall know of greater things than these. Behold, I am Moroni; and were it possible, I would make all things known unto you.*" "*Behold, I make an end concerning this people. I am the son of Mormon, and my father was a direct descendant of Nephi[who came out of Jerusalem in 600 B.C.].(Mormon 8:9-13, Book of Mormon)*

"*And I am the same who hideth up this record unto the Lord; the plates[gold sheets] thereof are no worth, because of the commandment of the Lord. For he truly saith that no one shall have them to get gain; but the record thereof is of great worth; and whoso shall bring it to light, him will the Lord bless.*" "*For none can have power to bring it to light save it be given him of God; for God wills that it shall be done with an eye single to his glory, or the welfare of the ancient and long dispersed covenant people of the Lord.*" "*And Blessed is he that shall bring this thing to light; for it shall be brought out of darkness unto light, according to the word of God; yea, it shall be brought out of the earth, and it shall shine forth out of the darkness, and come unto the knowledge of the people; and it shall be done by the power of God.*"(Mormon 8: 13-16, Book of Mormon)

Chapter 39

The depravity, by the Roman Catholic Church, upon the Nephites[Mayans]/ Lamanites[Aztecs]

then calling it Christianity?

1492 A.D.

Following the victory of *"El Sid"*, The Spanish Hero, in driving the Moors from the shores of Grenada, Spain, the King and Queen, Ferdinand and Isabella, granted Columbus's request in making a voyage across the Atlantic Ocean, in anticipation of new wealth. They funded his expedition by providing three ships, the Nina, the Pinta, and the Santa Maria, and paying and providing him sailors, and provisions.

Columbus set sail from the Canary Islands having the idea that he could sail west across the Atlantic and reach Japan, China, and India, etc.. However, although it turned out as a major miscalculation, due to not enough knowledge of the world at the time, He was put into a position of having very favorable winds, that carried him and his ships to the islands off of the East Coast bordering our Central America, today, more like the Gulf area. On October 12, 1492, he pressed onto Cuba and Haiti, and discovered an island that was home to a whole tribe of white natives/Mayans.

"And the angel said unto me:What beholdest thou? And I said: <u>I</u> <u>*behold many nations and kingdoms.*</u> *" "And he said unto me:<u>These are</u>* <u>*the nations and kingdoms of the* **Gentiles**</u>*[Europe]." "And it came* *to pass that <u>I saw among the nations of the Gentiles</u> **the formation** **of a great church**." "And the angel said unto me: **Behold the** **formation of a church which is most abominable above all other** **churches**[Catholic Church]**, which slayeth the saints of God, yea,** **and tortureth them and bindeth them down, and yoketh them** **with a yoke of iron, and bringeth them down into** captivity[Dark Ages]." "And it came to pass that I beheld this <u>great and abominable</u>* <u>*church;* **and I saw the devil that he was the founder of it.**</u> *" "And **I** **also saw gold, and silver, and silks, and scarlets, and fine twined** **linen, and all manner of precious clothing; and I saw many** **harlots**[whores]." "And the angel spake unto me, saying: **Behold the** **gold, and the silver, and the silks, and the scarlets, and the fine** **twined linen, and the precious clothing, and the harlots, are the** **desires of this great and abominable** church[the whore of all the earth].*"(1 Nephi 13:2-8, Book of Mormon)*

Of course, because of what Columbus had found, in the name of the Spanish government, opened up the doors for the Spaniards to come with their military to claim the new world for their own domination. Spain was dominated and under the control and were subject to the Catholic Church. The Catholic Church followed the military with their, alleged holy christian, Catholic priests, and Jesuit missionaries, to the detriment of the natives, especially to the islands inhabited by the remaining Nephites/Mayans, also with many records containing history of themselves, and of the Lamanites/Aztecs.

"And it came to pass that I looked and beheld many waters[Atlantic *Ocean];<u>And they divided the Gentiles[Europe] from the seed[posterity]</u>* <u>*of* **my brethren**</u>*[Nephites/Mayans and Lamanites/Aztecs]." "And it* *came to pass that the angel said unto me: Behold **the wrath of God** **is upon the seed of my** <u>brethren.</u>" "And I looked and <u>beheld a man</u>* <u>*among the Gentiles[Columbus], who was separated from the seed of*</u> <u>*my brethren by the many waters; and I beheld the* **Spirit of God,**</u> **<u>that it came down and wrought upon the man</u>***[spoke to his spirit]**;*

and he went forth upon the many waters, even unto the seed of my brethren, who were in the promised land[North and South America]."(1 Nephi 13:10-12, Book of Mormon)

Why would the Cardinal: Diego Durand, directly from the Vatican of the Catholic Church, want to burn all the records of the Mayans? Answer: They discovered that the Nephites/Mayans actually followed the teachings of Jesus Christ, and their records talked about Him often. They wanted to stamp out all existence of a people who at one time, were greatly blessed of the Lord, especially since their master, Satan was the source of their power, and their goal is to keep Christ impaled on the cross as a perpetual sacrifice, deceiving the people, wanting them to believe that Christ is not coming back. Therefore they must continue living their lie in order to keep their dominion over the people of their Roman, empire. (see: https://www.youtube.com/watch?v=Uho8VRLaOsA :)

….."At the time of the Spaniards' arrival, more than **200,000 people are believed to have lived in what had become the capital of the *Aztec* empire.** Its' settlers were named **Aztec** by the alleged experts, with the opinion, they came from the **mystical *Aztlan*** (in northern Mexico)." (see the book: "Mexico" by McCarta & Nelles Verlag; History and Culture).

This book describes the culture of these residents who once lived and prospered in Mexico as if they lived among them, therefore were able to tell you exactly what they believed, and what they did. However, many of the things they describe, are not any different than other experts wanting to paint credible pictures concerning the lives of these ancient peoples, regardless of the many names they come up with. Believing, or assumption, and opinions won't get it done. Fact or law is what you can hang your hat on. When alleged experts begin to mention terms like *"evolved"*, *"millions of years ago"*, *"pre-historic"*, *etc.*. Then don't believe it, they are lying to you. Search for the truth, and something that makes sense.

Ask God personally, by getting on your knees, and talking to him about your concerns, just like you talk to your best friend. I do this all the time, and I search, and as we show him that we really want and need to know, he never will let you down. As you look, search, pray, and are diligent, the Truth will come into your mind that makes sense. As you exercise your faith in him, by receiving the gospel of Jesus Christ, and enter into that straight and narrow gate of Baptism, by one who is in authority, will change your life.

At one time, these peoples worshiped and gave glory to Almighty God, and His Son, Jesus Christ. They observed the *"Law of Moses"*, as did the people back in Jerusalem before the coming of Christ. Their many sacrifices were mainly of the unblemished cattle, leading up to the death of Jesus Christ, after which the blood sacrifices ended. These reasons were why their temples were built with alters, for this purpose. It wasn't until several years before 400 A.D. when the Lamanites[Aztecs] turned to other gods. Satan had such control upon the hearts of the people, and they rebelled against God, and warred against the Nephites/Mayans, until nearly destroying them to extinction.

From 400 A.D. then to the year 1492 A.D., when the Spaniards began coming with their armies, to subjugate the natives, allows for plenty of time for a people once enlightened by God, to entirely go backwards into darkness, and ignorance, as did the people of the Americas. True to God's promise, was sent the Gentiles[i.e. Spaniards] to conquer these people at first. Over 1000 years had gone by, and they had spent that time going backwards, fighting among themselves, gathering into tribes, managing to stay alive by hunting, etc.. The native Lamanites/Aztecs were in darkness.

Many of the so-called pyramids that were built, were built as towers, so that the military of these people were able to look over their kingdoms and see in advance if any enemies were approaching. Some were built with alters on top so as all could see the offering of the sacrificial lamb, or bullock, or goat, in the observance of the *law of Moses,* which law ended at 34 A.D., because that was when Jesus Christ was hung on the cross, as the last blood sacrifice. If they continued any sacrifices after that, very well could have been human sacrifices, as it does describe in the Book of Mormon, of the many sacrifices of all their prisoners, especially women and children, captured from the Nephites/Mayans and sacrificed to their many gods. That didn't happen until hundreds of years later when the Lamanites/Aztecs, because of unbelieving, later generations, turned back to their old traditions. There were a lot of Nephites/Mayans who continually turned backwards and sinned against the truth, and also turned to witchcraft, and wizardry, etc., that could have been practicing human sacrifice, thinking the devil was more powerful than God. If this happened, it was really because the people became wicked and loved their vices, their riches, and lusts and possessions, more than they loved God.

It was in 200 A.D.--210 A.D. that the Catholic Church was organized, and they were more depraved than any native Lamanite/ Aztec, from the beginning. They murdered, and tortured their prisoners in many inhuman ways. They began with Christ, flaying him with a whip with bits of glass tied into it's strands, literally ripping pieces of flesh off of His body with every strike. Then nailing him to a cross, and publicly mocking and trying to humiliate him. Later the early apostles were killed and sacrificed in many different ways. One was boiled in oil, one crucified upside down, some had their heads cut off, etc.

In the book by: McCarta & Nelles Verlag titled: Mexico, an account is given of how "*Christian*" the Catholic Church really was.

"The 34-year-old Spanish Officer **Hernan Cortes** was among those who set off on exploratory voyages after **hearing Columbus's reports** of the **New World's riches.** By **1504**, he had already come to Hispaniola (the present-day Dominican Republic) and had become a major land-owner on the island of Cuba by **1517**. At roughly the same time, the first Spanish expeditions had reached the **Yukatan** coast under the command of **Francisco Hernandez de Cordoba** and **Juan de Grijalva**, discovering the white city of Tulum standing high above the sheer coastline. **Cortes also sailed from Cuba to Yukatan, where he vanquished a *Mayan tribe*...**"

"...The advance on *Tenochtitlan* began in the summer, with indigenous bearers guiding his small army into the highlands. En route, the first resistance from the native population was met in the city of *Tlaxcala*, 150 meters to the east of the **Aztec** capital. They were no match for Cortes' army. Thousands lost their lives, while the remainder joined the victor as auxiliary troops. The reception in *Cholula was friendly*, but the Spaniard nonetheless had some **5,000 of it's inhabitants <u>slaughtered</u>**, ..."

"...Cortes advanced into <u>western Mexico as well as</u> **Oaxaca and Yukatan**, subjugating, and enslaving the peoples who settled in these regions."

" **The Spanish conquerors committed the** *most gruesome atrocities* **against the population, recording even the smallest details of many of their misdeeds.** On the taking of a city, as many as possible of the **indigenous people were killed**, even when they **put up no resistance.** The soldiers were followed **by the <u>priests and monks of the Catholic Church, who sponsored a further series of bloodbaths.</u>** It is thus a matter of record that in the summer of **1562, <u>4500 Mayas</u> were tortured to their deaths** in one town in **Yukatan** *because they confessed <u>to having worshipped "foreign gods"[Jesus Christ?]</u>.* **6300 more of the town's inhabitants were inflicted the gravest injuries. <u>Burnings, roasting, crushing and breaking limbs, upsidedown hangings, setting bloodhounds onto</u>** *infants* **<u>and children, and other methods of torture</u>** applied by the **priests and soldiers, simply** *<u>defy description.</u>*"

"In this manner, Mexico became Nueva *Hispania,* or New Spain. An enigma which has scarcely been explained to this day is how Cortes managed, with just 700 men to conquer all of Mexico and Central America, an era comprising more than **20 million inhabitants....**"

"...Even after the conquest of Mexico, the Spaniards continued **waging their campaign <u>of destruction</u>, demolishing** countless palaces and temples. On their sites, colonial buildings were constructed from the old stones, Indigenous **slaves were forced to work** under the supervision of Spanish master builders and architects..."

"...All of this splendor stands in sharp contrast to the *actual origin* of the new Mexican *"nobility"*. Almost without exception, they were Spanish immigrants with few means who achieved their wealth and titles by **means of** *unscrupulous business dealings and exploitation of the native population."*

"Anybody who opposed the **Spanish was killed.** This fate **befell not only the indigenous chiefs(***kazics***), but native clerical elite as well.** The Spanish administrative system was established and *Christianity* [Democracy/Force] raised to the status of state religion. The conquerors and **Catholic church worked hand-in-hand. The Christian Orders [secret orders, i.e. illuminati, Jesuits] first** and foremost the *Franciscans*(from 1523) with the Dominicans, Augustinians and **Jesuits,** in train, were never far behind the conquering soldiers. In just a **century**[100-years] after the Conquest, hundreds of churches, cloisters and monasteries were erected, accompanied by the achievement of an almost **total Christianization [Catholicised by force and intimidation]"** *(1 Nephi 13:4-8, Book of Mormon)*

The question still remains: **Where is the Christianity in all of these actions by the Catholic Church?** Did Christ exercise force and dominion upon the people, or did He exercise kindness and long suffering, meanwhile teaching the people to love one another? Did Jesus Christ while He was on the earth not raise the dead, heal the sick, give sight to the blind, drive devils out of the mentally inflicted? Did He not teach the people that the two greatest commandments were first: Love God with all of your heart, might, mind, and strength, and that the second; is equal to it; love your neighbor as yourself?

Christ was against revenge, or lust of the flesh or for riches. He didn't need any of that, because He owned it all already, since He is the creator. He didn't need power, or control, but only wants your humble heart. He never uses force, but only long suffering and gentle persuasion through teaching. If this was not so, would an ever-powerful King allow Himself to be taken, flogged, and hung on a cross, so that you, if and when you repent can have something glorious in the world to come?

To be Catholic is not Christian. **Christ is a God of Truth and free-agency, whereas, Satan is a god of lies and force.** This is why today, South America, Mexico, and the Indian tribes of North America are predominantly Catholic today. You, Hispanics and natives of both North, Central, and South America, who read this book are from the remnants of the Tribe of Joseph, who was sold into Egypt. His two sons Manasseh and Ephraim went on to have large posterity, of whom the Nephites/Mayans, and Lamanites/Aztecs, are derived. My plea to you, is to turn back to Almighty God in the name of Jesus Christ, and He will hear your prayers and grant your desires as he has so often done in the past.

Years from now, when we stand to be judged in front of our true living, God the Father, and His Son Jesus Christ, we will receive our rewards based upon our actions in this life, and our actions are based upon the things we believed, from the knowledge we allowed to work upon our intelligence. The knowledge we have enables us to act, in order to receive the blessings upon which the law is predicated. Many are going to be disappointed and surprised when they didn't receive a reward for just a belief. They believe God is going to give them something, knowing they didn't deserve, but expect it, because they believe that they are special and God is all love. God is all love, but he is also a God of *Justice*.

For example: If you want Freedom, you must live the Laws of freedom; if you want good health, you must live the laws that provide good health; if you want to be spiritually blessed, and have your family blessed as well, you must pray, search the scriptures, and receive the gospel of Jesus Christ and live it. These principles are prerequisite, in order to receive the blessings of revelation and understanding. Even to those who think they have got it made, and to them who have been living the way they should, as told to them by their living *"Oracle"*, the prophet. There are going to be many who will be greatly surprised, and disappointed that they didn't acquire as much as they had supposed.

There will be those who have pinned their highest hopes and blessings on the sayings and words of men in positions of leadership, depending on him/them to get them to the highest kingdom, when they should have searched the scriptures for themselves, therefore procrastinated their change. Then standing before Almighty God and His Son, it will be revealed to them, that they do not belong to the *Church of the Firstborn,* because they have been deceived, and were not *valiant* in the testimony of Jesus Christ. Then shall there be weeping and wailing, and gnashing of teeth, and there is nothing that can be done, because all people have done it unto themselves, and no one will be able to say that the judgments of God are not just.

It is my most sincere and humble testimony, from the bottom of my heart, that God is alive and real, and His Son, Jesus Christ also lives and is so real. I am so grateful that God, through His Spirit of the Holy Ghost/Truth, has blessed me with the knowledge, that I am wanting the reader to see and understand. The truth of the Mayans and Incas and the Aztecs and Toltecs, and Olmecs/Giants, etc., is right in front of us waving a bright florescent banner.

I testify to you that the ***Book of Mormon*** is true, and that Joseph Smith was called of God in this Latter-Days to bring the record of the Nephites **[Mayans and Toltecs etc.]**; Lamanites **[Aztecs, etc.]**, and Jaredites/Giants **[Olmecs]** to light and has set the truth on a mountain top in flames, shouting to the world, to those who are in ignorance and darkness, to come to the light/truth, and receive understanding, and be saved in the Kingdom of God. The Book of Mormon is true, as has been proven, and the Spirit also tells the reader that the Book of Mormon is true, and if the Book of Mormon is true, then **everything** Joseph Smith has said and did is also true. I the author have satisfied my own search of the truth, and I have no doubt but what the contents and the facts, contained in this book are so true, and I say it, in the Name of: Jesus Christ, Amen.

*"And now I, Nephi, **cannot say more; the Spirit stoppeth mine utterance, and I am left to mourn because of the unbelief, and the wickedness, and the ignorance, and the stiffneckedness of men; for they will not search knowledge, nor understand great knowledge, when it is given unto them in plainness, even as plain as word can be."*** *(2 Nephi 32:7, Book of Mormon)*

*"My people are destroyed for lack of knowledge: because thou hast rejected knowledge, I will also reject thee, that thou shalt be no priest to me: **seeing thou hast forgotten the law of thy God, I will also forget thy children.** "As they were increased [became successful], so they sinned against me[decided they needed God no longer]: **therefore will I change their glory into shame."** (Hosea 4:6-7, KJV)*

BIBLIOGRAPHY

Holy Bible (KJV)

Book of Mormon

Doctrine and Covenants

Pearl of Great Price.

Published October 1993 by:

The Corporation of the President of The Church of Jesus Christ of
Latter-Day Saints

Salt Lake City, Utah.

Smith, Joseph. Joseph Smith's New Translation of the Bible.
Independence, MO: Herald Publishing House, 1970.

Joseph Smith's Testimony: Book of Mormon.

Testimony of the Three Witnesses: Book of Mormon.

Testimony of Eight Witnesses: Book of Mormon.

christianity.stackexchange.com: Old Testament Chronology: A return
to the Basics (pdf): by Dr. Floyd Jones.

Tower of Babel : March 9, 2012 https://en.m.wikipedia.org>wiki

https://reasons.org/explore/blogs/voices/does-the-tower-of-babel-confirm-
genealogical-gaps-in-genesis-11

H38 Virus – True Book of Mormon Geography Lands – Western New
York Model

https://www.bookofmormonhistory.com/post/rulebook-for-mapping-the-book-of-mormon-inside-out

http://www.mormonthink.com/mormonstudiesgeo.htm#map

https://www.churchofjesuschrist.org/bc/content/shared/content/images/gospel-library/manual/14419/book-mormon-land-map_1941052.pdf

https://www.fairlatterdaysaints.org/conference/august-2003/nephis-neighbors-book-of-mormon-peoples-and-pre-columbian-populations

https://sites.google.com/site/bomgeography/internal-map/new-world-commentary/d/desolation

https://upload.wikimedia.org/wikipedia/commons/e/e7/BRM3458-Weston-Map-of-Ancient-America_Mormon-1899_lowres-1888x3000.jpg

https://www.churchofjesuschrist.org/study/ensign/2011/10/book-of-mormon-time-line?lang=eng

http://bmaf.org/node/628

https://knowhy.bookofmormoncentral.org/knowhy/has-the-location-of-nephis-bountiful-been-discovered

Watch: Compelling Book of Mormon Evidence for Lehi's Journey through Arabia | Book of Mormon Central

http://www.supportingevidences.net/lehi-traveling-from-jerusalem

http://www.supportingevidences.net/thevalleyofnimrod/https://sites.google.com/site/bomgeography/internal-map/new-world-commentary/n/nehor-kingdom-of-shule

https://listverse.com/2009/09/21/top-10-fascinating-facts-about-the-mayans/

https://www.worldhistory.org/Maya_Civilization/

https://lds-tours.com/tours/multi-day-tours/yucatan-revealed-circuit-tour/

https://interpreterfoundation.org/blog-north-american-book-of-mormon-geography-the-river-sidon/

https://en.wikipedia.org/wiki/Magdalena_River#/media/File:Rio_ Magdalena_Delta_landsat.jpg

https://en.wikipedia.org/wiki/Magdalena_River#/media/File:Rio_ Magdalena_map.png

http://nephicode.blogspot.com/2010/07/where-lehi-landed-30-south- latitude-in.html

https://bookofmormoncentral.org/blog/archaeological-evidence-for-7-locations- on-lehi-s-journey-to-the-promised-land

https://en.m.wikipedia.org/wiki/lehi-nephi

bookofmormonevidence.org

America Unearthed: by Scott Wolter

https://whc.unesco.org/en/list/414/https://www.mapquest.com/travel/7- ancient-ruins-of-central-america/

https://bookofmormonevidence.org/lehis-first-landing-few-or-many- inhabitants/

Giants *https://www.st.croix360.com*

nbcnews.com-yukon'sbabymammoths

butchered Mammoth *https://shepherdexpress.com/news/features/ unearthing-wisconsins-lost-history/*

https://gizmodo.com/butchered-mammoth-bones-new-mexico-1849365357

https://www.nationalgeographic.com/animals/article/151007-woolly- mammoth-michigan-extinction-humans-science

https://gizmodo.com Butchered Mammoth: by Isaac Schultz

Hebior Mammoth-Milwaukee WI: photo by Timothy Rour-University of Texas@Austin

https://www.zenger.news/2022/08/09/pic-refile-newly-found-mammoth- butchering-site-proves-humans-were-in-north-america-much-earlier/

200 Mammoth Skeletons Found Buried Beneath Mexico Airport Site (businessinsider.com)

https://nationalgeographic.org MesoAmerica; also studentsofhistory.com

Richard J. Dewhurst, narrated by Nick McDougal; The Ancient Giants Who Ruled America; The missing Skeletons and the Great Smithsonian Cover-up.

Ancient Giants of the Americas: Suppressed Evidence and the Hidden History of a Lost Race by the Smithsonian Institute: by Xaviant Haze

Mexico City—Mayan Civilization in Central Mexico— https://gatewaytoalostworld.com

Maya, Inca& Aztec Organizer https://www.grangeharrow.sch.uk.com

https://www.culturalsurvival.org/mayan

There Were Giants on the Earth, by Manuel Ortiz Sepulveda; https://www.academia.edu

https://m.central.edu The Ancient Giants Who Ruled America: July 15, 2022

civilization.ca – Mystery Mayans from 2600 B.C. - 250 A.D.

historymuseum.ca Canadian Museum of History

worldhistory.org Maya Civilization-World; "Mayapan"

"Mexico" First edition 1993, printed in Slovenia; by Nelles Verlag Gmb, Munchen 45

"History of the Conquest of Mexico": by William H. Prescott: published by Random House

Anno Domini: https://en.wikipedia.org/wiki/annodomino jesus

Mohanri Moriancumr and his brother named Jared—by Dan R. Hender

https://huntercastle.com/peleg divide

https://nephicode.blogspot.com/Jaredites

*b*ookofmormonevidence.org/mohanrimoriancumr18stones

Joseph Smith the Prophet and His Progenitors For Many Generations
by Lucy Smith

Saints Herald, March 9, 1882, p. 258; Interview with William P. Smith

This Archeological Find Can Change The Entire World History:
https://youtu.be/s08AsRPbJ8M

*https://youtu.be/JL26r6kynI4 What Scientists Just Discovered at Grand
Canyon-Underground City*

*https://youtu.be/C2w-WSl3NN8 Ancient Mayan Secrets in Georgia
[Nephite-fortified city]*

*https://youtu.be/2vG-w4pctHI Huge Skeleton Buried in Mysterious
Cave— Giants[Olmecs]*

https://youtu.be/sVmOnwng6gs Giants Emerging Everywhere

*https://youtu.be/uPBgFAETrF4 Egyptian artifacts and symbols discovered
in Grand Canyon*

*https://youtu.be/XueMKFSbVcA Lost Relics of the Bible-America
Unearthed-Tennessee*

*https://youtube.com/playlist?list=PLob1mZcVWOai0TyJ23tul1mvk-
efO5-5C You tube play list*

*https://youtu.be/ZLi69vh1thU Legend of Appalachian Giant—North
Carolina*

*https://www.thearchaeologist.org/blog/when-archaeologists-explored-a-
ruined-aztec-temple-they-unearthed-a-gateway-to-a-lost-world Mayan
City and where their sacrificed children and women were placed.*

*https://www.cbsnews.com/amp/news/excavation-mayan-culture-human-
burial-grounds-bullets-ceramics-tayasal-guatemala/ Mayans[Nephites]
were already extinct from the Aztecs[Lamanites] Aztecs gave the
Spaniards resistance. Aztecs[Lamanites] inhabited what the Mayans
built.*

https://riobecdreams.com/2017/09/27/calakmul-inah-video-la-enigmatica-calakmul-el-antiguo-reino-de-caan/ This is a city of the Nephites[Mayans] in Book of Mormon-

Nephitehttps://play.google.com/store/audiobooks/details/Richard_J_Dewhurst_The_Ancient_Giants_Who_Ruled_Am?id=AQAAAEDM_ky-kM[Mayan]

https://www.amazon.com/Ancient-Giants-Americas-Suppressed-Evidence/dp/163265069X/ref=asc_df_163265069X/?tag=hyprod-20&linkCode=df0&hvadid=312115051380&hvpos=&hvnetw=g&hvrand=10018220811465073705&hvpone=&hvptwo=&hvqmt=&hvdev=m&hvdvcmdl=&hvlocint=&hvlocphy=9019241&hvtargid=pla-492212775551&psc=1#immersive-view_1667172686138 Northwest shore of Yukatan Penn

Giants in West Virginiahttps://www.thearchaeologist.org/blog and other places[Jaredites]

https://youtu.be/afPxLjfNooE Pennsylvania cave with Baptismal font[Nephites]

https://youtu.be/IOW2Z-oKlnQ Ancient Ruins Buried Beneath a Texas Town [Nephites]

https://youtu.be/Lde5NljBJk0 Minoan Connection to Bronze Age[Nephites or Jaredites]

https://youtu.be/IU1PpVO1SNs Ancient Swords Uncovered in America--Arizona[Nephites]

https://youtu.be/mNro9x3B7K4 Burials of Ancient People in Florida Swamps[Nephites]

https://youtu.be/8FCl2lbRvWY Ancient Ruins Discovered in California[Nephites]

https://youtu.be/sSiNhBhuBOU Giant Bones in Minnesota

https://youtu.be/3EXvsiKBLzA Ancient Pyramid Ruins under Rock Lake, near Madison Wisconsin[Nephites] Mocum *https://youtu.be/Mf3_PWprFS8 20 Surprising Giant Discoveries, several in U.S. And Mexico[Jaredites]*

https://youtu.be/T8MdIBHxjN0 Breakthrough Proof of Giants Bones in the Ozarks[Jaredites]

https://youtu.be/JzlSWzg-FkY Giants Buried in Goshen, Massachusetts[Jaredites]

https://youtu.be/hvqANniyRzI Polynesian Voyageurs of Mexico about 1000A.D.Mayan[Nephites]

https://youtu.be/WHn2GWjlK9Q Giants in the Ozarks Mountains of Missouri[Jaredites]

https://youtu.be/sVmOnwng6gs Giants Emerging Everywhere: Texas, Nevada, Mexico, etc.

https://youtu.be/I5GMVmsxKdY Bone Cave in Tennessee[Jaredites] more of Goshen Tunnel MA

https://www.youtube.com/watch?v=feGnocp8zJw 20 shocking things Scientists reveal about Antarctica; Pyramids larger than those of Ancient Egypt & Tropical forests

https://mail.google.com/mail/u/0/?pli=1#label/ America+Unearthed?projector=1 https://youtu.be/Cx_e4HXdtMk

https://www.google.com/maps/place/Campeche,+Mexico/@19.8305716,- 90.5448169,13z/data=!3m1!4b1!4m5!3m4!1s0x85f833 96176b136d:0xe93d8e4c95f26244! 8m2!3d19.8301251!4d-90.5349087

https://mail.google.com/mail/u/0/?pli=1#label/ America+Unearthed?projector=https://www.youtube.com/ watch?v=viaWo_0gXBc1 :

https://youtu.be/AcbC7V5KC9o Cahokia Ruins?[Mayan City]

https://archive.bookofmormoncentral.org/sites/default/files/archive-files/pdf/ sorenson/20

A Map of Mormon Geological Theology (kottke.org) Map of the lands of the Nephites/Mayans

24/part_2_summaries_of_models.pdf

25 Thousand-Mile Pre-Flood Ruin Exposed In Peru? (thearchaeologist. org) This video confirms the link just above, which is evidence of the map proving the settling of the Americas by the people of Lehi.

https://www.youtube.com/shorts/ZeRFGy6o27Y : Giants of Love-lock, Nevada

https://phys.org/news/2022-12-huge-year-old-mayan-civilization-northern. html : Zarahemla?

https://www.thearchaeologist.org/blog/when-scientists-discovered-a-ruined-aztec-temple-they-unearthed-a-gateway-to-a-lost-world

https://www.thearchaeologist.org/blog/scariest-archaeological-discoveries-no-one-was-supposed-to-see : shows how when people leave God, they become so depraved and evil.

https://youtu.be/Uho8VRLaOsA Spanish invaded the Mayans on the island Columbus first landed on.

https://youtu.be/KrpG1N0gf-M : Giant civilization having six fingers on each hand, and six toes on each foot.

"Mexico" by McCarta & Nelles Verlag; GmbH, Munchen 45, First Edition 1993, History and Culture

Printed in Slovenia

https://youtu.be/nE65Y8-CvQs :Engineering an empire.

https://www.archaeology.org/issues/494-2301/features/11025-maya-snake-queens

https://mexiconewsdaily.com/travel/cantona-an-impressive-but-underrated-archaeological-site/

https://youtube.com/shorts/UMLBq8Zheo8?feature=share : Discovery of Hidden Secret https://www.youtube.com/watch?v=otOfeaJB1DU Jaredites/Olmecs

https://mail.google.com/mail/u/0/?pli=1#label/America+Unearthed/ p3?projector=1

https://www.youtube.com/watch?v=I5GMVmsxKdY   Ohio   giants uncovered

https://mail.google.com/mail/u/0/?pli=1#label/Americahttps:// youthttps://youtu.be/JzlSWzg-FkY t15c 1ps://youtu.be/JzlSWzg-FkY giant skeleton tomb

unearthedhgiantgi151ttps://yougggggggggggtu.be/BEqxVPH9iXc

https://youtu.be/BEqxVPH9iXc 15giantdiscoveries

https://youtu.be/mpGes43ygGc

https://youtu.be/_UCTMKLiIzg giants emeging everywhere

https://youtu.be/7IEC3IA2kIQ 100 thousand year old discovery fantastic creations

https://yhttps://youtu.be/f0jP-Q_JuoY

https://youtu.be/TPeeI9yQfcQh arti

https://youtu.be/xCp8vhcUo54

hhttps://youtu.be/7ffnm4clPZA

https://youtu.be/w0gfRuU-YxM https://youtu.be/xCp8vhcUo54

https://www.thearchaeologist.org/blog/archaeologists-discover-ancient-mayan-city-on-construction-sitegist.org/blog/archaeologists-discover-ancient-mayan-city-on-conshttps://youtube.com/shorts/ZziGQjQMD5g?feature=sharetruction-site-discover-ancient-mayan-city-on-construction-

shorts/ZziGQjQMD5g?feature=share

https://youtu.be/3-AryIt5pQ

https://youtu.be/bq01lRiY1U

https://youtu.be/waPNLUYTkbM

https://youtu.be/LMpRuL6sR

https://youtube/Q4Po3fmmTls

https://youtu.be/lSO-bFwMx2I https://youtu.be/Q4Po3fmmTls

https://youtu.be/nE65Y8-CvQs

Cantona: an impressive but underrated archaeological site
*(mexiconewsdaily.com https://youtu.be/CvxP3ksCYHkoutu.be/
vhttps://mexiconewsdaily.com/travel/cantona-an-impressive-but-
underrated-archaeological-site/iaWo_0gXBc*

(602) Lost Mythical Mega–Metropolis Found Deep Inside Jungle?? –
YouTube *https://youtu.be/RcWcYCjtiJQ*

https://youtu.be/CvxP3ksCYHk

(603) Graham Hancock Explains the Mystery of the Olmecs | Joe
Rogan – YouTube

*https://youtu.be/RcWcYCjtiJQ7IEC3IA2kIQps/@19.8307194,-
https://youtu.be/iciOvaIm51M -a*

(603) Machu Picchu – What They Don't Show You – Check It Out! –
YouTube h

https://youtube.com/shorts/88Js7HyE65w?feature=share h

https://youtu.be/h5DFg7ECukQp.com Megaliths and city in
Guatemala

ABOUT THE AUTHOR

I, **Steven Sego,** was born in Alamosa, Colorado. My father was from Colorado, and my mother, originated from Missouri. I now had become the 13th child , out of later, to be a total of 16, having one younger brother, and the last two girls were half sisters. When I was still a very little boy, our father moved up to the panhandle of northern Idaho, and northwestern part of Montana. I really loved it there, hunting and fishing, trapping etc..

I worked hard on the little ranch, catching the bus every morning to school. I made many friends, that I will remember, and cherish their memories for the rest of my life. I ran on the track team, cross country, even basketball, when I could. I graduated from Noxon High School in Noxon, Montana, in 1976, then the following year I served a mission for the Church of Jesus Christ, and was called to Hong Kong, China, for two years, from May of 1977 through to June of 1979. I learned to speak the Cantonese dialect, and taught many of these people the gospel of Jesus Christ in their own language.

After completing that, and receiving an honorable release, I enrolled at Rick's College, in Rexburg, Idaho, now is known as BYU-Rexburg, for school, and not really having a direction of what

I really wanted to study, I signed up for a bachelors degree in business management. I didn't finish school right away, but after only half a year, I decided to move to Salt Lake City and work for a while then come back and finish school. One thing led to another, and I ended up getting married to my first wife in 1982, and having 5-beautiful children, all born under the covenant.

I went through the North American Van Lines truck driving school and certified, and have been operating equipment from the day I was old enough to see over a steering wheel. I always had a sense of adventure, and whatever I was involved in, I was committed, and always determined to do my best.

I held many responsibilities while growing up. I was a friend to all in school, and I loved my fellow students, on or off the school grounds. I had callings in church, being a Deacons quorum leader, Priests quorum Leader, on my mission, I was the personal secretary to the mission president, District leader, Zone leader. I also served in positions of Elders quorum president, counselors, athletics director, stake missionary, etc.. In college: Choir president. These are just some of the opportunities of leadership positions I had been called to serve in.

I really learned a lot of knowledge while on my mission, teaching the gospel and living it, but that was nothing compared to what I started learning when I returned home, and got involved in government. I became self taught about the Constitution, the IRS, Jurisdictions, etc. etc. too much to list. I have had numerous instances and responsibilities that have prepared me for preaching and teaching the gospel of Jesus Christ.

I have worked for myself in the timber industry, running my own logging business, and realty business, and I raised cows and sheep, and bees, and was an avid horse lover. I will admit that most people saw me as an Idaho Cowboy. I learned to exercise faith early on, and still marvel, that any young man growing up, and after all the abuse we put ourselves through, any of us are still alive to tell about it..

Today, in 2023, I have finished raising my second family of four beautiful children, and am still explaining and preaching the gospel of Jesus Christ. Even if I have to wear out my life, this is what makes life all worth it. It's for the children. The children, getting them born here on earth, into good families, and growing up themselves into fine, responsible adults, and being mindful also of helping God bring children here to earth, in order to grow, is the work and glory of God, and unless we become as one of these little ones, we can in no wise enter into the Kingdom of God. We will in no wise see the face of Almighty God forever more. We must take upon ourselves His attributes.

I, the author have received several revelations, from God making my eyes to see and ears to hear and understand many of the mysteries of God. I have authored two books Previously: Two Churches Only! & To Hell With the IRS. This third Book is to prove the Book of Mormon is true, but actually, I can't prove anything, unless the reader is able to see and understand. This is my prayer, That all will come unto the true knowledge of who we are, simply, by seeing with their eyes, hearing with their ears, and understanding with their hearts, and receiving the truth of this work through the Spirit of the Holy Ghost, into their minds, as the *"Mark of God"*.

> *" And now I give unto you **a commandment** to beware concerning yourselves, to **give diligent heed to the words of** eternal life."* *"For you shall **live by every word that proceedeth forth from the mouth of God.**"* *"For the **word of the Lord is truth, and whatsoever is truth is light, and whatsoever is light is Spirit, even the Spirit of Jesus Christ.**"* *"And the Spirit giveth light **to every man that cometh into the world**[devils kingdom when born]; and the **Spirit enlighteneth every man through the world**[during the days of probation], **that hearkeneth to the voice of the Spirit.**"* *"And everyone **that hearkeneth** to the **voice of the Spirit**[Christ]**cometh unto God, even the Father.**" (Section 84:43-47, Doctrine and Covenants).*